WOMEN AND GENDER IN POSTWAR EUROPE

From Cold War to European Union

Edited by
Joanna Regulska and Bonnie G. Smith

LONDON AND NEW YORK

First published 2012
by Routledge
2 Park Square, Milton Park, Abingdon, Oxon OX14 4RN

Simultaneously published in the USA and Canada
by Routledge
711 Third Avenue, New York, NY 10017

Routledge is an imprint of the Taylor & Francis Group, an informa business

© 2012 Joanna Regulska and Bonnie G. Smith

The right of Joanna Regulska and Bonnie G. Smith to be identified as author of this work has been asserted by them in accordance with sections 77 and 78 of the Copyright, Designs and Patents Act 1988.

All rights reserved. No part of this book may be reprinted or reproduced or utilized in any form or by any electronic, mechanical, or other means, now known or hereafter invented, including photocopying and recording, or in any information storage or retrieval system, without permission in writing from the publishers.

Trademark notice: Product or corporate names may be trademarks or registered trademarks, and are used only for identification and explanation without intent to infringe.

British Library Cataloguing in Publication Data
A catalogue record for this book is available from the British Library

Library of Congress Cataloging-in-Publication Data
Women and gender in postwar Europe : from Cold War to European Union / edited by Joanna Regulska and Bonnie G. Smith.
p. cm.
Includes bibliographical references.
ISBN 978-0-415-69499-5 (alk. paper)
ISBN 978-0-415-69500-8 (pbk : alk. paper)
ISBN 978-0-203-12623-3 (ebk)
1. Women–Europe–History–20th century. 2. Feminism–Europe–History–20th century. 3. Europe–Social conditions–20th century. 4. European Union countries–Social conditions. I. Regulska, Joanna. II. Smith, Bonnie G., 1940-
HQ1587.W626 2012
305.4209409'04–dc23
2011036035

ISBN: 978-0-415-69499-5 (hbk)
ISBN: 978-0-415-69500-8 (pbk)
ISBN: 978-0-203-12623-3 (ebk)

Typeset in Bembo
by Taylor & Francis Books

WOMEN AND GENDER IN POSTWAR EUROPE

Women and Gender in Postwar Europe charts the experiences of women across Europe from 1945 to the present day. Europe at the end of World War II was a sorry testimony to the human condition: awash in corpses, the infrastructure devastated, food and fuel in such short supply. From the Soviet Union to the United Kingdom and Ireland the vast majority of citizens on whom survival depended, in the postwar years, were women. This book charts the involvement of women in postwar reconstruction through the Cold War and post-Cold War years with chapters on the economic, social, and political dynamism that characterized Europe from the 1950s onwards, and goes on to look at the woman's place in a rebuilt Europe that was both more prosperous than before and as tension-filled.

The chapters look at broad trends across both eastern and western Europe such as the horrific aftermath of World War II, and also present individual case studies that illustrate those broad trends in the historical development of women's lives and gender roles. The case studies show difference and diversity across Europe while also setting the experience of women in a particular country within the broader historical issues and trends in such topics as work, professionalization, sexuality, consumerism, migration, and activism. The introduction and conclusion provide an overview that integrates the chapters into the more general history of this important period.

This will be an essential resource for students of women and gender studies and for post-1945 courses.

Joanna Regulska is a Professor of Women's and Gender Studies and Geography and the Vice President for International and Global Affairs at Rutgers University. Her publications include *Women and Citizenship in Central and East Europe* with Jasmina Lukic and Darja Zaviršek (2006), and *Cooperation or Conflict: State, the European Union and Women* with M. Grabowska, M. Fuszara and J. Mizielinska (2008).

Bonnie G. Smith is Board of Governors Professor of History at Rutgers University. Her publications include *The Gender of History: Men, Women and Historical Practice* (1998), *Imperialism* (2000), and *Europe in the Contemporary World* (2005). She is co-author of *The Making of the West: Peoples and Cultures* (1994, 2001, 2005, 2009) and of *Crossroads and Cultures: A History of the World* (forthcoming). She has edited *Global Feminisms since 1945* (2000) and *Women's and Gender History in Global Perspective* (3 vols., 2004–5).

Contents

Notes on contributors vii
Preface x

Introduction: Historical overview 1
Bonnie G. Smith

1 Battling for peace: The transformation of the women's movement in Cold War Czechoslovakia and eastern Europe 16
Melissa Feinberg

2 "Democracy could go no further": Europe and women in the early United Nations 34
Jan Lambertz

3 Women and social work in central and eastern Europe 52
Darja Zaviršek

4 Psychoanalysts on the radio: Domestic citizenship and motherhood in postwar Britain 71
Michal Shapira

5 Women as the "motor of modern life": Women's work in Europe west and east since 1945 87
Francisca de Haan

6 "What's new" and is it good for you? Gender and consumerism in postwar Europe 104
M. Jane Slaughter

7 Happy motherhood and lesbian spaces: Women's initiative and the sexual mores of postwar Europe 122
Cynthia Kreisel

8 Political participation, civil society, and gender: Lessons from the Cold War? 139
Belinda Davis

9 Gender, race, and utopias of development 156
Young-Sun Hong

10 Gender and reframing of World War I in Serbia during the 1980s and 1990s 176
Melissa Bokovoy

11 Post-Soviet masculinities, shame, and the archives of social suffering in contemporary Lithuania 194
Arturas Tereskinas

12 Post-1989 women's activism in Poland 212
Joanna Regulska and Magdalena Grabowska

Conclusion 231
Joanna Regulska

Index 238

Notes on contributors

Melissa Bokovoy is Associate Professor of History at the University of New Mexico. She is the co-author (with Jane Slaughter) of *Sharing the Stage: Biography and Gender in Western Civilization* (2003), *Peasants and Communists: Politics and Ideology in the Yugoslav Countryside, 1941–1953* (1998), and *State–Society Relations in Yugoslavia, 1945–1992* (1997).

Belinda Davis is Associate Professor of History at Rutgers University. Her published works include *Changing the World, Changing Oneself: Political Protest and Collective Identities in the 1960s/70s West Germany and U.S.*, ed., with W. Mausbach, M. Klimke, and C. MacDougall (2010), *Alltag–Erfahrung–Eigensinn: Historisch-anthropologische Erkundungen*, ed., with Thomas Lindenberger and Michael Wildt (2008), and *Home Fires Burning: Food, Politics, and Everyday Life in World War I Berlin* (2000).

Francisca de Haan is Professor of Gender Studies at the Central European University in Budapest and founding editor of the journal *Aspasia*. Her published works include *Een eigen patroon: Geschiedenis van een joodse familie en haar bedrijven, ca. 1800–1964* (2002), *The Rise of Caring Power: Elizabeth Fry and Josephine Butler in Britain and the Netherlands* with Annemieke van Drenth (2000), and *Gender and the Politics of Office Work, the Netherlands, 1860–1940* (1998).

Melissa Feinberg is Associate Professor of History at Rutgers University and currently works on the politics of fear in eastern Europe during the Cold War. Her monograph, *Gender, Citizenship, and the Limits of Democracy in Czechoslovakia, 1918–1950*, appeared in 2006.

Magdalena Grabowska is an Assistant Professor in the Institute of Ethnology and Cultural Anthropology at Warsaw University. Dr Grabowska is a fellow of the European Commission's Marie Curie International Re-integration grant and is currently conducting a research project entitled *Bits of Freedom: Gender Equality Through Women's Agency in State-socialist Georgia and Poland.*

Young-Sun Hong is Associate Professor of History at SUNY-Stony Brook. She is the author of *Welfare, Modernity, and the Weimar State, 1919–1933* and of the forthcoming *The Third World in the Two Germanys: Development, Migration, and the Global Cold War.*

Cynthia Kreisel is an Assistant Professor of History at Thiel College. She has published in French women's history and is completing her book on women's sexuality in postwar France to 1960.

Jan Lambertz serves as Contributing Editor for the Documenting Life and Destruction book series, a project of the Center for Advanced Holocaust Studies at the United States Holocaust Memorial Museum. She is a co-author of *Jewish Responses to Persecution: Volume II, 1938–1940* (Lanham: AltaMira, 2011).

Joanna Regulska is Vice President for International and Global Affairs and Professor of Geography and Women's and Gender Studies at Rutgers University. She is a widely published author in the field of women's and gender studies as well as an active participant in educational and NGO development around the world.

Michal Shapira is a Visiting Assistant Professor of History at Barnard College, Columbia University. Her book, *The War Inside: Child Psychoanalysis and the Democratic Self in Britain, 1930–1960s* is forthcoming.

M. Jane Slaughter is Professor of History at the University of New Mexico. Her published works include, among others, *Sharing the Stage: Biography and Civilization*, with Melissa Bokovoy, (2002/2003) and *Women in the Italian Resistance, 1943–45* (1997).

Bonnie G. Smith is Board of Governors Professor of History at Rutgers University. Her published works include *Women in European History since 1700* (1989), *The Gender of History: Men, Women, and Historical Practice* (1998), and *The Oxford Encyclopedia of Women in World History* (4 vols., 2008).

Arturas Tereskinas is Professor of Sociology at Vytautas Magnus University, Lithuania. He has written widely on the issues of gender, sexuality and popular culture. His publications include *Imperfect Communities: Identity, Discourse and Nation in the Seventeenth-Century Grand Duchy of Lithuania* (2005), *Culture, Gender, Sexuality: Essays on Different Bodies* (2007) and *It's a Man's World: Men and Wounded Masculinities in Lithuania* (2011).

Professor Dr Darja Zaviršek is Chair of the Center for Research of Social Justice and Inclusion at the University of Ljubljana, Faculty of Social Work, and the Chair of the Indosow-International Doctoral Studies in Social Work. She is honorary professor at the Alice Salomon University of Applied Sciences, Berlin, and a member of the Academic Network of European Disability Experts, ANED. She is an author of numerous books and articles in the area of mental health and disability studies, gender, history of social work and ethnicity.

Preface

The experience of women in Europe since 1945 is, as a whole, uncharted historical territory. This book looks at women's role in the grim situation across the region at the end of World War II, the beginnings of the Cold War, and the amazing economic, social, and political dynamism that characterized Europe from the 1950s on. We hope to help readers to see the ways in which women's contributions and constructions of gender shaped the "new" Europe right down to our present day.

This post-Cold War study is the first of its kind, encompassing eastern and western European perspectives on women's lives while simultaneously exploring a growing transnationalism and resulting new identities. The book both emphasizes broad trends across Europe – such as the horrific aftermath of World War II – and presents individual case studies that illustrate those broad trends in the historical development of women's lives and gender roles. The case studies aim to show difference and diversity across Europe and constitute microhistories within the broader post-war story. They show individual lives such as that of Milada Horáková in Cold War Czechoslovakia or present a range of French women's voices as they recount their recourse to abortion or their embrace of birth control. It focuses on activists in Germany but also charts the experiences of women immigrants there too. Professional women in Slovenia sought a place for themselves in social work as it was reconstituted after World War II, and a half century later women spearheaded the NGO movement to recreate civil society in eastern Europe. We believe that using individuals and microhistories can engage readers' interest and serve as useful illustrations to major themes. Microhistories also provide us with specific evidence that can lead them to draw more general conclusions about the period.

All of the discrete case studies in the book aim to give voice to particularisms and work to avoid the homogenization of experience that can flaw survey texts about Europe. Each chapter, however, sets the experience of women in a particular country within the broader historical issues and trends in such topics as work, professionalization, sexuality, consumerism, migration, and activism. This book uniquely presents the local within the context of a transnational European history and thus aims to show a manageable complexity that characterizes that history from World War II.

This book began as a conference for scholars for the specific purpose of creating such a current study of women in postwar Europe. The project has been financially supported from the beginning by the European Commission and Rutgers University. In addition, John Legrid of the Rutgers Department of Geography has provided invaluable expertise in preparing the final manuscript, and Kate Imy of the Rutgers Department of History, who worked assiduously to help with proofreading and compiling the index. We also thank Eve Setch of Routledge for her faith that this book will bring a wide audience up to date on the history of women in contemporary Europe.

Funding for this publication was received from the Delegation of the European Commission to the United States. The sole responsibility for the contents of this publication lies with the authors and the editors; the European Union shall not be responsible for any use that may be made of the information contained therein.

INTRODUCTION

Historical overview

Bonnie G. Smith

Awash in corpses, refugees, migrants, returning soldiers, the homeless, starving, and diseased persons, Europe was a sorry testimony to the human condition when World War II ended in 1945. Dwellings, factories, churches, government buildings, and infrastructure such as railroad tracks, roads, and airports had been devastated by years of bombing and heavy artillery fire. The worst conditions existed in the Soviet Union, which had not only endured the brunt of Nazi military power but had also taken the lead in bringing the Third Reich to its cataclysmic end. Eastern Europe had also been crushed by the Nazi invasion and retreat as well as the subsequent Soviet invasion. Western Europe was spared in comparison with the devastation from Germany to Moscow. Nonetheless, food and fuel were in such short supply that rationing continued well into the postwar period; so many lacked fuel to get them through the severe winters that followed the war that a new round of death from cold and disease followed in 1946 and 1947. The vast majority of citizens on whom survival depended in the postwar years were women.

The history of postwar Europe begins with this unparalleled situation in which literally millions of children, wounded men, and the aged depended on the survival skills of women. For a time, women were not only the principal breadwinners for their families but legislators in national governments, as well as mayors of cities and villages. They scrimped and stole to find food and clothing for their families; they cleared rubble to facilitate rebuilding. In fact, the wives of German officers and officials were forced to do so by the victorious allies to such an extent that Germans began to proclaim themselves the actual victims of the war. Those who had lost husbands often banded together setting up new forms of household in order to ensure survival. They also helped one another in neighborhoods and thus laid the foundations for citizen initiatives on the environment, feminism, antiwar protest, and other political activism of the postwar years in western Europe. Additionally, women in France and Italy received the vote for the first time ever at the war's end, though women in Switzerland would not gain suffrage for three more decades.

The politics of the postwar era was initially grim, both nationally and internationally. National governments had a hard time dealing with the problems of starvation, disease, wartime debt, and the incredible bitterness that often existed among citizens of the same country because of the war. There was immediate vengeance, for example, toward women who had slept with occupying soldiers. The problem of rape and violence toward women loomed large wherever occupying armies were stationed. Alongside that violence, the Cold War both divided Europe into Soviet and US-aligned blocs and raised political tensions to a frightening pitch, leaving many women to face dramatic changes in their lives. The victorious Allies partitioned Germany into two countries, creating a West Germany in the US bloc and an East Germany in the Soviet bloc. As the Soviets took control of most of eastern Europe, Communist-led purges killed leading women politicians and activists, and took the lives of returning soldiers who might have had too much of a good thing when they were stationed in the west of the continent. In the Soviet bloc as a whole, women's employment was close to 100 percent because of so many male deaths, but those jobs were the most menial and least well paid. Women with any property, including family farms, lost it to collectivization. Not only were individual women activists purged, but also women's organizations, including feminist ones, were closed down. Most activism was channeled into Communist Party-approved groups.

On the other side of the east–west divide, women became mayors and provided local leadership because of the absence of men or the Nazi past of many who survived. That situation quickly turned around. After the construction of the West German state, the new government enacted a constitution or Basic Law that severely handicapped women in the workplace and limited their access to social security benefits. Stores in West Germany closed by law at 5 pm so that a working woman could not find provisions for herself or her family. The result was that West Germany had one of the highest rates of women's poverty in old age and one of the lowest rates of women achieving good jobs or general social distinction. Other countries in western Europe hoped to get women out of the workforce to restore masculine pride after the battering it had taken during the war. The Netherlands had restrictions on store hours similar to those in Germany, with the result that it too succeeded in keeping women at home, achieving one of the lowest rates of full-time employment for women. Because so many lives had been lost, there was the additional goal across Europe of promoting a huge surge in births. This led to an emphasis on domesticity even where women were working more hours than ever. Soviet women, for example, were urged to make their men feel more masculine and to develop their femininity. Lacking some of the more costly beauty products that became abundant in western Europe under the consumerism of the era, Soviet women shared home recipes for facials and other treatments. They spent some of their small amount of time for sociability in the beauty parlor, trading news and domestic tips.

Another way of boosting the birth rate was to provide a better standard of living, because for those women lacking basic needs, having more children was unthinkable.

Thus, the welfare state continued to develop as a further way of encouraging women to give birth. The early welfare state had given pensions to veterans and insurance to working men. In the 1950s and thereafter, guided by the prewar programs established in Sweden, governments began giving women prenatal care, medical and hospital coverage, allowances to families with children, day care for working parents, and other encouragements to having children. There were differences, however: in Britain, family allowances were not given to women to help run households but to men as part of the tradition of giving them all the family's money. Until the 1960s and 1970s, most European nations outlawed birth control and abortion, and ran radio programs to promote good parenting as part of good citizenship.

Another component of postwar recovery across Europe was the rebuilding of cities and the updating of living conditions. From Moscow to London new housing appeared, some of it surpassing all standards of ugliness. One idea was to reward citizens and returning veterans for their sacrifices during the war; another was to prevent the flight to fascism such as occurred during the desperate days of the 1930s economic depression; still another was to encourage larger families by providing ample space for children. Whatever the case, new housing was in great demand because of both wartime damage and the siphoning off of monies during the war away from civilian well-being and toward military needs. Furnishing and equipping the household was also front and center during the postwar period. From the 1950s on, the eastern and western blocs carried out the Cold War over consumer issues such as which side could provide the best domestic appliances and styles in furniture, dishware, and household decoration.

The sexualization of popular culture echoed the need for boosting fertility. French films featured sexy teenaged women like Brigitte Bardot, clad in alluring, skimpy clothing. Promoters of consumer demand targeted young couples as part of the effort to rebuild and to repopulate Europe. Tracts with prefabricated bungalows arranged in suburban "subdivisions" sprang up overnight across western Europe to provide an intimate setting for young couples, while in the Soviet bloc modern apartment buildings went up with the similar aim of fostering intimacy. One sensational piece of literature was Marek Hlasko's *Eighth Day of the Week* (1956), a novel describing a Warsaw couple's attempt to find privacy for lovemaking when housing was in short supply. This resexualization and regendering entailed setting strict lines between masculinity and femininity to give society a heterosexual look. Here again consumerism played an important role. Consumer society's cultural leaders rebelled against some of these social and cultural trends, and in so doing they updated the image of artistic creativity as masculine and pronounced consumerism feminine. Male poets, artists, and performers created a non-conformist image of bad boys, gangsters, pornographers, and addicts who fanned out across Europe. These images, for all their seeming rebelliousness, echoed the stark heterosexual culture of the postwar years. Even in eastern Europe, the young demanded the highly sexualized "rock and roll," including its paraphernalia of tight blue jeans for men and sexy blouses for women.

Despite a brief surge in the birthrate, it became clear in the 1950s that in fact women were breaking the law by using birth control and obtaining abortions. The risks that women ran in the case of abortion were both emotional and physical: feelings of guilt and shame, along with the possible harm to health and even death. Lesbian circles and clubs also took women from the expected pool of fertile women. Moreover, there simply weren't enough men around for the blissful home life that official culture promoted by governments east and west – to say nothing of the traumatized state that many Europeans experienced for some years after the war. Even as films and advertising promoted domestic harmony and robust heterosexual relations for couples, in the 1950s and 1960s there were many sexual subcultures besides the dominant heterosexual and reproductive one, along with many obstacles to the hoped-for and speedy recreation of happy family life based on crowds of children. Publishing sensations chronicling and celebrating lesbianism, including Violette Le Duc's *La Bâtarde* (1964) and Monique Wittig's *Les Guérillières* (1969), provided evidence of these flourishing societies.

Because of the Cold War and the belief that the population needed to be replenished, homosexuality came under explicit attack, even being equated with communism. The French "good morals" law of 1946 forbade their employment in public service. In West Germany, the incarceration of homosexuals from the 1950s to 1965 took place at a higher rate than under the Nazis, with those surviving concentration camps imprisoned as "repeat offenders." The British persecuted gays as unmanly, feminine, and undermining population growth that was essential for a healthy nation – an outcome that led to labeling them as Communists. The Norwegian state church warned of a "world conspiracy of homosexuals," promoting the idea that democratic societies had been infiltrated by gay forces who were on the verge of overthrowing the government. The French Catholic church expressed similar views of a looming danger, issuing a warning of the "homosexual peril" that menaced free societies. An English Sunday paper in 1963 carried articles on "How to Spot a Homo" and "The Traitorous Tool of the Russians," referring to gay men.[1]

Recovery took several years of painstaking work and endurance of harsh conditions, but when prosperity returned it was unexpectedly robust. The surge in well-being from the late 1950s onwards encouraged tastemakers and social scientists to focus on women as mothers, homemakers, and consumers with somewhat greater success. Marketers and advertisers developed sophisticated new techniques for getting women to shop, even in spite of themselves, as a way of making cozy homes. Above all they encouraged women to set aside their wartime engagement with public issues and their work lives by which they had helped the war effort and supported their families. Alongside birthing many children, women were to inform themselves of the new appliances, fashions, and beauty-care products, and then purchase them. As American goods also flooded the European market, women were to learn about and buy those products too. The postwar world opened with tragedy and suffering, while the postwar era is seen as ending somewhere around 1960 with renewed abundance and better lives based on consumerism.

The postwar years saw women innovating in mass culture, writing novels, making films, and delving into fields like journalism. Women's magazines abounded at all levels of seriousness. East and west, there were magazines catering to the arts of the home, teaching women how to use the more plentiful consumer goods such as washing machines. In Spain, where women were supposed to maintain a properly ascetic Catholic life, magazines nonetheless filled their pages with advertisements for face creams and lavish, ultra-feminine clothing. Women's magazines took polls about sexual practices and married life, drawing women to participate in mass opinion-making. Françoise Giroud, who had once edited the premier women's magazine *Elle*, founded with her partner Jean-Jacques Servan-Schreiber the news magazine *L'Express*, which was modeled on the US weekly, *Time Magazine*. In the 1950s as well, soft-porn magazines like *Playboy* arrived on European newsstands and were incredibly popular with their depictions of air-brushed semi-nude women.

Beginning in the late 1940s, the turn toward the welfare state and consumerism opened doors for women's employment in the service sector, even as market culture emphasized their domesticity. There was advertising copy to be written, magazines to run – as seen in the case of Giroud – and goods to be designed and sold. The immense undertaking of building a welfare state also offered opportunities in hospitals, social work, teaching and child care, public health, and planning – all of them areas where women pioneered and helped society recover both physically and emotionally. As Europe went hi-tech with its scientific, medical, and other breakthroughs, the service sector of the economy became dominant, offering women new jobs. Women were among the early computer programmers, for example, although they would soon be pushed out as the industry developed into a lucrative one. They were active in health care and new fields such as reproductive counseling. But women also staffed factories and lower-level service work such as waitressing, sanitation, beautification, and clerking. Many were active in unions, working to improve conditions as soon as the war ended. It soon came to be seen, however, that more labor and cheaper labor were needed.

Everyday life was said to be better by the mid-1960s because of renewed prosperity. For women who worked, there were day care centers for children and vastly improved medical care in comparison to the war and immediate postwar years. Nonetheless, there was also the sense that everyday life for Europe's women provided less leisure and personal time than for men. Even though protests across the Soviet sphere in the 1950s had led to increasing the amount of available consumer goods, the daily schedules of eastern bloc women were exhausting. The day of a Hungarian architectural draftswoman in the 1960s showed her waking up at 5:45 am and ending the workday at 11 pm. This woman worker was busy the full seventeen hours, preparing and cleaning up for all the meals with no help, and finishing her day by doing laundry and ironing for the next morning. In the middle of her sleep, her son became ill and she had to change his clothes and get him back into bed. Though middle-class and relatively well off, there was no abundance of clothing or conveniences to eliminate daily shopping, cooking, laundering, and ironing in addition to a full day at work.

Even with women working, European recovery and the growing welfare state needed more laborers. Into this breach came tens of thousands of migrants from around the world – a migration that continues down to the present. Among the first arrivals were people from British colonies in the Caribbean. Many of the women arrivals were funneled into serving as cheap labor for the welfare state. Women with nursing degrees, arriving with high hopes of having good jobs, found themselves cleaning hospital floors and latrines. Racism was rife, despite the need for work. In other countries the immigrant workers were mostly men at the beginning, recruited to do the heavy work of rebuilding a continent where millions of potential male laborers had died in the war. By the 1950s, men from both north and sub-Saharan Africa and Turkey were being recruited through government agreements for this temporary displacement of workers. These male migrants initially came without their families and lived in barrack-like dormitories, mostly keeping to themselves. Asian migrants also came, often because of lethal civil turmoil, as in the case of decolonizing India. Many migrants from southeast Asia arrived in Europe to escape the Cold War devastation taking place in Vietnam, Laos, and Cambodia and were sheltered on both sides of the Cold War divide. By the 1970s most European cities had immigrant enclaves from the decolonizing world.

European society became more complex because of this immigration. For one thing there were many gendered innovations that took place. Mail order brides from emerging nations arrived as desirable commodities because of their supposed submissiveness to Western cultural norms. They were valued by men for not seeking the same kind of equality or emancipation as European women. These women lived liminal lives, neither one nationality nor the other in their own minds. Within immigrant neighborhoods, women were charged in many cases with upholding the home culture through cuisine, religious and holiday observances, and correct upbringing of children in the traditional ways of their native lands. Often women did not learn the new language nor take a job, while their husbands and children did. Simultaneously, there were many disadvantages: where domestic violence occurred, police often did not take immigrant women's complaints seriously, often seeing such violence as simply a manifestation of a different culture. Where women maintained non-European ways of life, such as arranging marriages either within their adopted country or with families in their country of origin, their children might see them as backwards – a view shared by native-born Europeans.

Nonetheless, women with non-European roots made notable contributions to an increasingly diverse culture. In 1961 Buchi Emecheta left her home in Nigeria where she worked in a government office to follow her husband to a new life in England. Emecheta was part of a swelling migration from former colonies that gained their independence in the postwar years. While her husband pursued a Western education in London, Emecheta herself would continue supporting the family – as she had done in Nigeria with the skills she had learned in high school. Conditions in London, however, did not provide immigrants – especially those of color – with the opportunities Emecheta expected. Instead she found discrimination in housing and getting a job: "Nearly all the notices had 'Sorry, no coloureds' on them," her fictional heroine remarks. "She was beginning to learn that her colour was something she was supposed to be ashamed of."[2] She also faced difficulties obtaining health care for herself and her five children, and instead of studying, her husband became involved with other women and left her bereft of any support. Emecheta came to the realization that in England, as in Nigeria, she was a "second-class citizen" – the title of a book she would later write. Perseverance and luck brought her a good job in a library and lifted her "head above water," as she titled her autobiography. Many books later, Emecheta was joined by dozens of other immigrant writers and their descendants: British-born Zadie Smith, daughter of a Jamaican mother, became a prize-winning author with her novel *White Teeth* (2000), which described post-imperial Britain through the lives of often bizarre and larger-than-life characters from many ethnic backgrounds. Outsized emotional wounds harbored by Indian, Caribbean, and even English characters, and weird but rollicking situations guided Smith's plots, which were also full of heartbreak.

The cold war between the United States and the USSR also affected Europe's recovery as well as shaping social, cultural, and political life across Europe. As the arms buildup of missiles and nuclear weapons advanced, women launched "ban the bomb" movements in the 1950s, claiming that radiation caused harm in children and boosted rates of cancer and other life-threatening illnesses. Some of these activists were long-standing pacifists from before World War II, though in the Soviet bloc younger women with few memories of World War II were active in peace demonstrations in the 1980s. A few women advanced their careers and even became heroines because of the Cold War space race: Valentina Tereshkova became one of the most admired people in the world after her 70-hour flight aboard Vostok 6 in 1963, another space "first" for Soviets, as the United States only let a woman go into space twenty years later. East German author Christa Wolf published *Divided Heaven* in 1963 to describe the lives of lovers torn between east and west. Even as many women themselves were divided in their allegiances, many of them supporting peace and social justice while simultaneously upholding the Cold War order, others were launching new movements that went beyond anything experienced before in postwar Europe.

The 1960s was a time when both male and female activists suddenly confronted the Cold War order directly and with force, including its patriarchal denial of equality to women. The back story to the eruption of activism comprised not only earlier peace activism and the powerful feminist movements from the nineteenth and early twentieth centuries, but postwar writings of thinkers such as Simone de Beauvoir. In 1949 de Beauvoir's *Second Sex* was published and became an immediate best-seller. Its message was that most women had avoided taking the kind of action essential to leading free and authentic lives. Instead, they lived in the world of nature or "necessity" – that is, following the dictates of biology by devoting themselves exclusively to reproduction and motherhood. Failing to create an authentic self through considered action and accomplishment, they had become the opposite – an object or "Other." Moreover, instead of struggling to define themselves and assert their freedom, women passively accepted their own "Otherness" and lived as defined by men. In the 1950s, there appeared in de Beauvoir's wake a number of influential and shocking books describing women's subjectivity and their intimate lives, including the novels of Doris Lessing, Françoise Sagan, Marguerite Duras, and Pauline Réage. By the 1960s, de Beauvoir's elaboration of the terms of "Otherness" became explosive in its influence on a powerful women's movement and on a variety of other liberation movements of that decade, as efforts for reform moved beyond the first wave of activism for legal and political reform to investigations of the psychological and cultural conditions of women's inequality.

Across Europe, which was now experiencing a great revival, women's activism exploded alongside that of men in the 1960s. At issue for men were superpower dominance, the war in Vietnam, and the increasing grip of technology and government on individual lives. Women participated in these movements but were consistently relegated to secretarial and domestic roles instead of sharing leadership positions – a situation they were not long in recognizing. Working-class and Communist women also understood their inferior status in the workforce and their failure to rise to managerial positions the way men did. After the threats against women in the British civil service who wanted equal pay during World War II, those women as well became activists in the postwar world. In Communist countries, women were acutely aware of the onerous burden of housework and shopping in an environment where consumer needs were seen to have little importance, mostly because women had to tend to them. In 1969 some of these issues came to a head in the Soviet Union with the publication of a heavily censored novella, *A Week Like Any Other* by Natalia Baranskaya. The work showed the harried life of a woman scientist who had to attend indoctrination sessions while attempting to do science. She then hurried home to care for her household and family with no help from her husband and always worried about becoming pregnant. Soviet citizens were astonished at the real-life depiction of life for women in the Communist utopia, where women's situation was supposed to be better than anywhere else in the world.

There was a similar outpouring of literature elsewhere in the Soviet bloc and also in the West. In the Soviet bloc, there were testimonials not only to the kind of burden described by Baranskaya but also to women's worth. In East Germany, Maxie Wander compiled testimonials from women in every walk of life, publishing them in *Good Morning, Beautiful* (*Guten Morgen, du Schöne*). Wander's subjects described their relationships with men, many of them unsatisfactory because they usually rested on men's, not women's needs: "Where do I fit in in all these stories? What's *mine* anyway?" Women wanted socialism to work on their behalf more than it did and they also talked about their dreams for more satisfying lives. As in the eastern block, women testified to their feelings and their oppression publicly even when it was dangerous. In Portugal, for example, three women met weekly to rewrite the *Letters of a Portuguese Nun*, a classic work of a young woman confined to a convent by her parents on the heels of an unrequited love. In this work, the "Three Marias," as the authors were known, explored life in the convent as a way of pointing to women's restrictions by domestic, religious, and legal standards. Their depictions of the nuns' eroticism caused such scandal that the Portuguese government banned the book and prosecuted the authors for writing it. There was hope that all this revealing conversation would help in rebuilding a truly public sphere of frank exchange of ideas beyond the reach of consumer or governmental propaganda.

In the 1970s, Tatania Mamonova, following Baranskaya's and others' lead, gathered writings from Russian women in all walks of life and packaged their testimony initially as a *samizdat* work – that is, one copied by hand and circulated among trusted friends and acquaintances. These amateur writers noted unequal conditions on the job and the unreported tragedies that shaped many women's lives in the Soviet Union. A woman railway worker described the impossibility for advancement because all good jobs were reserved for men, with women left at the bottom not only of the pay scale but of the job structure. There they did the most menial and disgusting kinds of work. At home, conditions were hardly better. One woman scientist vividly described life in her communal apartment where families lived in a single room: "I see a father slowly and monotonously beating the children, punishing them repeatedly, and they don't even cry anymore."[3] Alcoholic neighbors, difficulties provisioning their families, abusive sales clerks, and crowded living conditions tore at the fabric of life, revealing that many aspects of Soviet equality were not afforded women – and many others for that matter. The government sent Mamonova into exile for her public writing but women continued to agitate, some working within the Russian Orthodox Church to prevent their sons from serving in the Soviet war in Afghanistan that began in 1979.

This outpouring of public words from the 1960s on rested in part on Mao Zedong's idea of "speaking bitterness," which evolved in Western feminism into the practice of consciousness-raising. In this practice, women met in groups to describe – often in heart-breaking detail – the content of their lives and the ways in which they reacted to and felt about the inequities and even violence of their everyday situations. Alongside consciousness-raising, however, came practical and organized action for change. These efforts were sometimes prompted by outrageous expressions by men of their privilege and power. For instance, in the summer of 1970 French women held a women-only conference, which was interrupted by men shouting "Power lies at the tip of the phallus." Women's activities only escalated. Newspapers, anti-abortion marches, organizations to gain rights equal to those of men and to improve working conditions mushroomed and intensified their efforts. Union women took over factories and published their own newspapers, as feminism became a mass movement once again.

Sexuality also became a highly publicized activist issue, as lesbians felt their concerns marginalized by those of heterosexual women. Within the women's movement in the West, lesbians began announcing that they had a different agenda and that they were angry at being marginalized. The 1969 Stonewall riots in New York became another major force behind public activism, as gays across Europe decided that it was time to take a stand and announce a new kind of persona. While working for equal rights and access to jobs, housing, and parenting, they added a measure of affirmation of their identity. They also expressed the range of gay identities in mocking, exuberant, and circuslike performances, most notably in the "Gay Pride" parades that took place in European cities in the month of June and that continue to be held around the world to this day. Nonetheless, despite this enthusiasm, the male orientation of the gay rights movement made gay women wary; they came to work on their own, some even becoming separatists and not allowing men into women's bookstores, cooperatives, and the like. The movement reunited in the 1980s to face the AIDS crisis that initially imperiled gay men.

Practical measures on women's behalf were legion in the 1960s and 1970s. In West Germany women convened a national conference and began lobbying for abortion, receiving for their pains only a new law that denied women the right to abortion except when women's mental or physical health was at risk. Elsewhere the organized activism to obtain reproductive freedom had a different outcome. The Italian women's movement sought rights such as access to divorce, birth control information, and abortion, taking on the Catholic Church on these issues and even chaining themselves to the gates of the Vatican. Tens of thousands of women took to the streets of Italian cities to obtain these rights, which were granted in the 1970s. In addition, Italian feminists demanded equality in the family and in their careers. Italian feminism's program for reform was similar to that undertaken by women across western Europe.

While West German feminists gained far less than women elsewhere, they were successful in working on behalf of environmental safety and ecological well-being. At first men in the nascent "Green Party" wanted women to keep to their low-level positions doing office work and cooking for the male leadership. However, women began accusing the men of perpetuating the kind of masculinist atmosphere that caused the attack on nature to begin with. Her younger sister having died of cancer, Petra Kelly emerged as one woman leader, acting at first on behalf of purging the atmosphere of carcinogens. Then Kelly, like other women, saw that a sea change was necessary, and she began to espouse a far different approach when she emphasized attitudes toward the universe that were based in Indian philosophy and Buddhist approaches to life and nature.

Other west European women during these years took more extreme positions, joining terrorist groups such as the Red Brigades in Italy. Ulrike Meinhof, leader of the Baader-Meinhof terrorist group in West Germany, became politically active during her time in the university in the 1950s. Her first activism involved writing feminist articles for the Communist-funded journal *Konkret*. Soon she began lobbying for day care centers and jobs for women, but these efforts were short lived. In 1970, Meinhof and Andreas Baader started the Red Army faction, which committed robberies, arson, and even murder throughout West Germany. Most terrorism was extremely masculinist and aroused feminist opposition. Meinhof herself was captured by the police in 1972 and was found hanged in her prison cell. Nonetheless, terrorism continued to have some appeal for a handful of women.

In eastern Europe, women's activism increasingly revolved around the politics of everyday life. As trade with western Europe developed in the late 1960s and 1970s, governments in the Soviet bloc found themselves taking on increasing debt to get Western goods. The solution was to raise prices on food and other important commodities, which caused consumer protest, most notably in Poland where women along with men took to the streets to force a rollback in prices from the 1970s on. In 1980, workers in the Gdansk shipyards, led by electrician Lech Walesa and crane operator Anna Walentynowicz, organized the union Solidarity, which focused on a range of issues including the failure of the government to allow for decent everyday conditions. Tens of thousands of women marched in the streets yelling "We're hungry," but they also protested as workers and as the main caretakers of home and family. In 1981 the government outlawed Solidarity and jailed many of its leaders. During the harsh years of the subsequent military dictatorship, women kept the movement's networks functioning by communicating among union members and with those supporters outside Poland. Meanwhile, in East Germany women participated in peace vigils that implicitly criticized Cold War conditions, while across the eastern bloc rumblings of discontent grew. In this way, the road to a dramatic outcome in 1989 was opened.

Meanwhile, women came to head western European governments in the 1980s and to find a greater place in cabinets and other positions of political power. In 1979, Margaret Thatcher, head of the Conservative Party in the United Kingdom, became Prime Minister and immediately executed dramatic changes in social and economic policy. Thatcher's program involved rolling back the welfare state and its commitment to serve the needs of ordinary citizens. While many people backed the welfare state for its ability to aid those in need and thus lessen the appeal of fascism and communism, which had flourished during the Great Depression of the 1930s, Thatcher espoused a different program called monetarist or supply side economics. In that economic theory, inflation, such as existed in the 1970s and early 1980s, resulted from government programs that put too much money into economies. Monetarists and supply siders contended that a nation would flourish if businesses profited because those profits would then "trickle down" to make the entire society flourish. Holding to these principles, Thatcher cut taxes on businesses and the wealthy while simultaneously increasing taxes on the poor and cutting education and health programs. Her programs were labeled "neoliberal" because they harkened back to the nineteenth century when there was no welfare state and when liberalism promoted individualism (along with a concern for rights). Thatcher also attacked poor people and immigrants, saying that they were responsible for the country's ills, while only the rich and entrepreneurial could make the country thrive. She became the longest-serving British prime minister, only relinquishing her post in 1990, even as her legacy as schoolmaster of neoliberalism became a dominant influence for politicians and policy-makers.

Other women leaders took the helm in Scandinavian countries, maintaining and even advancing the commitment to welfare programs. These came to include parental leave programs that allowed men as well as women to stay home with newborns. Although conditions in the 1990s forced changes in the level of welfare state support in Scandinavia, programs remained alive and vital. Edith Cresson became France's first woman prime minister under president François Mitterrand, who also kept welfare state programs alive. In 1990, Mary Robinson became president of Ireland after building a coalition among many social groups including gays and feminists. In 1997 she became UN High Commissioner for Human Rights, criticizing China, Russia, and the US for their abuses of international standards.[4] However, as economic conditions became difficult, the welfare state, while not totally undone, was gradually seen as somehow wanting as a political platform, and programs that helped women were among those that were reduced, even as many western European governments added women to their cabinets. The legacy of racism that Thatcher promoted, however, also remained alive and well into the 1990s and the twenty-first century, causing Europeans to see people of color as costing taxpayers far too much. Meanwhile, as feminism declined in public visibility in the 1980s and thereafter, women's wages gradually declined as a percentage of men's wages and trended toward recreating the huge prefeminist wage gap.

During the 1980s in eastern Europe, activism and discontent built, promoted especially by the accession to power of Mikhail Gorbachev in the Soviet Union. Gorbachev introduced elements of a market economy into the USSR – many of these policies already practiced in Poland and Hungary – and promoted a program of "glasnost" or openness in political culture. At this juncture, ordinary people began bringing to light their discontent with the entire Soviet system. In the mid-1980s, the Soviet magazine *Ogonyok* ("Small Fires"), instead of making up patriotic "letters to the editor" as was the custom under communism, began printing actual mail from readers. Identifying herself as a "mother of two," one woman protested that the cost-cutting policy of reusing syringes in hospitals was spreading AIDS. "Why should little kids have to pay for the criminal actions of our Ministry of Health?" she asked. Other women readers complained of corrupt factory managers, of "the radioactive sausages" foisted on the public after the disastrous explosion at the Chernobyl nuclear plant in 1986, and of endless lines at grocery stores and the lack of food. Between 1989 and 1992, the entire Soviet system came crashing down, its foundations lethally damaged by the everyday activism of individuals like these.

As people across the Soviet bloc overthrew the Communist system, the inefficient factories were disbanded or bought up and reorganized, the level of social services declined and in some cases social services disappeared altogether, pensions were not paid, and as refurbishment of housing and other infrastructure proceeded, people lost not only their livelihoods but a place to live. Because the unequal West as opposed to the official equal rights commitment of the Communist past was seen as a model, women were the first to lose their jobs and came to constitute the vast majority of the unemployed. Hotel lobbies became clogged with prostitutes, and men and women alike sold their possessions on the street.

At the same time, the legacy of women's activism came to the surface, leading to an array of organizations not only on behalf of democracy but also in the causes of equality. Women were active in NGOs (non-governmental organizations) working to fortify a public sphere where issues were debated and action taken. These marked a break-out from the government-directed women's organizations under communism, which were tightly controlled and which ignored issues that were personally important such as rape and domestic violence. After 1989, women in NGOs worked to promote grassroots activism and to attend to neglected areas of public life that would bring about progressive improvements in living standards. Simultaneously, where religion had been a force in bringing down Communist regimes, women often participated in right-wing movements and in 2005 were essential to the victory of the ultra-conservative candidates in Poland. NGOs worked with many rural women, some of them backing conservative movements, to provide marketable skills such as knowledge of computers and other technology. Issues of sexuality came to the fore, as women made public discourse more diverse and pertinent to their lives. Activism for equal treatment of gays, lesbians, and transgendered and bisexual people also took place in a climate of deep homophobia.

Meanwhile, more of Europe's women were drawn under the umbrella of the European Union, as enlargement of this supranational body proceeded down to the present. Gender equality was one major part of the EU's objectives, and it was promoted across national borders. Women in the EU participated in an increasingly transnational economy, with women in eastern Europe and in less industrial countries such as Ireland, all of whose skills were being upgraded, working in call centers and other help-desk activities for global enterprises. As the economy globalized and eastern Europe opened up, migration – both legal and illegal – to all parts of Europe accelerated and with it racism rose simultaneously, with some women playing leadership roles in anti-immigrant politics. East to west migration was enormous, while the Chinese moved into parts of Russia that were being abandoned by Russians themselves. Migrants from Asia and African flooded the continent, making western Europe one of the most densely populated regions of the world. In these situations, women found themselves facing new problems in strange cultures.

As globalization proceeded, women's lives were shaped by other trends that had begun in the late nineteenth century. By the twenty-first century, the baby boom was long over and Europe as a region came to have the lowest fertility in the world and an aging population. The lowest levels of fertility in 2003 were in the Czech Republic and Ukraine with a rate of 1.1 children; Italy and Spain had only 1.3 children, all of these far below the replacement level of 2.1.[5] This meant, according to some predictions, that by 2050 the population of Europe would fall from 725 to 600 million, with economists predicting as a consequence the lack of young workers paying into the social security system to fund retirees's pensions. Women on average had their first child at age 28, and in countries such as Iceland and Sweden some 50 percent of those births were outside of marriage. In the 1990s high percentages of births outside marriages were also found in Denmark, Norway, and East Germany. Family relations were changing too. Single-parent households were becoming more common, as were households in which unmarried parents cohabited. Cohabitation was rarer in Ireland, Spain, and Italy, perhaps because they were heavily Catholic countries. The most prevalent kind of cohabitation was among young people, and these also tended to be the shortest-lived relationships. Yet unmarried couples with children were one of the fastest-growing family types, rising from 61,000 in the mid-1980s to 100,000 in Norway in 2004. In the 1980s in Denmark some 15 percent and in the United Kingdom 17 percent of all families with children were headed by a single parent and women headed some 80 to 90 percent of all such European families. These families were also among the poorest. But the trend to long-term cohabitation for both homosexual and heterosexual couples grew to such proportions that France, Portugal, Denmark, Germany, and the Netherlands had all legislated a variety of legal rights for partners in such relationships. The social results for women remained to be seen.

Amid these changes, women artists and thinkers of the global age abounded to bring new perspectives to the complexities of twenty-first century Europe. The collapse of the Communist system brought to light women who had hidden their work for decades for fear of censure – or worse: Galina Ustvolskaya endured utter poverty because she refused the Communist cultural system. She wrote music that would surface for the global public only after the USSR had disintegrated. Musicians expanded their compositions built on global patterns. To take just eastern European examples, Polish composer and percussionist Marta Ptaszynska absorbed the global culture around her, even though supposedly isolated behind an Iron Curtain in the Soviet Empire. In 1986 she composed "Moon Flowers," a work for cello and piano to commemorate the astronauts killed when the US spaceship *Challenger* exploded. Drawing on Asian art and Zen philosophy for her inspiration, she also composed "Concerto for Marimba," and used lights as an integral part of her musical works, as had composers influenced by theosophy at the beginning of the century. Best known of them was the internationally renowned composer, Russian Sofia Gubaidulina; attracted to Asian mysticism, she wrote for Asian instruments such as the Japanese koto and the Chinese shen. Gubaidulina's compositions straddled traditions, whether East or West, and were thus recorded worldwide by groups specializing in avant-garde and new music.[6]

Alongside the rollicking stories of gender roles among intermixed races and ethnicities, as in the novels of Zadie Smith, were authors such as English playwright Caryl Churchill. Her internationally acclaimed plays ran the gamut from considering what it took for women to be successful (*Top Girls*, 1982) to replicating life in pre- and post-Communist Romania (*Mad Forest*, 1996). In the early twenty-first century, Churchill pulled off one of her most disturbing if humorous works, *A Number*, which portrayed a cloned family that included a father and some of his twenty cloned sons. "I don't set out to find a bizarre way of writing," Churchill commented in an interview.[7] Smith's and Churchill's writing, however, had targeted some of the crucial issues in women's lives at the beginning of the twenty-first century: their role as leaders, the compulsion exercised over their bodies, and their relationship to ongoing technological development even as it cloned the species. For Smith, there were issues of diversity and the memories of past wrongs, which were legion since the war had ended. New nations had emerged, and the service sector – powered by women – had come to the economic fore. As Europe reunited, under uneven economic, political, and social conditions, the region's women adjusted to and participated in shaping the new millennium.

Notes

1 Barry D. Adam, *The Rise of a Gay and Lesbian Movement* (Boston: G. K. Hall, 1987), 163.
2 Buchi Emecheta, *In the Ditch* (Oxford: Heinemann, 1979).
3 "Interview with a Career Woman," in Tatyana Mamonova, ed., *Women and Russia: Feminist Writings from the Soviet Union* (Boston: Beacon Press, 1984), 18.
4 The US blocked Robinson's reappointment to the post in 2002 because of her criticism of US policies in Afghanistan and Guantanamo.

5 David Coleman, ed., *Europe's Population in the 1990s* (Oxford: OUP, 1996). *State of the World Population: People, Poverty, and Possibilities* (New York: United Nations Publications, 2003).
6 *Women and Music: A History*, Karin Pendle, ed. (Bloomington: Indiana University Press, 1991).
7 Quoted in *The New York Times*, December 5, 2004.

1

BATTLING FOR PEACE

The transformation of the women's movement in Cold War Czechoslovakia and eastern Europe

Melissa Feinberg

During World War II, the United States and the Soviet Union were allies in the fight against Nazi Germany. But even before the war was over, tension began to grow between the Soviet Union and its capitalist comrades in arms. The Soviets and the Americans, it turned out, had very different ideas about how to shape the peace that would follow Germany's surrender. In a remarkably short period of time, these former allies began to see each other as enemies. Each imagined that the other wanted to destroy it and its preferred way of life, creating either a completely Communist or capitalist world. In a speech given in the United States less than a year after the end of the war, former British Prime Minister Winston Churchill called Communism a "peril to Christian civilization" and declared that the Soviet Union had erected an "iron curtain" that cut western Europe off from the Soviet-dominated eastern half of the continent. Josef Stalin, the leader of the Soviet Union from 1929 to 1953, responded in kind, comparing Churchill and his American allies to Hitler and implying that they were simply imperialists who wanted to colonize Europe for their own gain.[1] Even though the conflict between the two sides did not devolve into actual battle, the animosity between them was so great that their struggle was likened to a war: the Cold War.

In postwar Europe, the Cold War became an inescapable part of life. After World War II ended in 1945, many European nations hoped to chart a course between the two superpowers, maintaining political and economic ties with both the United States and the Soviet Union. However, the possibility of neutrality quickly disappeared. By the end of 1948, the Iron Curtain imagined by Winston Churchill in 1946 had become a reality. The Soviet Union, feeling threatened by the West, decided to consolidate its influence over the countries of eastern Europe. With Soviet assistance, local east European Communist Parties created their own authoritarian socialist regimes that were allied with the USSR.[2] Meanwhile in western Europe, the United States created its own network of economic and military alliances, cemented together with the economic assistance of the Marshall Plan and the foreign policy of the Truman Doctrine, which declared that the United States would fight Communism all over the globe. Largely on the basis of their geographical location, most European governments found themselves compelled to join one of these two competing blocs, either Communist or capitalist. Alongside their governments, private organizations and ordinary people were forced to take one side in the conflict between the superpowers and show that they approved of their country's new allegiance. Those who failed to publicly support "their" side faced serious political, legal, and economic consequences, whether they lived in the capitalist West or in the Communist East.

As the conflict between the US and the USSR intensified, governments in both the capitalist and Communist camps began to insist that anyone who espoused their enemy's ideology was also their enemy. These enemies could be lurking anywhere: in the house next door, in the workplace, even within the government itself. During the first years of the Cold War, European and American governments alike urged their citizens to be constantly on the lookout for these potential traitors. In the heightened atmosphere of suspicion that reigned during the decade from 1945 to 1955, many people became convinced that there were indeed spies in their midst, actively working to sabotage their country for the other side. This rather hysterical fear of unseen enemies and saboteurs was present on both sides of the Iron Curtain, although it was more developed in the East, where newly established Communist governments spent the first years of their rule frantically trying to classify their subjects as either reliable or dangerous. Led by the conviction that "Western warmongering imperialists" were bent on destroying socialism and engulfing Europe in a nuclear war, eastern Europe's Communist cadres were committed to purging unreliable elements in their societies by any means necessary.

Women and women's organizations were also affected by the paranoid political atmosphere of the early Cold War. Like all other groups, women's organizations had to take sides and align themselves with one of the competing ideological camps. In eastern Europe, local women's movements were gradually forced to accept Cold War realities and accommodate themselves to Communist rule. This was often a violent process, as those who refused to adopt the Communist party line were forcibly removed from their places in public life. This chapter shows how this occurred within the country of Czechoslovakia. In this nation, conflicts over whether or not to support Communism split the once proudly non-partisan Czech women's movement, creating bitter enmities. After the Communist faction had taken over, it then used its victory to deal with those women it now considered its enemies.

The Cold War created conflicts between women not only within individual countries, but also internationally. This chapter illustrates this kind of conflict by looking at the so-called battle for peace. In Czechoslovakia, as in all of eastern Europe, the victorious Communists used the idea of peace to mobilize women as Cold War fighters. Taking part in the battle for peace was a requirement for anyone who didn't want to be branded as an enemy of socialism. The association of women with peace politics was certainly not new to the era of the Cold War. When they decided to build a peace movement dominated by women, European Communists were building on a long tradition of women's peace campaigns. In this case, however, they used that tradition for partisan purposes. The leaders of the Communist peace movement declared that only the Soviet Union could guarantee peace and prosperity in Europe. Their politicized stance caused the United States to condemn the peace campaign and castigate American women who wanted to take part in an international women's peace movement, calling them traitors and Communist fellow travelers. In the political climate of the Cold War, cooperation along gender lines, even in the name of peace, was largely jettisoned in favor of ideological loyalties.

Friends and enemies in the Czech women's movement

Events in Czechoslovakia, a small country located in the very center of the European continent, provide us with an excellent example of how the fears and enmities of the Cold War could affect local politics. Just after the end of World War II, Czechs and Slovaks largely agreed on what they wanted for their country: they hoped to achieve a mix of what each side in the Cold War represented. They wanted the right to personal freedom and to choose their leaders in free elections. But they also wanted their government to guarantee a basic standard of living for all of its citizens. In 1945, all four of the major Czech political parties, the Czechoslovak Communist Party (*Komunistická Strana Československá* or KSČ), the Czechoslovak Social Democratic Party, the National Socialist Party – a long-standing Czech party in no way related to the German Nazi party – and the Christian-oriented People's Party, claimed to support some combination of socialism and democratic government.[3]

Despite the fact that they supposedly had the same goals, these four political parties soon became suspicious of each other, largely over their links, real or imagined, to one of the two superpowers and their ideology. The Communist Party and the Social Democratic Party had close personal and ideological ties to the Soviet Union. This led them to distrust the National Socialists and the People's Party, which were more oriented toward the West. Further complicating this picture, the Communists feared that even their Social Democratic allies weren't loyal enough to the Soviet Union, and the People's Party worried that the National Socialists weren't sufficiently capitalist to be fully trusted. Soon these suspicions had grown to the point that each party doubted the motives of all those who didn't carry its own membership cards. By the time of the first postwar elections in May 1946, the partisan rancor had reached a fever pitch. During the election campaign, each party furiously attacked all the others. The KSČ called the National Socialists reactionaries and claimed that they harbored former Nazi collaborators. The National Socialists and the People's Party warned voters about the dangers of the "totalitarian" Communists, who would bring social justice only by taking away individual freedom. The National Socialists derided the Social Democrats for merely being Communists in poor disguise, and the Social Democrats responded by calling the National Socialists "a party without action, without a program, and without character."[4] Finally, the People's Party also attacked the National Socialists, even though this party was its most likely ally, and mocked them for claiming to be socialist while still supporting private property rights.

Part of this bitter contest between the parties was a battle to win women's allegiance. As the parties openly admitted in their appeals to female voters, women were a majority of the electorate and the party that could command their ballots would be the victor.[5] Every Czech party in 1946 angled for feminine support by claiming that it was the true champion of women's rights. It was, however, the Communists who were most successful in claiming women as new members, and this undoubtedly contributed to their spectacular performance in the 1946 elections, when they received more votes than any other party and won the prime minister's chair for their leader, Klement Gottwald.[6] For the next few years, the Communists continued to attract droves of new adherents. After a membership drive in May 1947, the KSČ was able to claim over 445,000 female members, a number that far surpassed the number of women who joined their closest competition, the National Socialists.[7]

This intense partisan competition for women's allegiance caused enormous rifts in the Czech women's movement. Before 1945, one of the remarkable things about Czech feminists was that they were often able to work beyond party lines. Women from the various socialist parties were able to make common cause with women from right-leaning parties in the name of women's rights.[8] After 1945, this was rarely the case. One woman, Milada Horáková, a lawyer who had been prominent in Czech feminist organizations since the mid-1920s, tried to create a new non-partisan feminist organization to work for the common interests of Czechoslovak women. It was called the Council of Czechoslovak Women (CCW). While the CCW did manage to bring some women together, it was not able to recreate the atmosphere of the prewar women's movement. Its meetings were soon made almost impossible by partisan infighting.[9]

Communist women leaders found it hard to accept the CCW because Milada Horáková, who became its president, was a member of the Czechoslovak National Assembly for the National Socialist party and therefore of dubious ideological character. At a meeting of the Communist Party's Central Women's Commission in 1946, the KSČ's leading women admitted that an organization like the CCW might be good for Czechoslovak women, but they could not countenance the idea of working seriously with Horáková. Women's Commission members were more concerned with defeating those they believed were their political enemies than with building a multiparty coalition to defend women's interests. Because they suspected that Horáková was led by a partisan desire to hurt the Communists, they did their best to hinder her and the CCW, even though they shared many of the same goals, including giving women greater access to the workforce, equal pay for equal work, and new marriage laws. Blinded by partisan warfare, they saw only enemies around them, and declared that "The reaction is concentrating, looking for ways to strengthen the reactionary front and disempower us" by blaming the Communist-led government for Czechoslovakia's economic problems. They put all their energy into fighting this political opposition, putting off other work until they had dispensed with their competition.[10]

The Communists were not the only ones to take this kind of attitude. The National Socialists, the party identified with the largest number of Czech feminists before 1945, also began to emphasize partisan loyalty over all else. The leader of the

National Socialist women's section, Fraňa Zemínová, was fiercely anti-Communist. She refused to allow her underlings to cooperate with Communist women's groups and instead directed them to battle the Communists at every opportunity. As one example, she sternly directed local National Socialist women's organizations not to participate in celebrations in honor of International Women's Day because it was a Marxist holiday. When one of her district-level leaders allowed National Socialist women in several towns to be "lured" to Women's Day events in March 1947, Zemínová angrily wrote to discipline her and make sure it never happened again. According to Zemínová, the Communist women were "double crossers" who were only interested in using events like Women's Day for their own partisan agitation.[11] Throughout 1947, she furiously organized her troops for political war, writing in a letter to one of her subordinates that the "biggest battle for democracy and the independence of the state lies in front of us."[12] As she told the head of the National Socialist women's group in the town of Horní Litvínov, the Czech nation did not take kindly to terror and would not easily submit to Communist domination. It was in resistance to such terror that they had "broken up Austria, fought Hitler to the death, and believe me, we will also disperse this red cloud over our borders."[13]

Throughout 1947 and into 1948, as the Cold War intensified and the conflict between the supporters of the United States and the Soviet Union became more heated across Europe, political animosities infected all areas of the Czech women's movement. Partisan infighting overturned old friendships and party loyalty came to mean more than feminist convictions. CCW president Milada Horáková, for example, was hurt that some women who had worked with her quite amicably before the war now saw her as an enemy. One of her former feminist colleagues, the judge Zdenka Patschová, initially tried to get Horáková to join the Communists and threatened her when she refused, saying, "If we win, we must arrest you, and if you are brought into my court, I must sentence you to death for all you have done to undermine the regime."[14] Horáková, for her own part, became convinced that Communists were a threat to democracy and vowed to fight them. According to one story, when a colleague complained that it seemed as if the Communists were gaining the upper hand, Horáková replied that they weren't going to gain the upper hand on her, adding, "A lot of people will still find me a hard nut to crack."[15]

The showdown between the Czechoslovak Communists and their opponents came in February 1948. An ill-fated attempt on the part of National Socialist ministers on February 13 to force new elections by resigning their posts provided the opportunity. Communist leaders decried the resignations as a reactionary attempt to divide the country and destroy the plan for a socialist democracy. As part of their successful bid to use the situation to gain absolute control of the government, Czechoslovak Prime Minister Klement Gottwald created the "Central Action Committee" of the National Front. The Action Committee was essentially a way of using the uproar to purge all dangerous "reactionaries" (meaning those who opposed the Communist Party) from public life. Subsidiary Action Committees sprang up everywhere, with the goal of rooting the supposed traitors out of every government ministry, political party, factory, union, and club. Within a few weeks, Communist Party members and their supporters would have control of the Czechoslovak government and all of Czechoslovakia's public organizations. From that moment on, Czechoslovakia would be under the Iron Curtain, part of the Soviet sphere in the Cold War.

Like all other organizations, the Council of Czechoslovak Women was forced to decide whether or not to join the Central Action Committee. Joining would mean publicly supporting the new Communist regime and assisting in its takeover of the country. The board of the CCW, which was composed of women from many different political parties, initially voted against doing so. But the CCW's vice-president, Julie Prokopová, was a Communist, and on her own initiative she added the CCW to the list of organizations that supported the Action Committee, despite the decision of the board.[16] CCW president Milada Horáková called an emergency meeting on February 25 to discuss Prokopová's unauthorized action. In the discussion, Communist members of the organization argued that there was no choice in the matter anymore. Not to participate in the Action Committee was, they said, the equivalent of rejecting the very idea of socialist democracy and all that it stood for. To stand aside was the same as openly declaring war against socialism itself. As Prokopová declared, "The things that are developing around us are of the type that the true women's movement represented by the CCW cannot remain outside of them."[17] Her words were dramatically underscored when the meeting was disrupted by a delegation of women workers and unionists who broke into the room to demand that the CCW support the republic by joining the Action Committee. While some board members rejected the Communist characterization of events, claiming that one could be against the Action Committee and for Czechoslovak social democracy, most of those present found the Communist argument persuasive, either because they believed it or because they were afraid of what would happen if they did not. The CCW board finally agreed to join the Action Committee by a vote of thirty to seven, with five abstentions.[18]

One of the few present to vote against joining the Action Committee was Milada Horáková. After the decision had been made, she boldly rose and denounced the Action Committee as an unconstitutional attack on Czechoslovakia's parliamentary system.[19] Yet, she declared, even though she had been defeated in the vote, she had every intention of staying in her post as president. "Maybe you think that I don't feel strong enough," she said, but "I will stay in charge until a plenary meeting removes me or until revolutionary circumstances force me to go."[20] But in the Czechoslovakia that was rapidly being created around her, Horáková's "no" vote had marked her indelibly as an enemy, not only of the KSČ, but of the state itself. The very next day, Horáková found herself locked out of the council offices. A self-proclaimed Action Committee of Czechoslovak Women took over the CCW and purged not only Horáková, but also all the other women who had refused to vote along with the Communists.[21]

At a meeting of the KSČ Central Women's Commission the next day, Julie Prokopová defended all that had just happened, saying that she and those who assisted her had acted in a completely correct manner. "The CCW," she said, "had feigned a progressive orientation against fascism on the outside, but in reality it was governed by reactionary elements that hindered every positive effort." Horáková and the National Socialists openly disagreed with KSČ goals, which, for Prokopová, meant they were enemies. Removing them, Prokopová noted, gave the Communists a wonderful opportunity to "direct the education and mood of women" without pernicious ideological interference from those who did not support Communism. The KSČ Women's Commission began right away to use the situation to liquidate its opposition. They dissolved the Czechoslovak Association of University Women, because of its "reactionary orientation," and promoted a complete shakedown in the Housewives' Union, which they considered a nest of National Socialists. They also purged the Council of Czechoslovak Women of anyone who had dissented from the Communist line and vowed to turn it into a mass organization that would follow the interests of the Communist regime.[22]

The battle for peace

The events of February 1948 allowed Communist women to remove all of their open competitors from women's organizations in Czechoslovakia. But despite this victory, they continued to describe their work in terms of war and remained preoccupied with creating ideological unity among women. From 1948 on, the women's movement in Czechoslovakia became increasingly identified with the "battle for peace" (*boj za mír*). Making war in the name of peace was not a Czechoslovak concept; the phrase came from the Soviets and was used throughout eastern Europe during the early Cold War.[23] The decision to focus Czech and Slovak women on working for peace was not made by women activists themselves, but came from the highest levels of government. Communist Party chief Klement Gottwald, the president of Czechoslovakia after 1949, himself pushed women into the peace campaign, repeatedly telling female functionaries that "peace was their greatest task."[24] As the KSČ used it, "peace" did not simply mean a state of non-violence. It indicated a world where socialism, the handmaiden of peace, could flourish, undisturbed by the warlike designs of western capitalist-imperialists. In the language of Communism, to fight for peace was synonymous with working for socialism. Gottwald made this link quite explicit by giving the women's movement the slogan "build the homeland – you will strengthen peace."[25] Gottwald and other KSČ leaders hoped that they could use the rhetoric of peace, which seemed an appropriately feminine cause, to mobilize women for political ends, even inspiring them to take on what might otherwise seem to be masculine tasks like being part of a work brigade.

As their use of the word "battle" or "struggle" implied, the Communists claimed that peace could only be achieved via hard work, both domestically and internationally. The first task was to convince women that socialism was indeed the essential protector of peace. In a speech given to commemorate the launch of the reorganized CCW, renamed the Czechoslovak Federation of Women (*Československý svaz žen* or CFW), KSČ Central Committee member Marie Švermová emphasized the need for women activists to work ceaselessly to instill the proper ideological commitment in their charges. If necessary, Švermová said, "We'll go from woman to woman, from house to house, in order to convince them."[26] And so, Švermová declared, the directive to battle for peace means "fighting over the soul of every woman who still isn't clear on what building socialism and defending peace means ... refuting the lies and calumnies spread by enemies, convincing (them) daily of our truth ... ."[27] No one could be allowed to stand on the sidelines of this struggle. Conviction and action, or at least compliance, would be required.

But peace would not come merely from belief in the cause, no matter how fervent. Peace would only be realized when socialism was secure, and this meant organizing women to work for the success of the socialist economy. Communist women planned big events, like the celebrations of International Women's Day on March 8, to mobilize women's labor for the cause of peace. During the years between 1948 and 1952, Women's Day was packed with activities designed to stress the connection between world peace and the physical labor of Czech and Slovak women. Their primary goal, planners of Women's Day admitted, was to get as many women into employment as possible, preferably in heavy industry or animal husbandry.[28] Women's Day organizers used all means at their disposal to persuade women that their sweat in the fields or on the production line would make the world a safer place for their children. They took their message of work for peace into every community, plastering the landscape with placards that declared "work – the weapon of peace" and "women in production – fighters for peace and happy families."[29] As they spoke about the need for world peace they presented honorary diplomas to women who had distinguished themselves by over-fulfilling their work quotas.[30] By 1951, Women's Day events were being held in even the smallest towns and villages across the country, as well as in thousands of individual factories. Party officials estimated that 2.5 million people attended formal celebrations of Women's Day in that year.[31]

In addition to activities on Women's Day itself, activists used the time surrounding it as an extended moment for popular mobilization. In the weeks before March 8, the Czechoslovak Federation of Women organized "agitation Sundays," where pairs of activists fanned out into individual communities and went from house to house, just as Marie Švermová had suggested. They were particularly interested in finding housewives, so that they could try and convince them to either join the CFW or sign up for industrial work. On one such Sunday in the Slovak district of Zvolen, 372 pairs of women set out. They reported that (perhaps unsurprisingly) they were welcomed wherever they visited, and that the women they spoke to understood the need to fight for peace, and promised that they would attend Women's Day events. Over the course of the day, they registered 193 new members of the CFW, and convinced 56 previously unemployed women to take jobs at the factory Bučina. All told, 10,208 pairs of women went out to pound the pavement across Bohemia, Moravia and Slovakia before Women's Day in 1951, and they persuaded 15,596 women to promise they would get jobs and convinced 43,448 to join the CFW.[32]

Building socialism at home in the factories and fields may have been the first step in the fight for peace, but it was not the only element in this campaign. The struggle for peace was international in scope, and it was presented as such in Czechoslovakia. The peace campaign was a weapon in the political education of the masses, one of many vehicles used to explain the new realities of the Cold War world to those who had only recently found themselves firmly on the Soviet side. As the KSČ explained it to their compatriots, the Soviet Union and its allies formed the core of the forces supporting peace; they worked in opposition to western political and financial interests that would willingly risk war in search of profit. But nationality on its own did not indicate who supported the peace cause and who did not. Ideology, in the form of a "progressive" orientation, was the key. Czech and Slovak women were encouraged to see themselves working in solidarity with the other progressive women around the world, part of a global peace camp. The CFW, along with other organizations, particularly tried to get local women to feel a connection to colonized women in Asia and Africa. For example, in September 1949, the group sponsored 627 parties and speeches in support of a conference of Asian and African women in Beijing (attended by KSČ leader and CFW president Anežka Hodinová-Spurná), and also published a brochure on their situation.[33] Articles about women in these regions, quite rare before 1945, became common in women's magazines. The plight of women in western Europe's colonies had multiple lessons for women in Czechoslovakia. It gave them a graphic illustration of the need to fight against the "war-mongering western imperialists," who might otherwise take over eastern Europe, treating it much as they had treated their other colonial possessions. It also provided east European women with a positive image of something to fight for – not only their well-being, but also the well-being of others across the globe, threatened by violence and ethnic oppression.

The primary vehicle for women's work in the Soviet-sponsored international peace movement was the Women's International Democratic Federation (WIDF). The WIDF was established shortly after the end of the war with the multiple goals of opposing fascism, working for world peace, and fighting for women's equality around the globe.[34] Although the group's ties to the USSR were strong from the start, the first leader of the Czechoslovak contingent was avowed non-Communist Milada Horáková. By 1949, however, Horáková had been removed from her post and the WIDF was considered a Communist front organization by western governments. Although it did represent women from 56 countries, and its president, Eugenie Cotton, was French, the WIDF did indeed take a pro-Soviet position on peace.[35]

What this meant was forcefully articulated by the Soviet delegate (and WIDF vice-president) Nina Popová at the WIDF board meeting in Helsinki in April 1950. In her speech, Popová began, as the Czechoslovak women often did, by emphasizing the essential connection between the health of socialism and world peace. Soviet women knew, she said, that when they worked to develop their national economy, they were also helping to strengthen the forces arrayed against the "instigators of war." As she went on, excoriating the Marshall Plan as a device meant to make Europeans beholden to American corporations and agriculture, Popová outlined a worldview in which war, profiteering, imperialism and capitalism were inevitable partners. As they schemed for new ways to "prolong their enormous [financial] gains," capitalists would always turn to war and the exploitation of others. In fact, she claimed, Western capitalist interests, in search of a means to keep their profits artificially high, were already preparing for a new war.

Women, Popová emphatically declared, needed to take an active role in international affairs in order to prevent such a war. She called on women from all parts of the world to protest arms production, sign international peace petitions and petitions decrying atomic weapons, and demand that using such weapons be considered a war crime. She asked women, especially women in capitalist countries, to work with the WIDF to organize mass campaigns in support of peace petitions, such as the Stockholm petition. Popová clearly did not think that gender alone was a firm basis for creating solidarity between those who claimed to support peace. She urged women to distinguish between those women's organizations that truly worked for peace and those that, whether knowingly or unwittingly, hurt the cause. She particularly lashed out at longstanding women's groups like the International Council of Women, the International Women's Alliance, and the Women's International League for Peace and Freedom for disingenuously claiming to be a political and to support peace, when they really served the interests of war-hungry imperialists. Popová exhorted her audience to choose their friends carefully and cautioned them to be alert to the possibility that even women who spoke in the name of peace could be their enemy.[36]

The (unnamed) Greek delegate at a meeting of the WIDF executive board about a year later returned to this theme. In her address, she blasted the International Council of Women for supporting the "monarcho-fascist" Greek government and allowing its April 1951 meeting to be opened by the Greek queen, who was, she said, "a friend of Hitler, murderer of our Greek children!" She was also incensed that the ICW had the temerity to demand that Greek children who had been evacuated to eastern Europe during the recent civil strife in Greece be returned from their safe new homes and handed over to the "fascist" Greek authorities. As she explained, "the participants of this gathering did not condescend to visit the monarcho-fascist prisons and concentration camps in order to see how men, women, the elderly and children are being cruelly martyred." The "reactionary" ICW, she charged, did not really work for peace, and did not know what was best for Greece. It had merely allowed itself to be led by the same Anglo-American interests the speaker believed were responsible for the outbreak of violence in the Balkans.[37]

The views espoused here certainly contained a politicized interpretation of "peace." The Greek delegate in 1951 declared that those who did not hew to the socialist side in the Greek civil war were against peace itself, just as the Soviet delegate Popová was prone to labeling all Western governments as warmongers. Perhaps not surprisingly, the WIDF's highly ideological stance made peace itself into a suspicious cause in the West. The United States government soon looked askance at any women's peace organization, easily assuming that it either was or could quickly become a tool of the Soviet Union. In the eyes of American cold warriors, the Soviet peace campaign's real goal was only to undermine the capitalist world.[38] No less an authority than Eleanor Roosevelt warned Western women of "Soviet inspired" peace groups like the WIDF, who wanted to "infiltrate and maneuver women's groups in various parts of the world," luring them to take part in "false peace propaganda."[39] For Roosevelt, there was no possibility of collaborating with a group like the WIDF, which she identified as an enemy organization, in the very same way that WIDF leaders rejected the International Women's Council and its allies for their Western ties.

This state of war in the middle of what was ostensibly a peace campaign had consequences for actors on both sides. Women in the West who seemed too close to the Communist side faced serious consequences for betraying their country's allegiance. At the WIDF executive board meeting in Berlin in December 1951, Italian delegate Maria Magdalena Rossi claimed that the Federation of Italian Women (allied with the WIDF) was being persecuted by the Italian government. Government authorities had, she said, closed down the summer camps her group had organized for children, citing either the lack of religious instruction, or the fact that the staff had organized collections of milk bottles for children in Korea, or, she claimed, simply because the children had sung a song with the refrain, "For Rome, for Italy, for the whole world – peace, peace, peace."[40] When placed into children's mouths, songs about peace had come to seem like an attempt to infiltrate the youth with Communist propaganda.

In the United States, the Council of American Women (CAW), the local affiliate of the WIDF, faced similar opposition. Founded in 1946 with the goals of working for peace, international cooperation, women's equality, social justice and anti-racism, CAW attracted a membership of 250,000 within a year. However, its refusal to see Soviet peace activists only as enemies and its skeptical stance on the Truman Doctrine as a force for peace just as rapidly attracted the notice of the House Un-American Activities Committee (HUAC). HUAC charged that the group was, perhaps unbeknownst to many of its supporters, really under the control of Communists who wanted to use CAW to "disarm and demobilize the US." A HUAC report attacked CAW leaders Susan B. Anthony II (the grandniece of the prominent suffragist of the same name) and Nora Barney (granddaughter of suffragist Elizabeth Cady Stanton), claiming that both were in league with the Communist Party. Tainted in the public mind by these accusations, CAW began to lose members, although the organization briefly continued to exist and protest US Cold War policy. In 1950, the battered group was effectively forced to close when it was ordered by the Justice Department to register as an enemy agent.[41]

There were many similar instances of American women being punished for not adopting a sufficiently militant anti-Soviet stance, even if they were sincerely working for peace or international cooperation. American journalist Dorothy Thompson's group WOMAN was prevented by opposition from both American women's groups and the US government from making a planned peace pilgrimage to Berlin because her rhetoric was too close to "Soviet" peace language and therefore bound to confuse German women, who needed to be trained to see that the discourse of groups like the WIDF was false.[42] The head of the American Association of University Women, Dorothy Kenyon, was accused of Communist sympathies by the infamous red-hunting Senator Joseph McCarthy when her organization suggested a slightly less bellicose policy toward the Soviet Union. Although Kenyon was eventually cleared of McCarthy's charges, the taint of the accusation had a lasting effect on her life and the lives of those who stood up to defend her.[43]

Such incidents could not but have a stifling effect on Western women who considered publicly challenging the now hardened battle lines of the Cold War. Although women in the West might face persecution and condemnation for expressing unpopular political views, their situation was still much easier than that of their counterparts in the Communist world, where public dissent was fraught with potential peril. In eastern Europe, there was no opportunity for women to organize publicly in groups outside of official outlets like the WIDF. Those who did dare to waver from the accepted stance on the evils of the west could face serious consequences, ranging from job termination to imprisonment, or even death. This was certainly the case in Czechoslovakia.

Dealing with the enemy: The trial of Milada Horáková

Before February 1948, Czechoslovak Communist women had considered feminist activist Milada Horáková their greatest enemy. In the course of the events that brought the Communists to power, they removed her from her various offices in the Czech women's movement.[44] Their sense of Horáková as a potential threat did not disappear, however. Among themselves, female Communist leaders spoke of the need to publicize an attack on Horáková as a "warning sign" to others who might consider opposing them, and they publicly denounced her as a reactionary element.[45] Within a few days, she had been removed from her other positions in public life and even found herself ceremonially thrown out of some associations she had never joined. She lost her job with the Social Office of the City of Prague, and her husband was fired from his job as well.

Despite this persecution, Horáková continued to resist the Communist version of international politics, especially its view of the capitalist world. Her refusal to accept the primacy of Communist ideology led her to meet secretly with other opposition politicians and correspond with some who had fled into exile in the West. It was for these kinds of activities that she was arrested in September 1949. While in prison, her case was chosen as fodder for what would become one of the first big political trials in Czechoslovakia. These trials, which were held all over eastern Europe in the early 1950's, were staged events in which supposed traitors were convicted of plotting against their governments according to a prewritten script, all for the benefit of the unwitting public.[46] Over the course of the next year, Milada Horáková and her fellow defendants (which included National Socialist women's leader Fraňa Zeminová) were slowly tortured until they would accept the parts written for them as the leads in this spectacular political theater. Their trial, which began on May 31, 1950, shows the most terrible consequences of the kind of logic adopted by the KSČ during its rise to power and made popular by the peace campaign.

According to the indictment, Milada Horáková was precisely the kind of enemy KSČ functionaries had claimed was lying in wait, ready to strike and destroy the people's democracy. Committed to the revival of capitalism at any cost and willing to do anything to see her aims realized, Milada Horáková, declared the prosecution, had become the ringleader of a vast conspiracy whose ultimate aim was to bring about a devastating imperialist war.[47] The presentation of Horáková and her fellow defendants had been carefully planned to meet the picture the KSČ had already drawn of its bloodthirsty enemies and create a sense of imminent danger facing the country. The story that the public heard was a lurid tale of fanatics so committed to the West and the triumph of the bourgeoisie over the masses that they would knowingly prepare the ground for a war of annihilation. According to the published transcripts of her testimony, Horáková freely admitted working toward the violent overthrow of the Czechoslovak government, claiming she was well aware her work might bring atomic bombs raining down on Prague, possibly killing even her own daughter.[48]

This part of her testimony was noted repeatedly by the press and used to make her seem like a cold and calculating monster, willing to sacrifice her own child for Western imperialism. In articles published during and just after the trial Horáková was constantly described in such a way as to make her seem as unfeeling and unfeminine as possible. She was referred to as "proud," "cold-blooded," and "uncontrollably ambitious and conceited," primarily concerned with her own personal advancement.[49] One book quite openly portrayed her as a perverted specimen of womanhood, titling its chapter about her deeds "Mother," as an ironic comment on her failure to embody the respect for peace that all women were supposed to have. The authors noted that Horáková had seen some of the destroyed cities of Europe during World War II, had met women who had lost children to bombs, and was a mother herself. Nonetheless, they wrote, "she helped those who wanted to drop bombs on the cities where tens of thousands of Czechoslovak children live, where even her own daughter lives?"[50] Contemporary commentators thus presented Horáková, who had let her feminine desire for peace be swallowed by her hatred for socialism, as a woman who had betrayed her gender – and therefore could not expect any leniency on behalf of her sex.

Implicit in the drive to present Horáková as a ruthless warmonger was the complementary discourse of the peace campaign. The very weeks before Horáková's trial had been filled with a major peace project: the drive to get every Czechoslovak citizen to sign the Stockholm peace pledge calling for a ban on atomic weapons. This campaign began with a gathering of 70,000 women packed into the Old Town Square in Prague to declare themselves ready to "fight for peace and the happiness of our children."[51] Between May 15 and 31, copies of the Stockholm peace petition were circulated in every school and factory, and armies of activists swarmed into every town and village collecting signatures. Millions around the country signed the petitions and went to peace rallies.[52] Especially in this context, Horáková and her companions in the courtroom did indeed seem "inhuman," as one of Horáková's own former colleagues from the CCW wrote, wondering what kind of woman would want "war to destroy the blooming land and growing towns, to betray defenseless children, who would want their death?"[53] Obviously, said Julie Prokopová, who had led the coup inside the CCW in 1948, Milada Horáková was motivated only by hate.[54]

Looked at from the cool, rational perspective of a different era, it seems preposterous to think that anyone could have seriously believed that a quiet lawyer like Milada Horáková had actually conspired to bomb the Czechoslovak Communist regime into oblivion. But this was a different time. While we can't know the private thoughts of individuals, the public reaction was one of shock and anger. Newspaper headlines screamed for the blood of the conspirators and thousands of resolutions poured into the prosecutor's office after the trial, demanding the death penalty for such a heinous traitor and spy.[55] While it is certainly possible that people signed these resolutions, as they may have signed the peace petitions, because they feared they would suffer the consequences if they did not, the ground had been well laid for such an emotional reaction to the Horáková case. Time and time again people had been told that the enemies of socialism were hungry for their blood, that they would use any opportunity to bring Europe into another war, this one made even more destructive by the power of the atomic bomb. In May 1950, Czechs and Slovaks were mobilized in great numbers in the name of this very fear, compelled to sign their names in support of protecting peace. Then, on May 31, the enemies of socialism actually appeared in the courtroom and even admitted their guilt. All the defendants were accordingly convicted, and five, including Horáková, received the death penalty.

In this atmosphere, protests from the West over Horáková's sentence could not have much of an effect. On June 28, 1950, Milada Horáková was executed.[56] She and her fellow defendants were casualties of a Cold War mentality that denied the possibility of compromise between different ideologies and insisted that those who were not in your camp necessarily wanted your death. This mentality, honed in the years of political infighting just after the end of World War II, made political work on the former basis of shared gender interests impossible, and even warped the cause of peace, making it instead into the battleground for partisan war.

Paradoxically, this very mentality would stain the victory of Communist women in Czechoslovakia. For a short while, they were able to transform the Czech women's movement as they wished, reshaping a multiparty coalition into a Communist-led machine, devoid of political difference. But, tied to the Communist Party, these women were unable to prevent the further transformation of their creation, from a set of organizations run by women to a mere arm of the male-dominated Communist state. From the earliest moments of their ascendancy they were forced to accept the dictates of male party leaders, who ordered them into the peace campaign. Soon afterwards, those same leaders voted to abolish the KSČ Women's Commission completely and disband all of the mass women's organizations they had worked to build, leaving female activists with no power base of their own and no foundation from which to work for women's interests. According to these male leaders, Czechoslovak women had already achieved equality and no longer needed their movement.[57] Communist women might disagree, but, trapped in a regime that had made public opposition into an enemy act, they had little choice but to quietly accept their own marginalization. This was characteristic of events in other Communist countries, where Communist Party women's sections were often eventually discarded as unnecessary elements in the socialist state.[58] Caught in an authoritarian regime that they had themselves helped to create, Czech Communist women were forced to watch the destruction of the women's movement they had worked so hard to conquer.

The hate-filled rhetoric of the early Cold War slowly receded after the death of Stalin in 1953. While there were still many moments of tension and fear, the two sides gradually settled down into an uneasy period of coexistence. The Iron Curtain remained intact, however, and the divisions created in the early years of the Cold

War only deepened with the decades of separation. The very different experiences of living under socialism and under capitalism meant that women in eastern and western Europe often had different priorities and concerns. When the Communist regimes in eastern Europe fell apart in 1989, allowing free travel across previously closed borders, some Western feminists found this difficult to comprehend and wondered why east European women did not have the same goals or beliefs as they did. Stung by this incomprehension, some east European women felt that Western women were indeed acting like imperialists, trying to direct the development of a post-socialist east European feminism. There was again anger and tension, albeit of a very different sort than had existed in the 1950s.[59] Working through these conflicts has not been easy. While the end of the Cold War did not mean the end of conflict, it has allowed the possibility of dialogue and compromise to replace the rhetoric of battle and war.

Notes

1 Churchill jumped the gun a little, since when he gave the speech much of eastern Europe still had democratically elected governments that included a variety of political parties. Exclusively Communist governments were not established in Czechoslovakia or Hungary, for example, until 1948. Austria, which Churchill placed behind the Iron Curtain in his speech, never had a Communist government. Winston Churchill, "Iron Curtain Speech," (March 5, 1946), from *The Modern History Sourcebook*, http://www.fordham.edu/halsall/mod/churchill-iron.html; Josef Stalin, "Reply to Churchill," from The Modern History Sourcebook, http://www.fordham.edu/halsall/mod/1946stalin.html.
2 This was the case in East Germany, Poland, Czechoslovakia, Hungary, Romania, and Bulgaria. Yugoslavia and Albania also had Communist governments, but were not in the Soviet alliance. For more on this see Vladimir Tismaneau (ed.), *Stalinism Revisited: The Establishment of Communist Regimes in East-Central Europe* (Budapest: CEU Press, 2009).
3 Bradley F. Abrams, *The Struggle for the Soul of the Nation: Czech Culture and the Rise of Communism, 1945–1948* (New York: Rowan and Littlefield, 2004).
4 "Volební bitva – a co potom?" *Právo Lidu*, May 22, 1946. The following section is largely drawn from Melissa Feinberg, *Elusive Equality: Gender, Citizenship and the Limits of Democracy in Czechoslovakia, 1918–1950* (Pittsburgh: University of Pittsburgh Press, 2006), 195–211.
5 Marie Hořinová, "Nedělní volby do parlamentu rozhodnou ženy," *Lidová Demokracie*, May 24, 1946; Mila Grimmichová, "Ženy rozhodnou ve volbách svou většinou," *Právo Lidu*, May 22, 1946.
6 The KSČ gained 38 percent of the vote. Their closest rival, the National Socialists, won only 18.3 per cent of the votes cast, trailed by the People's Party (15.6 percent), the Slovak Democrats (14.1 percent) and the Social Democrats (12.1 percent). Statistics from Paul Zinner, *Communist Strategy and Tactics in Czechoslovakia* (Westport, CT: Greenwood Press, 1975), 258.
7 "Jak plníme plán," *Rádkyně* 3:2 (1948), 29–30; Jiří Kocian, *Československá strana národně socialistická v letech 1945–1948* (Brno: Doplněk, 2002), 143.
8 See Melissa Feinberg, *Elusive Equality*, esp. Chapters 1–2.
9 For another perspective on the postwar Czech women's movement, see Denisa Nečasová, " 'Buduj vlast–pošíliš mír!' Ženské hnutí v českých zemích 1944–55," (Ph.D diss, Masaryk University (Brno), 2009).
10 Minutes from meeting of KSČ Central Women's Commission, December 11, 1947, Národní Archiv (hereafter NA), fond Ústřední Komise Žen KSČ (hereafter ÚKŽ-KSČ), aj. 1.

11 Letter from Zemínová to Smetanová, March 28, 1947, NA, fond Československá Strana Národně Socialistické (hereafter ČSNS), box 454.
12 Letter from Zemínová to Marie Srmšová. October 2, 1947, NA, ČSNS, box 453.
13 Letter from Zemínová to Marie Kostlivá, February 13, 1948, NA, ČSNS, box 453.
14 Quoted in Mila Lewis, "Milada's Living Heroism," in *Milada Horáková, k 10. výročí její popravy* (Washington, DC: Rada Svobodného Československo, 1960), 89–93.
15 Zora Dvořáková and Jiří Doležal, *O Miladě Horákové a Milada Horáková o sobě* (Prague: Klub Milady Horákové, 2001), 57.
16 Transcript from meeting of the Committee of the Council of Czechoslovak Women, February 25, 1948, 1–4, NA, fond UKŽ-KSČ, folder 65; transcript from meeting of extended KSČ Central Women's Commission, February 26, 1948. NA, fond UKŽ-KSČ, folder 1. Also see Eva Uhrová, "Národní fronta žen a Rada československých žen – dva proudy ženského hnutí v českých zemích a jejich zájem o sociální a právní postavení žen Květen 1945 až únor 1948," in Zdeněk Kárník and Michal Kopeček (eds), *Bolševismus, komunismus a radikální socialismus v Československu Sv. 4* (Prague: Ústav pro Soudobé Dějiny AV ČR, 2005), 105–12.
17 Transcript from meeting of the Committee of the Council of Czechoslovak Women, February 25, 1948, 5–7.
18 Transcript from meeting of the Committee of the Council of Czechoslovak Women, February 25, 1948, 8–14.
19 Transcript from meeting of the Committee of the Council of Czechoslovak Women, February 25, 1948, 14–17.
20 Transcript from meeting of the Committee of the Council of Czechoslovak Women, February 25, 1948, 17–19.
21 "Akční Výbor rady čsl žen a národní fronty," *Vlasta* 2:10 (1948), 15; "Vždy k lidem a národem a socialismu," *Vlasta* 2: 10 (1948), 15; Julie Prokopová, "Za mír a lepší zítřek," *Vlasta* 2: 9 (1948), 2.
22 Transcript from meeting of extended KSČ Central Women's Commission, February 26, 1948.
23 On the Soviet peace campaign generally, see Lawrence Wittner, *Confronting the Bomb* (Stanford: Stanford University Press, 2009), 40–44.
24 Marie Švermová, *Náš boj za mír* (Prague: Ministerstvo informací a osvěty, 1950), 7.
25 Olga Hillová (ed.), *Buduj vlast – posílíš mír. Z první celostátní konference údernic a vzorných zemědělek v Praze v březnu 1949* (Prague: Ministerstvo informací a osvěty, 1949) and also Vlastimila Drozdová (ed.), *Buduj vlast – posílíš mír* (Prague: Ústředí lidové tvořivosti a Rada žen, 1950).
26 Švermová, *Náš boj za mír*, 13.
27 Švermová, *Náš boj za mír*, 15. Ironically, less than a year after making this speech, Švermová would herself be arrested and tried as a traitor during the Soviet-sponsored purges of the KSČ.
28 "Zápis z porady poslankyň KSČ konané dne 19.12.1950 o MDŽ 1951," NA, ÚKŽ-KSČ, aj. 20.
29 NA, ÚKŽ-KSČ, aj. 20.
30 "Zprávy o výsledek MDŽ 1950," NA, ÚKŽ-KSČ, aj. 19; untitled report (in English) about Women's Day 1950, ÚKŽ-KSČ, aj. 95.
31 "Celkové výsledky oslav MDŽ 1951 podle hlášení na předsednictvu ÚV ČSŽ," NA, ÚKŽ-KSČ, aj. 20.
32 *Ibid.* While one might think that such reports are too good to be true, similar reports on the progress of campaigns to get both men and women to sign peace declarations carefully note whenever activists did not get a civil reception. It is therefore most likely that those who did not appreciate such house calls simply did not show it openly. See report from May 16, 1950, NA, fond Ústřední Akční Výbor Národní Fronty (hereafter ÚAV-NF), box 12. In Poland, historian Dariusz Jarosz finds that peasants tried all kinds of tricks to avoid signing the peace petitions, including hiding in the fields, or signed only under

threat. Dariusz Jarosz, "Polish Peasants under Stalinism," in Anthony Kamp-Welch (ed.), *Stalinism in Poland 1944–1956* (London: Macmillan, 1999), 67.
33 "Zpráva pro MDFŽ," NA, ÚAV-NF, box 67, 9–11.
34 Anna Šlechtová, "Mezinárodní události a boj za mír" NA, ÚAV-NF, box 67, 4.
35 Helen Laville, "The Memorial Day Statement; Women's Organizations in the 'Peace Offensive,'" *Intelligence and National Security* 18:2 (2003), 195–96; Mila Grimmichová, "II. Kongres MDFŽ v Budapešti," *Vlasta* 3:2 (1949) (from NA, fond Mila Grimmichová, box 12); Uhrová, "Národní fronta žen a Rada československých žen," 104.
36 Speech given by Nina Popová to the meeting of the executive committee of the WIDF in Helsinki, April 1950, NA, ÚKŽ-KSČ, a.j. 95.
37 "Zpráva řecké delegátky ke II. bodu 'Úloha žen v kampani světové rady miry' (červen r. 1951)," NA, ÚKŽ-KSČ, aj. 97, 1–2.
38 Helen Laville, *Cold War Women: The International Activities of American Women's Organizations* (Manchester, UK: Manchester University Press, 2002), 127–31.
39 Quoted in Laville, "Memorial Day Statement," 203.
40 Speech of Maria Magdalena Rossi at Berlin meeting of executive committee of WIDF, December 7–10, 1951, NA, ÚKŽ-KSČ, aj. 98.
41 Amy Swerdlow, "The Congress of American Women: Left Feminist Peace Politics in the Cold War," in Linda K. Kerber, Alice Kessler-Harris and Kathryn Kish Sklar (eds), *U.S. History as Women's History* (Chapel Hill: University of North Carolina Press, 1995), 296–312.
42 Laville, "Memorial Day Statement," 199–207.
43 Laville, *Cold War Women*, 102–5.
44 The following section is based on Feinberg, *Elusive Equality*, 211–22.
45 Transcript from meeting of extended KSČ Central Women's Commission, February 26, 1948, NA, UKŽ-KSČ, folder 1 and "Vždy k lidem a národem a socialismu."
46 On the political function of show trials, see Melissa Feinberg, "Die Durchsetzung einer neuen Welt. Politische Prozesse in Osteuropa, 1948–54," in Bernd Greiner, Christian Th. Müller and Dierk Walter (eds) *Angst im Kalten Krieg* (Hamburg: Hamburger Edition, 2009), 190–219 or George H. Hodos, *Show Trials: Stalinist Purges in Eastern Europe, 1948–1954* (New York: Praeger, 1987).
47 "Obžaloba proti pučistům a špionům usilujícím o válku proti republice," *Mladá Fronta* May 31, 1950; Miroslav Dvořák and Jaroslav Černý, *Žoldnéři války: soudní proces s dr. Horákovou a spol.* (Prague: Mír, 1950), 5–8. An English version of the trial transcripts was also published – Czechoslovak Ministry of Justice, *War Conspirators Before the Court of the Czechoslovak People* (Prague: Orbis, 1950).
48 Dvořák and Černý, *Žoldnéři války*, 16–18; "Špionka Horáková doznává své zločiny proti republice a míru," *Mladá Fronta*, June 1, 1950.
49 Dvořák and Černý, *Žoldnéři války*, 9–10; Vlasta Urbanová, "Zrádci lidu," *Vlasta* 4:20 (1950): 2; Karel Beran, *Před soudem lidu* (Prague: Melantrich, 1950), 108; Julie Prokopová, "Zločin a trest," *Rádkyně* no. 7 (1950): 105–6.
50 Dvořák and Černý, *Žoldnéři války*, 17.
51 "Slučovací sjezd našich žen zahájen," *Mladá Fronta*, April 1, 1950; Karel Marek, "Náš lid bojuje za mír," *Tvorba* 14, no. 7 (1950): 162; "Lid ozsuzuje rozvratníky a zrádce našeho národa," *Svobodné Slovo*, June 6, 1950.
52 "Zpráva o průběhu mírové podpisové akce" from May 27–29 1950, NA, ÚAV-NF, box 12.
53 Urbanová, "Zrádci lidu."
54 Prokopová, "Zločin a trest."
55 "Nejpřísnější tresty bandě rozvratníků," *Mladá Fronta*, June 4, 1950; "Týden údernických směn odpovídají stavaři na zločinné plány zrádců," *Mladá Fronta*, June 7, 1950.
56 Radotínský, *Rozsudek, který otřásl světem*, 74–84.
57 For information on the actual status of women in socialist Czechoslovakia, see Sharon L. Wolchik, "The Status of Women in a Socialist Order: Czechoslovakia, 1948–78," *Slavic Review* 38. no. 4 (1979): 583–602 and Alena Heitlinger, *Women and State Socialism: Sex*

Inequality in the Soviet Union and Czechoslovakia (Montreal: McGill-Queen's University Press, 1979).

58 For example, on East Germany see Donna Harsch, *Revenge of the Domestic: Women, Family and Communism in the German Democratic Republic* (Princeton: Princeton University Press, 2006) or on the Soviet Union itself, Elizabeth A. Wood, *The Baba and the Comrade: Gender and Politics in Revolutionary Russia* (Bloomington: Indiana University Press, 2001).

59 On these conflicts, see Hana Havelková, "Abstract Citizenship? Women and Power in the Czech Republic," *Social Politics* 3 (1996): 243–60; and Jasmina Lukić, Joanna Regulska and Darja Zaviršek, *Women and Citizenship in Central and Eastern Europe* (Burlington, VT: Ashgate, 2006), 225–98.

2

"DEMOCRACY COULD GO NO FURTHER"

Europe and women in the early United Nations[1]

Jan Lambertz

I invite you on an excursion to Long Island. Here, in the auspiciously named town of Lake Success, delegates and officials of the fledgling United Nations began to hold meetings in a converted airplane factory in 1946. The new organization had yet to choose and settle into its permanent home on the East River in Manhattan. And here the United Nation's Commission on the Status of Women also began its sessions in early 1947. Just a few days into the first session a blizzard crippled the New York metropolitan area, forcing most UN agencies to cancel their meetings. Alone, the members of the women's commission braved the Long Island railroad, "conscientiously mushed through the snow," and conducted business as usual. As one tongue-in-cheek news report concluded, "They must have thought … pityingly … of the soft, puny men delegates of the Security Council huddled in their warm hotel rooms back in New York, their meetings postponed."[2] We trail after these women, through snowdrifts and the cold, less to gauge the strength of their commitment than to capture a sense of their vision for the postwar settlement. The Commission on the Status of Women (CSW) allows us to take a measure of women's interventions – and European women's interventions – in the preeminent diplomatic and political debates emerging at the end of World War II. An anomalous political space, the CSW year in and year out brought together representatives from a range of states across the globe, each bearing her own traditions of public discourse and debate.[3]

The commission sparked controversy even before it first convened. At the founding conference of the UN, held in spring of 1945 in San Francisco, Bertha Lutz – a powerhouse Brazilian delegate and herpetologist in her professional life – allied with a female adviser in the Australian delegation, Jessie Street, to make women's rights more than just an afterthought to other human rights.[4] Still, when the organization as a whole began its work in early 1946, the women found that their project had been demoted to a subcommission, answering to the Commission on Human Rights rather than directly to the Economic and Social Committee. This interim subcommission convened in a temporary meeting space at Hunter College for several weeks early in 1946. In June, however, subcommission chair Bodil Begtrup (1903–87), backed by pressure from her fellow delegates and other women's rights advocates, was able to obtain full commission status for the body.[5] Its mandate was to

> prepare recommendations and reports to the Economic and Social Council on promoting women's rights in political, economic, civil, social and educational fields. The Commission shall also make recommendations to the Council on urgent problems requiring immediate attention in the field of women's rights with the object of implementing the principle that men and women shall have equal rights, and to develop proposals to give effect to such recommendations.[6]

The ranks of the women's group expanded from nine to fifteen members in February 1947 at its first session as a full-fledged commission, and grew to eighteen members in 1952. Their meetings would henceforth consist of annual gatherings of just a few weeks, although members spent the intervals between engaged in preparatory work, fact-finding, and promotion of UN work in their home countries. Appointments to the commission, arranged through a combination of UN member states' votes and individual government selections, came in two-year to four-year terms, and a considerable amount of lobbying about who would fill the position occurred in some countries.[7] Many of the early members came from mid-level government ranks in their respective countries and a few had even served as state ministers. Many came with strong ties to women's rights initiatives and leading political parties, and some had previous experience in international politics, including ties to the earlier League of Nations.[8] A handful had also actively fought in the anti-Nazi resistance or national liberation movements. Many of the Latin American delegates of the CSW's early years were linked to the powerful lobbying group for women's political rights, the Inter-American Commission of Women (IACW), formed in the late 1920s. Early delegates from India and later Pakistan shared a history of ties to the All India Women's Conference.[9] And not a few of these commission members seemed larger than life: Czesław Miłosz, for instance, paid affectionate tribute to one Polish delegate to the commission in the early 1950s, Zofia Dembińska (1905–89), remembering her as "a fanatic," a strong woman who seemed "like a character from a nineteenth-century novel."[10]

Despite this gallery of talent and despite some delegates' optimistic claim that women's issues transcended political boundaries, at least three contemporary realities would undermine the effectiveness and relevance of the body in its formative decade. First, in the chaos of the years immediately following World War II – a world food crisis, huge displaced populations, and ongoing militarized standoffs across the globe – the commission often latched on to issues that seemed far from urgent or far from the mainstream of contemporary international politics. Second, the growing Cold War climate created an unbridgeable divide between delegates about the status of women under socialist regimes. Third, the persistence of European colonial empires pitted apologists for empire – above all the delegates from France and Britain – against delegates from newly independent states and the USSR and its allies. The resulting fissures suggest the gradual dissipation of the power and moral authority of west European delegates, even as concerns about postwar Europe and specifically European issues continued to thread through the commission's agendas.

Europe at the United Nations

Europe maintained more than a foothold in the early CSW: European women never made up less than a quarter of its delegates and often occupied as many as a third of the commission's seats. Women from western Europe, notably French representative Marie-Hélène Lefaucheux (1904–64), were repeatedly elected to chair its annual meetings.[11] In almost every sense, however, meetings in the body's first decade remained a safe ocean away from the upheavals and ruined urban landscapes of postwar Europe.[12] When the commission finally did convene a round of meetings on European soil in 1952, the site chosen was benign Geneva, at that juncture an apparently "inexpensive" meeting place.[13] Many factors conspired to keep the continent's devastation from World War II a long arm's length from the women's agenda. First and most obviously was the division of labor within the United Nations itself. Jurisdiction for providing material relief for its displaced populations and upended economies lay well outside the realm of the women's commission. That task fell largely to such entities as the UN Relief and Rehabilitation Administration (UNRRA) and its successor, the International Refugee Organization (IRO); the Food and Agriculture Organization (FAO), established as a specialized UN agency in 1945; or even the international children's emergency fund, UNICEF, founded in late 1946.

European issues on which the commission was asked to intervene were either not foremost problems of sex discrimination, or affected only a small number of women. While these issues indisputably carried some symbolic purchase, the central place accorded them on CSW agendas also goes far in demonstrating how marginal the body was in dispatching the far larger problems left by World War II. For instance, the commission's delegate from Greece introduced a thorny "mother's right issue" in the 1949 and later sessions, asserting that children from northern Greece – kept in safety in Yugoslavia during the civil war – had not been repatriated to their homes or families.[14] In a slightly later appeal to the commission, French delegate and long-time chair of the CSW Mme. Lefaucheux in 1950 introduced "a rather specialized item which several women's organizations had asked her to bring before the Commission on the Status of Women," the lack of resources available to certain women who had been deported to Nazi camps and survived so-called scientific experiments.[15] The CSW chairwoman remained rather vague about the numbers involved, though at one point she conceded that probably less than ten women in France were thus affected. (Further inquiries helped bump the number cautiously up to seventy.) She implied that most of the survivors were stateless or displaced persons and had no ordinary legal channels through which to seek redress.[16] A brief discussion of the issue resumed at a later session. While several commission members expressed sympathy, some questioned whether their body was even competent to deal with the subject.[17] Others questioned the wisdom of pursuing an issue that apparently affected so few women, arguing, for instance, that "nobody has so far thought of helping" the purportedly nearly 1400 university women still lingering in displaced persons' camps.[18] And still others made clear that the controversy could not survive long as a "women's issue" alone.

Still, in the end the commission passed a draft resolution in May 1950 calling attention to the plight of these women survivors and calling for action.[19] The Economic and Social Council, under whose umbrella the CSW operated, forwarded the request to the UN secretary-general in July 1950, urging him to find a means for aiding such victims, but extended the injunction to cover both men and women. The request garnered a serious response, detailed in a 50-page report entitled "Plight of Survivors of Concentration Camps," issued in early February 1951. The secretary-general's staff had solicited names of victims of such medical atrocities and an account of their needs (inconclusive), and arranged for a legal study of compensation available under existing German provisions (which found them inadequate).[20] The Economic and Social Council ultimately adopted a resolution on March 19, 1951, appealing to the German authorities to make the fullest possible reparation for injuries suffered by such victims. The IRO, World Health Organization, and voluntary agencies were encouraged to find resources for this special group as well.[21]

These steps notwithstanding, it remains unclear whether the handful of stateless women survivors who had contacted Lefaucheux ultimately did receive the care and treatment they requested or desired. In truth, neither the CSW nor the United Nations was ever to be a major player in prosecuting medical crimes of the Nazi era or in setting up postwar mechanisms through which victims of Nazi persecution could seek redress.[22] And this illustrates a central limitation or characteristic of the early women's commission: while its members struggled to be relevant in the distress and chaos of the postwar world, it remained peripheral to the enormous tasks of reconstruction in Europe and elsewhere.

Cold War fissures

The Cold War stand-off soon trumped any sustained discussion of the recent war and erased common ground. Like the fledgling United Nations as a whole, the women's commission was engaged in international dialogue in a period when many of the doors that had briefly and cautiously opened at the end of the war were firmly closing. The UN's early years coincided with the confrontational, militarized benchmarks that we associate with the early Cold War, and many parts of the organization rapidly devolved into a staging ground for Cold War divisions; above all, the deepening distrust and rivalry between the United States and the Soviet Union.[23] (Lest we forget, the UN's host country itself soon became hostile to the organization, with many Americans viewing it, in Edward Luck's words, as a kind of "Trojan horse, offering a means for spies and subversives to infiltrate American soil.")[24] Acrimonious exchanges between the Soviets and the Americans in the General Assembly at times became so mesmerizing that debates and press conferences featuring the tough Soviet deputy foreign minister and UN delegate Andrei Vyshinsky reputedly became a minor tourist attraction in New York.[25] Trygve Lie, prominent Norwegian social democrat and labor politician, once remarked that he had suffered "Vyshinsky ulcers" during his years as the organization's first secretary-general.[26] And while Danish delegate Bodil Begtrup reportedly told her CSW colleagues that fortunately no "iron curtain" divided women "on the particular questions which concerned them," exchanges within the women's commission soon mirrored the tensions present in every corner of the United Nations.[27]

Delegates from the United States and Soviet Union proved to be the most reliable adversaries in the CSW, exchanging continuous barbs about Jim Crow and the Gulag, but European women – delegates from both sides of the continent – also readily entered the fray. One claim, an early signal of a growing divide between East and West bloc women (and their respective allies), was that Britain had been a kind of singular victim and victor in the late war. UK delegate Mary Sutherland (a Labour Party activist, anti-communist, and former teacher) ventured occasional arguments along these lines, steering a wide arc around the terrible war-time cost borne by occupied Europe and northern Africa or the Soviet Union.[28] In a discussion of educational opportunities for women, for example, she referred to her country's efforts since 1945 to replace or repair thousands of school buildings destroyed through bombing "at a time when that country was bearing the weight of enemy attack alone." And in a further display of insularity, she informed her fellow commission members, "as was well known, the United Kingdom, owing to the many sacrifices it had made during the war, was going through a difficult time. The United Kingdom had … mobilized more fully during the war than any other country, and had made the greatest sacrifices in material resources."[29]

Soviet delegate Elizieveta Popova in fact conceded no such setbacks. For her the war had soon become a distant memory. She chose instead to launch what soon became a familiar refrain deployed against her Western counterparts: "If one looks at the situation of women in the world at large, one sees that in some countries, such as mine, the problem usually called 'the problem of women' has been finally solved. From the moment the Soviet Authority was established, women have enjoyed all rights, with complete equality."[30] Soviet-allied delegates followed suit in their public pronouncements, with the Polish delegate to the commission, for instance, lauding her government's efficacy in eradicating high illiteracy rates at the end of the war.[31] The examples multiplied, surfacing in nearly every commission meeting, in every imaginable context. When the topic of veiling came up in passing during the 1952 sessions, the Byelorussian delegate triumphantly announced that "in certain Central Asian Republics forming part of the Soviet Union an end had been put to the wearing of the veil, another practice which was both humiliating to and unhealthy for women."[32]

The claim that socialist countries had "solved" the woman question became a central, long-lived Cold War tenet, contributing to a series of ideological divisions around gender that would heavily mark the next thirty or more years of debates about the role of women. Such rhetoric predated World War II, but in the first decade following the war this stance became ever more codified, particularly in new international venues such as the UN women's commission. And it arguably established an acrimonious pattern that inhibited many forms of international women's organizing and outreach for decades. Alongside this element of discord, another subject revealed and fed sharp, uncomfortable divisions in the early CSW, placing its west European delegates continually on the defensive: Europe's colonies. The commission became a locus for hot, intransigent debates in its first decade about women and imperialism, just at the juncture when long-established imperial power was gradually going to pieces.

Empire on notice

The processes now rather blandly labeled "decolonization" were not directly the business of the CSW, though its members, as extensions of their respective diplomatic corps, were part of the machinery of states. The quality of life in the remaining colonies and non-sovereign lands claimed a constant presence at the commission's table, be it in discussions of expanding political rights for women, equal work for equal pay, equal educational opportunities for girls, or gender discrimination in what was designated private law. And with it, the future of colonial rule also fell under scrutiny. Indeed, a number of the commission's early delegates represented former colonies, now independent states: India, Pakistan, Lebanon, and Syria. In a recent essay, historian Mark Mazower has argued that a number of the old European powers present at the founding of the United Nations were seeking to reassert colonial control, and that the organization, not accidentally, was designed to provide cooperation and stability "in a world of empires and great powers."[33] These founding premises soon eroded. With the advent of the Cold War, the world body was transformed, and advocates for independence began using its founding principles and institutions to challenge colonial rule and the old status quo. Membership expanded greatly from the mid-1950s and beyond, and by the early 1960s the UN would issue an explicit disavowal of colonialism.[34] Challenges to the old order and the legitimacy of empire began at many different locations within the halls of the UN; within formal meetings of the early CSW, it was the Soviet delegate and her allies who again and again led the charge, wielding their rhetorical slings above all against their colleagues from western Europe. I will address their strategies and responses in the text that follows.

In its daily operations the UN largely jettisoned an older vocabulary inherited from the League of Nations and from the long history of European colonial empires. The almost anodyne "Trust Territories" superseded what had been called mandates under the old League structure; for these, the UN's Trusteeship Council provided administrative oversight on the road to independence or sovereign status (for most, this began in the late 1950s and beyond). And the bland nomenclature of "Non-Self-Governing Territories" now bundled together the lands remaining under postwar European colonial rule; Mazower puts the population of these territories at no less than several hundred million.[35] These postwar aggregations of inordinately diverse lands and populations and forms of government represented a mental operation, a vision of the world that begs further scrutiny. Yet in practice critically minded CSW delegates appear to have treated even the differences between Trust Territories and the Non-Self-Governing Territories as somewhat academic.[36]

Almost from the outset members of the commission began inserting the question of women in Trust Territories and Non-Self-Governing Territories into their deliberations, above all in discussions of political or educational rights. They concurred that some representation by CSW members at Trusteeship Council meetings and ventures was worth pursuing. In an effort to educate themselves for the tasks ahead – for the challenge (indeed, hubris) of thinking in global terms – they also arranged for UN surveys to include questions about the status of women and girls in the territories, their voting rights and educational opportunities. If reporting from these surveys remained uneven, the sometimes finely detailed results that did come in confronted delegates with a bewildering array of arrangements and practices the world over, many in flux. In pages and pages of a March 1950 report, "Information Concerning the Status of Women in Non-Self-Governing Territories: Prepared by the Secretary-General," they learned, for instance, that women had the same voting rights as men in Curacao and Surinam (under Dutch administration), as they did in Greenland (under Denmark). In Mauritius (under British administration), the new constitution provided for equal franchise, albeit subject to a residence qualification and literacy test. In further territories under the UK – British Somaliland, Zanzibar, Brunei, North Borneo – no franchise or elected representative bodies existed. In Kenya, the report spelled out, women's rights depended on their "origin or descent," while in the Falkland Islands no women could vote. Women's eligibility for public office was likewise checkered and variable, in some places not prohibited, but "contrary to native law and custom" (Gambia) or subject to "marital authorization" (Seychelles). And in Hong Kong, "In certain cases, marriage disqualifies women for public office."[37] The commission's capacity to command this information demonstrated a new level of authority but at the same time, paradoxically, it underlined the drawbacks of "going global" in so thorough a fashion.

The breadth of postwar empires remained vast. Representing states with the lion's share of holdings, French and British commission members unsurprisingly bore the brunt of criticism from select colleagues (far more so than any representatives from the Netherlands). Summary reports of the first decade of women's commission meetings reveal that the barrage of critical comments held few surprises. Time and again east European and Soviet representatives invoked the "very hard conditions of life under colonial policies which allowed of no social and cultural developments" or the "feudal" or "simply catastrophic" situation and "widespread illiteracy" in Trust Territories and Non-Self-Governing Territories alike.[38] Women and girls there suffered from "acute" levels of discrimination. The showdown escalated in the early 1950s, with Mme. Popova arguing that many women in these territories were not "protected" but, rather, could claim "no corporal integrity" and were "mere slaves to vicious and pernicious customs … [such as the] mutilation of women and girls in the Sudan and other parts of Africa … ."[39] It remains unclear whether these critics had clear objectives beyond broadly shaming and discrediting the hold-out colonial powers, their opponents on so many other issues.

Delegates from the old colonial powers pushed back unapologetically and without hesitation. They invoked a set of surprisingly long-lived and shopworn arguments about the virtue and civilizing mission of colonial rule (particularly with respect to women and girls), and avoided explicit mention of national independence movements.[40] In one version of the script, they painted indigenous male prejudice as the main obstacle to female progress. Here they cast themselves as enlightened benefactors, pointing out that although their governments "had made strenuous efforts to develop women's education, they had had to fight against *the local populations' prejudices about education for girls*, and had had to go very slowly so as not to upset national tradition."[41] The French chairwoman also cast herself as a perfectly suitable spokesperson for indigenous wishes, insisting that women of any of the territories of the French Union would consider her as their compatriot and "would therefore feel that they were represented."[42]

In another version of the script – recited over and over – they simply denied that a real problem existed, again using the maddeningly obtuse rhetoric of metropolitan virtue and benevolence. Commission chair Lefaucheux, for instance, pronounced that "Administering Authorities, in particular France, had made great efforts to raise the level of education of the indigenous populations of their non-self-governing territories, without discrimination of sex." And Miss Sutherland echoed her colleague, insisting that compulsory education already existed in many a territory administered by the United Kingdom ("indeed, in many non-self-governing territories there were more educational opportunities available than in certain sovereign States") and that her government was struggling to overcome "old-established prejudices" against female education.[43]

In a further variant, both the UK and French representatives simply put problems down to details of a practical nature and lagging development, not the underlying fact of colonial rule. Again in a discussion of educational opportunities for women, Sutherland argued that the difficulties in the colonies were due to limited funds and a shortage of schools and teachers.

> Faithful to its tradition the United Kingdom had not wished to build up simply a legislative façade in these territories, before having the practical means to develop women's education. In recent years, however, considerable progress had been recorded in this matter ... The problem was the same for many small self-governing countries with limited financial resources. ... The real solution lay in the economic development of those countries.[44]

Lefaucheux similarly reported that both France and Belgium had made a considerable effort in territories under their authority, but the difficulties that remained were primarily due to a shortage of teachers.[45] And she announced to fellow CSW members that she had conducted her own research during several trips to Africa, reporting that in the Cameroons and French Togoland "the indigenous women took a lively interest in every aspect of the political evolution of their country. When it became administratively possible and when education became more widespread, they would undoubtedly be ready to exercise their rights freely and independently."[46] The implication here was that native populations were not quite ready to enjoy the fruits of self-determination.

A last resort in these narratives of benevolent colonialism was the inflammatory invocation of "native sexual practices," an argument used since the nineteenth century about the need for (white) women's intervention in colonial society and colonial affairs. For Lefaucheux, codification of monogamy, consent to marriage, and some minimum age of consent were the clear markers of acceptable social practices, and their absence at mid-century remained a sticking point. Describing her 1950 study tour of some dozen territories in Africa, she informed commission colleagues that she

> had had an opportunity to speak with relatively cultured African women including teachers, midwives, social service workers, university students and housewives. In almost every case their main desire had been for adequate protection, through monogamy, of their personal dignity as women, wives and mothers and for protection against the surviving vestiges of practices such as polygamy bride price, especially where those customs had become abusive.[47]

She hailed adoption of a September 1951 marriage decree, "which was likely to revolutionize living conditions for women in Africa, since henceforward as soon as they came of age they would have complete freedom of choice in the matter of their marriage ... The decree also allowed couples contracting marriage to opt for the French metropolitan civil code, which implied the recognition of monogamy."[48]

Tropes about sexual violence and exploitation in certain world regions arose in a slightly different but still powerful configuration at the outset of the annual 1952 meeting, held in Geneva. From summary reports we learn that the commission gathered in a closed session that evidently spelled out practices existing in some sovereign African states "in which large numbers of women were subjected to treatment which constituted an assault on their corporal integrity." (It is unclear who initiated and organized the meeting.)[49] The session left commission members disturbed and in agreement about the need to act on "inhuman customs that had been described at the closed meeting." However, confusion remained about where and when to issue a fitting resolution. Mary Sutherland again used the moment to segue into her own modest defense of empire, endorsing the fact that in some territories under UK administration, there were in fact "laws expressly forbidding the custom to which the proposed draft resolution related."[50]

While CSW representatives from the remaining colonial powers continued to reference an array of familiar arguments (for instance, the need to save "native women and girls" from "sexual barbarity"), they had also begun moving in some significant new directions. One was the promotion of women's enfranchisement and access to political participation. The UK and French delegates of course attempted to suggest that constraints on political representation had little to do with colonial rule per se. Sutherland, with utter seriousness, pointed out, "Women could be debarred from voting without there being discrimination. For instance, in certain territories for which the United Kingdom had been made responsible [sic], village councils had been set up which did not follow Western democratic procedure and did not grant the right to vote either to men or women."[51] She went on to point out that men and women had equal franchise rights in twenty-six of the (British) colonial territories. If in a few cases there was only limited franchise, "it could not be considered that non-self-governing territories were more backward than autonomous states in this respect."[52] Wielding effusive, upbeat generalities, Lefaucheux echoed her colleague's spin, insisting in 1950, for instance, that "the Frenchwoman in the metropolitan territory had obtained complete political rights for women in the overseas territories. Moreover, in future elections Europeans and indigenous inhabitants would vote for the same representatives, instead of there being separate lists as in the past." In what can be read as a double-edged statement today, the protocol continued, "In her opinion, democracy could go no further."[53]

At other junctures the chairwoman became more guarded, underlining the difficulties of organizing elections in vast territories, with scattered populations and no conventional means to verify voter identities (intact vital records).[54] Sutherland at least insisted that her government was paving a path to independence for its colonies, guiding colonial territories to full self-government

> "in conditions that ensure to the people concerned both a fair standard of living and freedom from oppression from every quarter." New constitutions, giving the franchise to women, had been introduced in recent years in eleven Territories ... It was the practice of the local governments in Territories where harmful, inveterate customs persisted to convince influential sections of the local population of the evils of such customs before introducing legal measures to deal with them ... [55]

She did not make clear at which date that prospective "full self-government" might be granted.

At a distance of sixty years, the claims of mid-twentieth-century colonial powers – here, issued and presented by women – feel disconcertingly self-righteous. In this public venue this handful of UN delegates appears to have seen no contradiction between continued colonial rule and pushing for vastly extended political rights for women.[56] Their constructions of rights and responsibilities – particularly concerning the Non-Self-Governing Territories – could also thrust allied delegates from other member states into fraught positions.[57] Their responses merit further analysis. And not least, the increasing number of CSW delegates from newly independent states raises the question of how their presence began to impact discussions, not only of colonial rule, but all CSW aspirations for the future. This, too, is a subject that deserves much closer scrutiny.

With the newly independent states' allegiances far from fixed, more established powers in the commission blew hot and cold, alternately courting and patronizing their delegates. The representatives of more powerful states, be it East bloc or West, quickly learned, however, that the condescending language of "backwardness" and "underdevelopment" would not pass without protest. Thus, for instance, the record shows Mrs Menon, delegate from (post-Partition) India, protesting during a March 1949 meeting on equal pay for equal work that an official document in circulation had spread erroneous statements and out-of-date figures about her country.

> India was several times described as a backward country. But a country whose economy was not fully developed *was not necessarily as backward as countries whose people could not enjoy civil freedom*, where most women were compelled to work against their wish and entrust their children to public institutions ... India was a relatively undeveloped country in a stage of political adolescence ... [58]

Menon's intervention echoed protests of her predecessor on the commission, Begum Hamid Ali, who the previous year had sparred with the Soviet delegate Mrs Popova about the role and meaning of the Koran; according to one meeting protocol she declared, "Since India became independent, the women of India were attaining equal rights in every possible direction. India's Constitution, however, was still on the anvil."[59] Over time delegates appeared to deploy such terms as "backward" or "barbaric" less frequently and more cautiously, while the seemingly more neutral language of "less-developed countries" and "under-developed areas" steadily gained favor.[60] Even the term "under-developed" could prove provocative, demonstrated, for instance, when the representative of Pakistan in 1953 pointed to women's high participation in provincial elections in her country, which "might be classed among the under-developed regions of the world."[61] Representatives of the newly independent states registered their disapproval of old prejudices with caustic efficiency: when on another occasion – in May 1952 – the Soviet Union's delegate declared that the status of women in Pakistan was "deplorable" in that country, that girls were being sold by their families and women treated as chattels, the representative from that country responded sharply that the allegations "applied to conditions *as they had been centuries earlier* and there could be no point in discussing them when they no longer exist."[62] The patronizing defenders of colonial arrangements and their adversaries had both been put on notice.

On the anvil

As I conclude this chapter, many large questions linger. I have shown here that tensions around the Cold War and European imperialism, which pitted delegates from France and Britain against those from newly independent states and the USSR, greatly diminished the effectiveness of the early CSW, its ability to improve the lives of women. Given the profound fissures under which it labored, could the Commission on the Status of Women tally any successes in its first decade? Offering aid and advocacy to women and girls across national lines in the mid-twentieth century was a perplexing task and the stakes were high as the world realigned into a largely new geopolitical order. Keenly interested in achieving equal voting rights for women and increasing women's access to public posts, the commission did launch a Convention on the Political Rights of Women as its first symbolic milestone; the General

Assembly adopted it in December 1952, opening it for signature and ratification or accession, and subsequently also urged member states to take all necessary measures "leading to the development of the political rights of women in all Territories in which women do not enjoy full political rights, including Trust and Non-Self-Governing Territories."[63] Without more detailed research, it remains difficult to gauge what impact such measures truly had, for the number of countries with equal voting rights on the books had increased steadily since the end of the war; only a handful of holdouts remained. Was the CSW effective in putting these nations on notice? We find skepticism at the time: the Byelorussian representative pointed out that the convention remained declaratory and contained no provisions for implementation or extending its provisions to the Trust and Non-Self-Governing Territories.[64] Her Soviet colleague expressed a willingness to sign the convention, but echoed her reservations, adding that in many places the rights would remain at best theoretical: in the Trust and Non-Self-Governing Territories, she insisted, women were "deprived of all rights and lived as real slaves of the family and of society."[65]

From the vantage point of 2012, it remains difficult to reconstruct the faith and aspirations that women on the commission placed in the ballot box. To argue that they collectively believed in the primacy of political rights solutions over other solutions is also too simple. What, after all, did the vote or political participation signify in the global turmoil that followed on the heels of 1945? Voting rights, endorsed from every side, had no transparent meaning. Soviet and US delegates to the commission mocked each other's duplicity in promoting equal voting rights, the Soviets repeatedly invoking the racist disenfranchisement of African Americans, successive US delegates slamming the Soviet Union for upholding an "equality of slaves."[66] The French delegate – representing a nation that had only extended an equal vote to women in 1944 – could long reconcile promotion of an expanded franchise with the prolongation of colonial rule. For others at the commission's gatherings, anything resembling transparent, irreproachably conducted national elections would long remain out of reach.

As we have seen, the specter of devastating mass violence and civil war shadowed CSW proceedings almost from the outset, as representatives from war-torn China, Greece, and India (later India and Pakistan) all intermittently sat at the table in the late 1940s and beyond. A representative from Costa Rica took part in the commission's January 1948 meetings just two months before a short-lived but bloody civil war broke out in her country; she did not return the following year. Many representatives on the women's commission in its first decade were also thrown into the position of de facto representing military governments, even if the term "junta" was politely avoided at meetings: in the late 1940s and 1950s the CSW included delegates from Venezuela, Syria, the Dominican Republic, Haiti, and Cuba.[67] We lack much information about how these women reconciled their international engagement with their circumscribed domestic positions. If belonging to the commission conferred some measure of prestige, it remains less clear what kind of leverage that prestige gave these members at home.

A second preoccupation of this chapter has been whether European women could stake a position in decisive postwar policy circles and could use the UN toward that end. Europe's troubles continued to vex and transfix the international community long after the defeat of Hitler's armies. Still, if the earlier League of Nations had been something of a "European club," the United Nations soon provided evidence that a new era had arrived.[68] Following suit, in its first decade the UN's Commission on the Status of Women rarely became the province of explicitly "European issues," even while Europe remained one of the most visible battlefields in a growing global Cold War. CSW delegates from a number of European countries stood on the periphery of many battles for Europe's future, instead promoting a global expansion of civil society, accessible to women and men alike. They skirted evidence of enduring racist barriers, even while pursuing a broad set of precepts that aimed to make women and men everywhere equal legal subjects. They were hardly pioneers in this project; their Latin American colleagues affiliated with the Inter-American Commission of Women had arguably mobilized for their interests much more effectively and continuously than women from any other world region in the interwar years. Other colleagues in the commission could claim similarly impressive histories of engagement. And finally, the arrogance of explicitly or tacitly upholding a postwar colonial order – even as it was fraying, even as it was being torn down – meant that a number of formidable west European women at the United Nations had by and by depleted their moral purchase.

Notes

1 I am indebted to Margaret R. Hunt and Jürgen Matthäus for their comments on an earlier draft of this chapter, and to staff members of the Sophia Smith Collection at Smith College and the United Nations archives in New York for their generous assistance.
2 *The Washington Post*, February 27, 1947, 6.
3 In 1960 at their fourteenth annual gathering, however, members voiced concern that "no African country had ever been represented on the Commission." *Yearbook of the United Nations, 1960* (New York: Columbia University Press, 1961), 343.
4 After returning from her studies at the Sorbonne as a young woman, Lutz (1894–1976) had become an instigator of Brazil's women's suffrage movement. She served as president of the main suffrage organization in Brazil from 1922 to 1942, on the committee that drafted a new constitution for the country (1934), and briefly in the Chamber of Deputies until the dictatorship in 1937 ended electoral politics. See June E. Hahner, *Encyclopedia of Latin American History and Culture*, vol. 3 (New York: Charles Scribner's Sons, 1996), 474–75; Robert M. Levine, *Historical Dictionary of Brazil* (London: Scarecrow Press, 1979), 132; Alzira Alves de Abreu et al. (eds), *Dicionário histórico-biográfico brasileiro*, vol. 3, ed. 2 (Rio de Janeiro: FGV, 2001), 3343–44. Jessie Street (1889–1970), an Australian Labor (and later Independent Labor) politician, was the only female member of Australia's delegation to the San Francisco founding conference of the UN, attending as an adviser. She subsequently served as a member (and deputy chair) of the CSW for a two-year term, beginning in 1947, but was not reappointed. She ran into increasing problems with her government because of her left-wing political rhetoric, work for Soviet friendship and peace initiatives, and trips to the Soviet Union, including one during which she was an official guest at Stalin's funeral. See her memoir, *Truth or Repose?* (Sydney: Australasian Book Society, 1966), 266; Heather Radi (ed.), *Jessie Street: Documents and Essays* (Broadway, NSW: Women's Redress Press, 1990), 2–4.

5 Exchanges between the women's commission and the Human Rights Commission, as well as the HRC's other subcommissions (for instance, the Subcommission on Prevention of Discrimination and Protection of Minorities), continued both formally and informally.
6 See *Yearbook of the United Nations, 1946–47* (Lake Success, NY: [UN] Department of Public Information, 1947), 529, and cf. 530–31. A range of authors have described the commission's first steps in detail, including Johannes Morsink, *The Universal Declaration of Human Rights: Origins, Drafting, and Intent* (Philadelphia: University of Pennsylvania Press, 1999), esp. 116–29; Mary Ann Glendon, *A World Made New: Eleanor Roosevelt and the Universal Declaration of Human Rights* (New York: Random House, 2001), 32, 92; Deborah Stienstra, *Women's Movements and International Organizations* (New York: St. Martin's Press, 1994), 75–87; Laura Reanda, "The Commission on the Status of Women," in *The United Nations and Human Rights: A Critical Appraisal* (ed.), Philip Alston (Oxford: Clarendon, 1992), 266; Leila Rupp, *Worlds of Women: The Making of an International Women's Movement* (Princeton: Princeton University Press, 1997), 223–24; Street, *Truth or Repose*, 274–75, 306; the chapters by Margaret E. Galey in *Women, Politics, and the United Nations*, (ed.) Anne Winslow (Westport, CT: Greenwood, 1995), 6ff.; and Virginia Crocheron Gildersleeve, *Many a Good Crusade* (New York: Arno, 1980, orig. 1954), 351–53.
7 In the US case, see memo of telephone conversation, Alice Paul (World Council of the World's Women's Party) and Mr Mullikan (US State Department), August 30, 1946: US National Archives, RG 59, CDF 1945–49, 501.BD-Women/8–3046, box 2202; Florence Kitchelt (Connecticut Committee for the Equal Rights Amendment) to Harry S. Truman, January 3, 1950, letter denouncing Dorothy Kenyon, RG 59, CDF 1950–53, 340.1-AGB/1–350; letter, Florence Kitchelt to Dean Acheson, January 7, 1950: RG 59, CDF 1950–54, 340.1 AGB/1–750.
8 Jessie Street attended a few Assembly meetings in the 1930s, apparently in an informal capacity, and promoted the League back home. Dorothy Kenyon, the first US member of the 1947 CSW, had served on a late 1930s League committee for conducting a comprehensive study of the legal status of women around the world, a project cut short by the war. And Bodil Begtrup was a delegate for her native Denmark. See Radi (ed.), *Jessie Street*, 2, 11, 119–21, 192–93, 226; Biographical Note, finding aid for the Dorothy Kenyon Papers, Sophia Smith Collection, Smith College, Northampton, Massachusetts. In her early days as a delegate to the UN, Eleanor Roosevelt complained of the presence of "too many old League people here and far too many elderly states-men. They are accustomed to diplomatic ways, secrecy appeals to them, and this will only succeed if everyone says what they really think." Letter, Roosevelt to Lash (January 20, 1946), quoted in Joseph P. Lash, *Eleanor: The Years Alone* (New York: Smithmark, 1972), 49.
9 On the IACW, see *Inter-American Commission of Women, 1928–1973* (Washington, DC: General Secretariat, Organization of American States, 1974). We catch glimpses of Begum Shareefah Hamid Ali, Hansa Mehta (1897–1995), Lakshmi N. Menon (1899–1994), and Hannah Sen in Aparna Basu and Bharati Ray, *Women's Struggle: A History of the All India Women's Conference, 1927–1990* (New Delhi: Manohar, 1990), 116a–116b, 175, 180, 182, 188, and B. K. Vashishta, (ed.), *Encyclopaedia of Women in India* (New Delhi: Praveen Encyclopaedia Publications, 1976), Part II: 97–98, 158.
10 Czesław Miłosz, *Miłosz's ABC* (New York: Farrar, Straus and Giroux, 2001), 96–98.
11 Lefaucheux won the Legion of Honor for her work in the resistance. After the war she became a member of the body that drew up the new French constitution, a vice president of the Municipal Council of Paris, and a member of the Christian democratic Mouvement republicain populaire in the French assembly, devoting energy to examining the status of women in economically underdeveloped areas, particularly overseas. She served with the French UN delegation from 1946 to 1959. See entries in Jennifer S. Uglow, compiler/ed., *International Dictionary of Women's Biography* (New York: Continuum, 1982), 275; Melanie Parry (ed.), *Larousse Dictionary of Women* (New York: Larousse,

48 Women and gender in postwar Europe

   1996), 391–29; and *Current Biography 1947* (New York: H. W. Wilson, 1948), 385–86; Margaret Collins Weitz, *Sisters in the Resistance: How Women Fought to Free France, 1940–1945* (New York: John Wiley & Sons, 1995), 175, 244–45, 323; "58 on Jet Killed in Crash," *New York Times,* February 26, 1964, 1.
12 One departure from routine was a convening of the 1948 annual meeting in Beirut at the invitation of the Lebanese government and designed to provide some inspiration or encouragement for the advancement of women's rights and groups in that region.
13 In discussions of alternative venues to New York, the Indian CSW delegate Begum Hamid Ali had already back in 1948 ventured that the Swiss city might be appropriate "because it was economical and yet it was in Europe where many women still did not have as many rights as the women of the New World." See United Nations document E/CN.6/SR 27 (1948): 7. I will be citing summary reports (SR) of the commission's meetings in this chapter; verbatim transcripts have not survived.
14 E/CN.6/SR 44 (1949): 3; on May 17, 1950, the commission devoted a whole session to the problem, see E/CN.6/SR 78 (1950) and cf. E/CN.6/L.19 (1950).
15 E/CN.6/SR 69 (1950): 13.
16 See E/CN.6/SR 79 (1950): 4–6, and cf. E/CN.6/L.23 (1950). The discussions left unclear whether any of them were Jewish survivors.
17 E/CN.6/SR 80 (1950): 6–7.
18 *Ibid.*: 5.
19 E/CN.6/L.23 (1950).
20 UN document E/1915; E/CN.6/SR 91 (1951): 5–7.
21 Paul Weindling offers a fuller account of the journey these cases took through the UN in his *Nazi Medicine and the Nuremberg Trials: From Medical War Crimes to Informed Consent* (Basingstoke, UK: Palgrave Macmillan, 2004), 336–40, 459n141. He writes that by 1953 the number of claimants had risen to 468, and by 1958 to over 1,000.
22 See Arieh J. Kochavi, "United Nations War Crimes Commission," in *Encyclopedia of Genocide and Crimes Against Humanity* (Detroit: Macmillian Reference USA, 2005), 3:1100–107. The Caroline Ferriday collection, US Holocaust Memorial Museum Archives, also documents efforts by survivors of Ravensbrück experiments to receive compensation from the West German government (in part through UN intervention). Cf. Christian Pross, *Paying for the Past: The Struggle over Reparations for Surviving Victims of the Nazi Terror* (Baltimore: Johns Hopkins University Press, 1998, orig. 1988), esp. Chapters 3–4.
23 On the UN as a Cold War institution, see Brian Urquhart, *Ralph Bunche: An American Life* (New York: W. W. Norton, 1993), 234–35 and 246–47; on the witch hunt for "disloyal" American officials in the Secretariat since 1950, see Edward C. Luck, *Mixed Messages: American Politics and International Organization, 1919–1999* (Washington, DC: Brookings Institution Press, 1999), 83–89; and cf. Dean Acheson, *Present at the Creation: My Years in the State Department,* rev. ed. (New York: W. W. Norton, 1987), 619–714 passim.
24 Luck, *Mixed Messages,* 84.
25 Obituary, *New York Times,* November 23, 1954, 14. After Stalin's death, he appeared to become more conciliatory.
26 Quoted in Lie's obituary, *New York Times,* December 31, 1968, 24. Andrew Boyd, *Fifteen Men on a Powder Keg: A History of the UN Security Council* (London: Methuen, 1971), 30–31, writes, "It was Andrei Vishinsky who personified Russia at the UN during the organisation's first decade – until his sudden death in 1955, in New York … This tense little man gave the impression that, while he enjoyed being obstructive well enough, what he particularly enjoyed was a virulent onslaught. Some of his polemical feats in New York gave his audience the chilling reminder that he had served Stalin as chief prosecutor in the rigged show trials of the great pre-war purges."
27 Begtrup is cited in E/CN.6/20 (1948): 2.
28 On postwar conditions, see David Kynaston, *Austerity Britain, 1945–51* (London: Bloomsbury, 2007). For Sutherland, "Sense and Sensibility," *Times* (London), May

12, 1958, 13; obituary, *Times* (London), October 23, 1972, 14; *Times* (London), October 26, 1972, 18; Margaret l'Espinasse, "Mary Elizabeth Sutherland (1895–1972), Labour Party Organiser," in Joyce M. Bellamy and John Saville (eds), *Dictionary of Labour Biography*, vol. 6 (London: Macmillan, 1982), 245–49. She was British representative on the CSW from 1947 to 1952.
29 See E/CN.6/SR 23 (1948): 6, and E/CN.6/SR 25 (1948): 9.
30 Quoted here is the opening salvo of an article she penned, "Women's Status in USSR," *United Nations Bulletin* 6 (June 15, 1949): 648–49. Cf. similar statements, e.g., E/CN.6/SR 24 (1948): 2; E/CN.6/SR 25 (1948): 5; E/CN.6/SR 44 (1949): 2 and E/CN.6/SR 48 (1949): 6–7; E.CN.6/SR 102 (1952): 14.
31 See UN documents E/CN.6/SR 86 (1951): 10; E/CN.6/SR 104 (1952): 6; E/CN.6/SR 105 (1952): 7. Cold War fissures in the CSW were not confined to the East–West divide alone. Between meetings Dorothy Kenyon commiserated with her friends and Bodil Begtrup over the problematic sympathies of the Australian on the commission, Jessie Street. See letter, Begtrup to Kenyon, February 20, 1949, Kenyon papers, box 57, folder 7; and letter, Margery Corbett Ashby to Kenyon, November 2, 1948, and Kenyon to Corbett Ashby, (carbon copy) letter, July 9, 1948, both box 58, folder 4.
32 E/CN.6/SR 121 (1952): 15.
33 Mazower, *No Enchanted Palace: The End of Empire and the Ideological Origins of the United Nations* (Princeton: Princeton University Press, 2009), 150–51. Cf. Carol Anderson, *Eyes Off the Prize: The United Nations and the African American Struggle for Human Rights, 1944–1955* (New York: Cambridge University Press, 2003), 35–39, 53–55; Elizabeth Borgwardt, *A New Deal for the World: America's Vision for Human Rights* (Cambridge, MA: Belknap Press, 2005), 261ff.
34 Mazower, *No Enchanted Palace*, 188, 198–99, and cf. 194. On UN disavowal of colonialism, see also Wm. Roger Louis, *Ends of British Imperialism: The Scramble for Empire, Suez and Decolonization. Collected Essays* (London: I. B. Tauris, 2006), esp. Chapter 17 (written with Ronald Robinson) and Chapter 27; on UN Resolution 1514, see 700ff.
35 Mazower, *No Enchanted Palace*, 150. The General Assembly acquired more extensive supervisory powers over the trust territories (encompassing some 20 million people) than in the League's mandate system. Cf. Wm. Roger Louis (ed.), *National Security and International Trusteeship in the Pacific* (Annapolis: Naval Institute Press, 1972), and the discussion in Morsink, *Universal Declaration*, 96–101.
36 The latter were technically protected from direct UN oversight or interference. The French chair of the commission complained about her colleagues' conflation of the two categories, and reminded her colleagues that while the administering authorities of Trust Territories were required to furnish the United Nations up-to-date information about these lands, the same was not true for governments overseeing Non-Self-Governing Territories. E/CN.6/SR 117 (1952): 12.
37 See E/CN.6/137 (1950), and cf. E/CN.6 /138 (1950) and E/CN.6/163 (1951). The CSW organized many similar subsequent surveys.
38 E/CN.6/SR 92 (1951): 14; E/CN.6/SR 93 (1951): 17; E/CN.6/SR 97 (1951): 4; E/CN.6/SR 117 (1952): 13; E/CN.6/SR 137 (1953): 12.
39 E/CN.6/SR 119 (1952): 15.
40 For a useful overview of this history, see Barbara Bush, "Gender and Empire: The Twentieth Century," in *Gender and Empire*, ed. Philippa Levine (Oxford: Oxford University Press, 2004), 77–111.
41 My emphasis, E/CN.6/SR 23 (1948): 6.
42 E/CN.6/SR 142 (1953): 7–8. And cf. E/CN.6/SR 119 (1952): 18, "In the darkest hours of French history, when the metropolitan country had been occupied by the enemy, the entire population of French African territories had spontaneously rallied to the French people."
43 E/CN.6/SR 25 (1948): 2; E/CN.6/SR.31 (1948): 6.
44 E/CN.6/SR 42 (1949): 3–4.

45 *Ibid.*: 5.
46 See E/CN.6/SR 65 (1949): 8.
47 E/CN.6/SR 98 (1951): 12.
48 E/CN.6/SR 117 (1952): 19. On the complicated ways that issues such as child marriage played out at the intersection of international interests, colonial and homegrown feminist politics, see Mrinalini Sinha, "Unraveling Masculinity and Rethinking Citizenship: A Comment," *Representing Masculinity: Male Citizenship in Modern Western Culture*, ed. Stefan Dudink et al. (New York: Palgrave Macmillan 2007), esp. 269–70.
49 E/CN.6/SR 121 (1952): 11.
50 *Ibid.*: 12. Islamic societies did not seem to be under specific attack in this apparent escalation of anxiety within the women's commission.
51 According to the summary report that survives of this meeting. E/CN.6/SR 40 (1949): 7.
52 E/CN.6/SR 41 (1949): 7. For a slightly earlier period, see Mrinalini Sinha, "Suffragism and Internationalism: The Enfranchisement of British and Indian Women under an Imperial State," in *Women's Suffrage in the British Empire: Citizenship, Nation, and Race*, ed. Ian Fletcher, Laura E. Nym Mayhall, and Philippa Levine (New York: Routledge, 2000), 224–39. Dorothy Kenyon, US representative to the commission, had just before this noted that 21 countries remained where women did not yet possess the right to vote, 9 in the American hemisphere and the remaining 12 in countries with mostly quite small populations.
53 E/CN.6/SR 96 (1951): 4; cf. E/CN.6/SR 117 (1952): 19: "Again, since the entry into force of the latest French Constitution, the right of citizenship had been granted to all subjects of the French Republic." By contrast, some of her colleagues appeared to hold much more extreme, racially charged views of "local customs" and were not above arguing "how easily Non-Self-Governing Territories could revert to barbaric customs when they became independent." See E/CN.6/SR 117 (1952): 14–15.
54 E/CN.6/SR 134 (1953): 8.
55 E/CN.6/SR 117 (1952): 22–23.
56 The French delegate also resisted any attempt to tie condemnations of racial discrimination to resolutions on political rights. E/CN.6/SR 84 (1951): 15–16.
57 See Louis, *Ends of British Imperialism*; on US views of postwar British (and French) colonial claims, 455–63, 466–67, 479, 500–501, and on Britain's reputation at the UN, 696ff.
58 My emphasis; E/CN.6/SR 49 (1949): 2–3. On Menon, see S. N. Visranath, *Profiles of Lakshmi N. Menon* (Bangalore: All India Women's Conference, 1995), esp. 202.
59 E/CN.6/SR 26 (1948): 4, my emphasis; and cf. E/CN.6/SR 17 (1947): 8, and E/CN.6/SR 17/Corr. 1 (1947), for a discussion of the Koran and "customary law."
60 See, e.g., E/CN.6/SR 41 (1949): 5; E/CN.6/SR 75 (1950): 5–6; E/CN.6/L.18 (1950); E/CN.6/SR 79 (1950): 8; E/CN.6/SR 108 (1952): 19; E/CN.6/SR 110 (1952): 15; E/CN.6/SR 117 (1952): 22–23.
61 E/CN.6/SR 132 (1953): 16.
62 E/CN.6/SR 101 (1952): 15; E/CN.6/SR 102 (1952): 7, my emphasis.
63 *Yearbook of the United Nations, 1953* (New York: Columbia University Press, 1954), 426–29. The CSW continued campaigns on multiple fronts, however, promoting improved female educational and economic opportunities, expanded nationality rights for married women and improved status of women in private law, equal pay for equal work, and greater opportunities for women at the UN itself.
64 E/CN.6/SR 133 (1953): 5. US officials decided this was not the desired stuff of treaties and did not become signatories.
65 And the Polish representative weighed in to remind the commission again that in some places only white women had gained access to the franchise. E/CN.6/SR 134 (1953): 5.
66 See, e.g., Dorothy Kenyon papers, box 1, folder 17, *Post Intelligencer*, April 1949. The liberal Democrat Kenyon was not above inquiring bluntly whether women received equal pay for equal work in the USSR's slave labor camps.

67 Commission protocols reveal that Mexican delegate Amalia C. de Castillo Ledon did use the word on at least one occasion. See E/CN.6/SR 66 (1950): 14. On living with the Trujillo regime, see the intriguing article, Ellen DuBois and Lauren Derby, "The Strange Case of Minerva Bernardino: Pan American and United Nations Women's Right Activist," *Women's Studies International Forum* 32 (2009): 43–50.
68 Mazower, *No Enchanted Palace*, 90, 145.

3

WOMEN AND SOCIAL WORK IN CENTRAL AND EASTERN EUROPE

Darja Zaviršek

Introduction

This chapter focuses on the importance of women's agency in the development of professional social work, social welfare activities, and social work education in Yugoslavia during the interwar and Communist periods (1920–40 and 1945–91, respectively).[1] Setting the Yugoslav case in comparison with that of the Soviet Union, this chapter will examine the processes by which Yugoslavia's Communist leadership established a system of social work education in the 1950s, with key roles played by women in its founding. However, the Communist Party then closely supervised women's activities and legitimized gender inequality. In spite of women's significant contributions to public health and social innovation in the drive to modernize the predominantly rural countries of central and eastern Europe, their work was ignored by the leadership of newly developed Communist states.

Cold War methodology in the history of social work

The history of social work in central and eastern Europe has been dominated by two methodological fallacies: one, that men were the founders of the profession; and two, that the development of professional social work in eastern Europe was the same in all Communist countries. The latter has been described by some researchers as "Cold War methodology." The major characteristics of Cold War methodology are, first of all, the construction of eastern Europe as a homogeneous entity, and second, the production (whether deliberate or unintentional) of the alterity of its peoples. Until the late 1990s, most researchers believed that professional social work had been something of a modern humanist mission, imported from the West only after the collapse of Communism. Most Western academics share the oversimplified view that in denouncing "Western" bourgeois ideas, Communist nations also dismissed the profession of social work. Instead of looking on indigenous, culturally specific traditions in different eastern European countries, researchers have focused primarily upon the Western humanitarian and developmental organizations which entered in large numbers after 1991.

In addition, Western feminist writers have tended to overlook women working in the social sphere. Unlike their compatriots who moved into traditionally male sectors of employment, Eastern women welfare workers appeared familiar and ordinary to Western writers, who were fascinated by the exotic idea of eastern women working in factories or on immense collective farms. The construction of the eastern woman as "Other" can be seen in the iconic image of the *traktoristka* (woman on a tractor), which the Western gaze embodied with the essence of eastern European womanhood. With these preconceptions, researchers were drawn to the larger body of written material about women's work in "masculine" fields, not recognizing that in order to destabilize the old (bourgeois) gender order, Communist leaders were deliberately silent concerning women's welfare work. Even eastern European scholars have approached their topic as "the history of western social work" rather than exploring central and eastern European traditions and foundations. In consequence, there are a limited number of studies that would provide a fruitful comparison to the material presented here.

This research is based on a multifaceted methodological approach that includes a comparative analysis of literature on the history of social work in Europe, with special attention paid to eastern Europe. Primary source material provides the basis for a unique analysis of Yugoslavia and its former constituent nation, Slovenia. This source base is comprised of archival documents from 1945 to 1970, interviews with early Yugoslav teachers, welfare and social workers, examination of photographs, site visits, and early academic theses. Interviews used in this article were conducted by the author between 2005 and 2008. Those interviewed included two pioneers of social work education in Slovenia, early instructors of social work, "field visitors," and older professional social workers from Slovenia and Macedonia. Field research included visits to the largest semi-closed asylums in Slovenia and Croatia, where social workers have been sending the disabled since the early 1960s. Major focus is placed on Yugoslavia because it was the only nation in central and eastern Europe to establish schools of social work after the Communist rise to power, and is therefore unique in the development of social work education under Communism.[2]

It is important to note that the Soviet and Yugoslav undertakings to be discussed here were defined as "socialist social work," and therefore differed fundamentally from Western social work until the early 1980s.

Parallels and variations in development

The early twentieth century witnessed the foundation of a number of institutions whose goal was to train women to work in the social sphere – the antecedents of modern professional social workers. These schools of social education developed not only in western Europe, but also in central and eastern European nations, and progressive women were often at the helm. In 1908, Alice Salomon (1872–1948) established the first women's school for social work in Berlin. That year, Edith Farkas founded a Catholic organization that gave work to religious and laywomen in Hungary.[3] Both Salomon and Farkas were driven by the desire to replace alms work for the needy with what would later become known as professional social work, and their work inspired others. Salomon's fellow "welfare theorist" Ilse Arlt (1876–1960) opened a school of social work in Vienna in 1912.[4] After World War I, social education further expanded in east central Europe. Margit Slachta, one of the members of Edith Farkas's Hungarian Catholic organization, opened a school for social work in Budapest in 1926, while Helena Radlinska set up the School of Education and Social Work at the Free Polish University in Warsaw in 1925,[5] and Princess Ileana of Romania established a school for social work in Bucharest in 1929.[6] In the Kingdom of Serbs, Croats and Slovenes, efforts were made to establish the Royal School of Social Work (*Kraljevska zemaljska socialna škola*) in Zagreb in 1920.[7] In 1921, pedagogue and children's author Ljudevit Krajačić published an article entitled "The Social School and the Need to Educate Social Workers" in the Croatian journal *National Defense* (*Narodna zaštita*). Krajačić claimed that the necessity for "theoretical social education" arose from the needs of survivors of the war, who were struggling with physical privation and mental scars. The Royal School aimed to meet this need, setting up vocational training and scholarships designed to attract the best potential social workers from all parts of the kingdom: Croatia, Slovenia, Serbia, Dalmatia, Bosnia, and Montenegro.

These examples show that in a number of central and eastern European countries, attempts to professionalize social work were present from the beginning of the twentieth century, especially after World War I. This is similar to the development of the field in Western nations. The founders of social education in both the West and the East prior to World War II did not simply understand social work as aiding the poor or seeking to address individual pathologies. To the contrary, they believed that their work should improve social justice in the nation as a whole. Amidst the quick and at times brutal industrialization and urbanization of their societies, they struggled against the economic, social and symbolic inequality experienced by women and other marginalized populations.[8]

While western and eastern European social work and welfare systems showed similarities in chronology and intent, they diverged in several fundamental ways. Western countries generally had larger urban populations, lower poverty rates, better medical care, and more extensive existing educational systems.[9] Meanwhile, it was only after 1945 that the more rural eastern European countries developed public institutions to care for a burgeoning urban population. Such institutions were a key element of urban development, and were seen as a sign of the modernization of social welfare initiatives. After World War II, when western Europeans were calling for a more humane means of dealing with the disabled and mentally ill, the type of closed and semi-closed institutions that they condemned had just begun to appear in eastern Europe. Additionally, western social education and practices after 1945 were based on foundations developed before the war, while eastern Europe experienced an ideological rupture with prewar theories. The profession, where it existed, was channeled into a state-directed activity, while prewar educational entities were closed down and erased from public memory.[10]

In most of central and eastern Europe, professional social work did not develop systematically until the 1990s. Having been an occupation for petit-bourgeois women in the early twentieth century, it was deemed an unsuitable activity by the Communist regimes that came to power following World War II. The belief that socialism's capacity to guarantee the well-being of all citizens would eradicate the need for intervention by social workers was also prevalent at the time. It should therefore come as no surprise that in Hungary, some university-level social work courses were terminated in 1948, and the Ministry of Welfare and the Social Policy Institute terminated their activities the following year.[11] In 1952, departments of social work at universities in Czechoslovakia and Poland also ceased to operate.[12] The aforementioned Princess Ileana Superior School for Social Assistance in Romania was first transformed into the Institute for Social Assistance in 1948 and then into the Institute for Social Provision in 1951, before finally being shut down in 1952.[13] In postwar Yugoslavia, however, the situation was different. Yugoslav Communists ensured the establishment of schools for social workers throughout Yugoslavia (in 1952 in Croatia, in 1955 in Slovenia, in 1957 in Macedonia and Serbia, and in 1958 in Bosnia and Herzegovina). These developments served political aims as much as they did people's needs, as will be shown later in this study.

Disappearing knowledge

In presocialist Yugoslavia, numerous women's groups and feminist organizations were similar to their western counterparts in their articulation of issues, demands for rights, and attention to social reform. Women's organizations in the Kingdom of Yugoslavia advocated voting rights, equal pay for equal work, and civil marriage. They also deliberately referred to "social work" (rather than "welfare") when speaking about social justice.[14] Since 1931, the Yugoslav Women's Association had had a "Section for Social Work," and many of the women who promoted social work in the Slovenian part of the Kingdom of Yugoslavia were also activists in feminist organizations.[15]

In eastern Europe, there had been a long history of the interconnectedness between women working in social spheres and the so-called "woman question." In Slovenia, the idea first appeared in 1884 when Pavlina Pajk, a poet and songwriter, published an essay entitled "Some Notes on the Woman Question," in which she endorsed gender parity (specifically, equal pay for equal work) and encouraged more extensive social equality among various segments of the population. Later, public discussions about the "woman question" appeared in the first women's journal, *The Slovenian Woman* (*Slovenka*), which was issued in Trieste between 1897 and 1902. The "woman question" was nearly always linked to broader social issues and with what is today called the "welfare regime."

Slovenian and other Yugoslav women were knowledgeable about key activists and currents of thought in western social work. Slovenian feminists and professionals within the sphere of social welfare, like Angela Vode and Alojzija Štebi, praised Alice Salomon and Jane Addams, and the Slovenian women's press introduced its readers to their work. For instance, two different women's magazines published articles about the life and the work of Alice Salomon in 1912 and in 1932. They presented Salomon as a leading figure in international social work whose assistance to the needy was complemented by her advocacy of social reform in the name of equality and justice for all. It is probable that the 1912 article appeared in connection with the establishment of the first welfare school in the Austro-Hungarian Empire, Ilse Arlt's institution in Vienna (the *Vereinigte Fachkurse für Volkspflege*, or United Specialist Courses for Primary Care).[16] Slovenia, at that time still part of the empire, would have been well aware of that event, though they could not yet hope for a similar development closer to home. In 1930, another women's journal, *The Woman's World*, praised Jane Addams' efforts to secure rights and better living conditions for workers, and went on to praise her pacifism.

However, World War II overturned all of this. Although the political demands of prewar feminists found their demands almost identical to those of Communist Party programs in the early 1940s, feminists and professionals who had been active in prewar welfare politics vanished from the public sphere after 1945. Women in the Communist Party usually gave class issues priority over gender issues as they focused on universal workers' rights,[17] and postwar Communist leadership erased public memory of the few Slovenian women who had worked in the social sphere. Angela Vode, a former president of the Women's Movement of Yugoslavia, emerged from a Nazi prison camp only to be expelled from the Communist Party and arrested after opposing party leadership. Non-Yugoslav women like Alice Salomon and Jane Addams were similarly excluded from future discussions of social intervention.

Erasing the legacies of women pioneers was not a specifically Communist undertaking. Some of the most influential western European founders of social work were overlooked and forgotten for decades. The work of Ilse Arlt, for instance, was rediscovered only in the 1990s. Arlt, a Viennese Jew, saw her school of social work (the first in Austria) destroyed by the Nazis. It was never reestablished. Alice Salomon, also Jewish, was given three weeks by the Gestapo to flee Germany while her books were burnt and her school closed down in 1937. She remained a refugee in New York until her death in 1948. This void in the history of social work was not filled until the 1980s, when some of Salomon's writing began to be republished.[18]

There were different political reasons for the careful engineering of public knowledge of about the history of the social work profession in post-Nazi Germany, Austria and in the Communist Yugoslavia. In Germany and Austria, the silence grew out of Holocaust-related shame and a fear of encouraging sentiment critical of social work. Meanwhile, in Yugoslavia the new Communist elite constructed the "new people's era" by suppressing the past achievements of women working in the social sphere. The establishment of the schools of social work across Yugoslavia was to be seen as a unique and original intervention by the Communist Party, without any historical predecessors. As Katja Vodopivec, one of the founders of social education in Yugoslavia, recalled, "We could write about what happens in the west and about social work abroad, but always in such a way that it was obvious that ours [The

Communist Party of Yugoslavia] had written or said that already before them [westerners]. We always had to be in front of everyone else" (interview by the author, 2005).

From field visitors to social workers in Yugoslavia

Following World War II, social aid across Yugoslavia was mainly provided by the Antifascist Women's Front (AFŽ), a major women's organization with over 4,000 members in Slovenia and 2 million members in Yugoslavia.[19] Known as "field visitors" (*terenske obiskovalke*), these unpaid workers were usually individuals who had played an active role in the partisan struggle. The AFŽ was established by the Yugoslav Communist Party in 1942 (1943 in Slovenia) in order to mobilize aid to partisans fighting against Nazism and to ensure a wide loyalty base among women, in particular among peasant women, for the forthcoming Communist rise to power.[20] After 1945, its work focused on three basic activities: "collecting information" about individuals and families in need and reporting the "situation in the field" to higher local authorities; distributing material aid to the most needy and organizing housing for war orphans; and organizing educational seminars on hygiene, infant mortality, and childcare.[21] Apart from providing aid to "all those in need" and carrying out certain modernization processes like anti-tuberculosis campaigns and registering children for medical examinations, the work of the AFŽ was supposed to foster a new socialist subjectivity.

The AFŽ represented the beginning of social work education in Yugoslavia, as the recruitment of paid female social workers began within this organization. In the early days of Communist leadership, women were at first readily encouraged to engage in various unpaid voluntary activities, then to take up paid jobs in social work. However, patriarchal Communist leaders did not automatically "confer" the right for paid employment to women. They emphasized that women had "earned" their rights during the liberation struggle, when they had showed their "maturity" and had justified their equality, fighting "shoulder to shoulder" with men against the enemy. Formal equality was thus a reward for their self-sacrifice. (Such an attitude was not unknown elsewhere in Europe. In Ireland, for example, women's philanthropic work justified their entrance into the public sphere.)[22]

Despite its initial importance, the AFŽ was disbanded by the Communist leadership in 1953 on the grounds that it had become historically irrelevant. At this time, schools of social work throughout Yugoslavia had begun to train professional social workers in order to replace the AFŽ, and in 1958, social work was officially recognized as a profession.[23]

Yugoslav welfare workers and female volunteer workers in the Soviet Union – a comparison

Although the Yugoslav Communist Party severed political ties with the Soviet Union under Stalin in 1948 (in the conflict known as *Informbiro*[24]), the Communist system in the Soviet Union remained a model for leading Yugoslav political figures, most of whom had been trained in Soviet party schools (cf. *Soviet Women Among Us*, 1945).[25]

A number of similarities with the Soviet Communist system could therefore be found in Tito's Yugoslavia.[26]

In both early Soviet Russia and postwar Yugoslavia, many so-called "modernization processes" were carried out by women.[27] In Stalin-era Russia, women played an important role in the *kul'turnost'* (culturedness) campaign, while Yugoslav women carried out activities pertaining to hygiene and public health. Likewise, the role of the AFŽ had several similarities with that of two Soviet women's organizations, the *Zhenotdel* and the *obshchestvennitsy* (civic-minded women). The *Zhenotdel,* the women's department of the Central Committee of the Communist Party, was created in 1919 in order to spread the party's message among women[28] or, in Lenin's words, to "rouse the broad masses of women, bringing them into contact with the Party and keeping them under its influence."[29] Two decades later, Yugoslav Communists established the AFŽ with the same ideological objectives.

On January 5, 1930, the Politburo eliminated the *Zhenotdel* on the grounds that it was inspired by "bourgeois feminism," and in 1953 the Yugoslav Central Committee dismissed the AFŽ, claiming that it was no longer needed. Both organizations had been active for eleven years. The real reason for the dissolution of the Yugoslav AFŽ was the desire to curb demands for the reestablishment of women's organizations, which were, to use the words of national hero Mitra Mitrović, full of "bourgeois ladies."[30] Both Yugoslav Communists and Soviet party leaders feared that by linking their activities to those of prewar feminists, women would subvert the objectives of the state. The political life of women, which had flourished before the war, had to be channeled into a single women's organization under party control.[31] Following the elimination of the *Zhenotdel,* the Soviet *obshchestvennitsy* movement was founded in the late 1930s, and began to carry out activities very similar to those of early welfare workers from the AFŽ.[32]

At least four significant similarities between these two women's movements can be found. Both organizations promoted literacy, the construction of kindergartens, playgrounds and summer retreats (*kolonije*) for children, cleanliness and hygiene, and seminars on cooking, housekeeping, and other domestic tasks. Both organizations were formed under the auspices of the Communist Party to mobilize women to perform social tasks outside of the family unit and to influence "less advanced" women to abandon gendered activities (and consequently gender identity). Neither organization received payment for the work it did. Finally, workers from both organizations were often unpopular. *Obshchestvennitsy* workers were turned away from factories and public kitchens, where they tried to promote cleanliness and moral behavior, while AFŽ workers (known as *afežejevke*)[33] earned the wrath of the rural population by allegedly trying to destroy village life. Both organizations also continued to arouse negative connotations long after they had ceased to exist.[34] As one teacher remarked, "calling [women] '*afežejevke*' was like calling women 'feminists' today; it was a pejorative term, something to ridicule them."

Many Slovenes were apprehensive about the work being done by the AFŽ in part due to its Soviet inspiration (it is highly likely that the Communist leadership in Yugoslavia followed the example set by the *Zhenotdel* and *obshchestvennitsy* when mobilizing women to join the AFŽ in 1942). Interviews with early social workers from Slovenia showed that joint activities, and especially organized childcare in the first decade after the war, were seen as potentially dangerous. Women feared that their children would be sent not to summer retreats but to Russia.

However controversial they became, the Zhenotdel and the AFŽ provide interesting examples of how Communist Parties used gender politics to influence vast sections of the population during their rise to power, attempting to "mobiliz[e]" a key section of the population in the service of the new state, and extending the sphere of control into the private household.'[35] The conviction that "social work carries out the goals of social policy"[36] remained prevalent well into the 1970s.

The liberalization of everyday life in Yugoslavia after 1948

Certain processes of the liberalization of everyday life went hand in hand with Yugoslavia's ideological rift with the Soviet Union. When the Yugoslav Communists ended their close relationship with Stalin, they were forced to find other political allies, and linked themselves with the United States in the social field. The development of schools of social work was, to a large extent, a product of the Cold War equilibrium. Yugoslavia had positioned itself as the most open of all Communist countries, a phenomenon sometimes called "socialism with a human face."[37] American experts provided advice on the first social work curriculum in Croatia in the early 1950s, and helped to establish social welfare institutions called "centres for social work" throughout Yugoslavia in the early 1960s. Some foreigners were allowed to enter the country, and certain citizens were sent abroad by the Communist Party in order to "learn more about social services." One of the pioneers of social work education in Slovenia, Katja Vodopivec, was given a passport and granted permission to visit the USA to bring back information on workers' legislation. Instead, she learned social work methods from this "western ally", and intended to share her newly acquired knowledge once she returned. Another pioneer of social work education, Nika Arko, was sent to Sweden to observe social service workers in action. In Croatia, prominent founders of social work education were sent abroad through UN exchange programs in order to acquire knowledge for the establishment of the Croatian School of Social Work.[38]

It seems that this "third way" political system had initially allowed greater freedom in the reestablishment of certain prewar structures in everyday life, especially in the social sphere. The liberalization of everyday life was also reflected in the 7th Congress of the League of the Communists of Yugoslavia in 1958, where prominent party members stressed the need for a general improvement of living standards, more activities in local communities, and the development of "professional social workers".[39] This was the first time the expression 'social worker' was used at the highest level of Yugoslav politics.

Intellectuals, party activists, and peasant women – the three orders of society

Slovenia, as part of Yugoslavia, was the second of the five socialist republics (the others being Croatia, Macedonia, Bosnia and Herzegovina, and Serbia) to institute social work education.[40] The opening of the School of Social Work (*Šola za socialne delavce*) in Ljubljana took place on November 7, 1955, on the anniversary of the October Revolution. On the morning of November 8, 1955, all Slovenian newspapers published a short commentary on the modest ceremony. One newspaper summed up the school's activities by saying that it would "qualify its cadre for duties in the spheres of social insurance and social protection and medicine, and will combat criminality and alcoholism."[41] Another newspaper stressed that future social workers would toil for "protection of the family," dealing with issues such as foster care, divorce, and single motherhood.[42] These periodicals noted that there remained room for expansion: while 30 students were enrolled in the school, Slovenia needed an estimated 900 social workers.

Three women symbolizing the "three orders" of the new society were present at the opening ceremony of the School of Social Work: a Communist intellectual, a party member with a working class background, and a party member with a peasant background. They represented a fundamental shift from the pre-Communist period, when the ranks of female social activists were composed primarily of Catholic nuns and laywomen, wealthy philanthropists, and professionals from bourgeois families. Their impact on social work education demonstrates that individuals, not only women from mass organizations, occupied important places within the public sphere. Their biographies are intertwined with personal agency, but also political instrumentalization.

The first, Katja Vodopivec (b. 1917), was an intellectual with a bourgeois background (her father was director of the City Bank of Ljubljana).[43] As an expert on workers' rights legislation, she went on to become a leading figure at the University of Ljubljana's Faculty of Law. Her major contribution to the field was a textbook on social work methods, the first of its kind to appear in Slovenia. The second, Nika Arko (b. 1914), came from a working class family and simultaneously served as deputy director of the Council for Health and Social Policy of the People's Republic of Slovenia, an important institution, which initiated formal social work training in the country. Nika had begun her career as a member of the AFŽ.[44] The third, Marija Jančar (1913–91), was born a peasant. She would serve as director of the School of Social Work for its first seventeen years (1955–72). As a school teacher from rural Slovenia, she was neither an intellectual nor an important figure in the Communist Party. She did, however, represent the third order of socialist women, and was meant to serve as a role model to future social work students from rural areas. In an interview, one of the first social work teachers remarked that Jančar learned of her assignment through a late-night phone call from a Communist Party official: she was to immediately ready herself to begin the important project of educating social workers in Slovenia.

While the party intellectual, Dr Vodopivec, was sent abroad to learn and write about workers' rights, Marija Jančar was sent to the city to carry out another important socialist project: the development of the School of Social Work. Sending teachers from rural areas to cities was a common occurrence in many Communist countries. Educated women recruited peasant women into the Communist Party, and peasant women shook their urban colleagues out of the bubble of the private sphere. That is, women with a "higher intellectual and political consciousness" were asked to influence their benighted counterparts. In Yugoslavia, members of the AFŽ were asked to become role models for other women and were assigned the task of educating and inspiring those with an impoverished rural background. Marija Jančar, herself an AFŽ member, was a hard-working woman, a modest teacher, and a firm believer in Communism. Living in Bela Krajina, a liberated territory since 1943, she had helped find homes for displaced children and provisional housing for people who had lost their homes in the war. Social work teachers who knew her speak fondly of her, saying, "She was mother to us all."

The School of Social Work was meant to educate welfare workers (called social protection officers) who were already active within the welfare system. It was developed as a two-year post-secondary school and did not become an institution of higher learning until 1960, when its name was changed to the College of Social Work (*Višja šola za socialne delavce*). It became a part of the University of Ljubljana in 1975, and began offering a four-year degree programme in 1992. In 2003 it was officially renamed the Faculty of Social Work (*Fakulteta za socialno delo*).[45] During Communist times, all teaching materials were written by Yugoslav writers; literature on social welfare from before World War II had fallen into oblivion. As Katja Vodopivec observed, Communist politicians required that foreign input be used only in such a way that it reinforced "novel" Yugoslav thinking. Vodopivec's 1959 *Handbook of Social Work Methods,* written upon her return from the United States, focused on case work, social reeducation, and group work, but Vodopivec was not allowed to mention the individuals who had contributed to the development of these methods. Instead, most of her citations were taken from speeches by leading party figures, such as Tito and economist Edvard Kardelj, as well as from Yugoslav sociologists, psychologists, lawyers, and medical professionals who wrote about "Marxist personality," "Communist morale," and "building socialist consciousness." International authors, such as Hamilton Gordon, L. de Bray, and Herbert Latthe, were mentioned throughout the book, but never directly quoted. The Communist leadership censored any traces of knowledge of social welfare that had existed prior to the implementation of socialism in Yugoslavia.

The conflict between what was desired and what was permitted is evident in Vodopivec's book, and the reader can feel that one layer has been superimposed upon the other, as if it were a palimpsest tablet. The first layer was meant to present a collection of existing social work methods, based on therapeutic knowledge and self-reflexivity, in order to avoid the imposition of the "truth" of the social worker onto that of the "client." The second layer served to justify the one-party system: "The aim of the core subjects in social work education is to teach the future social workers the political and legal-organizational principles of our societal system and the principles of the formation of a healthy personality within this societal system."[46] Furthermore, whenever Vodopivec wrote a passage that might be considered unacceptable, she justified it by citing party politicians. For example, "The aim of social work is to balance the relationship between persons who are in need of special protection and the society in which they live, and *vice versa*, between society and individuals"[47] was followed by a footnote from a speech Tito had delivered in 1958: "Comrades, we will not be mistaken if we look at the human being with the same care and understanding with which we look at the factory!"[48] When she wrote that "the social worker has to be human ... it is not about imposing our life-style on another person,"[49] she proceeded with a quotation from Kardelj, the architect of socialist self-management: "the state apparatus has to serve the people, not impose power upon them – this is the basic principle of socialist democracy."[50]

Today, Vodopivec's text reads like a patchwork of western social work methods, consciously and over-cautiously packaged in the canonized ideas of Communist Party politics. When asked why she had quoted so many Communist authors, Vodopivec said that she knew she would have to send the book to the Ministry for review: "It was probably read by Vida Tomšič[51] and certain other politicians. They got back to me and requested that I use more of our writers, because everything the foreigners said had already been said by us." Nonetheless, her ideological acrobatics did not prevent the book from being removed from libraries and social work curricula. The manual was ultimately banned, never to be used again by students of social work. A librarian at the School of Social Work remembered finding a cache of unused copies of the book in a locked closet; in the 1970s all but two were promptly thrown away. After her book had been demonized, Vodopivec moved to the Faculty of Law: "They wouldn't let me work in social work any more. I had to go, but I also wanted to be closer to my initial discipline" (interview, 2005).

From 1959 to the early 1990s, not a single textbook on social work methods was written, and some teachers recall that methodology was considered a touchy subject within Yugoslav social work. Nonetheless, social workers trained in the 1960s and 1970s who were employed at the centers for social work remembered how they "worked with their hearts," happily working overtime without regard to their pay (Interviews, 2005–7). "We were full of enthusiasm and even had more resources than our colleagues have today!" (social worker employed at one of the centres for social work in Skopje since the mid-1960s; interview by the author 2008).

The influence of social work education on the new gender and social order

One of the most surprising elements of social work training throughout Yugoslavia after 1952 was that a large number of the first students were men, many of whom had already worked as social protection officers.[52] A 1957 survey showed that 41.3 percent of Slovenia's 293 accredited social workers were men who had jobs pertaining to social issues in their local municipalities.[53] Such a gender ratio shows that although caring work was still considered an inherently feminine activity, professional training was desirable for men as well. There are several reasons for this unusual blurring of gender lines. Increased interest in welfare work was probably bolstered by the stipends that were offered for professional study; combined with a lack of paid unemployment elsewhere, this made social work a desirable option for men. A professional diploma conferred symbolic social mobility, making it an attractive path for men who had already worked within the field. Moreover, eastern European patriarchal societies had long held the belief that only men could turn an activity into a profession.[54] The high concentration of male students was not only the consequence of a structural focus on men's needs, but a deliberate move to counter the prewar tradition of female charity and philanthropy. A large number of men in a traditionally female profession could change the gendered, bourgeois image of welfare and reshape both the gender and social orders. An amalgamation of these factors could therefore ensure that welfare work would finally shake off the concrete and symbolic characteristics of feminine charity or alms work to become a formal profession. A similar blurring of gender lines for the sake of the implementation of a new gender order had precedent in the Communist East: for a short period in Stalin-era Russia, the *obshchestvennitsy* had more male than female members.[55]

It is clear that modernization also encompassed an attempt to reformulate the gender and social orders. On one hand, the socialist state declared its support for women's liberation. On the other hand, it used women to further its own aims. Attempts to put an end to the subordination of women to the patriarchal family, especially in rural areas, were primarily meant "to 'free up' both men and women to serve the communist cause."[56] The state guaranteed women certain formal rights, such as the right to enter the workforce, but at the same time exploited women in order to achieve hegemony through the collapse of the old gender order. In exchange for bearing the burden of having to perform both paid and unpaid work, women would receive "protection" from the state.

From the 1960s onwards, however, the number of men at schools for social work throughout Yugoslavia declined rapidly, and social work again became a feminized profession. One reason for this change stems from an increase in job opportunities for men and a lack of opportunities for promotion – most of the leading positions within the profession were already occupied by men. From the 1950s onward, the majority of the directors of welfare institutions were male.

A historical analysis of the development of social work in Yugoslavia shows that a combination of pragmatic and implicit goals led to the establishment of social work education.[57] The liberalization of everyday life and the genuine wish of some professionals and educators to provide those working in social welfare with a formal education were the key pragmatic goals. No less important were implicit goals. Buttressing "third way" Communism meant that the Yugoslav Communist leadership had to prove to the West that Yugoslavia was not a typical Communist country: "We were totally convinced that the West was wrong and that the Soviet Union was wrong. We were the only socialist country."[58] Additionally, providing education and a suitable occupation for women was intended to ensure the continuity of the revolution. Yugoslavia's leaders mobilized women and men who had worked with communities during the partisan struggle, making sure that the first diplomas in social work were issued to those who had both proven their loyalty to the cause and who had experience as social protection officers. Through the school, the state rewarded both women and men who had served in the partisan struggle and helped carry out modernization processes in the socialist state. Eugen Pusić (b. 1916), a leading figure in Croatian social work, pointed this out when he explained why the first school had been established in Croatia:

> [S]omething unique to Croatia, something that others did not have, was perhaps of crucial importance – a group of [female] social activists who participated in the national liberation movement and the National Liberation War. I'm referring to women such as Tatjana Marinić, Jana Koh and Valerija Singer. These partisan women, who later came to Zagreb and worked on social policy, wielded authority even over the Party. Only in this way was it possible to overcome the regime's strong opposition to the idea of educating social workers ....[59]

Schools of social work were aimed at women from peasant and poor rural areas, and brief vocational training provided an ideal opportunity to spread socialist ideology among women from disadvantaged social backgrounds. As one early student remarked, "My brothers went to the university; I had to study social work, because it was only a two-year education and we couldn't afford anything more."

Social work also created new jobs for women through the establishment of large-scale welfare institutions (nursing homes, boarding schools for disabled children, and asylums for people with disabilities). These segregated institutions, which could accommodate between 100 and 800 residents, gave Communist Party leaders an opportunity to demonstrate their devotion to social change and women's employment. At the same time, these large, semi-closed places of public care were meant to replace unpaid home care, in line with the view that paid employment was an important factor in women's emancipation. Institutions of public care were not only meant to provide employment for poor women, but also to free domestic caregivers for employment outside the home. Mothers remember that social workers during the Communist period encouraged and sometimes even forced them to place their disabled children in long-term closed institutions.

It must also be stressed that in spite of the Communist drive for a new gender order, the Communist leadership never abandoned the idea that women were responsible for domestic harmony; paid work was to complement rather than replace a woman's role in caring for the household and bringing up children. When Tito spoke about the necessity of participation in the Anti-Fascist Women's Front at the end of the 1950s, he also emphasized that "this does not mean at all, that they would alienate themselves from home, family and everyday work, which they are obliged to perform as wives/women (žene). No, just the opposite, they must also manage their duties toward the home and their own family."[60]

As a "reward" for this double burden, women in all eastern European countries received some "protection" from the state in the form of jobs and subsidies for children, and some independence through their access to paid work.[61] This was true also in Yugoslavia. "Protection" also occasionally involved state intervention in cases of domestic violence. Violence against women, often explained as a consequence of alcohol abuse by men, reflected traditional male control over women in a cycle that had been repeated continuously since prewar times. The Communist state's intercession took two forms: either police and local party officers were called upon to intimidate the perpetrator, or the children from affected homes were put into foster care. Offending husbands could expect to be asked to visit the municipal offices, and were warned that good Communists must not lose their tempers. In one interview, an elderly welfare worker recounted: "I remember a violent man who was a respected war veteran, but after the war he became a drinker. […] Once he was visited by someone from the party committee, and he was warned that they would solve the issue in a political way. The man calmed down and stopped being violent. If you had a bad record at the committee, you didn't get a job; they could also put you in prison."

These examples demonstrate both the traditional gender dynamic between men and women, as well as the gendered relationship between the state and socialist citizens. Significantly, it was not social workers but police or state party representatives who intervened in cases of known violence. Violent men were required to change their behavior not to defend women's safety or equal rights, but under pressure from state apparatuses of scrutiny, repression and guilt. Ashwin has called this phenomenon a "triangular set of relations in which the primary relationship of individual men and women was to the state rather than to each other."[62] The socialist state became "a universal patriarch to which both men and women were subject."[63]

Additionally, social work education and practice sustained social control. The institutionalization of social work training gave the Communist Party power not only over welfare and gender regimes, but also "in the field," where "deviant" behavior such as alcoholism, work-hatred, and prostitution could be carefully monitored. In practice, rather than aiding those in need, social work constructed a fresh set of "social problems" based on the new gender order. Foster care, which constituted one of the primary activities of professional social work during its first two decades, provides a good example: it was often to "help" single mothers enter the work force. "We resorted to foster care for the protection of children. Mothers had to return to work after two months, so we often placed the children of single mothers in foster homes" (interview with a social worker employed at the centre for social work since 1967). In this case, social work was defined as a "protective measure" against economic vulnerability, but ended up separating families.

The implicit and pragmatic goals of social work training show that the gender and welfare orders overlapped; developments in the social welfare system, such as the rise of public institutions and particular forms of intervention (like foster care), facilitated developments in the gender system. Although social workers in Slovenia were initially seen as capitalist remnants in a profession that was likely doomed to disappear, they were needed for three objectives: to maintain the momentum of the Communist revolution, to institutionalize the new welfare regime, and to complete the regendering of society.

Conclusions

This chapter shows that there are strong connections among the implementation of welfare regimes, social work instruction, and the position of women during the

Communist period in Yugoslavia. Although – or perhaps because – social workers were needed to implement societal change, they found themselves susceptible to exploitation by the state. In spite of its formal criticism and nominal efforts to break down the "patriarchal family," the Communist program of "family socialization" (*podružbljanje družine*) was no less oppressive to women. At the educational level, the new Communist leadership established institutional social work education in order to accomplish the goals of broader education and employment for women, but ensured that no social work methodology was taught. In contrast to developments in western Europe, social work education in socialist Yugoslavia was imposed from above in order to influence the everyday lives of people below.

In most of eastern and western Europe, the history of social work was connected to feminist and workers' struggles for rights, equal citizenship, and everyday justice. In prewar eastern Europe, class and feminist struggles intertwined. In tandem with their western counterparts, Yugoslav feminists discussed and fought against poverty, social suffering, and marginalization. Yet after World War II, the move to a "medical diagnostic model of social work" became favored for its capacity to extend state control over the people. Therefore, while women social workers in Yugoslavia might be considered powerful agents in the realm of supporting the poor and managing those who stood outside of social norms, they were also powerless instruments of the state, subject to the management of a male-centered political and social elite.

Notes

1 A shorter version of this article appeared as Darja Zaviršek (2008): Engendering Social Work Education under State Socialism in Yugoslavia. *British Journal of Social Work*, June 2008, vol. 38, no. 4, pp. 734–50.

2 Zaviršek, Darja (2005): "You will teach them some, socialism will do the rest.!": The History of Social Work Education 1945–60. In Kurt Schilde and Dagmar Schulte, eds., *Need and Care. Glimpses into the Beginnings of Eastern Europe's Professional Welfare.* Opladen: Barbara Budrich. pp. 237–74.

Zaviršek, Darja (ed.) (2005): *"With a Diploma it was Easier to Work"! A Scientific Textbook for the Fiftieth Anniversary of Social Work Education in Slovenia* [orig: "Z diplomo mi je bilo lažje delat!": *Znanstveni zbornik ob 50-obletnici izobraževanja za socialno delo v Sloveniji.*] Ljubljana: Faculty of Social Work.

Zaviršek, Darja (2005): Between Unease and Enthusiasm: The Development of Social Work Education in Yugoslavia. In Sven Hessle and Darja Zaviršek, eds., *Sustainable Development in Social Work – The Case of a Regional Network in the Balkans.* Stockholm: University of Stockholm. pp. 26–34.

Zaviršek, Darja (2006): Gender, Social Protection and Social Work Education in Slovenia [orig.: Spol, socialna skrb i obrazovanje za socijalni rad u početku socijalističke vlasti u Sloveniji]. *Ljetopis studijskog centra socialnog rada.* Zagreb: Faculty of Law, Department of Social Work. 13, 1, pp. 63–74.

Zaviršek, Darja, and Vesna Leskošek (2006): *The History of Social Work in Slovenia. Between Social Movements and Political Systems.* [orig.: *Zgodovina socialnega dela v Sloveniji. Med družbenimi gibanji in političnimi sistemi].* Ljubljana: Fakulteta za socialno delo.

Zaviršek, Darja (2008): Engendering Social Work Education Under State Socialism in Yugoslavia. *British Journal of Social Work*, June, vol. 38, no 4, pp. 734–50.

3 Juhasz, Borbala (2003): The Unfinished History of Social work in Hungary. In Hering, Sabine and Berteke Waaldijk, eds., *History of Social Work in Europe (1900–1960)*. Leske + Budrich, Opladen.
4 Frey, Cornelia (2005): "Respect vor der Kreativitaet der Menschen"–*Ilse Arlt: Werk Und Wirking*. Barbara Budrich Verlag, Opladen. See also: Staub-Bernasconi, Silvia (2003): Ilse Arlt: Enjoying Life on the Base of a Scientific Theory of Needs (Austria). In Sabine Hering and Berteke Waaldijk, eds., *History of Social Work in Europe (1900–1960)*. Opladen: Leske + Budrich. pp. 23–34.
5 Malek, Agnieszka and Szczepaniak-Wiecha, Izabela (2005): Female Organisers of Social Care in Poland: From Charity to Professional Social Assistance. In Kurt Schilde and Dagmar Schulte, eds., *Need and Care: Glimpses into the Beginnings of Eastern Europe's Professional Welfare*. Opladen: Barbara Budrich. pp. 25–36.
6 Cheschebec, Roxana (2003): "Nationalism, Feminism and Social Work in Interwar Romania: The Activities of Princess Alexandrina Catacuzino." In Hering, Sabine/ Waaldijk, Berteke (eds.), *History of Social Work in Europe (1900–1960)*. Opladen: Leske + Budrich. See also: Rachieru, Silvana (2005): "Humans Capable of Compassion": The Challenge of Training Professional Social Workers in Inter-War Romania. In Kurt Schilde and Dagmar Schulte, eds., *Need and Care. Glimpses into the Beginnings of Eastern Europe's Professional Welfare*. Opladen: Barbara Budrich. pp. 221–36.
7 Ajduković, Marina and Branica, Vanja (2006): Beginnings of Social Work in Croatia Between the Two World Wars [orig. Počeci socialnog rada u Hrvatskoj između dva svjetska rata]. *Ljetopis studijskog centra socijalnog rada*. Zagreb: Faculty of Law Zagreb, Department of social work. 13, 1, pp. 29–45.
8 Hering, Sabine, and Berteke Waaldijk, eds. (2003): *History of Social Work in Europe (1900–1960)*. Opladen: Leske + Budrich.
9 Ibid.
10 Zaviršek, Darja (2005): "You will teach them some, socialism will do the rest.!": The History of Social Work Education 1945–60. In Kurt Schilde and Dagmar Schulte, eds., *Need and Care. Glimpses into the Beginnings of Eastern Europe's Professional Welfare*. Opladen: Barbara Budrich. pp. 237–74.
  Zaviršek, Darja (2006): Gender, Social Protection and Social Work Education in Slovenia [orig.: Spol, socialna skrb i obrazovanje za socijalni rad u početku socijalističke vlasti u Sloveniji]. *Ljetopis studijskog centra socialnog rada*. Zagreb: Faculty of Law, Department of Social Work. 13, 1, pp. 63–74.
11 Juhasz, Borbala (2003): The Unfinished History of Social work in Hungary. In Hering, Sabine and Berteke Waaldijk, eds., *History of Social Work in Europe (1900–1960)*. Opladen: Leske + Budrich.
12 Seibel, Friedrich W. (2001): "Ziale Arbeit in Mittel-und Osteuropa". In H. J. Kerstoing and M. Riege, eds, *Internationale Sozialarbeit,* Band 29. Moenchengladbach: Fachhochschule Niederrhein.
13 Rachieru, Silvana (2005): Humans Capable of Compassion: The Challenge of Training Professional Social Workers in Inter-War Romania. In Kurt Schilde and Dagmar Schulte, eds., *Need and Care. Glimpses into the Beginnings of Eastern Europe's Professional Welfare*. Opladen: Barbara Budrich. pp. 221–36.
14 Leskošek, Vesna (2005): The Role of the Slovenian Women's Movement in the Development of Social Work: the History of Social Work in Slovenia 1900–1940, in Kurt Schilde and Dagmar Schulte, eds., *Need and Care. Glimpses into the Beginnings of the Eastern Europe's Professional Welfare*. Opladen & Bloomfield Hills: Barbara Budrich. pp. 149–60. See also: Leskošek, Vesna (2006): The Women's Movement and Social Work [orig.: Žensko gibanje in socialno delo]. In Darja Zaviršek and Vesna Leskošek, eds., *The History of Social Work in Slovenia: Between Social Movements and Political Systems*. [orig.: Zgodovina socialnega dela v Sloveniji. Med družbenimi gibanji in političnimi sistemi]. Ljubljana: Fakulteta za socialno delo.
15 Ibid.

16 Staub-Bernasconi, Silvia (2003): Ilse Arlt: Enjoying Life on the Base of a Scientific Theory of Needs (Austria). In Sabine Hering and Berteke Waaldijk, eds., *History of Social Work in Europe (1900–1960)*. Opladen: Leske + Budrich. pp.23 – 34.
17 Vode, Angela (2006): *Hidden Memory [Skriti spomin]*. Edited by Alenka Puhar. Ljubljana: Nova Revija.
18 Wieler, Joachim (1987): *Er-Innerung eines zerstoerten Lebensabends: Alice Salomon waehrend der NS-Zeit (1933–1937) und im Exil (1937–1948)*. Darmstadt: Lingbach.
19 Arko, Nika (1958): 'Organisation of Welfare Services' [Orig.: Organizacija socialnih služb]. In *Association of Social Workers of Slovenia: Welfare Services in Slovenia [Organizacija socialnih delavcev Slovenije: Socialne službe v Sloveniji]*, Ljubljana.
Milić, Andeljka (1993): Women and Nationalism in Former Yugoslavia. In N. Funk and M. Mueller, eds., *Gender Politics and Post-Communism: Reflections from Eastern Europe and the former Soviet Union*. New York, London: Routledge. pp. 109–22.
20 Jancar Webster, Barbara (1990): *Women and Revolution in Yugoslavia, 1941–45*. Denver: Arden Press.
21 Zaviršek, Darja, and Vesna Leskošek (2006): *The History of Social Work in Slovenia. Between Social Movements and Political Systems. [orig.: Zgodovina socialnega dela v Sloveniji. Med družbenimi gibanji in političnimi sistemi]*. Ljubljana: Fakulteta za socialno delo. See also: Zorn, Jelka (2006): Social Protection after the Second World War: New Ideology and Old Values [orig.: Socialno skrbstvo po drugi svetovni vojni: nova ideologija in stare vrednote]. In Darja Zaviršek and Vesna Leskošek, eds., *The History of Social Work in Slovenia: Between Social Movements and Political Systems. [orig.: Zgodovina socialnega dela v Sloveniji. Med družbenimi gibanji in političnimi sistemi]*. Ljubljana: Fakulteta za socialno delo.
22 Luddy, Maria (1995): *Women and Philanthropy in Nineteenth-Century Ireland*. Cambridge: Cambridge Univ. Press.
23 Before 1955, persons doing paid welfare work were called "administrative workers" (*administrativni delavci*) and "social protection officers" (*referenti za socialno skrbstvo*).
24 *Informbiro* refers to the Cominform Resolution of June 1948, when Tito and Stalin ended the official alliance between their two nations. The Communist Party of Yugoslavia was accused of departing from Marxism–Leninism when Tito opposed the submissive relationship that Stalin demanded.
25 Kriškova, Marija (1945): *Sovjetska žena v veliki domovinski vojni*. Ljubljana: Partizanska tiskarna.
26 Josip Broz Tito [1892–1980], commonly known as Tito, was the leading commander of the National Liberation Army of Yugoslavia from 1941 to 1945, and became the president of the Socialist Federative Republic of Yugoslavia in 1945. In 1953 he was made president for life.
27 Kiaer, Christina and Naiman, Eric. eds. (2006): *Everyday Life in Early Soviet Russia*, Bloomington and Indianapolis: Indiana Univ. Press.
28 Ashwin, Sarah (2000): "Introduction: gender, state and society in Soviet and Post-Soviet Russia," in Ashwin, S. (ed.), *Gender, State and Society in Soviet and Post-Soviet Russia*. London, New York: Routledge. Also see: Bridger, Susan (1987): *Women in the Soviet Countryside*, Cambridge: Cambridge Univ. Press.
29 Quote from Lenin; found in Stites, Robert (1991): *The Women's Liberation Movement in Russia: Feminism, Nihilism, and Bolshevism, 1860–1930*. Princeton: Princeton University Press.
30 Jancar Webster, Barbara (1990): *Women and Revolution in Yugoslavia, 1941–45*. Denver: Arden Press.
31 Sklevicky, Lidija (1996): *Horses, Women, Wars [Konji, žene, ratovi]*. Edited by Dunja Rihtman Auguštin. Zagreb: Ženska infoteka.
32 Buckley, Mary (2001): The Untold Story of the *Obshchestvennitsa* in the 1930s. In Ilič, M., ed., *Women in the Stalin Era*. Basingstoke and New York: Palgrave.

33 *afežejevke* is a noun made from the phonetic pronunciation of the acronym AFŽ plus the -jevka termination, a rough equivalent of the English -er termination. This practice is quite common in colloquial Slovene, but relatively rare in English. One example would be "PCer", which, in colloquial American English, denotes a person who makes an effort to ensure that his actions are politically correct (PC).
34 Buckley, Mary (2001): The Untold Story of the *Obshchestvennitsa* in the 1930s. In Ilič, M., ed., *Women in the Stalin Era*. Basingstoke and New York: Palgrave.
35 Ashwin, Sarah (2000): Introduction: Gender, State and Society in Soviet and Post-Soviet Russia. In Ashwin, S. (ed.), *Gender, State and Society in Soviet and Post-Soviet Russia*. London, New York: Routledge.
36 Vodopivec, Katja (1959): *Handbook of Social Work Methods [Priročnik iz metodike socialnega dela]*. Ljubljana.
37 Zaviršek, Darja (2005): "You will teach them some, socialism will do the rest.!": The History of Social Work Education 1945–60. In Kurt Schilde and Dagmar Schulte, eds., *Need and Care. Glimpses into the Beginnings of Eastern Europe's Professional Welfare*. Opladen: Barbara Budrich, pp. 237–74.
38 Ajduković, Marina and Branica, Vanja (2006): Beginnings of Social Work in Croatia Between the Two World Wars [orig. Počeci socialnog rada u Hrvatskoj izmedu dva svjetska rata]. *Ljetopis studijskog centra socijalnog rada*. Zagreb: Faculty of Law Zagreb, Department of Social Work. 13, 1, pp. 29–45.
39 *Programme of the League of Communists of Yugoslavia* 1958, pp. 213.
40 The School of Social Work in Zagreb, Croatia was the first to be established in 1952.
41 *Slovenski poročevalec*, year XVI, no. 262, 9 Nov. 1955.
42 *Ljudska pravica*, no. 262, 8 Nov. 1955.
43 In 2005 Nika Arko was present at the national celebration of the 50th anniversary of the opening of the School of Social Work. When she was asked to comment on a presentation about the institution's history, she remarked "Comrade Zaviršek spoke correctly about all of these things!" Her lapse into socialist language caused a ripple of silent laughter among the audience of 500 social workers and educators.
44 It remains the only institution of higher education to offer social work education (up to the doctoral level) in the country.
45 Vodopivec, Katja (1959): *Handbook of Social Work Methods [Priročnik iz metodike socialnega dela]*. Ljubljana.
46 *Ibid*. p. 78.
47 *Ibid*. p. 78.
48 *Ibid*. p. 86.
49 *Ibid*. p. 86.
50 *Ibid*. p. 86.
51 Vida Tomšič (1913–98) was a prewar Communist, one of the national heroes of Yugoslavia and one of the few women who became part of the Communist elite and member of the Central Committee. She remained a leading figure in social welfare and family activism until the end of her life.
52 Ajduković, Marina and Branica, Vanja (2006): Beginnings of Social Work in Croatia Between the Two World Wars [orig. Počeci socialnog rada u Hrvatskoj izmedu dva svjetska rata]. *Ljetopis studijskog centra socijalnog rada*. Zagreb: Faculty of Law Zagreb, Department of Social Work. 13, 1, pp. 29–45.
Zaviršek, Darja (ed.) (2005): *"With a Diploma it was Easier to Work!" A Scientific Textbook for the Fiftieth Anniversary of Social Work Education in Slovenia* [orig: "Z diplomo mi je bilo lažje delat!": Znanstveni zbornik ob 50-obletnici izobraževanja za socialno delo v Sloveniji.] Ljubljana: Faculty of Social Work.
Zaviršek, Darja (2005): Between Unease and Enthusiasm: The Development of Social Work Education in Yugoslavia. In Sven Hessle and Darja Zaviršek, eds., *Sustainable Development in Social Work – The Case of a Regional Network in the Balkans*. Stockholm: University of Stockholm. pp. 26–34.

53 Arko, Nika (1958): "Organisation of Welfare Services" [Orig. Organizacija socialnih služb], in: *Association of Social Workers of Slovenia: Welfare Services in Slovenia [Organizacija socialnih delavcev Slovenije: Socialne službe v Sloveniji]*, Ljubljana.
54 Lukić, Jasmina and Regulska, Joanna and Zaviršek, Darja, eds., (2006): *Women and Citizenship in Central and Eastern Europe.* Burlington: Ashgate.
55 Buckley, Mary (2001): The Untold Story of the *Obshchestvennitsa* in the 1930s. In Ilič, M., ed., *Women in the Stalin Era.* Basingstoke and New York: Palgrave.
56 Ashwin, Sarah (2000): Introduction: Gender, State and Society in Soviet and Post-Soviet Russia. In Ashwin, S. (ed.), *Gender, State and Society in Soviet and Post-Soviet Russia.* London, New York: Routledge.
57 Zaviršek, Darja (2008): "Engendering Social Work Education Under State Socialism in Yugoslavia." *British Journal of Social Work*, June, vol. 38, no 4, pp. 734–50.
58 Jancar Webster, Barbara (1990): *Women and Revolution in Yugoslavia, 1941–45.* Denver: Arden Press.
59 Ajduković, Marina (ed.) (2002): *50 Years of Education for Social Work: 1952–2002* [orig.: *50 godina Studija za socijalni rad: 1952 – 2002*]. Zagreb: University of Zagreb.
60 Jeraj, Mateja (2005): *Slovenian Women in the Transition to Socialism* [orig: *Slovenke na prehodu v socializem]*. Ljubljana: Arhiv Republike Slovenije.
61 Ashwin, Sarah (2000): "Introduction: gender, state and society in Soviet and Post-Soviet Russia," in Ashwin, S. (ed.), *Gender, State and Society in Soviet and Post-Soviet Russia.* London, New York: Routledge.
62 *Ibid.*
63 *Ibid.*

4

PSYCHOANALYSTS ON THE RADIO

Domestic citizenship and motherhood in postwar Britain

Michal Shapira

During World War II, British psychoanalysts developed a social role and public engagement that led to their widened recognition in postwar society. The second generation of psychoanalysts after Sigmund Freud, a diverse group of both native professionals and continental Jewish refugees, included prominent individuals like Melanie Klein, Anna Freud, John Bowlby, Susan Isaacs, and Donald Winnicott, as well as now-forgotten personalities such as Edward Glover, Barbara Low, and Melitta Schmideberg. These experts had a profound role in making the understanding of children and the mother–child relationship key to the successful creation of democratic citizenry in this formative period.[1] Psychoanalysts informed understandings not only of individuals but also of broader political questions in an age of mass violence. Through their emphasis on mother–child relations and on diverse "separation theories" (stressing the risk of separation of mother and child, often a reality in wartime), they offered influential answers to the pressing need for cultivating harmonious and cooperative citizens. Working during the war beyond their own private clinics, they contributed to the emergence of a modern psychological definition of childhood and parenthood in relation to warfare and democracy.[2]

For Anna Freud and her staff in London's Hampstead War Nurseries, for example, the war was an exceptional occasion to work with "infants without families."[3] Most harmful to the child, for Freud and her staff, were not bombings and real-time violence but the separation from the mother. Handling several houses in London and its vicinity, they worked under fire, developing ideas that would come to be used in peacetime. John Bowlby's career was also formatively influenced by the war. Before the war, he had been involved in thinking about aggression and democracy. He spread his ideas about the least harmful way to conduct the evacuation of children and publicly warned against mother–child separations. During the war, he served as an Army psychiatrist in a War Neurosis Center and was later involved with Donald Winnicott and Melanie Klein in the *Cambridge Evacuation Survey*, edited by Susan

Isaacs.[4] Winnicott was a Consultant Psychiatrist for the Government Evacuation Scheme in Oxfordshire responsible for the mental care of evacuated children in five different hostels.[5]

After the war, psychoanalysts continued to work with children, combining practical and theoretical work with public commitment to a degree greater than in other countries. Anna Freud and her circle worked at the new Hampstead clinic serving the local community. Bowlby wrote his famous works on the effects of mother–child separation at the Tavistock Clinic.[6] He there conducted the investigations and filming of the Separation Research Unit together with James Robertson, himself a student of Anna Freud's War Nurseries. These psychoanalysts and many others all helped establish the notion of the child's mental health as one of critical importance. Their psychoanalytic work had practical effects on society, contributing to changing procedures for child hospitalization, ideas about juvenile delinquency, the roles of parents, and the perception of the child in the emerging welfare state.[7]

During this transition between war and peace, Winnicott appeared to the British public through psychoanalytic broadcasts he was invited to deliver on the BBC (British Broadcasting Corporation) radio. Focusing on these broadcasts, this essay examines the relationship between psychoanalysis and the British mass media, and the process of popularization of psychoanalytic ideas on the child, as well as the gendered concepts of the parental responsibilities of the mother and the father. It shows how the presentation of psychoanalytic ideas was influenced by the encounter with the BBC and its staff and the ways in which the BBC audience was imagined and constructed during this period. Specifically, it illustrates how many of Winnicott's ideas were influenced and directed by the BBC's pioneering female producers Isa Benzie and Janet Quigley, themselves little studied. The essay also explores the ways in which, in a democratic context, Winnicott shaped his expert authority and the manner in which the everyday life of ordinary citizens now fell under psychoanalytic purview. Looking at the BBC programs targeted at women and children, the essay affirms the shift in notions of citizenship in this period. During the war, emphasis was placed on "collective citizenship" – that is, on doing one's bit and sacrificing for the nation. The end of the war and the postwar period, however, saw a new focus on "domestic citizenship" – that is: an understanding of citizens' contribution to the nation as related to establishing the correct home and family. Being a good citizen now meant taking care of one's family and the next generation of children. Through radio broadcasting, psychoanalysis reached the hearts and minds of millions of British people, helping to form links between citizenship, home, and the notion of the child as a future citizen whose stable mental health, "normalcy," and ability to collaborate with others democratically were dependent on good parenthood.[8]

Winnicott's radio talks were broadcast in a period when the family across Europe was paradoxically seen as both stable and fragile. Since the 1930s stabilizing new demographic family patterns emerged: birth and death rates were falling, babies had a higher chance of living to adulthood, and rates of marriage were rising. While family patterns were interrupted by wartime, the underlying trends remained unchanged and were accompanied by a "baby boom" after the war. The mid-decades of the century were the golden age of what was celebrated as "the normal family," with a near universal marriage rate, controlled fertility, growing state welfare benefits, and a new cult of motherhood, domesticity and housekeeping with the help of new facilities. This normal family was envisioned as headed by a male worker whose wife's paid work, if she engaged in any at all, was secondary.[9] Along with this perceived stability there was also a growing anxiety about the fragility of the family, which was associated with a growing rate of divorce, changing patterns of women's work, and fears of "war babies" turning into "juvenile delinquents" due to the wartime absence of their fathers or the working hours of their mothers.[10]

After the cataclysmic violence of World War II, the family played an important role in discussions emerging in postwar continental Europe about democratization, welfare, and the keeping of the peace. If World War II destroyed the structure of the family and Nazism distorted intimate relationships, the way back to civilized democratic life required the rehabilitation of such relationships, or rather a "psychological Marshall Plan."[11] Reeducation for democracy required a transformation of individual psychology. However, the seemingly universal emphasis on the heterosexual family, proper parenthood and childhood had specific meanings in different national and ethnic contexts and among diverse social actors.[12] This essay tries to answer what the family might have meant in psychoanalytic thinking about the self and in relation to the reconstruction of Britain. Numerically speaking, the scale of death in World War II Britain was far less than in mainland Europe. On a moral level, for Britons the war did not include many of the murderous experiences and ethical compromises that were the lot of so many of their European neighbors. Nevertheless, the war did bring an unimaginable level of destruction to the British home front, with approximately 60,000 civilians killed, millions of houses damaged, mass evacuation, and scenes of horror in everyday life. Many in Britain believed that the war had interfered with family, home life and gender relations in alarming ways as men, women, and children were scattered from each other around the country and the world. As in other countries, millions of men in the armed services were away during the war and no longer served as breadwinners, while many women "left behind" in Britain itself did essential work in war industries and served as heads of their family units. Children were separated from their fathers or both parents during the waves of evacuation or were placed in nurseries. Between the Battle of Britain and the end of 1942 in particular, when civilians endured the primary brunt of enemy blows, a strange inversion of gender roles took place, as it was frequently the male–soldier who waited for news from his wife and children rather than the wife and children worried if the husband was alive. Peacetime conditions did not bring immediate relief as the demobilization of soldiers took time and was seen to be creating "a crisis at home" with members of the family needing to adjust to a husband and father who had been away. Adding to this situation was the housing shortage and the continuation of austerity.[13] Creating a "happy home" and a "normative" heterosexual family dynamic (where women of all classes were expected to embrace full-time domestic life rather than paying jobs) was indeed a challenge in postwar Britain. Nevertheless, it was on the basis of their reconstruction along conservative social norms and clear gender boundaries that the new society was to be rebuilt, or so insisted different public officials and experts.[14] This common idea was to reinforce and extend democracy in the 1940s as the true alternative to Nazism, Fascism and Communism.[15] Psychoanalysis contributed to this specific historical experience of democracy while reformulating visions of the self and mental health that tied together patriarchal family life and the management of aggression. The mother–child bond became central to insuring normal family dynamics that would, in their turn, guarantee a tranquil democratic citizenry for the future. More than ever before, motherhood and childhood required expert knowledge and guidance.

The BBC between war and peace

If the reading of newspapers and novels in the nineteenth century, as Benedict Anderson argues, helped promote an imagined sense of national community, the radio became *the* consolidator of cultural unity from the 1930s to 1950s.[16] The role of the BBC in developing the notion of collective citizenship during World War II cannot be understated.[17] While the BBC was shaping the "People's War," it was also attentive to its audiences, which included servicemen and women, and workers in war factories, in new and profound ways. When war ended, this populist tendency was irreversible.[18]

By 1945 there were 10.8 million radio licenses in Britain, which represented a large majority of households across social classes.[19] The BBC created a tripartite system of networks: The Light Programme (lowbrow), the Home Service (middlebrow) and the Third Programme (highbrow).[20] The popular Light Programme had roughly two-thirds of the BBC's listeners tuned in to productions such as *Woman's Hour* and Children's Hour. These programs marked an important shift in the BBC's assumptions – a transformation that is central to the understanding of Winnicott's radio work. Whereas the direction of wartime programming had been collaborative, the tendency of postwar programs was domestic and individual. The latter were designed not for women at war, but women at home.[21] While from its advent radio listening was a domestic activity,[22] the war tightened this connection between the private and the public, emphasizing collective citizenship and individual self-sacrifice for the sake of the community at war.[23] When the war ended, radio reverted to its domestic role.[24] Psychoanalytic experts like Winnicott played a crucial part in this shift, forming new connections between the family, citizenship, media, and expertise.

Winnicott's broadcasts were conducted in a period in which the BBC dedicated more attention to children and women as listeners and as important participants in democracy. For example, the director of *Children's Hour* explained how during the war the BBC pooled all its resources in an endeavor to project this daily popular program for the younger listeners.[25] It was a program for the "citizens and the license holders of the future."[26] The BBC's image of citizenship increasingly included women in new and sometimes conflicting ways.[27] By 1951, *Woman's Hour*, which was created in 1946, was described to be "a stable feature in the lives of millions of housewives."[28] The *BBC Yearbook* of 1958 clarified that *Woman's Hour* "is addressed to one section of listeners, the women at home in the early afternoon, and it included items that are of immediate practical service to such women in the running of their homes and in caring for the welfare of their families." The program also aimed "to entertain, inform, and refresh women listeners with subjects and people that they may have little opportunity of meeting elsewhere." Yet starting in 1953, the immensely popular *Woman's Hour* was supplemented by the Sunday morning *Home for the Day*, which was addressed primarily to women who worked outside the home and focused on their professional interests.[29]

Another popular show, addressed to both mothers and young children, was titled *Listen with Mother*. According to BBC producer Olive Shapley, the show, which started in the early 1950s, soon "had found its way, like an arrow, straight to the heart of the audience for which it was intended." Shapley shared the growing postwar concern for children's emotional needs and explained that "there is no doubt that this small and rather special section of the BBC's listeners [children under five] has a right to its own programme, and takes it very seriously."[30] The radio was seen to play an active role in family life, even helping in parenting. It is in this context of increased attention to the family, women, and children that I want to look at the work of Winnicott at the BBC to expose the development and popularization of psychoanalytic ideas in relation to the needs of a postwar society and the project of domestic citizenship.[31]

Winnicott and the BBC

Donald Winnicott (1896–1971) was born into a middle-class family in Plymouth, England. In 1923, after studying at Cambridge, he started working as a pediatrician at the Paddington Green Children's Hospital in London where he had been involved in some 60,000 mother–child consultations. In 1923 Winnicott also started psychoanalytic treatment with James Strachey, Sigmund Freud's English translator. Winnicott began training with the British Psycho-Analytical Society in 1927. While Winnicott had additional analysis with Melanie Klein's disciple Joan Rivière, he later helped develop the independent, "middle" group in the society, standing between the Anna Freudians and the Kleinians. After the war, Winnicott continued to work at the Child Department of the Institute of Psychoanalysis and at the Paddington Green Children's Hospital. He lectured widely and, in the atmosphere of growing focus on domestic citizenship, he was called upon by producers Janet Quigley and Isa Benzie to deliver almost sixty broadcasts on BBC radio from 1943 to 1966.[32]

Happy and difficult children

The first series Winnicott delivered was titled *Happy Children* and was transmitted on the Home Service on Friday mornings starting in 1943.[33] Through this series, a close working relationship developed with Janet Quigley, and Winnicott cultivated his expertise on parenthood.

Quigley (1902–87), born in Belfast and educated at Oxford, joined the BBC in 1930, where she became a pioneering female producer and broadcaster. Quigley made her mark producing groundbreaking wartime radio features for women such as *Calling the Factory Front*; *The Kitchen Front*; *Calling All Women*; *Your Health in Wartime* and *Talking it Over*.[34] Quigley extended the frontiers of women's broadcasting through her editorship of *Woman's Hour* from 1950 to 1956.[35] Alongside a return to "traditional" women's issues, she brought to the air topics such as divorce, homosexuality, and prostitution, "so that the less-educated … listeners," she explained, "may get used to the idea that no subject which concerns them as citizens need be taboo."[36]

Quigley first wrote to Winnicott asking if he would take part in a BBC series in which he would have "a completely free hand" to develop his subjects. She added, "All we really want is agreement amongst the speakers that we are aiming at the same object in the end, and agreement too on the subjects which should be included."[37] This, however, did not always remain the case as Quigley and Winnicott quickly developed a dialogue regarding content. For example, Quigley asked Winnicott if he would want to give a talk on *Getting to Know Your Baby*. The title and topic of the talk were hers.[38] As a matter of control, Winnicott was to presubmit script drafts for approval. Quigley wrote to him that she liked his submitted draft but that it was "not factual enough."[39] As producer, she had a dynamic involvement in the direction of the expert talk. Characteristic of the BBC at the time was the concern not only for educating but also speaking to the audience, significantly here composed of many female listeners.

In the final script of *Getting to Know Your Baby* Winnicott revealed the ways in which he saw women as mothers by default. His tone shifted from one of expert observation to direct address of the mothers among the listeners. Winnicott started by using a universal description according to which every woman would eventually become a mother. He then shifted from these generalizations to the second person, addressing an imagined woman/listener directly to say "as you become more and more sure that you'll soon be a mother … you begin to take the risk of allowing yourself to be concerned with one object, the little boy or girl human being that will be born." Nevertheless, he said to his mother/listener, "you may very well need support from those of us who study your subject, because superstitions and old wives' tales come along and make you doubt your own true feelings."[40] Psychoanalytic expertise was here privileged over the common advice that other women – here in the derogatory – could provide the mother.

Quigley directed Winnicott's next lecture in this series, titled *Why Does Your Baby Cry?* After Winnicott submitted a draft, Quigley responded by offering that Winnicott should break it into two parts. She believed that anecdotes would make the script easier listening and suggested that the talk should more practically tackle questions of how to deal with crying.[41] Winnicott followed Quigley's instructions and established his authority in the talks in a peculiar way. He aimed to communicate directly with mothers, telling them that they were already "the real experts." Winnicott explained the causes for crying, stemming from pleasure, pain, rage, and grief, demonstrating his sense of authority as emerging from what a mother knows but perhaps does not articulate: "if you have a pencil handy you might want to write down pleasure, pain, rage and grief, so that tomorrow, when you are wondering what on earth the psychologist was saying, you will be able to see that really I was only saying quite obvious things, the sort of things that every mother of an infant knows naturally, though she hasn't usually tried thinking out how to express what she knows in words." Offering an internal explanation for crying out of rage and using more psychoanalytic logic than before, Winnicott suggested that "if a baby cries in a state of rage and feels as if he has destroyed anyone and everything, and yet the people round him remain calm and unhurt, this experience greatly strengthens his ability to see that what he feels to be true is not necessarily real, that fantasy and fact, (both are important) are nevertheless different from each other."[42] These words reflected the psychoanalytic notion of the child as innocent and in need of care, yet aggressive and requiring control. This notion emerged in the interwar period and developed during and after the war. Violence was seen to be part of the child (an emerging self) and as something to be contained by good parenting. While interwar hygienist and behaviorist literature focused on children's bodies, the importance of habits, and the dangers of excessive parental love, psychoanalysts instead proffered that emotions be understood rather than managed and that the parent-child relationship was central for social stability. The problem of war for psychoanalysts could only be solved by recognition of inner aggressiveness.[43] Accordingly, in his script Winnicott also addressed the mother/listener with the following lines that were apparently edited out by Quigley from the broadcast itself: "You can get a lot of interest out of watching your infant for the first signs that he knows he can hurt you, and that he intends to hurt you."[44] This editorializing of statements deemed too negative appeared in other talks as well.

Indeed, in a letter Quigley wrote to Winnicott she said, "one has to be very careful in talks of this kind not to alarm people unduly." She also suggested the possibility of a talk on *Where Does Dad Come In?*[45] The title and theme of the talk were again hers.[46] Winnicott agreed, and seeing himself as an adviser on family dynamics aiming to prevent harm to the future generation of citizens, began his draft script by warning that the war was dangerously depriving children of contact with their fathers.[47] Quigley was not altogether happy with Winnicott's draft script. She wrote that it was depressing to wives whose husbands are still away, and wondered whether Winnicott could provide more encouragement to women whose husbands are at home on how to draw them into the picture.[48] Her comments reflected the ambiguity of the changing notion of the father at the time, especially among working class families, from a distant figure within the family to a more participatory one.[49]

In his draft script Winnicott thought of the father in a few ways, none of them requiring full – or equal – participation. First, he saw the father as an important person in the child's life whose main job is "representing mother's authority."[50] The father takes over feelings that the infant partially has toward the mother, including hatred. The father, for Winnicott (here influenced by the ideas of Melanie Klein on the complex feelings stored in the child's mind), was valuable because the child has a fantasy of the union of the mother and the father, a rock to which he can cling and against which he can kick. The father does not have to be present all the time but he opens up a new world when he gradually discloses the nature of his work or "when he shows the gun that he takes with him into the battle."[51] The father, therefore, signifies authority and the outside world, he mitigates the child's fantasized negative feelings, and he participates in violence in the name of democracy under certain terms.

In contrast, a woman's main role in democracy was motherhood for Winnicott. In the talk *Their Standards and Yours*, he saw motherhood and housekeeping as sites of freedom and expression for women.[52] In *What Do We Mean By A Normal Child?*, a later talk that Quigley helped simplify for the listener, Winnicott explained what would be reasonable to accept from a newborn, a prime concern in a society that experienced the break-up of families.[53] He presented theoretical psychoanalytic ideas describing the dynamics of the child's difficulties as existing between the reality of the external world and that of the personal inner world. A normal child was one who "can and does employ every device that nature has provided for avoiding too painful feelings, and for dealing with pain that can't be avoided."[54] The normal child was an aggressive being that could learn to manage his destructiveness with the help of others. Despite this theoretical language, Winnicott received supportive letters from listeners after the broadcast. Quigley wrote to Winnicott saying that the letters showed how well his sincerity and sympathy had been conveyed to listeners and expressed her wish to do further talks.[55] This was fulfilled in the series *Difficult Children*, broadcast in 1945. Quigley first wrote to Winnicott that in this series she wanted to concentrate on "the slightly difficult child or perhaps, more accurately, the child where circumstances are difficult," and asked for his help as she "must be guided by the experts."[56] When Quigley suggested this series to the Director of Talks, she explained that this idea arose from a Ministry of Health conference pushing for "better parentcraft."[57] As a transformative editor, Quigley saw the radio's role as one of "indirect propaganda," as she called it, responsible for conveying useful social messages.[58] Childrearing and parenthood during this time were the most pressing issues for her as well as for many others emerging from the war. Quigley, rather than Winnicott, again chose the titles and directed the content of the talks as she rejected his script about children who were difficult in ways other than she imagined.[59] Throughout the series, the problem of insuring stable human relations – both inside the family and later in civic democratic life – was a central one. The solution was envisioned through specific gender roles.

In a broadcast titled *Home Again* on the BBC Health Magazine, Winnicott emphasized the irreplaceable importance of the home to the child's well-being.[60] He assigned psychological value to the concept of home that was already seen as the center of life and of comfort for many middle class families and increasingly more working class families.[61] In late 1945, Quigley informed Winnicott that she was leaving the BBC and that her manager Isa Benzie would be looking after the health talks.[62] Benzie (1902–88), another pioneering BBC female broadcaster, joined the BBC in 1927 and became a producer at the BBC Talks Department in 1943. She produced programs such as *Taking Stock of Health* and *Is There a Doctor in the House?*

and oversaw the health items on programs like *Woman's Hour*, becoming something of a legend at the BBC.[63]

How's the baby?

During the months of October and November 1949, Winnicott gave another series of talks on the Home Service, this time produced by Benzie. This series was titled *How's The Baby*.[64] In the first talk on Wednesday morning, 5 October 1949, Winnicott again placed his expert authority in relation to what he saw as the mother's "natural" role. He started by saying to the mother/listener, "You will be relieved to know that I'm not going to be telling you what to do. I'm a man, and I have never been a mother, and so I never really know what it is like to see wrapped up over there in the cot a bit of my own self, a bit of me living an independent life, yet at the same time dependent and gradually becoming a human being. Only a woman can experience this … " Winnicott imagined the mother as forever knowing what to do with the baby and added, "sometimes the urine trickled down your apron or went right through and soaked you as if you yourself had let slip, and you didn't mind it. In fact, by these things you could have known that you were a woman, and what I have … called an ordinary devoted mother … " Explaining his own role he said, "I can't tell you what to do, but I can talk about what it all means."[65] His position, as he saw it, was therefore as an interpreter of motherhood, shaping it as a social, rather than natural, institution.

Winnicott connected the mother's individual childrearing tasks to their social benefits in a democratic society. He said, "If human babies are to develop eventually into healthy independent and society-minded adult individuals they absolutely depend on being given a good start; this good start is assured in nature by the experience of the bond between the baby's mother and the baby, the thing called love." He further claimed that it is "vitally important that society should get to understand the part played by those who care for the infant … " Yet fathers, as discussed earlier, also had a place in Winnicott's social vision. He saw them as able to be "good mothers" for limited periods of time, and as helping to protect the mother and baby from whatever tends to interfere with the mother–child bond; a tie which was "the essence and very nature of child care."[66] In the following talk on October 2, 1949, Winnicott empowered a woman's role as a mother by saying "You are founding the health of a person who will be a member of our society. This is worth doing." He advised mothers to "Enjoy letting other people look after the world while you are producing a new one of its members … Enjoy the way in which your man feels responsible for the welfare of you and your child."[67] In Winnicott's vision of the family – one that went hand in hand with the British model of the welfare state – the father was the breadwinner and protector of the family, while the woman was the main caretaker of the nation's future citizens. Speaking on November 9, 1949 against behaviorist theories that aimed to give mothers recipes for the right behavior, Winnicott said, "No book's rules can take the place of this feeling a mother has for her infant's needs, which enables her to make at times an almost exact adaptation to those needs."[68] His notion contrasted with the behaviorist model of writers like John Watson, who believed that institutions could be ideal environments for children, that love should be done mechanically to avoid invalidism or a "mother's boy syndrome," and that mothers should leave their children alone for a large part of their day.[69]

The mother portrayed in those radio talks did not completely exist as a person in her own right, but rather as a person *for* the baby, giving it individual attention and a setting for its needs as part of a human relationship where the baby was prioritized.[70] In a later talk from January 9, 1952, Winnicott even stressed that "A mother who is enjoying herself is probably a good mother from the baby's point of view."[71] Winnicott connected the mother's flexibility toward the child to the development of a civilized adult. He claimed that if the mother was sensitive to the child, it would decreasingly need to gratify its primitive needs for greediness, messiness, and control, and "civilization would start again inside a new human being." He added, "It's for you to catch on to their (the babies') primitive morality and to tone it down gradually to the humanity that comes from mutual understanding."[72] This way, the dyadic relationship between mother and child became for Winnicott a relationship on which democratic society was dependent. Women's role in democracy was motherhood, but motherhood in its turn was creating and making democracy.[73] To Sigmund Freud's account of life in society as fraught with frustration and human conflict, Winnicott added the figure of the mother as a mediator of aggression.[74]

Winnicott discussed the difference between "what the mother has to learn" and "what she knows." He explained that while there are some things about childcare that are known naturally to the mother, there is a great deal that the mother could learn from doctors' research. Demonstrating how ideas on everyday activities of ordinary individuals were now under scrutiny and management through psychoanalysis, Winnicott connected the trivial tasks of baby care, mental health, and society. He meticulously studied, for example, the way the "wise mother" holds her baby. The naturally devoted mother, who is not anxious and so does not grip the baby too tight and is not afraid of dropping the baby to the floor, can adapt the pressure in her arms to the baby's needs and move slightly or perhaps make sounds and breath to show that she is alive. He insisted that handling the baby well "is part of the way in which you give a good foundation for the mental health of this new member of the community."[75]

Another talk focused on "healthy symptoms" in "ordinary children" and dealt among other things with a letter from a mother who described the troubles of her baby during weaning. Winnicott claimed that even if he took for granted the mother's management of the baby to be skilled and consistent, the infant might still have all sorts of symptoms that had to do with the working of instincts, terrific feelings that belong to them and to the painful conflicts that result from the child's imagination.[76] Winnicott again drew connection between the inner and external worlds, and (unlike behaviorist writers) stressed that the child could be in conflict with the environment. Before this talk aired, Benzie required Winnicott to make changes in his submitted script. In a letter from March 27, 1950, she expressed concern that mothers might feel blamed for the baby's problems. She asked him to change this impression (which would indeed bother later feminists). She also provided a set of comments noting that she would not want to "frighten mothers."[77]

The ordinary devoted mother and her baby

Winnicott's talks were a great success. In December 1951, Benzie invited Winnicott to re-broadcast live his previous series of talks in a shorter format as part of *Woman's Hour*. She called his earlier broadcasts "notable" and mentioned how they were done "superbly," and were greatly "valued – by very many listeners and very many outside interests and connoisseurs."[78] Winnicott rewrote his talks to explain that by "ordinary devoted mother" he did not expect the mother to be perfect. Instead, he psychoanalytically argued that every mother has mixed feelings of love and hate toward the baby. Despite possible strain in the first weeks, the mother would usually be able to devote herself to the baby without resentment. He warned his listener/mother, "every bit of experience of your baby affects eventually the personality of a human adult." Winnicott also included a paragraph that seems to have been cut by Benzie, saying that in the first days of life "it is the mother and not the doctors and nurses who knows how to manage the baby."[79]

During the last talk in the series, Winnicott discussed his "fan mail," as he called it (i.e., the letters he received from listeners).[80] Letters were frequently discussed during the *Woman's Hour*, a fact that indicates the responsiveness of the BBC to its listeners. One such letter, among the eight that Winnicott received during this particular date, came from a woman in Liverpool who argued against his implication that books on childcare are not worthwhile and claimed instead that she had learned a great deal from them. Winnicott clarified that what he meant was to say that the early "management of a baby" goes deeper than book-learning, "that it comes naturally under suitable conditions just because of the fact of the mother's motherhood." In a section that was crossed out in the script and probably censored by Benzie, Winnicott agreed with a grandmother from Streatham (London) who wrote that breastfeeding was the loveliest thing of her married life. He offered again that the mother, and not doctors and nurses, is the one to know what is right for the baby "since the baby needs exactly what the mother and no one else is shaped for." Yet answering another letter of a mother from Kent who complained about the nursing staff's interference after her delivery, Winnicott said that many mothers should still be grateful for doctors' and nurses' help.[81] By February 28, 1952, more letters from listeners arrived. One woman wrote, for example, that his early series was the finest she had ever heard on motherhood.[82]

Conclusion

The psychoanalytic ideas broadcasted on BBC radio contributed to the shift from a collective wartime citizenship toward a postwar domestic citizenship and to a focus on conservative family relationships in general and the mother–child bond in particular as important to the functioning of democracy. Winnicott's public discussion of psychoanalytic ideas on the child and the parents was shaped though an active dialogue with the BBC staff and with a particular vision of citizenry.[83] Winnicott constructed his expert authority as a psychoanalyst in relation to an audience of mothers that was imagined according to particular gender roles. He believed that he was mostly elucidating the "deep" reasoning behind what mothers were already "naturally" doing with their babies. He was willing to work with the BBC producers and shape his ideas according to their instructions to make an immediate connection with the public. Through his talks, new behaviors and troubles of "normal ordinary people" – and not only those of people labeled mentally ill or disturbed – became topics for expert guidance.

Winnicott was not alone in turning women into symbols of the return to normalcy after the war, but the contribution of his radio talks lay in their claim that full-time motherhood was crucial to the democratic national community in a particular way. Good motherhood would ensure the creation of a healthy "mature democracy." Instead of being a haven from the political world, the home here was the very place where democracy was being produced. Childhood was valued as the period of initiation into selfhood and of proto-democratic tendencies. Winnicott envisioned normative family dynamics and adequate parenting that would breed healthy, cooperative, normative, sociable, and non-aggressive children (i.e., the future democratic citizens). Women were seen as mothers and natural caregivers whose subjectivity was almost entirely directed toward providing for children's needs so that aggression on a personal and social level would be diminished. Men, on the other hand, were envisioned as financial providers, and as only partial and secondary, albeit important, caregivers of babies. This vision, which we would now recognize as heterosexist and middle class, was developed together with the female producers of the BBC talks who were themselves radio pioneers and who helped develop new radio genres targeting women, and were remembered as radicals for their time. Indeed, it is important to note that the ideas that Winnicott presented, now seen as simplistic, were new and seen as progressive for their time as they were set against behaviorist childrearing advice. During the mid-century these views were seen as innovations that reassured mothers of their importance and authority as parents. The voices of women producers and mother listeners suggest that many women of the time were embracing these ideas.[84] Interestingly, no letters of protest or criticism against Winnicott's ideas were sent to the BBC. Winnicott warned that without the mother's love and care the baby would grow to be a troubled adult, yet following BBC's instructions not to upset parents, he mostly spoke in a positive manner, emphasizing the importance of good mothering as something that comes naturally to a woman. Nevertheless, the threat of damage to mental health and the democratic regime was there.

The heritage of World War II in Britain was less tainted than that of other countries in the European continent. British women and men did not experience the results of violent occupation, annihilative racism, rape, mass deportation and murder, and did not have to deal with the question of collaboration with or resistance to an enemy. While other countries had to deal with more complex national wartime pasts of either victimizing or being victimized (and sometimes both), Britain's legacies of war centered on notions of heroism and the worry for the future stability of its democratic regime. This stability was seen as tied to the promotion and maintenance of mental health. Ideas about mental health, significantly advocated by psychoanalysts, were often described in gendered terms that made full-time motherhood – for better and for worse – a milestone in the process.[85] Evacuated, delinquent or "democratically immature" children, as Juliet Mitchell noted, were all seen by psychoanalysts to be "maternally deprived," while bombs, poverty, absent fathers, or a critique of the welfare state were not part of this description. The early Freudian triadic relationship of the Oedipus complex and the more radical psychoanalytic debates on femininity from earlier in the century were now replaced by a preoccupation with the mother–child bond, one that fit the political demands of the era.[86]

Notes

1 Despite infamous theoretical differences between them, I look at psychoanalytic discourse as collectively forming a certain image of the child that emphasized his or her vulnerability and aggression, the importance of the relationship with the parents and the mother in particular (whether real or imaginary), the link between inner and outer realities, and the connection between experiences of early life and the future fragility of mental stability and social relations.
2 A comprehensive history of psychoanalysis in Britain is largely unwritten. See Sandra Ellesley, *Psychoanalysis in Early Twentieth Century: A Study in the Popularisation of Ideas* (Ph.D dissertation, University of Essex, 1995); Dean Rapp, "The Reception of Freud by the British Press: General Interest and Literary Magazines, 1920–25," *Journal of the History of the Behavioral Science* Vol. 24 (1988), 191–201.
3 Anna Freud and Dorothy Burlingham, *Infants Without Families: The Case For and Against Residential Nurseries* (New York: International Universities Press, 1970 [1944]).
4 Suzan van Dijken, *John Bowlby, His Early Life: A Biographical Journey into the Roots of Attachment Theory* (New York: Free Association Books, 1998), 103–28; Susan Isaacs, (ed.), *The Cambridge Evacuation Survey: A Wartime Study in Social Welfare and Education* (London: Methuen, 1941).
5 Brett Kahr, *D. W. Winnicott: A Biographical Portrait* (Madison: International Universities Press, 1996), 83–85.
6 Dijken, *John Bowlby*, 129–52.
7 Michal Shapira, *The War Inside: Child Psychoanalysis and Remaking the Self in Britain, 1930–1960* (forthcoming). Cf. Denise Riley, *War in the Nursery: Theories of the Child and Mother* (London: Virago, 1983).
8 I am grateful to the BBC scholars Paddy Scannell, Jean Seaton, David Hendy, Siân Nicholas, Kristin Skoog, Kate Murphy, and Suzanne Franks for their help. Thanks to Bonnie Smith for her insight and guidance. D. W. Winnicott quotes reproduced by kind permission of The Winnicott Trust and with the help of Lesley Caldwell. Permission on behalf of the BBC was granted for quotes related to its work and with the kind help of BBC Written Archives Centre archivist Trish Hayes.
9 This "normal family life" to which many people aspire and which was promoted in the media and through psychoanalysis after the war was in fact a new rather than traditional model of the family, although it quickly came to be represented as traditional. Pat Thane, "Family Life and 'Normality' in Postwar Britain," in Richard Bessel and Dirk Schumann, (eds), *Life After Death: Approaches to Cultural and Social History of Europe During the 1940s and 1950s* (Cambridge: Cambridge University Press, 2003), 193–210.
10 *Ibid.*

11 Tara Zahra, "Lost Children: Displacement, Family, and Nation in Postwar Europe," *The Journal of Modern History* (March 2009), 45–86.
12 See for example Robert Moeller, *Protecting Motherhood: Women and Politics of Postwar West Germany* (Berkeley: University of California Press, 2003).
13 Alan Allport, *Demobbed: Coming Home after the Second World War* (New Haven: Yale University Press, 2009).
14 William Beveridge's conviction that married women should be housewives and that adult women would normally be economically dependent on their husbands "became embodied in the postwar social security legislation which in turn had a prescriptive effect," Jane Lewis, *Women in Britain Since 1945* (London: Blackwell, 1992). 21.
15 Mark Mazower, *Dark Continent: Europe's Twentieth Century* (New York: Vintage, 1994).
16 Benedict Anderson, *Imagined Communities: Reflections on the Origin and Spread of Nationalism* (New York: Verso, 1991), 35–36.
17 Angus Calder, *The People's War: Britain 1939–1945* (New York: Pantheon Books, 1969), 358–59; Ross McKibbin, *Classes and Cultures, England 1918–1951* (Oxford: Oxford University Press, 1998), 468.
18 Andrew Crisell, *An Introductory History of British Broadcasting* (London: Routledge, 2002), 54. See also Siân Nicholas, "From John Bull to John Citizen: Images of National Identity and Citizenship on the Wartime BBC," in Richard Weight and Abigail Beach, eds, *The Right to Belong: Citizenship and National Identity in Britain, 1930–1960* (London: I. B. Tauris, 1998), 36–57; James Curran and Jean Seaton, *Power without Responsibility: The Press and Broadcasting in Britain* (London: Routledge, 1997), 128–60.
19 McKibbin, *Classes*, 457; Crisell, *An Introductory*, 56.
20 Crisell, *An Introductory*, 63.
21 McKibbin, *Classes*, 471–72.
22 *Ibid.*, 457–76; Paddy Scannell and David Cardiff, *A Social History of British Broadcasting* (Cambridge, Mass.: Blackwell, 1991), 14–15.
23 Calder, *The People's War*, 358.
24 Crisell, *An Introductory*, 54; 64.
25 *BBC Yearbook 1945* (London: BBC, 1945), 67–69.
26 *BBC Yearbook 1947* (London: BBC, 1947) 57.
27 Cf. Nicholas, "From John Bull," 46. See also Siân Nicholas, "'Sly Demagogues' and Wartime Radio: J. B. Priestley and the BBC," *Twentieth Century British History* Vol. 6 (1995), 115–24 and 139.
28 *BBC Handbook 1951* (London, BBC, 1951), 135.
29 Both programs were heard by a considerable number of men as well. *BBC Handbook 1958* (London: BBC, 1958), 103–4.
30 *BBC Yearbook 1952* (London: BBC, 1952) 49.
31 I use the unexplored archival correspondence between Winnicott and BBC producers and the scripts of Winnicott's talks. Many of the talks are now published, yet I also cover unpublished ones. I stick to the archival scripts for those talks that have been published, as there are differences between the archival and published versions, with the quotations referring to the war or to listeners usually omitted from the published version. The archival scripts also allow one to follow the immediate context in which the talks were transmitted, to explore the sections that were censored (and that at times made it to the published version), and to study the discussion of listeners' letters. See BBC Written Archives Centre, Caversham, UK (hereafter BBCWAC): Scripts Index Cards for broadcasts by other psychoanalysts.
32 See BBCWAC: Scripts Index Cards: DW Winnicott; Talk Booking Requisitions in Talks: Winnicott, Donald Woods, File LA, 1943–59 (hereafter TW). Some talks were also published as popular pamphlets costing one shilling.
33 The Home Service was the main network during the war before the BBC created the three network system.
34 Kate Murphy, *Women in the BBC: A History 1922–2002* (unpublished report).

35 "Miss Janet Quigley," *The Times* (February 12, 1987).
36 Qtd. in Paul Donovan, "Quigley, Janet Muriel Alexander (1902–87)," *Oxford Dictionary of National Biography* (Oxford: Oxford University Press, 2004).
37 TW: Letter, October 12, 1943.
38 TW: Letter, November 15, 1943.
39 TW: Letter (date unclear) November, 1943.
40 BBCWAC: Microfilm (hereafter MF) T659/T660: Script "Happy Children: Getting to Know Your Baby," (December 12, 1943), 1–6.
41 TW: Letter, January 16, 1944.
42 MF: T659/T660: Script "Why Does Your Baby Cry?" (1) (February 4, 1944). Winnicott used the third person "he" for baby or child but he meant both sexes. I follow him here for the sake of simplicity.
43 Cathy Urwin and Elaine Sharland, "From Bodies to Minds in Childcare Literature: Advice to Parents in Inter-war Britain," in Roger Cooter (ed.) *In the Name of the Child: Health and Welfare, 1880–1940* (London: Routledge, 1992), 174–99.
44 MF: T659/T660: Script "Why Does Your Baby Cry?" (1) (February 4, 1944), 2–7.
45 TW: Letter, February 25, 1944.
46 See also TW: Letter, March 1, 1944.
47 MF: T659/T660: Script "Where Does Dad Come In?" (March 17, 1944), 1.
48 TW: Letter, March 13, 1944.
49 Allport, *Demobbed*, 70–71.
50 MF: T659/T660: Script "Where Does Dad Come In?" 2.
51 Ibid., 4–5. Winnicott also implicitly referenced to the Oedipus conflict.
52 MF: T659/T660: Script "Their Standards and Yours" (May 12, 1944), 2.
53 TW: Letters, June 20–22, 1944.
54 MF: T659/T660: Script "What Do We Mean by a Normal Child?" (June 1944), 5–8.
55 TW: Letter, July 11, 1944.
56 TW: Letter, November 1, 1944. The popular *Radio Times* described the series saying, "Some 'difficult' [children] are not really difficult if rightly handled, but if they *are* difficult then they need special care." "Difficult Children in Difficult Times," *Radio Times* (January 26, 1945).
57 Qtd. in Donovan, "Quigley."
58 *Ibid.*
59 TW: Letters, January 5 and 16, 1945. See also February 2; March 26, 1945.
60 MF: T659/T660: Script "Home Again" (June 22, 1945), 5–6. When Winnicott and his wife Clare Britton reported to the Government's The Care of Children Committee they expressed concern over the aggressiveness of the institutional child; D. W. Winnicott and Clare Britton, "The Problem of Homeless Children," *Children's Communities: Experiments in Democratic Living* (London: NEF Monograph, 1944), 2.
61 The wartime geographical mobility of many civilians and soldiers further intensified a romance with home life; see Claire Langhamer, "The Meaning of Home in Postwar Britain," *Journal of Contemporary History* (April 2005), 341–62.
62 TW: Letter, October 3, 1945; Paul Donovan, "Benzie, Isa Donald (1902–88)," *Oxford Dictionary of National Biography* (Oxford: Oxford University Press, 2004).
63 *Ibid.* and Kate Murphy, *Women in the BBC: A History 1922–2002* (unpublished report).
64 The talks were also published as pamphlets for the price of one shilling. Winnicott received 15 guineas for each talk. See BBCWAC: File LA: Letters, February 1 and 2, 1950.
65 MF: T659/T660: Script "How's the Baby (1)" (October 5, 1949), 1–2.
66 *Ibid.*, 3.
67 MF: T659/T660: Script "How's the Baby (2)" (October 12, 1949), 2–3.
68 MF: T659/T660: Script "How's the Baby (6)" (Nov. 9, 1949), 1.
69 Urwin and Sharland, "From Bodies to Minds," 179–80.
70 *Ibid.*, 1–6.
71 MF: T657/T658: Script "The Ordinary Devoted Mother and Her Baby" (January 9, 1952), 4.

72 MF: T659/T660: Script "How's the Baby (8)" (November 23, 1949), 4.
73 See D. W. Winnicott, "Some Thoughts on the Meaning of the Word Democracy," *Human Relations* Vol. 3 (1950), 175–86.
74 Sigmund Freud, "Civilization and its Discontents" [1930] *The Standard Edition of the Complete Psychological Works of Sigmund Freud,* Vol. XXI, 57–146.
75 MF: T659/T660: Script "How's the Baby (7)" (March 22, 1950), 5.
76 MF: T659/T660: Script "How's the Baby (8)" (March 29, 1950), 3.
77 TW: Letter, March 27, 1950.
78 TW: Letter, February 5, 1952.
79 MF: T657/T658: Script "The Ordinary Devoted Mother and Her Baby (2), The First Weeks: By a Doctor," (January 16, 1952), 1–3.
80 Letter from May 3, 1951.
81 MF: T657/T658: Script "The Ordinary Devoted Mother and Her Baby (5)" (February 20, 1952), 1–4. Winnicott gave many more talks on the BBC: He delivered three talks in 1955, one talk in 1956 and 1959, thirteen talks in 1960, one talk in 1961, two in 1962, and one in 1966. See BBCWAC: Scripts Index Cards: DW Winnicott.
82 TW: Letter, February 28, 1951.
83 Cf. Peter Miller and Nikolas Rose, "The Tavistock Programme: The Government of Subjectivity and Social Life," *Sociology* Vol. 22, No. 2. (May 1988), 171–92.
84 See Elizabeth Wilson, *Only Halfway to Paradise: Women in Postwar Britain* (London: Tavistock, 1980).
85 Dolly Smith Wilson, "A New Look at the Affluent Worker: The Good Working Mother in Post-War Britain," *Twentieth Century British History* Vol. 17 (2006), 206–29.
86 Juliet Mitchell, *Psychoanalysis and Feminism* (New York: Basic Books, 1974), 228–29.

5

WOMEN AS THE "MOTOR OF MODERN LIFE"

Women's work in Europe west and east since 1945

Francisca de Haan

> A woman who contributes materially to the support of the family, cannot be treated in the same contemptuously tyrannical manner as one who, however she may toil as a domestic drudge, is dependent on the man for subsistence.
>
> Harriet Taylor Mill, 1851[1]

> The quintessential prerequisite for [women's] economic independence is work ... Once women have attained their economic independence from men, there is no reason why they should remain socially dependent upon them.
>
> Clara Zetkin (around 1900)[2]

> I said [to my husband], we are both people, we both work, we both bring in money, we will do everything together.
>
> Corina, looking back on her life during state socialism in Romania.[3]

"I love my work. I value my independence," Olga Voronkova thinks, in Natalya Baranskaya's novella, *A Week Like Any Other*. The novella caused a stir when it was published in Moscow in 1969. The official view in Soviet Russia was that women were liberated, and a very important part of that liberation was that they worked outside of the home. In practice this meant that most Soviet women were workers as well as mothers, but without sufficient social services or an equal sharing of the paid and unpaid work with men. *A Week Like Any Other* exposed women's difficulties with what became known as their "double burden."[4]

Two years earlier, in 1967, the Dutch writer Joke Kool-Smit published an article about "Woman's Discontent" that equally created a stir. Her article, though, was not about women's being overburdened due to the combination of full-time work outside of the home and being a housewife and mother, but about the extent to which an existence as a full-time housewife, economically dependent on one's husband – generally the Western model – was unfulfilling and damaging for women's self-respect.[5]

This chapter focuses on women's work outside of the home in Europe since 1945. The Cold War, the US–Soviet struggle for global power and influence that dominated most of that period, fundamentally was a competition about which system, capitalism or Communism, offered a superior way of life. Therefore, the Cold War was more than an "arms race and … space race," it was also a "living-standards race," with a very strong ideological competition about what the good life consisted of.[6] Gender was one of the key components in the Cold War discourse. With both sides emphatically believing that their system represented what was best for women, competing views on women's work and role in society were part of the Cold War contestation.[7]

The Soviet Union claimed to have solved the so-called "woman question," arguing that it had given women full economic, political, and legal rights. In 1963, for example, Soviet leader Nikita Khrushchev proudly stated to a large international congress of women that in the Soviet Union "woman … is a full-fledged member of the society … Soviet women have all the opportunities to fully participate in the political, cultural, and social life of their nation."[8] At the time of Khrushchev's speech, dominant thinking about women in most Western countries went the other way around: women's place was in the home, this is where they belonged and were happy, and "staying at home" was what the capitalist system allowed them to do. It was "natural" for women to be full-time housewives and mothers, with a breadwinner–husband earning the family income. Although with different emphases between varying types of Western welfare states, overall these systems were geared toward supporting this particular middle-class heterosexual arrangement and making it seem natural, desirable and inevitable.[9] Simultaneously, women's paid work outside of the home was constructed as something secondary, temporary, and, in any case, less desirable. It was deemed unnatural for women to have any other wishes than to get married and become a full-time housewife, let alone to aspire to a career, and children needed to be with their mother.[10]

The aim of this chapter is to provide a balanced account of the history of women's work in Europe east and west since 1945, with a focus on some main trends. This allows us to see Baranskaya's and Kool-Smit's texts as representative for women's plight in their respective societies at the time. What have been the main developments in women's paid employment in Europe east and west since 1945? How have women themselves viewed their paid work? And what have been the consequences of the changes in Europe since the 1980s for women's labor market position?

Women's work In Europe after 1945: major trends and developments

Following the end of World War II in 1945, and in a process that on the Communist side may have been less centrally planned than it looked in retrospect, the European continent became divided into a capitalist west and socialist East.[11] The human and economic consequences of World War II were immense. The United States experienced relatively moderate losses, saw its gross domestic product double between 1941 and 1945, and emerged as the most powerful nation in the world. The losses of the Soviet Union, however, were so big as to be almost unimaginable. In its struggle for survival with Nazi Germany, the Soviet Union lost up to 27 million people, with another estimated 20 million children not born in the 1940s as a consequence of the war.[12] Besides the Soviet Union, Poland and Yugoslavia also lost 10 to 20 percent of their populations; whereas between 4 and 6 percent of the total populations of Germany, Italy, Austria, and Hungary perished. About 50 million people were uprooted by the war, and much of Europe lay in ruins.[13] With all the differences that existed between the two main social, economic and political systems, in both western and eastern Europe, it is possible to argue, women were the "motor of modern life," though initially with different emphases on what was expected of them.[14]

Eastern Europe

From 1945, the economies of the Soviet-dominated countries in eastern Europe were modernized on the basis of the model of central planning and rapid industrialization of the Soviet Union in the 1930s. Even though eastern Europe was economically more advanced than the Soviet Union had been, this particular way of development still meant a profound social revolution. In the years between 1948 and 1951, all countries in eastern Europe introduced a five- or six-year plan. The achievements of central planning in eastern Europe were impressive, at least until the early 1960s. "A revolutionary transformation of the industrial structure has been carried out," wrote the Economic Commission for Europe. "East European governments have on the whole planned successfully."[15] The forced industrialization was financed out of domestic savings and based on an intensive use of labor, which also included forced and slave labor. Millions of peasants, men and women, moved to the cities; in less than two decades the region became a predominantly urban society.[16]

The labor-intensive strategy of economic development and the rapid industrialization were dependent on a large-scale inclusion of women in the labor force. Throughout the region, the effects of state-socialist policies toward women were a significant increase in their levels of education, and a large-scale entry of women into paid employment outside the home. Both the levels of women's education and of their employment outside the home generally were higher in the "more developed northern countries in the region" (GDR, Czechoslovakia, Poland, and Hungary) than in the Balkans, as Table 5.1 shows.[17]

The two reasons why state-socialist governments strongly encouraged women's paid employment outside of the home were their commitment to the principle of women's equality – of which women's economic independence was seen as a necessary precondition – and their need for women's labor power. Whatever the

TABLE 5.1 Women Workers as a Percentage of the Labor Force, in Eight State-Sociolist Countries and the OECD, 1950–1988

Year	Albania	Bulgaria	Czechosl.	GDR	Hungary	Poland	Romania	Yugoslavia	OECD
1950		27.4 (a)	38.4	38.4		33 (b)		23.2 (c)	31.4
1960	25.1	33.5	42.8	44.3	32.5	32.8	27.1	27	33.6
1970	38.7	41	46.7	47.7	40.6	40	30.1	31	35.2 (c)
1980		47.1	45.4	51.0	45.7 (d)	44.5		35.5	38.7
1988		49.5 (e)	46	50.3	46.0 (e)	46.8		38.3 (e)	41.6 (f)

Notes:
OECD = Organisation for Economic Co-operation and Development (born after WWII as the Organisation for European Economic Co-operation to coordinate the Marshall Plan).
(a) 1951; (b) 1955; (c) 1971; (d) 1985; (e) 1986; (f) 1989
Sources:
S. L. Wolchik, "Women and Work in Communist and Post-Communist Central and Eastern Europe," in H. Kahne and J. Z. Giele (eds) *Women's Work and Women's Lives. The Continuing Struggle Worldwide*, Boulder etc.: Westview Press, 1992, table on 121. L. Paukert, "The Economist Status of Women in the Transition to a Market System: The Case of Czechoslouakia," 1991.

relative weight of these two components – and many scholars would argue that the second reason was by far more important[18] – together they resulted in

> efforts never seen before [in the countries in eastern Europe] to include women into the labor force, using the wage system [keeping the wages low, thus requiring two-income earners to make a reasonable family income] as well as centralized political pressure and propaganda to [their] ends. Following the ideas of Lenin and Engels, the initial ideological assumption was that women should not be differentiated from men in the workforce in any way.[19]

Along these lines, the Hungarian Constitution of 1949, for instance, proclaimed that women were entitled to the same work under the same working conditions as men, followed by a harsh campaign to mobilize women for paid work. "The new family laws in 1952 – preceding the revision of the Austrian family law by almost two-and-a half decades – supported the independence of women."[20]

It is clear that the lives of women in the Soviet Union and eastern Europe were fundamentally different from those of their mothers and grandmothers. How did they experience these changes, and what, in particular, did their paid work mean to them? I entirely agree with those who argue that there is not one coherent or representative narrative of women's lives under state socialism. There are multiple and competing stories, and there is no reason to privilege one view.[21] In both contemporary sources and later interviews, some women emphasize the ways in which socialism or the Communist Party liberated them. Others foreground their sacrifices and suffering, whereas yet others convey both dimensions. In 1969, when Natalya Baranskaya published her novella *A Week Like Any Other*, the official discourse in the Soviet Union still strongly maintained that the socialist superpower had liberated women (remember Khrushchev's 1963 speech). *A Week Like Any Other* was important because it showed the limitations of that liberation. In the Soviet Union and across eastern Europe, women were structurally overburdened and put in many more hours than men.[22]

However, at the same time women made it very clear that they did not want to give up their paid work. In 1960 in Hungary, for example, only 13 per cent of 4,828 working women interviewed said they would have preferred to work solely at home, just as women interviewed in the late Soviet Union said they did not want to give up their work outside of the home.[23] Many women realized the possibilities that socialism had created for them; they only had to look at their own family histories to see the difference. Alevtina Fedulova, born in 1940, for example, compared the illiteracy in "old Russia ... especially among women," with the progress made since then.[24]

Most of the Russian women interviewed by Anastasia Posadskaya-Vanderbeck realized that the Soviet period had opened many doors to them; they appreciated the gains they had made and were proud of their achievements. Work was seen as inherently valuable and was a source of self-realization.[25] Jill Massino, in her research on state-socialist Romania, similarly found that women's labor force participation "did dramatically alter women's roles, self-identities and relations with men – often in positive ways. While some women found paid work exhausting, time-consuming and wholly unfulfilling, others found it empowering, intellectually stimulating and personally validating." Despite many shortcomings, she further argues, the social services and other benefits that work offered "decisively affected women's ability to support themselves and their families."[26] Importantly, Massino also maintains that women did not just passively accept the positive and negative sides of state socialism, but actively engaged with the regime's policies, practices and discourses.[27] Among the women who felt they had a good life during state socialism was Tatiana, who grew up in a poor rural area in Romania and then became a factory worker in a big industrial city. Tatiana said:

> For me, I have the impression that the period was good ... it was very good ... I believe that, regardless of the regime, if you are diligent and you work, you will live well. I liked it because I worked eight hours ... I came home ... I put a meal on the stove ... and I had time to read ... I read a lot then ... I led an ordered life. Yes ... we worked on Saturday and sometimes Sunday, but to be honest that didn't disrupt anything.[28]

Elvira, another former factory worker, described how work provided her with companionship and a sense of purpose and belonging.

> Work ... oh, it was very good. We were well paid ... we worked with pleasure because of our co-workers ... we had an extraordinary relationship. It was a collaborative effort. Everybody collaborated and when work is like that it appears easy. Also we saved money ... there were two salaries coming in and we were able to put one salary into the bank and off the other salary we lived very well, we went to plays and to restaurants.[29]

The importance of the workplace collectives for working-class women also comes through in material about Soviet Russia, the German Democratic Republic and

Hungary, as does women's pride in their achievements. In an article called "'I Am Somebody!'" (based on materials from the 1970s and 1980s), for example, Maria Barbara Watson-Franke showed the positive impact of GDR women's participation in work collectives on their sense of self.[30] There is no doubt, therefore, that for many millions of women their labor force participation was a deeply formative and positive experience, opening up horizons, increasing their standard of living, positively influencing their self-respect, and empowering them in a number of ways.

However, that does not mean that women were fully equal to men in the sphere of paid work. Although there was equal pay for the same work, a wage gap of upwards of 30 percent in the earnings of men and women existed everywhere in the state-socialist world.[31] This significant wage gap was caused by a number of factors. Women, by and large, remained concentrated in branches of the economy (education, the service sector, retail trade, medicine, and light industry) that had lower wages than the high-priority branches of the economy where men predominated (such as mining and heavy industry). The differences in wages and occupations also reflected men and women's different educational trajectories: much more men than women chose a technical education, which was valued higher because of the focus on industrialization. Other factors that explain women's lower wages were outright discrimination against them, the fact that few women held leading economic positions, and women's willingness to accept positions for which they were overqualified in order to be nearer to their homes. The reason for the latter was that, although women had been proclaimed "equal," in all socioeconomic groups, domestic work and care for children remained women's responsibility.[32] One scholar has summed up these issues in the statement that "the [state-socialist] world of men ... defended its advantages in the spheres of paid work and unpaid care work ... just as it did in other industrial societies."[33]

From the early 1960s, the birthrates dropped significantly across eastern Europe. Political leaders interpreted this as a reaction by women to the fact that they were overburdened in the new situation (though one might note that a decline in birth rates always happens when women's education increases), and therefore took steps to make the combination of paid work and motherhood somewhat easier.[34] The paid maternity leave and mothers' allowances, in some cases allowing women with more than one child to remain at home until their children were three, were widely used.[35] While these measures did alleviate women's burden, they also reinforced the identification of women as a group with family and the home. In the 1970s and 1980s, women's paid employment rates continued to be high, or increased even further. But in that period of economic and political crises, so-called women's issues remained low on the list of politicians' priorities.[36]

Western Europe[37]

In the first fifteen to twenty years after World War II, the height of the Cold War, a conservative social and political climate predominated in western Europe, characterized by a "widespread desire ... for political quiescence, family stability and domesticity."[38] Instead of the socialist ideal of women's equality with men (based on the notion of their essential sameness as human beings), in the west *sexual difference* was emphasized or even celebrated in all domains of life, from fashion (Christian Dior's incredibly successful 1947 "New Look" for women), to popularized social science (Freud) and politics (the Cold War propaganda about western women's "soft and true femininity" versus the tough Communist female factory workers and tractor drivers).[39] There was an overwhelming consensus, in which women shared, that marriage and motherhood were women's natural vocations, and that women – especially mothers – belonged not on the labor market but in the home.[40] In the Netherlands, for example, in 1947, 98 percent of married women were full-time housewives.[41] At least until the 1960s, single and independent women who worked outside of the home throughout their adult lives were exceptions and pitied for their "empty lives."[42] Complementing this was the equally widely held belief that paid work was *men*'s natural right, and that men were entitled to a breadwinner's wage, enough to support a wife and dependent children. This was the period when regimes in western and eastern Europe diverged the most.

While women in state-socialist countries contributed to building up their societies by participating in the labor force, getting children and daily taking care of themselves and their families, women's primary role in western Europe in this period was decidedly different, though equally crucial. Between 1950 and the early 1970s, life in western Europe was transformed by a historically unprecedented period of economic growth – the so-called "economic miracle" – the causes of which remain disputed.[43] In addition to bearing children and taking care of everybody's daily needs, women in capitalist societies from the 1950s were strongly encouraged to develop a consumer identity, and thus build up the new consumer society. "Women ... were spotlighted as the 'motor' of 'modern life': advertisers saw them in the 1950s chiefly in domestic terms and concentrated on 'hitting the housewife'. 'You can't do any longer without electricity, espresso and Cola', ran one German ad. 'But you can do without cooking! All these wonders are now yours, dear housewife! What your grandmother and mother had to suffer through by hand, a tiny miracle machine will handle in seconds ... Tell your husband to dig a little deeper into his pocket!'"[44]

Simone de Beauvoir had already in 1949 published her groundbreaking feminist book *Le deuxième sexe* (*The Second Sex*). From the early 1960s middle-class Western women became increasingly disillusioned with their "home-bound isolation," and started to protest their "continuing social and economic subordination."[45] Publications such as Betty Friedan's *The Feminine Mystique* (published in the United States in 1963, but quickly hitting Europe as well), Hannah Gavron's *The Captive Wife: Conflicts of Housebound Mothers* (UK, 1966) and, in the case of the Netherlands, socialist feminist Joke Kool-Smit's earlier-mentioned article about "Woman's Discontent" (1967), sharply criticized the notion that "woman" found happiness within four walls and by devoting herself to the well-being of others. These works and the ensuing public debate contributed enormously to the development of a strong women's movement, which forever changed women's lives – in the context of and entangled with other social, cultural and protest movements, as well as other fundamental changes in the lives of women in western Europe. Women's educational levels began to rise, as did their labor market participation, in an economy that increasingly needed their labor power. Encouraged by the women's movement on the one hand, and international bodies such as the United Nations on the other (which in turn had been spurred by the international women's movement),[46] western governments abolished laws that cemented women's subordinate position. In 1970, for example, the rule that the husband was the head of the married couple was abolished from Dutch marital law; in 1977, the West German Marriage Law did away with the clause which permitted a wife to work only with her husband's permission.[47] They also adopted policies to support women's equal treatment in the labor market, the tax system, social security programs, and society in general.[48]

Women's labor force participation in western Europe continued to increase from the 1960s through the 1990s. However, most of this increase took the form of part-time employment. The western European postwar "economic miracle" came to an end in 1973, to be followed first by slow growth (1975–80), and then a shrinking economy (until 1986). Inflation and unemployment increased, and many countries adopted so-called "austerity policies" to combat inflation. In this period of the spread of neoliberal thinking and the onset of the current wave of globalization, the very concept of "paid employment" also changed. Neoliberal policies emphasize the importance of a flexible labor market, privatization, and a slim-down of the welfare state to increase "competitiveness" in the global economy. The norm of "life-long employment," which mainly had been men's prerogative, thus from the 1980s became replaced by "job mobility" and "flexibility" as the new keywords. The new labor regime was characterized by a huge increase in part-time work, mostly done by women. As emphasized by the French sociologist Rose-Marie Lagrave, "the sexual division of labor was fundamental to the way firms managed [these 1980s'] changes in the labor process. Statistics showed that women definitely wanted to work." What they got, to a large extent, were various forms of "flexible work," and in the first place, part-time work. In 1986, "90 percent of all part-time workers in Belgium, the United Kingdom, and Germany were women, as were 80 to 90 percent in Denmark, Norway, Sweden, France, and Luxembourg." Part-time work was characterized by more insecurity, lower pay, and less workers' rights. Hence, the employment of women on a part-time basis – which only a third of women wanted, but was the available option for many more – contributed to keeping women in the position of secondary workers.[49]

Generally, when women wanted part-time work, it was to enable them to combine paid and unpaid work. Despite women's higher levels of education, their greater focus on paid work, and western governments' professed support for gender equality (pressured by the UN-proclaimed International Women's Year, 1975, and the women's movement more broadly), women remained responsible for most of the work related to reproduction.[50]

In addition, western women also continued to be paid significantly less than men, notwithstanding laws mandating equal pay for equal work. In 1982, women in western Europe on average earned 20 to 40 percent less than men, with the wage gap narrowing everywhere.[51] Figures collected by international organizations such as the United Nations, the OECD, and the EU continue to show that women everywhere earn less than men. In twenty countries listed under the heading "Developed regions" for the years 1992/1997 women in manufacturing earned between 10 to 37 percent less than men (the 10 percent, in Sweden, was exceptionally "positive"; the 37 percent, for Luxembourg, exceptionally bad); the average difference was 22.8 percent.[52] Across industrialized countries in 2010, men's median, full-time earnings were 17.6 percent higher than women's. The smallest "gender wage gap" was in Belgium, where the gap was 9.3 percent.[53]

Europe as a whole

Since 1945, then, women's labor force participation has increased significantly across Europe. What is striking is the extent to which the developments described above – the increase in women's paid employment in both parts of the continent after 1945 – have resulted in *convergence*. More recent data, such as those published by the UN under the title *The World's Women 2000*, continue to show that convergence, which, however, does not apply to the level of wages, which is very uneven between eastern and western Europe [54]

The figures in Table 5.1 (earlier) further indicate that the levels of women's labor force participation reached in Czechoslovakia and East Germany in 1960 (more than 40 per cent), and by most other state-socialist countries in 1970, were reached in the OECD countries only in 1989; in general, the state-socialist countries in Europe reached this level twenty to thirty years earlier than the capitalist ones.

Women's labor force participation since 1989

In November 1989 the Berlin Wall fell and at the end of 1991 the Soviet Union ceased to exist. As a consequence of these changes and how they were managed, people in the Soviet Union and eastern Europe were confronted with an enormous decline in overall living standards,[55] huge unemployment, severe cutbacks on social services, a lack of prospects in the short run, and deep insecurity about the longer term. As one woman from Moldova dramatically but succinctly put it: "Our future collapsed with the Perestroika."[56]

Women were particularly hard hit, both by higher unemployment rates (though not everywhere) and by the cuts on social spending. Even if social services under state socialism had been insufficient, they were still important in allowing women to work, helping them cope with their "double burden," and maintaining a certain standard of living. As pointed out by Pascall and Kwak, some ten to fifteen years after the system change, the overall picture in the former state-socialist countries was one of "economic turmoil and recovery," many countries retaining high public spending (higher than in western Europe, though on a lower level than before), fewer people in the labor force, and "a growth in inequality and unemployment through policies influenced by international agencies such as the World Bank and the International

Monetary Fund."[57] How did women in eastern Europe react to these changes? Are there signs of a "retraditionalization" – expected by some, feared by others – of gender relations, including a "return of women to the home?"

Feminist scholars, such as Barbara Einhorn in her influential book *Cinderella Goes to Market*, initially emphasized that women in eastern Europe did not so much deplore the loss of their jobs because their paid work had been more of a duty than a right. According to Einhorn, many women in the former state-socialist countries did not perceive the "right to work" as liberation. Rather, "the right to work was degraded by state compulsion into an obligation to be endured. It subjected them to the rigours of the double burden – long days, exhaustion, feelings of guilt and inadequacy toward their children, lack of career satisfaction."[58] Along the same lines, Mirjana Morokvasic in 2003 wrote that "when they became the first ones to lose their jobs in the process of post-Communist economic restructuring, women did not consider it worthwhile to fight against this locally."[59] However, we have meanwhile seen and will further substantiate here that the picture of how women perceived their work during state socialism was more diverse, and the same applies to how they reacted to the post-1989 changes.[60]

As noted above, the heroine of Natalya Baranskaya's novella *A Week Like Any Other*, Olga Voronkova, in the midst of exhaustion and stress still said to herself: "I love my work. I value my independence." Many women will have understood the complexity of her situation. Romanian former factory worker Corina felt that her paid work entitled her to insist on an equal sharing with her husband of all the work: "I said, we are both people, we both work, we both bring in money, we will do everything together."[61] For some women their work outside of the home was so important that they – defying all expectations and/or stereotypes – felt justified in "neglecting" their family when their work demanded so, as Luana quoted here: "I liked this work very much, even if, at certain times, I had to neglect my family, because I stayed in so late. Sometimes we stayed as late as nine o'clock or even into the next morning. I would go home, maybe I'd only clean up, change and go back again."[62] Clearly, these women not only valued their work but felt that, despite the difficulties, it empowered them.[63]

The idea that women did not consider it worthwhile to fight against their job loss, articulated by contemporaries as well as scholars such as Morokvasic, has also been explicitly questioned. In "Do Russian Women Want to Work?", Sarah Ashwin and Elain Bowers observed that "it is by no means clear that Russian women are as passive as is implied by these arguments, and they are in fact attempting to hold onto their jobs for a number of reasons, something which is reflected in the employment statistics."[64] Recent work by economists about women's work in Europe underscores this. Thus it was concluded in 1999 about Europe as a whole: "There is little evidence from women's own behaviour of any major change or rupture to their continued integration into wage work and their conversion into more permanent and continuously committed employees,"[65] and in 2000 about central and eastern Europe that "the high level of women's inclination toward and participation in the workforce has been maintained."[66] In 2005, Gillian Pascall and Anna Kwak concluded that neither overall policies in central and eastern Europe nor women's everyday behavior and expectations were going in the direction of a "retraditionalization."[67] They found no evidence of a change toward male breadwinner assumptions in the region, but noticed instead that many women whom they interviewed were angry about the post-1989 decline or loss of services that supported families and expressed strong expectations regarding gender equality and men's responsibility within households. Pascall and Kwak interpreted the latter as a profound social change that had taken place in a relatively short time.[68] This is not to say that there is no danger at all of what has been called "repatriarchalization" and "retraditionalization," but it may be worthwhile to distinguish between dominant, conservative discourses and what the evidence indicates about women's behavior and expectations.

Conclusions

This chapter has explored main trends in women's paid employment outside of the home in western and eastern Europe since 1945, sketching the initial divergence and more recent convergence in this area. First, the percentage of women working outside of the home is now roughly the same across Europe, though the numbers in central and eastern Europe are still slightly higher. In addition, many more women in western Europe work part-time than in the former state-socialist countries, where, on the contrary, women and men often have more than one job in order to survive, because the wages are so low.

Second, despite the earlier emphasis on women's negative experiences with paid employment outside of the home, let alone a "career" (either by pitying women who remained single and worked full-time, or by depicting "women in eastern Europe" as oppressed and exhausted, and their work as generally unfulfilling), there is reason to believe that women across Europe have looked at their paid work in a more positive way and continue to do so, notwithstanding the neoliberal hardships and insufficient male sharing of the unpaid work.

Third, the collapse of state socialism had disastrous economic and social consequences and hit women even harder than men because of higher unemployment rates (though not uniformly) and loss of support of social services.

Fourth, women have not been passive recipients or victims, either of state-socialist discourse and policies or of the system's collapse. They tried to find ways to make the system work for them, and when it broke down and they lost their jobs, they reacted by making ends meet in all sorts of ways, by migrating in large numbers to find work in other parts of Europe and beyond,[69] and also by anger, perceiving the post-1989 loss of social services, the poverty and the economic insecurity as an infringement of their citizenship rights.[70]

Finally, some conclusions regarding the EU: In the late twentieth and early twenty-first century, women's paid employment has become the norm in Europe; indeed, it is now stimulated, for economic reasons, by Western governments and the European Union (joined by Cyprus, the Czech Republic, Estonia, Hungary, Latvia, Lithuania, Malta, Poland, Slovakia and Slovenia in 2004, and Bulgaria and Romania in

2007). As we have seen, though, the picture is not just positive, and the inequalities described above still exist in 2012. The ongoing gender inequality in the labor market has many causes, but a crucial factor is women's continued responsibility for household tasks and childcare, a conclusion that applies to the whole of Europe. In various countries men have somewhat increased their share in the household and caring tasks, but that is a very slow development, to say the least. Meanwhile, the EU does not offer women any substantial support to deal with their reproductive (household and care) work, and there are at least two fundamental problems with its approach.[71] First, although the EU has accepted "gender" as a category and "gender mainstreaming" as one of its policy instruments, it treats the responsibility for household and care-giving work as a *women's* issue.[72] There is no serious pressure on men to take up their part. Second, the EU policies that do exist to assist women with their double burden focus on *childcare*.[73] As important as this is, women's responsibilities related to the home consist of more than taking care of children. Nowadays, actual household labor, with its physical, planning, and time-consuming dimensions, seems to have disappeared from public and political discourse; nobody mentions "household drudgery" any more, the concept once so central to feminist–socialist theorizing about women's oppression (from William Thompson in 1825 to August Bebel, Clara Zetkin and V. I. Lenin).

What happens in this context of making invisible the reality of household work is that women who can afford it buy the services of other women to do the domestic work, thus freeing themselves from this demanding and undervalued work and enabling themselves to partake in the regular labor market. Hence, across Europe women of color and women from former state-socialist countries work in the houses of (mainly white) middle- and upper-class women, where they do both household work and take care of children and (increasingly) the elderly;[74] similarly, Polish women work in Germany in the domestic and care-giving sector, women from Ukraine work in Poland, and so on.[75] Migrant women, especially those from developing countries, often lack labor and other rights and are in a vulnerable position. The last strategy more affluent women revert to when trying to deal with all the pressure in their own lives and that of their children is the car – which has been referred to as the latest "domestic assistant."[76] While having a car may help individual women cope with the logistics of their complicated lives, it is also clear that the various strategies mentioned here allow men to continue avoiding their responsibilities, reproduce global, regional, and class inequalities, and are detrimental from the perspective of people's health and the environment.

At the same time, the official EU language is that "women are free" and "equal," making us wonder where we have heard that before … Researchers Pascall and Kwak still see reason to hope that EU gender policies will become more progressive and more helpful to women, first of all because "Europe" needs women's labor force participation, but needs them to have children as well.[77]

Let us end on a cautiously optimistic note by expressing the hope that in the long run Pascall and Kwak will prove to be right, and that a broad range of progressive social policies and equal citizenship status for all will be the outcome.

Notes

My sincere thanks to Eva Fodor, Yana Knopova, Raluca Popa and Susan Zimmermann for their comments and suggestions.

1 H. Taylor Mill, "Enfranchisement of Women," *The Westminster Review* (July 1851), quoted in M. Schneir (ed.), *The Vintage Book of Historical Feminism*, London, Vintage Books, 1996 (first edition 1972), xvii–xviii.
2 C. Zetkin (1857–1933), quoted in C. Sowerwine "Socialism, Feminism, and the Socialist Women's Movement from the French Revolution to World War II," in R. Bridenthal, Susan Mosher Stuard and Merry E. Wiesner (eds), *Becoming Visible: Women in European History*, 3rd ed., Boston and New York: Houghton Mifflin, 1998, 370.
3 Quoted in J. Massino, "Workers under Construction: Gender, Identity, and Women's Experiences of Work on State Socialist Romania," in S. Penn and J. Massino (eds), *Gender Politics and Everyday Life in State Socialist Eastern and Central Europe*, New York and Basingstoke: Palgrave Macmillan, 2009, 29.
4 N. Baranskaya, *Nedelya Kak Nedelya*, published in the *Novy Mir* in 1969; in English *A Week Like Any Other*. See F. du Plessix Gray, *Soviet Women: Walking the Tightrope*, New York, London, Toronto, Sydney, Auckland: Doubleday, 1989, 28–31, 210, and http://en.wikipedia.org/wiki/Natalya_Baranskaya (accessed June 30, 2011).
5 J. Kool-Smit, "Het onbehagen bij de vrouw," *De Gids*, 1967, Vol. 130, No. 9/10, 267–81.
6 S. E. Reid, "'Our Kitchen is Just as Good': Soviet Responses to the American Kitchen," in R. Oldenziel and K. Zachmann (eds), *Cold War Kitchen. Americanization, Technology, and European Users*, Cambridge, MA, and London: The MIT Press, 2009, 83–112, quotes on 86.
7 *Ibid*. On gender in the Cold War competition see also J. Withuis, "Over sekse en Koude Oorlog. De gelaatstrekken van de minister en de jurk van de kosmonaute," in J. Withuis, *De jurk van de kosmonaute. Over politiek, cultuur en psyche*, Amsterdam/Meppel: Boom, 1995, 85–113.
8 Nikita Khrushchev's address to the fifth WIDF Congress, June 24, 1963, GARF, Fond 7928, opis 3, number 946. As quoted and translated in A. Kadnikova, "The Women's International Democratic Federation's World Congress of Women, Moscow, 1963: Women's Rights and World Politics during the Cold War," MA Thesis, CEU, Budapest, 2011.
9 J. Jenson, "Friend or Foe? Women and Welfare State in Western Europe," in Bridenthal et. al. (eds), *Becoming Visible*, 493–513. G. Pascall and A. Kwak, *Gender Regimes in Transition in Central and Eastern Europe*, Bristol: The Policy Press, 2005, 4, point out that the Scandinavian regimes began to encourage women's labor market participation from the 1960s.
10 For the Netherlands, see M. Moree, "Mijn kinderen hebben er niets van gemerkt," *In Buitens-huis werkende moeders tussen 1950 en nu*, Utrecht: Jan van Arkel, 1992.
11 See M. Mazower, *Dark Continent: Europe's Twentieth Century*, London: Penguin Books, 1999, 255 and further; as well as McMahon, *The Cold War*.
12 McMahon, *The Cold War*; N. V. Riasanovsky and M. D. Steinberg, *A History of Russia. Vol. 2: Since 1855*, New York and Oxford: Oxford University Press, 2011, 547–48; O. Verbitskaia, "Tragic Numbers: The Lives Taken by the War (1995)," in A. Barker and B. Grant (eds), *The Russia Reader: History, Culture, Politics*, Durham and London: Duke University Press, 2010, 520–22; R. Overy, *Russia's War*, New York: Penguin Books, 1997, 287–89.
13 Since the focus is on Europe, I am leaving aside the huge losses elsewhere. McMahon, *The Cold War*, 6, 1, quote on 2.
14 M. Mazower, *Dark Continent*, 307.
15 Quoted in M. Mazower, *Dark Continent*, 272.
16 For this whole paragraph, see *ibid*., 270–99; and R. J. Crampton, *Eastern Europe in the Twentieth Century and After*, London and New York: Routledge, 1997.
17 S. L. Wolchik, "Women and Work in Communist and Post-Communist Central and Eastern Europe," in H. Kahne and J. Z. Giele (eds), *Women's Work and Women's Lives*.

The Continuing Struggle Worldwide, Boulder: Westview Press, 1992, 119–39, quote on 120. The exception was Bulgaria, where women's outside employment was among the highest in the region.
18 For example, M. Buckley, "Women in the Soviet Union," 84; Yana Knopova argues that, whatever the motivation, the official Soviet support for women's emancipation as part of its Bolshevik platform had a certain impact abroad. See her "The Soviet Union and the International Domain of Women's Rights and Struggles," MA thesis, CEU, Budapest, 2011.
19 Eva Fodor, *Working Difference: Women's Working Lives in Hungary and Austria*, Durham and London: Duke University Press, 2003, 114.
20 *Ibid.*, 114–15, quote on 117. All state-socialist countries adopted the principle of equality between men and women in their new constitutions.
21 B. Alpern Engel and A. Posadskaya-Vanderbeck (eds), *A Revolution of Their Own: Voices of Women in Soviet History*, Boulder, CO: Westview Press, 1998, 221; J. Massino, "Constructing the Socialist Worker: Gender, Identity and Work under State Socialism in Braşov, Romania," *Aspasia: The International Yearbook of Central, Eastern, and Southeastern European Women's and Gender History*, 2009, Vol. 3, 131–60, esp. 135.
22 See for example N. Rimashevskaia, "Perestroika and the Status of Women in the Soviet Union," in S. Rai, H. Pilkington and A. Phizacklea (eds), *Women in the Face of Change. The Soviet Union, Eastern Europe and China*, London and New York: Routledge, 1992, 11–19, esp. 14; M. Buckley, "Women in the Soviet Union," with some fantastic cartoons.
23 I. Volgyes and N. Volgyes, *The Liberated Female. Life, Work, and Sex in Socialist Hungary*, Boulder, CO: Westview Press, 1977, 55. Rimashevskaia, "Perestroika," in Rai et. al. (eds), *Women in the Face of Change*, 15. According to du Plessix Gray, *Soviet Women*, 38, in the second half of the 1980s "one out of five Soviet women would willingly give up work if they could so afford," which means that 80 percent would not.
24 Quoted in L. Racioppi, and K. O'Sullivan See, *Women's Activism in Contemporary Russia*, Philadelphia: Temple University Press, 1997, 86–87.
25 Alpern Engel and Posadskaya-Vanderbeck (eds), *A Revolution of Their Own*, 220–21. See also A. Rotkirch, "'Coming to Stand on Firm Ground'. The Making of a Soviet Working Mother," in D. Bertaux, P. Thompson and A. Rotkirch (eds), *On Living Through Soviet Russia*, London: Routledge, 2004, 146–75, esp. 167. The interviewees in C. Hansson and K. Lidén (eds), *Moscow Women. Thirteen Interviews*, New York: Pantheon Books, 1983, similarly viewed their work as a source of status and personal satisfaction.
26 J. Massino, "Constructing the Socialist Worker," *Aspasia*, 2009, Vol. 3, 132.
27 *Ibid.*, 132 and 141; for a similar emphasis on women's agency, but then for rural women, see D. L. Ransel, *Village Mothers. Three Generations of Change in Russia and Tataria*, Bloomington and Indianapolis: Indiana University Press, 2000.
28 J. Massino, "Constructing the Socialist Worker," *Aspasia*, 2009, Vol. 3, 144.
29 *Ibid.*, 145.
30 E. Zs. Tóth, "'My Work, My Family, and My Car': Women's Memories of Work, Consumerism, and Leisure in Socialist Hungary," in S. Penn and J. Massino (eds), *Gender Politics and Everyday Life*, 20–30; S. Ashwin and E. Bowers, "Do Russian Women Want to Work?" in M. Buckley (ed.), *Post-Soviet Women: From the Baltic to Central Asia*, Cambridge: Cambridge University Press, 1997, 21–37, see esp. 27; M.-B. Watson-Franke, "'I Am Somebody!' – Women's Changing Sense of Self in the German Democratic Republic," in M. J. Boxer and J. H. Quataert (eds), *Connecting Spheres: Women in the Western World, 1500 to the Present*, New York and Oxford: Oxford University Press, 1987, 256–66.
31 M. Molyneux, *Women's Movements in International Perspective: Latin America and Beyond*, New York: Palgrave, 2001, 100 and 131.
32 *Inter alia* S. Wolchik, "Women and Work," in H. Kahne and J. Giele (eds), *Women's Work and Women's Lives*, 122–24; M. Molyneux, *Women's Movements*, 100; S. Zimmermann, "Gender Regime and Gender Struggle in Hungarian State Socialism," *Aspasia*, 2010, Vol. 4, 1–24.

33 S. Zimmermann, "Gender Regime," *Aspasia*, 2010, Vol. 4, 17; a similar statement by J. Massino, "Constructing the Socialist Worker," ibid., 2009, Vol. 3, 143. For a lot of important data, see G. Warshofsky Lapidus (ed.), *Women, Work, and Family in the Soviet Union*, Armonk and London: M. E. Sharpe, 1982.
34 For these "pronatalist measures" see S. Wolchik, "Women and Work," in H. Kahne and J. Giele (eds), *Women's Work and Women's Lives*, 126.
35 For Hungary, see E. Fodor, *Working Difference*, 122; and S. Zimmermann, "Gender Regime," *Aspasia*, 2010, Vol. 4, 8–11, who also discusses differences among women in this respect.
36 S. Wolchik, "Women and Work," in H. Kahne and J. Giele (eds), *Women's Work and Women's Lives*, 128. E. Fodor, *Working Difference*. M. Molyneux, *Women's Movements*, 134–35.
37 For a longer overview, see D. Simonton, *A History of European Women's Work, 1700 to the Present*, London and New York: Routledge, 1998.
38 M. Mazower, *Dark Continent*, 295.
39 J. Withuis, "Over sekse en Koude Oorlog."
40 M. Moree, "Mijn kinderen hebben er niets van gemerkt."
41 R. Oldenziel and C. Bouw, "Huisvrouwen, hun strategieën en apparaten 1898–1998. Een inleiding," in R. Oldenziel and C. Bouw (eds), *Schoon genoeg. Huisvrouwen en huishoudtechnologie in Nederland 1898–1998*, Nijmegen: SUN, 1998, 16.
42 See, for example, J. A. Wttewaall van Stoetwegen, *Ongehuwd* [1953]; A. Franssen and N. van Heezik, *Ongehuwd bestaan: Ongehuwde vrouwen in de jaren vijftig*, Amsterdam: SUA, 1987.
43 See M. Mazower, *Dark Continent*, 296–302; R.-M. Lagrave, "A Supervised Emancipation," in F. Thébaud (ed.), *A History of Women in the West. V. Toward a Cultural Identity in the Twentieth Century*, Cambridge, MA, and London: The Belknap Press of Harvard University Press, 1994, 467.
44 Of course, there was a considerable female working force, but in countries such as the Netherlands, the UK and West Germany, this consisted overwhelmingly of young and single women. See C. van Eijl, *Het werkzame verschil: Vrouwen in de slag om arbeid, 1898–1940*, Hilversum: Verloren, 1994; D. Simonton, *A History*, 192; H. A. Pott-Buter, *Facts and Fairy Tales about Female Labor, Family and Fertility: A Seven-Country Comparison, 1850–1990*, Amsterdam: Amsterdam University Press, 1993. Quote from M. Mazower, *Dark Continent*, 307.
45 M. Mazower, *Dark Continent*, 319 and 318, respectively.
46 F. de Haan, "A Concise History of Women's Rights," *UN Chronicle* XLVII no. 1, 2010, *Empowering Women: Progress or Not?*, 56–59.
47 F. de Haan, *Gender and the Politics of Office Work*, 157, note 12; M. Mazower, *Dark Continent*, 358.
48 See esp. Lagrave, "Supervised Emancipation," in Thébaud (ed.), *A History of Women in the West*.
49 Ibid., 481–82.
50 Dutch women, for example, seem to have embraced working outside of the home, but based on the "part-time work" scenario: in 2000, 70 percent of employed women worked part time, allowing them to combine a job with household and childcare responsibilities, but clearly undermining any notion of economic independence. *Eurostat Yearbook 2002: The Statistical Guide to Europe. Data 1990–2000*, Brussels: European Commission, 2002, 105. H. Kahne, "Progress or Stalemate? A Cross-National Comparison of Women's Status and Roles," in H. Kahne and J. Giele (eds). *Women's Work and Women's Lives*, 279.
51 Lagrave, "Supervised Emancipation," in Thébaud (ed.), *A History of Women in the West*, 485–86. See also H. Kahne, "Progress or Stalemate?", 281–82 on wage differentials.
52 My calculation on the basis of United Nations, *The World's Women 2000. Trends and Statistics* (New York: United Nations, 2000) 123, Chart 5.23.

53 *The New York Times*, March 9, 2010, "The Gender Wage Gap, Around the World," based on data provided by the OECD.
54 United Nations, *The World's Women 2000*, 147–48, Table 5.D. For figures about 2003, see G. Pascall and A. Kwak, *Gender Regimes*, 40. For further data about women's economic position, see also the 2006 UNIFEM report *The Story Behind the Numbers: Women and Employment in Central and Eastern Europe and the Western Commonwealth of Independent States*, available at http://www.unifem.org/attachments/products/StoryBehindThe Numbers_eng.pdf
55 For numbers, see G. Pascall and A. Kwak, *Gender Regimes*, 11 and 19, Fig. 1.1. Hungary has been hit very hard by the 2008 world economic crisis.
56 Quote from C. Onica, "Women Migrating from Post-Soviet Moldova: Performing Transnational Motherhood," MA thesis, CEU, Budapest, 2008, 41. See further M. Rueschemeyer (ed.), *Women in the Politics of Postcommunist Eastern Europe*, Armonk and London: M. E. Sharpe, 1994; B. Łobodzińska (ed.), *Family, Women, and Employment in Central-Eastern Europe*, Westport, CT and London: Greenwood Press, 1995.
57 G. Pascall and A. Kwak, *Gender Regimes*, 23.
58 B. Einhorn, *Cinderella Goes to Market: Citizenship, Gender and Women's Movements in East Central Europe*, London and New York: Verso, 1993, 114. See also her "The Great Divide? Women's Rights in Eastern and Central Europe since 1945," in R. Bridenthal et. al. (eds), *Becoming Visible*, 515–48.
59 M. Morokvasic-Müller, "Transnational Mobility and Gender: A View from Post-Wall Europe," in M. Morokvasic-Müller, U. Erel and K. Shinozaki (eds), *Crossing Borders and Shifting Boundaries Vol. I: Gender on the Move*, Opladen: Leske + Budrich, 2003, 101–33, esp. 121.
60 For a broader discussion, see Racioppi and O'Sullivan See, *Women's Activism in Contemporary Russia*. A rich collection of essays about the gendered consequences of the changes after 1989 is S. Gal and G. Kligman (eds), *Reproducing Gender. Politics, Publics, and Everyday Life after Socialism*, Princeton, NJ: Princeton University Press, 2000.
61 See note 3.
62 J. Massino, "Constructing the Socialist Worker," *Aspasia*, 2009, Vol. 3, 146.
63 For a broader, positive assessment of state socialism on women's sense of self, see Dubravka Ugrešić, "Women's Cultural Canon?" *Aspasia*, 2008, Vol. 2, 172–73; Maca Jogan refers to the "economic empowerment of women" in Slovenia during state socialism. See her "The Decomposition of Sexism in the Second half of the 20th Century in Slovenia," in E. Saurer, M. Lanzinger, and E. Frysak (eds), *Women's Movements. Networks and Debates in Post-Communist Countries in the 19th and the 20th Centuries*, Cologne/Weimar/Vienna: Boehlau, 204.
64 Ashwin and Bowers, "Do Russian Women," in Buckley (ed.), *Post-Soviet Women*, 23.
65 J. Rubery, M. Smith, and C. Fagan, *Women's Employment in Europe. Trends and Prospects*, London and New York: Routledge, 1999, 15.
66 *Problems of Economic Transition* Vol. 43 No. 7 (November 2000). S. Gal and G. Kligman, *The Politics of Gender after Socialism*, Princeton, NJ: Princeton University Press, 2000, 112–13: "Polls across the region show that ... most women want to continue working for wages, even if their families do not need the money."
67 Pascall and Kwak, *Gender Regimes*, 29, 184 and 186.
68 *Ibid.*, 186–189. Jogan similarly mentions for Slovenia that the majority of respondents in both 1992 and 1998 "rejected a one-breadwinner ideology and accepted egalitarian standards." See her "Decomposition," in Saurer et. al. (eds), *Women's Movements*, 209.
69 The post-1989 job losses and lack of prospects forced millions of men and women from eastern Europe to migrate abroad, as has been extensively documented. See, for example, L. Passerini et. al. (eds), *Women Migrants from East to West: Gender, Mobility and Belonging in Contemporary Europe*, New York and Oxford: Berghahn Books, 2007.
70 As pointed out by Pascall and Kwak, *Gender Regimes*.

71 The general lack of progressive social policies in the EU is a fundamental problem; see, e.g., Pascall and Kwak, *Gender Regimes*, 180–81.
72 J. Rubery, "Gender Mainstreaming and Gender Equality in the EU: The Impact of the EU Employment Strategy," *Industrial Relations Journal* 2002, Vol. 33, No. 5, 500–522.
73 *Ibid*.
74 H. Lutz (ed.), *Migration and Domestic Work: A European Perspective on a Global Theme*, Farnham and Burlington, VT: Ashgate, 2008; J. Andall, *Gender, Migration and Domestic Service. The Politics of Black Women in Italy*, Aldershot: Ashgate, 2000.
75 Morokvasic, "Transnational Mobility and Gender," 109.
76 "De auto als nieuwe hulp in de huishouding," *NRC Handelsblad* (April 6, 2011).
77 Pascall and Kwak, *Gender Regimes*, 181–82; they specifically talk about women in central and eastern Europe; I have broadened the point.

6

"WHAT'S NEW" AND IS IT GOOD FOR YOU?

Gender and consumerism in postwar Europe

M. Jane Slaughter

As World War II in Europe ended in May 1945, Europeans rejoiced in the cessation of hostilities, and were overcome by the magnitude of human and material destruction the war had wrought. They also had to consider the question of what lay ahead in their political, social and economic worlds, either tomorrow or in the future. Some longed for a return to "normalcy," while others saw an opportunity to transform their nations and societies. Political and economic leaders from Milan to Moscow, Belgrade to Berlin, and west to the Atlantic coasts, all faced the daunting tasks of reconstruction and recovery, and hoped that these might lead to the building of modern, progressive democratic nations, though the definitions and incarnations of these terms varied dramatically. Like men, women had been mobilized during the war years as they were called upon to make their contributions to the nation, and had suffered the same deprivations, fears and destruction of the war. In some areas like Italy, Yugoslavia and France, women had served in significant numbers in resistance movements. Thus women also held a variety of hopes for the futures of their nations. Many felt that "the end of the war signaled the beginning of a new epoch for the country, an epoch in which ... traditional injustices, among these the problems of women would be eliminated."[1]

The menu of women's desires included the hope that the double burden of working in the home and in the public sphere, often exacerbated during the war, would be eased. Equally important were hopes for education, better jobs and economic security, while in some nations political rights were high on the list. In Italy and France, for example, women gained the right to vote at the close of World War II, thus joining the majority of their European sisters in the exercise of political rights. There is no doubt that postwar Europeans experienced considerable social, economic and political change, but plans for reform or transformation were complex processes with contradictory results for women. In the political realm, for example, Italian Marisa Rodano, herself a participant in the Resistance, a deputy from 1948–68, and later president of the Union of Italian Women (UDI), noted that while women were organized and included in political life, this was not necessarily the beginning of an inevitable march to emancipation.[2] In postwar Italy, as in other European nations, nearly equal civil rights coexisted with social inequality, and debates about appropriate behaviors for women made these even more contradictory.

Renovation, innovation, and expanding productivity were goals common to political leaders of all stripes after the war, and one marker of their success was the ability to improve standards of living for all citizens. By the early 1950s most European countries had regained much of their prewar economic stature, and in some cases like Italy and Germany, this recovery was remarkable enough to be called "an economic miracle." As postwar cities were rebuilt, new housing projects were planned that had indoor plumbing, central heating and electricity. Technological innovations in the domestic sphere accompanied these changes, and new visions of life in the home focused on women. These developments had the potential to transform daily life and individual expectations, and women often were on the front lines of these changes.

What had been emerging as "aspirational societies" in the prewar world now reacted positively to the promises of the "good life" and by the 1950s welcomed the possibility of mass consumption. In the 1950s and 1960s a continuum of consumer values and practices ran throughout Europe, and as political contests between the US and the USSR heated up in the 1950s, the different models of consumerism were important battlegrounds in the Cold War. The works by Victoria de Grazia and Lizabeth Cohen, as well as other important studies of Europe and the United States, have described the relationship between the state and the "consumer citizen." They argue that popular democracy and mass politics joined hands with the independent "sovereign consumer" who exercised her or his freedom in marketplace choices.[3] Slightly different models appeared in the USSR, and the "people's democracies" under its influence, where a command economy mandated that the state might well set the boundaries of individual consumption. Even in those cases, the state never had total control over consumer behavior, and with the "thaw" in the USSR after 1953, new goods and practices were tentatively introduced. While both Western and Eastern models associated scientific modernization, rationality and efficiency with the modern consumer process, there were significant differences in their narratives of consumption. For the West, pleasure, individual choice, and the constant expansion of products and opportunities were associated with the action of consuming; in the socialist states, standardization, equality, and frugality derived from a moral social conscience were often used to describe ideal consumer practices and values.[4] But the lines of meaning between the East and the West were always permeable, and in the socialist states material goods and improved lifestyle could be considered rewards for hard work on behalf of one's society, while the eastern European satellite nations were "proving grounds for experiments in socialist consumer modernity."[5]

Few doubted the power of consumerism or limited it to simple marketplace exchanges. It was seen as a force that could prompt changes in values, social and political relations. Some embraced the possibilities of modernity, while others held on to traditions with tenacity.[6] Concern for standards of living, which were frequently a starting point for discussions about the value of consumerism, usually focused on the home and family, and quite often targeted the importance of women as consumers. Because women could be both instruments of modernity and symbols of tradition, their place was central to the debates. Is the consuming woman a danger or an asset? In the USSR, according to Susan Reid, technological modernization in the home and "scientific consciousness" in the housewife, could help to emancipate women from the double burden on the home front. In Western countries women were transformed from being "ration-card holders to valued consumers," and grudgingly some conceded that even married women might have to enter the workforce in order to afford the new domestic technologies that were essential to modern living standards.[7] Without doubt women were both targets and instruments of the modernization that consumerism promised.

The act of consuming can involve material goods, bodies, services or spaces. Consumption might best be seen as a point of intersection – a nexus of work, productivity and market, of time and money, of politics, identity, and culture. The pages that follow will consider modern consumer society in terms of goods, practices and meanings. We begin by recognizing influential and powerful actors who set forth the policies that encouraged consumption, and the agents who produced, advertised and distributed the goods, but the focus will be the consumers, and eventually the people, many of them women, who worked in the expanding service and retail economy. Detailed examples from Italy will be joined by comparative materials in order to broaden the discussion. The conclusion of the chapter will illustrate popular responses to the emerging regime of consumption, and make clear the ambiguities, contradictions, and frequently unintended consequences that grew out of this new "empire."

Competing views about the values of consumerism were expressed in the centers of European political power and economic development. Political leaders in Italy in the 1950s were interested in economic stability, often tended to be fiscally conservative, feared inflation (which they linked to higher wages and private consumption), and were cautious about embracing "modernity." At the same time, in Italy and throughout Europe, pressures from other internal and external centers of power often pushed political leaders to accept some of the new ideas of the "regime of consumption." Private businesses, professional business organizations and their publications, Chambers of Commerce, United States Department officials and its commercial agents all promoted productivity and consumption. In doing so they used the language and practices of modernity, and wove gender images and expectations into these, sometimes intentionally, sometimes not.

The United States' postwar role in recovery and modernization across western Europe is well-known. As the 1950s unfolded, US economic and diplomatic goals were tied to programs for reconstruction and recovery, and for security and defense. Hallmarks of modernity – increases in production and an improvement in standards of living – were considered "to be the best possible answer to communism."[8] When the Cold War heated up in the 1950s, the battleground between East and West was often situated in the politics of consumption. Which side could deliver the goods that were considered essential to human happiness and well-being? Which economic and political system could produce the technology that would improve daily life as well as military prowess? Women were viewed as key players in the politics of well-being, because their interests were served by a society where their work was lessened through availability of more goods and services. Few would question the importance of US interests and influence in western Europe in these years. Nevertheless, it is critical to remember that regardless of what the US hoped to accomplish, local actors played "autonomous and creative roles ... in the reception – both positive and negative – of American techniques and methods."[9] The best way to assess US postwar reconstruction and Cold War policies and their effects is to look for the coexistence of assimilation, adaptation and rejection.

A major agent for the dissemination of the US message of productivity and prosperity in western Europe were National Productivity Committees, initially funded and launched by the Mutual Security Agency. Their agendas provide a guide to the efforts to promote a consumer society in Europe in the Cold War era.[10] Their goals were evident in a number of different arenas of industry and commerce, where creativity and vision in marketing, and rationality and understanding in approaching the consumer, became key principles. The Committee's magazine in Italy, *Produttività*, stated in a 1963 article quiet simply: "Only a nation that consumes – albeit within the limits of its own potential – can be a productive nation."[11]

Visions of gender were also evident in arguments advocating "rationalization" and standardization in the home. *Produttività* in April 1957 described the possible benefits of rationalization in daily life for a middle-class family in which "the husband is an ordinary employee, the wife a smart housewife who took care of the housework," and the two children were in school. Both in terms of motion and efforts, time and labor are saved in a home that is "unified" efficiently. The article concluded that consolidation of functions and goods in the home "contributes in notable measure to civic progress."[12] In the 1950s new roles and images were articulated for women in West Germany as propaganda campaigns led by industry described female consumerism and male productivity as "civic duties that defined and strengthened the newly formed West German State."[13] In the same period, state policies in the USSR, which were designed to bring the transition to Communism, also intervened in the practices and experiences of everyday life. In particular, "the female domain of good housekeeping had become a public affair, requiring codification, education and professionalization."

In Italy and other nations in western Europe, the expanded use of advertising linked private enterprise, the rise of consumerism, and the gendered dimensions of modernity. Advertising became more "democratic" and less oriented to the elites, used "target groups," and often focused on women. Italian firms, for example, used a variety of forms of advertising in the 1950s. Radio and direct mailings were popular, but also more and more ads appeared in a wide variety of print media. The vast majority of goods advertised were connected to home and family – usually considered the domain of the woman. Advertising directed to women was heavily concentrated in what were increasingly "slick" women's magazines where, throughout the 1950s, more ads with a more sophisticated message appeared for more new products, both Italian and foreign made. In the May 11, 1958 issue of *Época*, Zoppas stoves ran an advert that spoke to women who "having many responsibilities and loving the 'bright life' [*vita brillante*] had little time to devote to the kitchen." Other Zoppas ads a year later launched a new model of their refrigerator, noting that experts in industrial design and company technicians had been able to harmonize the most modern structures developed by the Americans with "*il gusto latino*" [Latin taste]. With this new, ultra-modern line, "one leaves the kitchen and enters into true home furnishing."[14] The consumer they had in mind was not a "kitchen slave," or a domestic drudge, but a "modern woman." Extolling the virtues of home appliances, and selling an independent and mobile lifestyle were designed to encourage women to consume in order to become modern.

The promotion of new images of modern women was not confined to western Europe. In the USSR after 1954, the popular press encouraged women to "prettify themselves ... [and] cultivate physical attractiveness," through their dress, hairstyles and especially their shoes.[15] Perfume also entered the lists of desirable purchases as state planning expanded the production of cheaper "modern, synthetic scents" like "Sputnik" and "Red Moscow," and these were featured in photo-essays and other visual documents in Russian magazines. By 1959 the effects of the "thaw" were evident when the Party Congress promised to shift economic priorities to consumer goods, domestic appliances, and housing, arguing that "consumption and comfort comprised an important dimension of the socialist promise and the failure to supply them had become a source of humiliation internationally." In other eastern European socialist nations, state-sponsored media encouraged "moderate consumerism [that] sparked desires."[16] In Poland in the 1960s the media promoted the "so-called modern girl" who was financially independent, enjoyed an improved standard of living which included travel, and consumption of fashions and cosmetics.

Public officials and their propaganda, businesses and their advertising constituted a significant force in the growth of a regime of consumption. But possibly even greater impact on the consumer came in the opportunity to see the new goods first-hand, perhaps to touch them, and eventually even purchase them. Trade fairs, supermarkets, self-service markets, and modern department stores were important bridges between the material examples of modernity, and popular responses to these. The trade fair in particular shows the relationships between desires and reality, between fantasy and the fascination with things that are new.

The economic and political possibilities offered in these venues were not lost on US leaders. By 1950s, the USA had become a regular participant at trade fairs throughout the world, and shows portraying community and home life in the United States appeared in fairs from Asia to Europe.[17] One of the earliest of these efforts was the Berlin Industrial Fair in 1950. Author Greg Castillo argues that before "television could beam images of Western lifestyles directly into East German homes," the State Department used the trade pavilion in divided Berlin to publicize consumer marvels abundant in the United States such as "the electric washing machine, illuminated electric range, vacuum cleaner, mix-master."[18] It became increasingly common to show off US culture and consumption in pre-fabricated homes that could be put on display and easily moved from one fair venue to another. A large two-bedroom house was the center of the Berlin Fair in 1952, publicized with the catchy slogan – "we're building a better life." The US exhibit at the 1957 Milan Fair once again reproduced a model American home with its "ultra-modern kitchen." This kitchen was actually a standard exhibit in various international expositions, and the responses to it are telling. When this home was shown at a British exhibition, the *Daily News* reported that "wonderfully impossible dreams" came closer to reality in the display, and that it was a "treat to watch the faces of the large number of housewives who had flocked round to watch it – their faces were studies in mingled expressions – envy, wonder, even disbelief."[19] Such domestic concerns gained international political attention in 1959 when Vice President Richard Nixon and Premier Nikita Khrushchev engaged in the famous "kitchen debate" at the US exhibition in Moscow. Standards of living and the position of women were used to measure the relative successes of American capitalism and Russia socialism.[20]

Advertising and displays like those at the fairs were accompanied by greatly expanded efforts to distribute and sell the goods in new self-service stores and American-style supermarkets. In 1948, there were no such stores in Italy; according to the International Chamber of Commerce, by 1956 there were four, and by 1960, over 200.[21] This expansion in new sorts of retail outfits in Italy was actually quite modest when compared with similar growth in France and Germany, where thousands of such businesses existed by 1960. In Britain, the first supermarkets opened in the 1950s; by 1958 there were 175 such stores; by 1967, 2,803. The extent of the appeal of these shopping venues is illustrated by the introduction of supermarket and self-service stores in Poland by 1959, after a decade of state control over shops and what was sold in them, and an accompanying black market economy.[22] Although consumers in these establishments were supposed to be "empowered" through greater choice of goods and access to them, in many of the eastern European stores, scarcity was still the norm.

Large department stores often symbolized the height of consumer possibilities and desires. Such emporiums had existed throughout western and eastern Europe before the war. The most prominent in Italy was Rinascente, and its accompanying single-price, cheaper store, UPIM. In the 1950s, Rinascente owners recognized the need to "modernize" and, using the expertise of the Harvard Business School, set up offices for research and organization and began training courses for managers. They were obviously successful as the main store in Milan on Piazza del Duomo had sales of over 13 billion lira in 1952, and over 37 billion in 1957. A study of buying practices between 1950 and 1960 indicated that about 20 percent of income was spent on goods sold by stores like Rinascente, and purchased by women. Rinascente was clearly a model for distribution and sales in the 1950s.[23] These developments were duplicated in the major cities of Europe, and one of the largest department stores in the world was Moscow's GUM (State Universal Store) which was modeled after similar emporiums in the West.[24]

But who were the consumers reading the advertisements, entering the stores, and purchasing the goods? And what were their motives, consumer needs and desires? While women were certainly important actors in the drama of acquiring goods, market research indicated that when large and expensive items were being considered, men were important in the decision-making. That same market research showed that young people were also good targets for consumer propaganda. The most important and obvious feature of the new regimes of consumption and their consumers was that they were urban. Urban populations had greater access to visual, printed, and electronic advertising; trade fairs took place in cities, and supermarkets and department stores were located in urban environments. In Italy, the new kinds of merchandising did not reach into the countryside, and, in fact, over half of the provinces of Italy did not have a supermarket or a department store in the period we are considering. The backwardness of rural commercial activity was commented upon by a journalist in Rome in 1961, when he noted that market practices were outdated and goods more expensive in a system that dated back to the eighteenth century.[25]

In 1950s Italy there was considerable migration from southern to northern areas and from the countryside to the city. Men were usually the first to migrate, leaving women to maintain the rural economy and family. By the later 1950s women began to move as well, but for most of them the benefits of a modern consumer society seemed quite remote. A series of interviews with rural women born before 1945 points to the demands and harshness of their lives: one woman said if she could leave the country she would never come back. Instead she would marry an urban worker and move to the city because "the wife of a worker had only to think about running her house. A woman in the city when she has ten minutes free can read a magazine, she can amuse herself a little with nice things, permit herself a few luxuries, dress like a lady. That is not my life."[26] Another woman who lived in the south said that she rarely left her home. Their amusement was through the radio, and later TV, but she had never seen a movie. "We don't have a washing machine, and I wash everything by hand. We don't have a car, we have a tractor. I have a bicycle! Eh, for a car other incomes are necessary." These women were aware of the possibilities of the "economic miracle" but their dreams were relatively modest. Even if they had been able to move to a large city, could they have taken advantage of the goods and the standards of living associated with modernity in the 1950s?

Actual conditions and the record of consumption throughout Europe in the 1950s indicate that dreams and promises usually outran reality. Throughout the decade gross national products improved enough to constitute the "miracle" of economic recovery already mentioned. Unemployment dropped and wages also improved. Nevertheless, during the 1950s average incomes did not allow consumers to acquire many of the items advertised and distributed. In Italy, by 1960, 84 percent of families did not possess a television, refrigerator or washing machine; only about 1.1 percent owned an automobile (although 66 percent said they wanted one), and only 23 percent of homes had electricity and modern plumbing.[27] For the time period under consideration here, there was still "a scarcity of resources available to most people," and "the economic miracle had not yet touched the majority of Italians."

Gender and consumerism **111**

Memories of a generation of men and women born between 1935 and 1955 illustrate the mixed or partial successes of the new consumerism. Giovanna (b. 1943) had worked in an outdoor restaurant, and remembered that frugality was the rule in her family. Because ready-to-wear clothing was still not easily available or affordable, her and her sister's clothes were made by a local seamstress, but the family could only afford one pattern and so the two girls were always dressed the same. Her father purchased a car, but a very small one, in which the whole family did not fit.[28] Luciana (b. 1940), who was a public relations person for a large company, recounted that her family "had a car and a regular serving woman, but my mother ... wore the same coat for thirty years. It didn't have holes, so why throw it away? It is also true that fashion didn't change as quickly then. Everything was made to last. From cloth to electric appliances." Aldo (b. 1951), a store manager, grew up in an apartment building constructed in 1948, but without heating. "There was a large coal burning stove in the corridor for all the rooms. The doors were left open. But at night, on going to bed, the bedclothes were cold and damp." In 1960 they finally began a remodel of the building to introduce oil heating and radiators. Modest changes and a good deal of practicality governed much of the consumerism of the 1950s.

Surveys and polls, as well as records of spending and consumption for Italy, and other parts of Europe, indicate that women were especially interested in owning a refrigerator. In the Federal Republic of Germany, "Of the new durable goods in the kitchen ... the most coveted item during the 1950s was the refrigerator."[29] In 1958 only 29 percent of German households owned a refrigerator; by 1961 39 percent did. Figures for Britain and Italy mirror this assessment: in 1956 only 8 percent of households in Britain had a refrigerator but that figure rose to 38 percent in 1964. In 1958 13 percent of Italian families had a refrigerator; the figure for 1965 was 55 percent. The Italian press commented on the "desire" for a refrigerator. In September 1958, the magazine *Il Giorno* reported on new products available and what was selling or not. The major news was that "At last more refrigerators than automobiles are sold in Italy."[30]

In the USSR refrigerators were also sought-after appliances, and by the mid-1950s the state promised that "new technology would come to the aid of the Soviet housewife, struggling under her double burden."[31] Regardless of efforts to expand production and availability of household appliances, by the mid-1970s only about half of Soviet families owned a refrigerator, and only two out of three a washing machine; women were expressing more dissatisfaction with public failures to ease the double burden. Generally, women were quite pragmatic about the possibilities of socialist consumer societies. Soviet ads that had appealed to women's "wish to be beautiful," didn't convince Russian women who "often said they wanted more children's clothes and modest and practical clothes for themselves."[32] In more general terms, in the USSR and other eastern European states, demand usually exceeded supply, and choice of models was quite limited. But even in western Europe, large numbers of households could not purchase many of the domestic goods they saw advertised. Across Europe, consumer goods were often in the world of dreams, not reality. If women did own a refrigerator, it could represent status or economic success, but it also could alter women's lives dramatically. As Italian women consumers were quick to note, they could save time and effort, and take advantage of sales, if shopping did not have to be a daily activity. Advertisers like Zoppas might claim that the "bright life," or the American way of life symbolized by the newest kitchen technology were what drew women to their products, but evidence of consumer practices and values would indicate that there was nothing glamorous about the purchase of items such as the refrigerator or the washing machine. Instead, these items saved time, energy and money. Here, two sides of consumerism – pleasure and utility – are intimately linked.

If consumerism can vary depending on access to goods and motives to acquire them, the world of work supplies another vantage point for measuring the impact and the possibilities of consumption in these years. The growth of consumption brought with it new businesses and new jobs. Who were the employees in the supermarkets, self-service and department stores, financial and credit institutions, advertising agencies, offices, food businesses, and the whole range of enterprises that catered to the use of leisure time? Throughout the countries discussed in this chapter, in the postwar era, more women were integrated into the workforce, often constituted a large percentage of the clerical, service, and food and entertainment workers, continued to be in jobs lower in the hierarchy than men, and were paid less than men were paid.[33] What was it like to work in such places, and how did aspirations for a better life, and the benefits of a modern economy, fit with experiences in the workplace? Did this work empower women and make them feel that they were participants in the new "regimes of consumption?"

In Italy in the 1950s, while the male work force increased by 5.6 percent, the female workforce grew by 25.2 percent, and by 1961 women were 27 percent of the overall workforce.[34] Articles in popular magazines that proclaimed the "economic miracle" also noted the "new generation" of young women entering the work force. An essay in 1956 entitled "Beatrice Goes to the Office," described a variety of jobs from hairdresser, to tourist office clerk, to secretary and teacher, that young women held. Later that year an article appeared in *Grazia* that marveled at the more than 200,000 lira spent on ads for stenographers and argued that such work was readily available for she who specialized. Speaking particularly to women, the author listed various state-sponsored commercial training courses that could lead to jobs as models, window-dressers, retail clerks, secretaries and stenographers, interpreters, and sales clerks in boutiques. These were the kinds of employment that could be linked to the new consumer culture. But were these jobs fulfilling or empowering? Did they live up to the expectations of a "new" generation of "modern" women? A survey in 1964 asked young women about their jobs and their use of leisure time. Twenty year-old Giuseppina worked at a commercial company in Bari. She worked ten-hour days, and had no vacations. She told the interviewer that her "kind of work hits hard on the nerves after a few years. It depends on the need for constant self-control in front of the public, and the fact of being controlled by the boss or the department head."[35] A nineteen-year-old clerical worker in Milan recorded that she had "little free time. I leave the house at 6:30 a.m., arrive at the office at 8:00 where I stay until

I leave at 6:00 p.m. Sometimes during the winter I go to the skating rink. In the summer I watch TV or go to the movies." Another commentary on women's work written in this same period noted the contradictions between young women's desires for independence and freedom, and the reality of being poorly paid, working from morning to night, and often having to live with their parents. What was the result? They had "no alternative but to dream about success at the movies, or to complain."[36]

When one enters the doors of Rinascente, and other retail establishments like it, whether in Italy, the USSR, or France, we encounter even more starkly the contrast between consumer dreams, and the hard work of making those dreams a reality. Department stores for some time had used women clerks, but the tremendous growth of retailing after 1945 meant an even greater reliance on young women to staff the growing number of stores. In the case of Italy, the large stores tended to employ many more women than men. For those workers under the age of twenty, there were nine women to one man; for employees aged forty to fifty, there were two men for one woman – clearly, this was not a lifetime "career" for many of the women.[37] In the late 1950s and early 1960s an Italian sociologist did a study of *la commessa* [retail clerk] that included a fairly large number of interviews. The women interviewed were asked what it meant for women to work in these "palaces of consumption," and their responses are testimonials to what it was like to live and work in the postwar age of consumerism.

One young woman answered with resignation: "I only lack two exams to graduate in commercial and economic science. Only two exams, but I am beginning to think I won't finish. I am already thirty years old. I began here at Standa, thinking it was a matter of a year or two, then I would leave, get my degree and a job. Instead, here I am." For another the work and the commute to her job added up to fatigue: "Nine hours on my feet behind a counter. Two hours on the trolley on my feet. You know what we call ourselves – *le donne-cavallo* [Women Workhorses]. I, however, could sleep standing on my feet like the horses, I am so tired." Another didn't feel the physical strain, but eventually the tedium set in: "The work isn't hard ... at the beginning everything was easy: the lights, the music, the people, the things to sell; everything happy and the smile came easily. Then, as the hours and days passed, smiling becomes a duty, but you have to do it in this job. It's part of the rules." One young woman who found the work decent, also found that it cost her a great deal: "The job is good: fixed hours and a pretty good salary. When I took the job, we were about to get married. We got married anyway, but secretly. Two times I was pregnant – two times I had an abortion. In the store I told them I had stomach trouble." Most stores preferred not to hire married women, and certainly would have fired a pregnant woman on the spot. Larger stores like Rinascente, Upim and Standa offered training courses for the new employees. There they were prepared "psychologically" to approach and handle customers, and they were given training books with rules of behavior they should follow.[38] In Italy in overall terms, in the 1950s, the numbers of young women who entered the tertiary sector did grow significantly. For them consumerism meant employment that paid relatively well, had regular hours and a workplace that at least wasn't dangerous or dirty; nevertheless, few intended to stay in the job for life. Were they really as different from an older generation of women who had worked in retailing, as the final testimony from *la commessa* reveals? In 1960, Rinascente held a "*Festa dell'anziano*," to honor long-time employees of the company. One woman commented on the younger generation of postwar workers:

> They are better than we were, I think. ... in appearance, their clothes, their manners ... are different. I admire the young ones. They have their defects – sometimes they look too far ahead, they are too ambitious. But in general they know what they want, and they know how to look people in the face, they know how to value their rights. ... None any longer think of the store as their family, none has the love for the store that I had ... they come, and are already thinking of when they can leave.

This older woman had the notion that something had changed – that the younger generation had a stronger sense of themselves, which she admired. If we return to the words of the young women, it is not clear that they saw themselves in the same way. We can perhaps extrapolate something of their desires and hopes from their words, but it would be hard to conclude that they saw themselves as "modern" or identified with women's new public role as consumer. What does that tell us? First, in order to fully understand the meanings of the new practices of consumerism in this era, we need to have the subjective accounts to complete the picture. Second, it forces us to acknowledge that reactions to consumer practices and possibilities are more often contradictory, or ambivalent, than straight-forward models of satisfied desires and personal freedom. Finally, while the woman consumer and the shop girl operate in the same worlds of goods, what they get from the exchange and what it means to them varied dramatically.

The complicated meanings and impact of the growth of consumer society show up in the differences between urban and rural lives, in the gaps between dreams and reality, in the contrasts between the roles of buyer and seller. But the unintended consequences and the mixed blessings of consumerism are revealed even more directly in studies at the time that reacted quite specifically to the impending consumer revolution. What were some of the responses to the new domestic technology, possible changes in family relations, and rationalization of life in the home? One answer can be found in the 1955–56 Italian *Parliamentary Inquiry into the Conditions of Life and Work*, which describes difficulties facing working class people in an urban environment. A portion of the inquiry focused on life outside the factory for workers in Milan. The typical family described was a father, mother and two children, and the concerns that were listed included the distance between home and workplace, and the costs of transportation. But the report also noted that the rent most workers paid absorbed 20–30 percent of their income, and that usually meant that the wife had to go to work to make up the difference. According to the report, this presented "grave problems deriving from the absence of the woman from the home without the necessary support in services and modern domestic goods." Among the feared results of this situation were: "neglected children, pasta prepared often in haste with ingredients from a can, ... thus producing other difficulties for the reproduction of the labor force that requires not only suitable material conditions, but also tranquility and relaxation."[39] This report was highly critical of the conditions of modern life and their impact on the family. Ironically, the problems of disruption of traditional family life and in gender roles in the home could be solved through the application of some of the services and technology of modernity.

Several years later, similar issues were addressed by the two major women's organizations in Italy, UDI (affiliated with the Italian Communist Party) and the Christian Democratic Center of Italian Women (CIF). The UDI study re-asserted the connection between women's emancipation and their entry into the workforce, but it also argued that women needed modern social services in order to support their work at home and in the family. What the study focused on especially were the methods of distributing goods. Although they liked the large supermarkets and department stores that made shopping easier and goods available to all, they also proposed "consumer cooperatives," and envisioned a system that was "not just technologically modern, but part of a political and social economy that is also new."[40] The CIF study hoped to discover why women engaged in paid work outside the home, and what impact this had on "the structure of the family and on social attitudes about women." They concluded that women entered the workforce largely for economic necessities, although increasingly to maintain the family's class status, and to take advantage of "the prospect of satisfactions that are appropriate to a modern life." As these examples illustrate, consumerism was an essential factor in debates about gender roles and the family, and about the advantages of change or the desirability of maintaining tradition. Across Europe political leaders and activists debated whether consumerism brought with it general well-being and civic progress, or dangerous individualism, amorality, and social instability. Critiques of the growing tide of consumerism were often couched in political terms, and the act of consumption itself could symbolize a political stance.

In Italy in the 1950s the Italian Communist Party (PCI) was doing fairly well at the ballot box. But, as historian Stephen Gundle points out, it "was having serious difficulties resisting the call of television and consumption that would become dynamic elements in a broad process of social and cultural reorganization."[41] The effects of this dilemma are borne out in the experiences of a Communist woman, Bianca Secondo, who was born into a working class family in Turin in 1919, went to work at twenty, participated in the Resistance and married a left labor union official after the war. They had two children, and in her interview she indicates that by 1954 she was well aware of the new consumerism making its appearance in Italy. She was impressed by the number of well-dressed people on the streets, and her children liked to look in the store windows, often asking if they could have whatever product was on display. She would tell them, "tomorrow, children, tomorrow."[42] In 1958, she and her family moved to Rome where she worked on *Noi donne*, the UDI women's magazine. The family did acquire a car, but she wanted other improvements in their standard of living and these caused problems with her husband who "resisted any new form of consumerism that was seen as incompatible with the communist ethic."

Eventually the party would have to face the fact, as Bianca noted, that party women were "sighing outside the [boutique] windows of Via Roma."

Earlier in this chapter, differences in political ideologies that played out in the arena of consumerism appeared in the discussion about gender and consumerism in the trade fairs and the Cold War, but the following examples point more directly to the links between consumption and ideological positions in eastern Europe and the USSR. The Soviet government had reacted to the American exhibition in 1959 by trying to restrict public access to the show, and it "forbade the organizers" from giving away cosmetic samples or "building modern restrooms with flush toilets." The American display of a modern kitchen in Russia was described as "a tacky display of excess and bourgeois trivia," while new housing that provided more modern one-family flats, was not to "foster individualistic tendencies," but instead to "propagate a new regime of austere 'contemporary' taste in home furnishings."[43] In East Germany, party leadership and intellectuals argued that what was "best for the working people ... were price and function." Standardization rather than individuality was the goal, as were "alternatives to limitless consumption, the throw-away society, and consumerism as compensation for boredom." The politics of consumption had another face as well, as the consumption of particular articles could represent resistance – of young people to an older generation, or of citizens against repressive governments. In East Germany, consuming West German shampoo and keeping the bottles on display was a sign of protest; in Warsaw a 1954 article reported that "amongst the young, socks with coloured stripes are a uniform and, at the same time, a manifesto ... These socks stand in recent years as the sign of a holy war over the right to have your own taste ... ."[44] In Poland, state support for the "modern girl" was briefly suspended in the late 1960s as young women and men began seeking new definitions of modernity and Communism, while East German authorities waged a "constant struggle against the allure of consumer abundance" coming from the West, and eventually abandoned the reformist consumer society. But lest we see these behaviors as peculiar to the socialist states, we need only remember that in Italy rebel teenagers consumed American music and movies and drank Coca-Cola, while in the US itself young girls' responses to Elvis Presley were seen as threats to social order.

What kinds of conclusions can we draw about gender and consumerism in postwar Europe, and particularly the connections between women and the new standards of "well-being?" Reports from the early 1950s had argued that women would support economic and social changes that lessened their work and rewarded them with more goods and services. That would certainly seem to be borne out in the evidence we have considered. We can conclude that most European women were exposed to the new possibilities of consumption, even if they lived in rural areas, and most were anxious to use the new stores and to acquire goods like the refrigerator, even if economic constraints meant they could not take advantage of these opportunities until the mid-1960s and even the 1970s. But the changes that occurred were not unequivocal or simple. Unintended consequences, debates rather than consensus, and acknowledged contradictions marked discussions about the meanings and portent of the newly emerging consumer societies.

The generations of women who lived through the postwar period of recovery and the miracle of new standards of living and an expanding world of goods "experienced profound changes in everyday life, to which the blanket term 'informal emancipatory movements' may be applied. These include ... changes in consumption [that] concerned the body, home and transport."[45] But the meanings attached to these changes, and the reactions of women to these new conditions, varied dramatically. In 1964, the PCI's publication *Vie Nuove* conducted a survey of young women and men born after 1945. A seventeen-year-old hairdresser was asked about her expectations for the future. She said, "I hope for a better life – the most important thing, not to work. I will be able to do that by getting married or else having a fortune." On the one hand, some of her expectations and goals might have meshed with those who hoped to maintain traditional family life in a technologically modernized household. On the other hand, she was the worst nightmare of an older, politically active generation of women like Ada Gobetti. In 1953, at the dawn of the "economic miracle" and with modernity on the horizon, she had lamented the goals and values that modern women were encouraged to adopt. She asked, what were their ideals? "To catch a man who offers them nice gifts, and dinners in elegant and expensive places. ... She wants a man with a solid position, slightly older, who has a car, possibly not Italian. Then she needs to make him marry her. To realize that noble goal all means are appropriate: deceit, duplicity and lies."[46] Ada Gobetti was part of the generation of women who participated in the Resistance and who had great expectations for postwar politics, society and reforms that would benefit women. Neither she nor her political peers would have seen consumerism as it influenced the next generation as liberating or citizenship measured by or connected to the accumulation of goods. Like the women of UDI, they might have seen the advantages of a "revolution of well-being" but equal pay for equal work, and political equality would have been described as more important than equality of desires or rights in terms of consumption.

In the immediate postwar world, women across Europe had more educational opportunities and were more present in the work force, even though in segregated jobs that were not well-paid. Many were able to take advantage of emerging state welfare schemes, and certainly they benefited from new housing that included heat, water, sewer and electric systems. Thus to some degree they shared the benefits of the consumer revolution. One study that assesses the changes in women's lives in the 1950s argues that there is evidence of the impact of ideas of social mobility as well as new publicity about private behaviors and attitudes. These changes had mixed or contradictory impact and reception on the part of housewives who saw them as risky and confusing. From this there emerged "a female protagonist who was bold and determined, but at the same time, confused in her goals." A second study maintains that the 1950s witnessed "a significant process of emancipation in the daily behavior of women, from consuming fashion to striking a pose in public." This constituted "an informal movement of emancipation" that included "how to live, to go out, to walk on the streets, to travel, smoke, up to uncertainty about sexual behavior."[47] At the same time women were expected to maintain a "feminine equilibrium" that balanced their public lives with their responsibilities as wives and mothers.[48]

Whatever women's increased visibility in the public world might be was countered by "the limitations the social order placed on both women's occupational and workplace opportunities." Just as the promises of democracy remained unfulfilled for women, so too one could argue that the freedoms and transformations promised by the "democracy of consumption" also remained unrealized. If we ask the societies of postwar Europe the question, "What's new" and is it good for you? The answer is multi-vocal. Some voices, like those of the major businesses I have mentioned, adopted the powerful language and practices of modernity as they expanded their concerns and persuaded the population to consume their products. Some political leaders lent their support to this vision of modernity while others adopted a more conservative and cautious narrative of progress. Individuals reacted differently depending on their age, gender, economic circumstances, education and where they lived, and expressed a diversity of aspirations and dreams. Desires mixed with pragmatism, and for many consumerism was a mixed blessing. Enthusiasm for many aspects of a modern consumer society was balanced by ambivalence when it came to the possibility of accompanying redefinitions of women's place and changes in personal and family relations. The end result was a chorus that sometimes sang in unison, but was often dissonant in the face of the tumultuous and contradictory events of the post-World War II era. One conclusion that we can draw about the postwar world is that consumption meant much more than acquiring a refrigerator or other goods. As a young East German woman commented several decades later: "I go shopping, not necessarily to buy things, but to look. I can do what I want."[49]

Notes

1 Aida Tiso, *I comunisti e la questione femminile* (Rome: Editore Riunti, 1976), 62.
2 Marisa Rodano, "Un difficile processo di emancipazione nella Resistenza italiana," *Donne e politica* 5:5 (December 1974), 41–43.
3 Cohen uses the phrase "consumer citizen," in *A Consumers' Republic: The Politics of Mass Consumption in Postwar America* (New York: Vintage Books, 2004) and de Grazia's "the sovereign consumer" appears in *Irresistible Empire: America's Advance through Twentieth Century Europe* (Harvard University: Belknap Press, 2005). Other important works that expand this discussion are Martin Daunton and Matthew Hilton (eds), *The Politics of Consumption: Material Culture and Citizenship in Europe and America* (Oxford: Berg, 2001); and Susan Strasser, Charles McGovern and Matthias Judt (eds), *Getting and Spending: European and American Consumer Societies in the Twentieth Century* (Cambridge: Cambridge University Press, 1998).
4 For a discussion of the broader contours of and changes in socialist consumerism, see David Crowley and Susan Reid, "Style and Socialism: Modernity and Material Culture in Post-War Eastern Europe," in Reid and Crowley (eds), *Style and Socialism* (Oxford: Berg Publishers, 2000), 2–4; Andre Steiner, "Dissolution of the 'Dictatorship of Needs'? Consumer Behavior and Economic Reform in East Germany in the 1960s," in Strasser et. al. (eds), p. 167, and Ina Merkel, "Consumer Culture in the GDR, or How the Struggle for Antimodernity Was Lost on the Battleground of Consumer Culture," in Strasser et. al. (eds), 281–83, 297; Susan Reid, "Cold War in the Kitchen: Gender and the De-Stalinization of Consumer Taste in the Soviet Union under Khrushchev," *Slavic Review*, 61:2 (2002), 218–19.
5 Greta Bucher, "Struggling to Survive: Soviet Women in the Postwar Years," *Journal of Women's History* 12:1 (Spring 2000), 138; Greg Castillo, "Domesticating the Cold War: Household Consumption as Propaganda in Marshall Plan Germany," *Journal of Contemporary History* 40:2 (April 2005), 284.

6 Guido Crainz, *Storia del miracolo italiano: Cultura, identita, trasformazione fra anni Cinquanta e Sessanta* (Rome: Ed. Donzelli, 1996), vii.
7 Susan Reid, "The Khrushchev Kitchen: Domesticating the Scientific Technological Revolution," *Journal of Contemporary History* 40:2 (2005), 291; Mark Spicka, "Political Discourse and the CDU/CSU Vision of the Economic Miracle, 1949–54," *German Studies Review* 24:2 (2992), 319; and Ida Blom, "1945: Change or Continuity in European Gender Politics," in Sue Bridger (ed.), *Women and Political Change: Perspectives from East-Central Europe* (London/New York: Macmillan/St Martin's, 1999), 38.
8 United States Congress, House Committee of Foreign Affairs. MSP Hearings, House of Representatives, June 1951, Vol. IX, 157.
9 Jonathan Zeitlin and Gary Herrigel (eds), *Americanization and Its Limits: Reworking US Technology and Management in Post-War Europe and Japan* (New York: Oxford University Press, 2000), 4. They suggest using the idea of "cross-fertilization" to explain these interactions. Recent works by Guido Crainz, David Ellwood, Stephen Gundle, Richard Kuisel, and Federico Romero have made similar arguments.
10 The history of the influence of the productivity committees was laid out by Charles Maier in "The International Politics of Productivity: Sources of the US Foreign Economic Policy After World War II," *International Organization* 31:4 (Fall 1977), 607–34.
11 Lorenzo Tozzoli, "Le ricerche di mercato nel commercio al dettaglio," *Produttività* (February 2, 1963), 35–37.
12 *Produttività* (April 1957), 364. An in-depth examination of the reality of this scenario can be found in Luisa Tasca, "The Average Housewife in Post-World War II Italy," *Journal of Women's History*, 16:2 (2004): 92–115.
13 Spicka, 308; for the USSR see Reid, "Cold War in the Kitchen," 249.
14 *Época* (May 11, 1958), 112; *Domenica del Corriere,* (March 8, 1959), 10; and (April 27, 1959), 20.
15 This and information on consumption of Soviet perfume are in Susan Reid, "Cold War in the Kitchen," 230, 232, and 233–35. For the 1959 Party Congress and new consumer policy see Barbara Alpern Engel, *Women in Russia, 1700–2000* (New York: Cambridge University Press, 2003), 238.
16 For Poland see Malgorzata Fidelis, "Are You a Modern Girl? Consumer Culture and Young Women in 1960s Poland," in Shana Penn and Jill Massino (eds), *Gender Politics and Everyday Life in State Socialist Eastern and Central Europe* (New York: Palgrave/Macmillan, 2009), 172–73.
17 See R. Harrow, *Pavilions of Plenty* (Washington, DC: Smithsonian Institution Press, 1997) for an excellent overview of US participation in trade fairs.
18 Castillo, 263, 268–69.
19 RG 40, International Trade Fairs, Historic Document File, 1957, Box 2, File Clippings, *Daily News*, January 30, 1956, "When (Kitchen) Dreams Come True."
20 For a good discussion of the "kitchen debate" in the USSR, see Susan Reid, "Cold War in the Kitchen," 223–28. Also useful is Walter Hixon, *Parting the Curtain: Propaganda, Culture and the Cold War, 1945–1961* (Basingstoke: Macmillan, 1997), 206.
21 International Chamber of Commerce. Italian Section, *Il supermercato nel sistema distributivo italiano* (Milan: Ed. Giuffre, 1962), 9; Emanuela Scarpellini, *Comprare all'americana: Le origini della rivoluzione commerciale in Italy, 1945–1973* (Bologna: Il Mulino, 2001), 133–36; and Andrew Rosen, *Transformation of British Life* (Manchester University Press, 2003), 21, 23, 150.
22 David Crowley, "Warsaw's Shops, Stalinism and the Thaw," in Reid and Crowley (eds.), *Style and Socialism*, 31–33, 42–43.
23 This and the previous information on Rinascente is from Amatori, *Proprietà e direzione*, 177, 166, 185–86.
24 Julie Hessler, *A Social History of Soviet Trade: Trade Policy, Retail Practices and Consumption, 1917–1953* (Princeton: Princeton University Press, 2004), 219, and Susan Reid, "Cold War in the Kitchen," 228.

25 Marco Cesmini Sforza, "La battaglia dei supermercati," *Il Giorno* (June 21, 1961).
26 Nuto Revelli (ed.), *L'anello forte-La donna: Storie di vita contadina* (Turin: Einaudi Editore, 1983), xxv. He and his team did 260 interviews in the late 1970s of rural women, asking them about their lives. The second interview is on xl.
27 Maria Cacioppi, "Condizione di vita familiare negli anni cinquanta," Special Edition, *Memória* 6 (1982), 87; Pier Paolo D'Attorre, "Anche noi possiamo essere prósperi," *Quaderni storici* 58 (April 1988), 79; and *Bollettino della DOXA* 15:13/14 (July 1961), 162.
28 This and the two following recollections are from Serena Zoli, *La generazione fortunata* (Milan: Longanesi and C., 2005), 24–26.
29 For Germany see Michael Wildt, "Changes in Consumption as Social Practice in West Germany During the 1950s," in Strasser, et. al. (eds), *Getting and Spending*, 307–9; for Britain see Rosen, 13; for Italy see Francesca Carnevali, "State Enterprise and Italy's 'Economic Miracle': The Ente Nazionale Idrocarburi, 1945–62," *Enterprise and Society* 1:2 (June 2000), fn. 3, 250.
30 The polls on refrigerators in Italy are quoted in Crainz, *Storia del miracolo económico*, 140.
31 Reid, "The Khrushchev Kitchen," 311; see also Hessler, *A Social History of Soviet Trade*, 319 and Engel, 237, 243.
32 Bucher, 151.
33 For general views of women's work in this era see Jane Jenson (ed.), *Feminization of the Labor Force* (New York: Oxford University Press, 1988); Rose-Marie Lagrave, "A Supervised Emancipation," in Françoise Thebaud (ed.), *A History of Women in The West*, Vol. V, *Toward a Cultural Identity in the Twentieth Century* (Cambridge, MA: The Belkanp Press, Harvard University Press, 1994), 453–89; and Svetlana Aivazova, "Liberty and Equality for Women in the Socialist Countries of Eastern Europe, 1960–80," in Christine Fauré (ed.), *Political and Historical Encyclopedia of Women* (New York: Routledge, 2003), 407–21.
34 Data from *Documenti di vita*, CXXIII (February 1962), 9693–94. The article "Beatrice Goes to the Office," is in *Época* (January 8, 1956), 32, and the "Work is Not Lacking for Those who Specialize," is in *Grazia* (November 6, 1956), 31–36.
35 These two accounts appear in "Nati dopo il diluvio," *Vie Nuove*, Special Edition (June 11, 1964), 54, 40.
36 Lorenza Mazzetti, "Chi dice donna," *Vie nuove* (May 5, 1962), 27.
37 This information, and the personal testimonies that follow are from M. Pastorino, *La commessa* (Florence: Vallechi Editore, 1962).
38 Ibid., 40–41; Most of the stores had house magazines for employees that provided guidance and advice for the workers.
39 Archivio della Camera Confederale del Lavoro di Milano e provincia (CCdL), Commissione Económico. "Condizioni di vita e di lavoro." Commissione parlamentare d'Inchieste, 1955–56, Seg. 13-II/19, Pt.1, Riporto di Silvio Leonardi, Milano, 19 Gennaio 1956, 1–3.
40 Neva Cerrina, "I servizi sociali indispensabili alla vita moderna della donna e la funzione delle cooperative," in Unione Donne Italiane, *Per l'emancipazione della donna una grande associazione autonoma e unitaria. Atti del VI Congresso dell' UDI*, Rome 7–10, May 1959, pp. 226–32. The CIF study is Tullio Tentori, *Donna, famiglia, lavoro: Inchiesta promossa dalla presidenza central del c.i.f.* (C.I.F.: Rome, 1960), 9, 12.
41 Stephen Gundle, *I comunisti italiano tra Hollywood e Mosca: la sfida della cultura di massa, 1943–1991* (Milan: Giunti Gruppo Editoriale, 1995), 149.
42 Interview with Bianca Secondo in Simona Lunedei, Lucia Motti and Maria Luisa Righi (eds), *E brava, ma ... donne nella CGIL, 1944–1962* (Rome: Ediesse, 1999), 357.
43 For Soviet reactions see, Engel, p. 241; Susan Reid, "Cold War in the Kitchen," 224, 244. For East Germany see Ina Merkel, "Consumer Culture in the GDR," 288–89.
44 See Merkel, 284; the article is cited in David Crowley, "Warsaw's Shops: Stalinism and the Thaw," 39. Fears aroused by modernity in Poland are in Fidelis, 183–84, while East German reaction is in Mark Landsman, "The Consumer Supply Lobby: Did It Exist?

State and Consumption in East Germany in the 1950s," *Central European History* 35:4 (2002), 478 and Castillo, 287.
45 Luisa Passerini, "The Women's Movement in Italy and the Events of 1968," in Mirna Cicioni and Nicole Prunster (eds), *Visions and Revisions: Women in Italian Culture* (Providence; Oxford: Berg, 1993), 168–69.
46 "Nati dopo il diluvio," *Vie Nuove* (June 11, 1964), p. 37. Ada Gobetti, "Panorama della stampa femminile," in A.V., *Le donne e la cultura* (Rome: Edizione "Noi Donne," 1953), 16.
47 The first study is S. Piccone Stella, "Donne all'Americana? Imagini convenzionale e realtà di fatto," in Paolo D'Attorre, *Nemici per la pelle: Sogno americano e mito sovietica nell'Italia contemporanea* (Milan: Franco Angeli, 1991), 273; the second is Luisa Passerini, *Storie di donne e femministe* (Turin: Rosenberg and Sellier, 1991), 141–52.
48 Simonetta Piccone Stella, *La prima generazione: Ragazze e ragazzi nel miracolo económico italiano* (Milan: Franco Angeli, 1993), 109; Rose-Marie Lagrave, "A Supervised Emancipation," in Thebaud (ed.), *A History of Women*, 470.
49 Daphne Berdahl, *On the Social Life of Post-socialism: Memory, Consumption, Germany*. Edited with an introduction by Matti Bunzl. (Bloomington, IN: Indiana University Press, 2010), 40–41.

7

HAPPY MOTHERHOOD AND LESBIAN SPACES

Women's initiative and the sexual mores of postwar Europe

Cynthia Kreisel

Women in post-World-War-II Europe lived in societies that sought desperately to return to a prewar sense of normalcy and calm. In order to stabilize the postwar world, many European countries experienced a postwar backlash, which attempted to return women to their homes and into contrived roles of domestic tranquility after their heavy and essential participation in the Allied war movement. This return to traditionalism greatly affected women's ability to control their sexual and reproductive lives. For instance, in both France and Italy abortion and advertising for birth control were illegal in the 1950s and 1960s.[1] In Germany, the politics of postwar occupation and the Cold War also greatly influenced women's reproductive options. In the Soviet Union, debates about birth control and abortion centered primarily on their harmful effects on the state. Meanwhile, some European countries followed a different path. Some took advantage of scientific improvements in birth control in order to ensure the health of their female citizens; others legalized same-sex relationships; while still others granted women access to abortion.

The ambiguous nature of sexual behavior and values in postwar Europe becomes especially clear in France, where there existed multiple sexual and reproductive regimes. A woman from an eastern European country explained that she had immigrated to France in the postwar period because she knew early on that she liked women and that same-sex love was not possible in her own country. She stressed, "France represented a country that was liberated in terms of its mores."[2] The French are said to have invented the art *de l'amour* (of love); however, in post-World-War-II France the reality of French sexuality in everyday practice was often far removed from this image. On the one hand, there was the hyper-sexualized France of the Place Pigalle, with its prostitutes, sex shows, and famous cabarets like the Moulin Rouge.[3] This was the France that foreign tourists visited in order to "walk on the wild side" and see "deviance" under the cover of darkness in certain Parisian neighborhoods. On the other hand, a great number of women in France were by no means "sexually liberated." Instead, they were largely occupied with concerns about feeding and sheltering their families, and raising well-developed and "dignified" children in the adverse postwar conditions. There were many women in France who were boldly heterosexual and applied themselves whole-heartedly to French President Charles de Gaulle's suggestion that French women bear "12 million bouncing babies" in the immediate postwar era. However, there was also a competing sexual and reproductive regime in which women flouted tradition and conservatism and resisted outside attempts to control their fertility and sexual lives. Some French women chose to love other women secretly, others visited family planning clinics (which were illegal at the time), and still others practiced clandestine abortion.

The many women who happily procreated contributed to the postwar baby boom in France and the rest of Europe. For almost a century (from the 1850s to the 1940s) France had had one of the lowest birth rates in Europe, reaching its nadir in the interwar years when the French population decreased from zero growth to more deaths than births.[4] France's birth rate began to accelerate during the Occupation, when the Vichy wartime government built on the pro-natalist policies of the Third Republic by awarding subsidies to large families; punishing abortionists as murderers; and portraying depopulation as a moral failing in their ubiquitous wartime propaganda.[5] Subsequently, France's birthrate rose from 612,000 in 1939 to 869,000 in 1949.[6] Relying only marginally on outside stimulation – for instance intra-European immigration – France's population increased by a full 30 percent between the first postwar census of 1946 and those conducted in the late 1960s. This was the most rapid rate of increase ever recorded in France.[7] Elsewhere in Europe, there were similar trends. Between 1950 and 1970, the population in Italy rose by 17 percent and Britain's population rose by 13 percent. During the same time span, the population of West Germany rose by 28 percent, Sweden by 29 percent, and the Netherlands by 35 percent.[8] Other women, however, took illegal or socially reprehensible steps to make their lives safer, healthier, and happier, by struggling to control their fertility or to practice their sexuality by claiming social space. Despite the harsh conditions after World War II, a weak sexual education, and a revival of traditional and religious mores, European women in the postwar "dared" to push for reproductive and sexual change.

Contraception in France

Women in many parts of the world had access to modern means of birth control long before the French legalization of contraceptives in 1967. Countries in Europe and overseas had already established centers for "family planning" in the late nineteenth and early twentieth centuries, including the Netherlands in 1882, Denmark in 1905; the United States in 1916, and England in 1921. In 1936, the United States, England, and Sweden officially organized the importation and regulation of contraceptive devices.[9] Yet after World War II France remained embroiled in controversy over providing women with a means to control their pregnancies.

Although French women had been familiar with contraceptive techniques for centuries, French legislation in the interwar years curtailed women's access to contraceptives. The law of July 23, 1920 punished the dissemination of information surrounding birth control and the sale or distribution of remedies, substances, or objects that could impede pregnancies with both fines and imprisonment.[10] In the 1950s a small core of participants in the French birth control debates had tapped into the pulse of French women, assessing their needs and desires by serving them in their various professions as doctors and lawyers and by reading their letters. The young gynecologist Dr Marie-Andrée Lagroua Weill-Hallé disrupted the silence surrounding contraception. Dr Weill-Hallé's first experience with what she termed the "injustice and hypocrisy that passed for 'Morality'" was during her first internship in surgery in the mid-1920s. There, she witnessed a woman suffering during an operation without anesthetics after a faulty attempt to abort herself.

After the surgery, the woman lay in the waiting room, streaming with sweat and shaking with violent tears, which she tried to stifle in her pillow. Overcome, Weill-Hallé went to comfort her by holding her head and stroking her hair and after the woman calmed, she walked silently away "under the reproving eye of the supervisor."[11]

In the 1950s and 1960s, many birth control advocates like Weill-Hallé argued that women's access to birth control would decrease the number of abortions in France and the consequent collateral damage that women suffered from their misuse. Many politicians denied the landslide of abortions occurring in France after World War II, because illegal abortions did not figure into formal statistics. However, doctors who dealt with women and couples on a daily basis realized that repressive legal measures against abortion had little effect on their prevalence. In fact, although estimates varied wildly because of the illegality of the procedure, most experts agreed that the number of abortions in postwar France ranged anywhere between 500,000 and 1,200,000 per year.[12] According to contemporary studies, the number of deaths resulting from illegal abortions was between 10,000 and 50,000 women per year in the 1950s and 1960s.[13] Doctors like Weill-Hallé argued that sexual education and access to contraception would not only stem the tide of abortions in the present, but that the women who might otherwise have been killed or rendered sterile, would live to procreate in the future.[14]

Facing the fierce opposition to her efforts staged by the Catholic Church, the French Medical Association, and most parliamentarians, Weill-Hallé found strength in numbers. Under a cloak of secrecy, Weill-Hallé worked with sociologist Evelyne Sullerot and twenty-one more like-minded women to form the association *Maternité Heureuse* (Happy Motherhood) in March 1956.[15] The association's primary goals were to give couples the right to make their own decisions regarding birth control and to promote the "desired child," conscious maternity, and the happy family.[16]

Weill-Hallé strengthened the cause by turning to the victims of law of 1920. Women from all over France and from all walks of life had confided to Weill-Hallé their life-shattering reproductive experiences and had begged for a solution to their burden of constant childbirth. Weill-Hallé began to publish their letters with the hopes that their stories and plights could inspire debate, educate a wary public, and persuade politicians and doctors to push for change. Weill-Hallé declared, "The daily drama of thousands of French women finally emerges from secrecy."[17]

Women's letters to her journal, *Maternité Heureuse*, as well as other French journals and publications, contained several recurring themes.[18] Some of these themes included: the idea of the child-as-catastrophe; women's mental and physical health; the effect of the fear of pregnancy on conjugal relations; the imperative to have children at a later date due to situation, circumstance, or means; the solitude and mental anguish women experienced over the topics of sexuality and contraception; and the formation of networks to help other women in need. For instance, in a letter to *Maternité Heureuse*, Madame L. and her husband (both devout Catholics from the Haute Savoie) bemoaned the fact that the Ogino-Knaus method had broken down completely in their case (she had already had four live births).[19] As a preventative measure, the couple agreed to have sex only at the commencement of her menstrual cycle; however, Madame L. became pregnant yet again. Feeling completely defeated, the woman sank into a deep depression. She disclosed that her children were always sick, her house was in disrepair, the finances were perpetually disrupted, and she had renounced even the slightest personal pleasure. She had become "a woman who knows nothing more than vomiting and crying," who was beneath any ambition to educate her children, and for whom life had become unlivable.[20]

For many women, the fear of pregnancy also destroyed all hope of conjugal intimacy, causing deep rifts in the family lives of many of the writers. A young woman wrote to *Marie-Claire* expressing her fear at having to tell her newly wed husband that she was pregnant. The couple had hoped to spend their first year of marriage "as lovers," and although her husband wanted children later in life, he had told her that he would be jealous if she ever had an infant to care for. She was frightened at his reaction to her pregnancy after only two months of marriage, exclaiming, "What if he does not love me anymore?"[21]

A woman from a provincial area emphasized that for her, true love was a thing of the past because she had grown to hate her husband. She blamed him for her continual pregnancies, stating:

> Don't talk to me about conjugal relations, it is a real ordeal for me; as soon as I have to have them with my husband, the idea of having another child obliterates all pleasure and any abandon I might experience.[22]

Women living in an agricultural setting lived a particularly hard lot, because rural French society was deeply religious and enforced traditional gender roles. One woman from the countryside conveyed her desperation:

> At twenty-three I have four children. ... The life that I live is saturated with fatigue and irritation. ... Every month there are the same days of anguish when one waits for one's period to arrive. ... In these conditions, is life worth living? Me, I cry out no, and what can I do?[23]

When she became pregnant for the fourth time, this woman hid her pregnancy and tried to abort it. She stated, "Me, who would have been ashamed to even think of such a thing, I had arrived at this."[24]

Despite the dire circumstances of some, many of the women who wrote letters were so inspired by the work of Weill-Hallé and her associates that they made it their mission to throw lifelines to the women around them by spreading the knowledge of family planning. French women created networks in order to pass on information that had been kept from them by the government and by the medical establishment. For example, one female accountant, whose husband had told her about family planning, dedicated herself to sharing the information with her female colleagues at work. This middle-class woman explained, "Once I started speaking on the subject, the reactions were very good, I could address it fully, easily, and they were very pleased to hear a solution. It made them happy!"[25] After learning of the existence of *Maternité Heureuse,* an older widow from Marseille wrote that she had suffered three "tragic and voluntary miscarriages"[26] in her life, but she celebrated that perhaps "the younger generation is ... saved."[27] She declared that she would work tirelessly in the service of publicizing their cause.[28] Madame R. as well vowed to distribute the association's flyers in her H.L.M. (*habitation à loyer modéré*, or low-rent housing), where scenes of misery surrounded her, including a 23 year-old mother of three, a young father with five children, and a young mother in a tiny apartment, who had risked her life trying "all sorts of foolish things" to abort her third child.[29] Tired of being denied the information on contraception that could change their lives, many French women took the matter into their own hands and circumvented the law of 1920 by writing letters and by joining *Maternité Heureuse.*

The French movement for family planning

The association *Maternité Heureuse* metamorphosed into the *Movement Français pour le Planning Familial* (MFPF; the "French Movement for Family Planning") in 1960, setting forth several formal statutes which concentrated on: studying the problems of maternity and its social, familial, and national repercussions; researching global scientific information on birth control; and spreading sexual information and education. The MFPF orientation centers were inundated with clients who lined the halls and waited for up to two hours. One center in Paris had so many demands that the hostess had to work three days without resting, breaking only to eat a meal that the concierge was kind enough to bring up.[30] By January of 1963 the MFPF in France had 16,000 members.[31]

The women that visited the planning centers with the hope of obtaining birth control took bold steps to change their own lives. First, they had to be strong enough to overcome years of repressed fears and shame surrounding their bodies and their sexualities. They had an intense fear of speaking of things that were "forbidden" and things they had never discussed before, even with their husbands. Hostesses struggled over how to best introduce technical terms such as: contraception, diaphragm, vagina, sexual relations, and speculum, since traditionally women did not talk about "things like that." Another difficult challenge laid in the fact that in order for women to use vaginal contraception, they needed to become acquainted with and claim ownership of their bodies, particularly their female anatomy which they had been told "was dirty."[32] Women also had to have the nerve to submit to an intense, interactive gynecological exam, which many of them had never experienced before. The hostesses had undergone the examination themselves and understood that patients might be deeply "troubled" because they would be naked and forced into a "humiliating" posture during the examination. One hostess described the examination and the feelings she experienced during the procedure. She explained:

> The gestures of the gynecologist are simple, neat, and precise. But, despite that, one's spirit remains troubled and one winces when one hears "Here is your size diaphragm, try it yourself." The woman is left alone in her discomfort, her shame. Why? She does not know.[33]

It became necessary for clients to take a solid assessment of their sexual lives in order to represent themselves effectively.

In 1966, Gaullist deputy Lucien Neuwirth submitted a proposal to abolish articles 3 and 4 of the law of 1920, which dealt with contraception. The government accepted the proposal, but wanted to wait for the findings of the Committee on Population and the Family. In January 1967 this committee acknowledged the need for contraceptives, but only in order to fight against the dangers of illegal abortions. At the same time, the committee officially denied the endorsement of contraception in principle and the idea that access to birth control was a woman's right. The committee also insisted that it did not support a reassessment of gender, or the changes in women's social and sexual roles that many believed would be promoted by the use of the pill. Minors would still need the written consent of their parents and all publicity for contraception was still banned. Additionally, President Charles de Gaulle refused to reimburse the cost of contraception through social security because he believed that the pill's intended use was for pleasure. After much parliamentary debate, the *Loi Neuwirth* (Neuwirth Law) was finally passed in December 1967.[34]

In Germany, reproductive politics were similar to France in the interwar period, but veered away from the French model at the end of World War II, due to Germany's history of division and occupation. The interwar Weimar Government (1918–33) set in place the Weimar Constitution, which on paper seemed to assure women in Germany a certain level of protection and equality. However, the penal and civil codes, which preexisted the Weimar Republic, added a certain level of ambiguity to the status of women. Although it was legal to sell and manufacture contraceptives, paragraph 184.3 forbade the promotion or exhibition of contraceptives meant to be used for "indecent" activities. Additionally, paragraph 218 banned all abortions that were not medically necessary for the health of the mother. According to the German State, the goals of these measures were to protect the German family, to raise the birth rate (which had been declining steadily since the nineteenth century), and to replace the loss of a generation of young men to World War I.[35]

Access to birth control and abortion in postwar Germany depended on which side of Germany one called home, either the Soviet Occupation Zone in the east (the SBZ), which in 1949 became the German Democratic Republic (GDR),[36] or the western half of Germany, which became the Federal Republic of Germany, or

FRG, in 1949.[37] In the SBZ, the laws against abortion were undermined by the bleak physical and social conditions of the postwar period and by the wave of pregnancies generated by Russian soldiers' assaults on German women. Although there is extensive variation in the statistics, it is estimated that approximately 500,000 of the 1.5 million women residing in Berlin at the war's end were the victims of rape.[38] In the end, doctors in Berlin ignored paragraph 218 and worked feverishly to abort women who said that they had been raped, sometimes as late as in their ninth month of pregnancy.[39]

After the immediate crisis of rape-induced pregnancies had subsided, the debate on abortion that had been suppressed by the Nazis recommenced in the press, women's conferences, student meetings, and provincial governments.[40] For a brief spell, reformers in the SBZ advocating abolition won the day. By December 1947, the Soviet Occupation Zone had abolished paragraph 218, the 1941 police ordinance that restricted the distribution of contraceptives, and the 1943 law legalizing the death penalty for abortion.[41] However, when the GDR was formed, the government declared that the essential conditions for the "healthy upbringing" of children had been "assured." Therefore on September 27, 1950 the state abrogated the recently established social justification for abortion with paragraph 11 of the Law for the Protection of Women and Children and the Rights of Women.[42]

In the FRG in the West, the politics of reproduction transpired differently based on the residual influence of the defeated Nazi regime, the presence of the Allied Occupation forces, and the strength of the Christian Democratic Party on the right and Christian intellectuals on the left. The political culture in the FRG hindered the open discussion of contraception and contraceptive practices. For instance, many states still had Heinrich Himmler's 1941 order forbidding the sale and advertisement of all birth control products except condoms in effect. Additionally, many of the medical experts in the FRG had been trained under the Nazi regime and had subsequently inherited a negative perception of contraceptive practices.[43] Birth control was also attacked by conservative Christian segments of the population who believed that condom machines in particular and contraception more generally were "an offense to morals and decency." This argument was then used to hinder the access of both youths and adults to modern and reliable forms of birth control.[44]

On the other hand, the mores of the West German population at large differed greatly from the more conservative doctors, officials, and intellectuals. For example, one 1949 survey found that 44 percent of those regularly attending church accepted premarital sexual relations.[45] Additionally, in the 1950s and 1960s, several informal inquiries indicated that somewhere between 80 and 90 percent of West German youths were engaging in premarital intercourse.[46]

One way that women fought to control their fertility in West Germany was by procuring illegal abortions. Immediately after World War II (1945 to the end of 1946), the "special regulation" allowing abortions for women who had been raped was extended to several western regions. However, after the acute calamity had passed, the legal justifications for abortion in the western sector narrowed dramatically.[47] The illegality of the procedure, however, did not stop women in the FRG from having abortions. In the 1950s and 1960s in West Germany, abortion was the second most common method of controlling family size after the withdrawal method.[48]

In the Soviet Union, Joseph Stalin had prohibited abortion in 1936 and all contraceptives were removed from sale as part of an effort to increase the Soviet population. When Nikita Sergeevich Krushchev rose to power after the death of Stalin in March 1953, there was a shift in gender politics in the Soviet Union. In 1955, the government under Krushchev legalized abortion again in order to protect women's health. On the other hand, the state (which had the sole power over production in the country) refused to increase the availability of contraceptives, and therefore most women were still forced to use abortion to limit their pregnancies.[49] In fact, it was estimated that the average Soviet woman living in the postwar era would have over ten abortions in her lifetime.[50] These statistics show, however, that despite the grim limitation of their choices, Soviet women (as well as women in East Germany, West Germany, and France) refused to succumb to government pressure and coercion and instead took direct action to control their reproductive lives.

Lesbian spaces in Europe[51]

Many women in postwar Europe, whether by having abortions, by procuring illegal contraception, or by their sexual choices, did not accept the sexual mores of the societies in which they lived. French, British, and other European lesbians' efforts to define themselves and to live lives of their own choosing in a conservative postwar environment were also important examples of women's postwar resistance.

In France, homosexual men and women began pressing for legal rights and recognition in the late 1960s. These men and women were fighting against legal discrimination that dated back to the French Revolution. At the Liberation, the provisional government fortified anti-homosexual policies by signing into law an article on February 8, 1945, which punished anyone committing "acts against nature" with members of their own sex under 21 years of age. The penalty for this offense was six months to three years in jail and a fine. Continuing in this same vein, the French government passed the law of July 30, 1960 which authorized the government to take specific measures to battle against various ills in society such as alcoholism, prostitution, and tuberculosis, but also to "fight against homosexuality." Finally, in 1968, France adopted the classification of the *Organisation Mondiale de la Santé* (OMS), or Global Health Organization, which considered homosexuality a mental illness, along with fetishism, exhibitionism, voyeurism, and necrophilia.[52] In addition to French legal discrimination, the Catholic Church's denunciation of homosexuality also greatly influenced popular attitudes in France.

In Sweden, on the other hand, gay and lesbian relations were decriminalized in 1944. However, the age of consent in Sweden remained higher for homosexual interactions than for heterosexual. Additionally, in the 1950s in Sweden there was an extreme social backlash against homosexuals including police raids and witch-hunts in the media. Swedish homosexuals responded to this infringement on their personal freedoms by organizing in the 1950s, and by consolidating these informal networks into a full-fledged movement in the 1960s. Swedish men and women formed the *Risförbundet för sexuellt likaberättigade* or RFSL, an organization open to all men and women who wanted to fight for the rights of gays and lesbians. This organization strove to strengthen the gay identities, to create a sense of solidarity between gays and lesbians, and to build a social environment for the gay community in Sweden. The federation also fought against the oppression and discrimination against gays in Swedish society by lobbying the government and other authorities. Perhaps because Swedish society was at least nominally more open than the more traditional France, the gay and lesbian population in Sweden was able to organize against social repression nearly two decades earlier than the gay community in France.[53]

Lesbian women in postwar France nonetheless took advantage of their cloak of invisibility to claim social space for themselves in the 1950s and 1960s. These women found other women in a multitude of ways. Some connected with women in their daily lives, for instance, at the outdoor market, on the metro, or at the movies. Parisian lesbian Patricia liked to pick up women boldly on the streets of Montmartre. On the other hand, Geneviève (who lived in Provence) observed that one could not simply "drag" for women in cities outside Paris, because one could not just "do what one pleased" in the countryside.[54] Geneviève suggested that if she had moved to the capital, she might have been able to meet more women, perhaps participating in "adventures without tomorrows," or perhaps not, but, "at least [she] would have lived."[55] However, Geneviève used other opportunities in her life to meet women. For instance, Geneviève became an ambulance driver and entered the army in the 1950s, meeting the love of her life, Françoise, in the barracks. Geneviève recounted, "The barracks, they were great, no problems! If I had believed in God, I would have been a nun, I love being like that, among women. Truly, one is free in the army ...."[56] For women like Patricia and Geneviève, however, finding other women who loved women in one's everyday life was difficult because there were few signs or references by which one could tell a homosexual from a heterosexual. Yet these women, and many others like them, refused to submit to France's postwar gender and sexual norms, choosing to fly just under the radar of the surrounding society.

Perhaps the most important venue in which lesbians fashioned their own world was in the clubs and bars for women. There is much ambiguity surrounding these clubs in the memories of French lesbians. Many women complained about the clubs, bemoaning the ghettoization of lesbian sexuality, the level of voyeurism of straight couples, and the behavior of les *garçonnes* (in this case, lesbians who transgressed "traditional" gender roles by dressing and acting like men). However, most lesbians were familiar with these clubs and had visited them, if not frequented them, at some point in their lives. For instance Patricia, who later owned her own club in Paris, insisted that in the 1960s the only place to meet other women was in the clubs, but that the choice of clubs was very limited. Patricia recalled that there were two primary all-woman bars in Paris, *Monocle* and *Pousse-au-Crime*, describing *Pousse-au-Crime* as a spot where both *garçonnes* and very feminine women passed time together and where she always "felt at home."[57] Geneviève, as well, recounted that she had visited the bars and clubs of Paris between 1953 and 1960. She said that when she was young (in her thirties) she frequented bars like the *L'Entre nous* (Between us) in the *Pigalle*, "from time to time, but not too much."[58]

Bars were also an essential element in the lesbian subculture budding in England in the 1960s. According to Bee Zed, there were certain bars where "everyone" went to dance such as the bar "Gateways" in Chelsea.[59] However, she recounted that lesbians frequently formed "clubs" in the pubs as well. She explained that in large pubs there were always rooms reserved for private parties such as marriages and dinners and that British women often used these rooms to "form a space reserved for women." In this way, they made sure that women had "a place to go." She recalled that women would learn about the address and pass it on to their friends, forming lesbian networks in which "everyone knew everyone."[60]

Although many lesbians visited the bars, with varying levels of comfort and varying measures of success, another essential means by which lesbians met other women was through the "*annonces*" or personal ads. It is evident that these were an important means by which women met other women not only by the frequency with which they were mentioned in oral interviews, but also by the strenuous effort the *Brigade Mondaine* (a special branch of the police ensuring public morality) made to shut these publications down as quickly as they appeared. In 1955 28 individuals were investigated, apprehended, and underwent public hearings for placing licentious and "perverted" ads in the "Dates" section of the journal *Les Annonces*.[61] The 1950 report from the *Brigade Mondaine* confirmed that "more and more" lesbians (and male homosexuals) were searching for other lesbians (and "pederasts") through personal announcements that "had currently gained the favor of perverts." The police report also expressed an intense concern that the volume of the announcements had grown from five or six individual ads, to between three and four columns of ads over the space of a few months.[62] According to the report, homosexual men and women were researching homosexual partners with whom to enjoy nights out, weekend trips, or holidays, and that these "perverse" propositions were hidden behind such benign phrases as: "exchanging ideas, sorties, theatre, vacations, etc."[63] However, of all the ads posted in the publication, lesbians were more likely to use the announcements in order to find a female companion than were male homosexuals. Seventy-five percent of the notices by women were for lesbian encounters whereas only two out of 24 men were looking for other men for a homosexual rendezvous.[64] Most women were less likely to "drag" the streets looking for partners, so personal ads became an important way to come into contact with other women in the 1950s. Women professed as well that the personal ads had changed their lives because they realized that they were no longer alone. The *annonces* were part of the lesbian subculture in Britain as well. One woman in Britain described the coming of personal announcements in the press as "the turning point" in the lesbian existence.[65] Bee Zed remembered that in 1964 an association for women started a journal in which women could place personal ads looking for other women. She explained that the formation of the association corresponded with the decriminalization of homosexuality by the British government. Bee Zed remembered that the possibility of placing personal ads "was the start of a new life for all the women of England."[66] She continued:

> Many women thought that they were the only person in the world that felt like they did. They were always alone, so the idea that there were many others like them, clubs, parties ... transformed everything, bit by bit women started living with one another.[67]

Other women participated in homosexual networks disguised in the media. For instance Rachel saw an advertisement for the Mick Michel club in the journal *Cinémonde* (Cinema World). Rachel knew that Mick Michel was "*comme ça*" because she was familiar with Michel's genre (Michel was an artist, song-writer, and producer of cabarets) and because Michel already had a loyal following of female admirers. Rachel wrote to the club and was then visited by a young man. The man proposed a correspondence with two women who were interested in finding other women, one in Lyon (in the southeast of France) and one in Villers-Cotteret (just northeast of Paris). She chose Michèle, the woman who lived in Villers-Cotteret, because she was greatly moved by the letter she had written. When Michèle wrote back and said that she too, "felt instant sparks" when reading Rachel's letter, they agreed to meet. Despite many trials and tribulations (including an indictment for public indecency), Rachel was with Michèle for eleven years.[68] Women like Rachel needed to perform a bit of detective work to find other women who were attracted to women.[69]

Tradition and progress

Even while resisting, many women in postwar Europe were deeply influenced by traditionalism. For instance, although they were still expected to work outside the home, most Soviet women embraced their domestic roles, believing themselves more suited to the private sphere, taking pride not only in their housework, but also in their ability to please their husbands by looking pretty. Many accepted male domination (especially in the home) despite the Soviet doctrine of gender equality.[70]

Similarly, many French women were just as embroiled as French men in the conventional social and sexual mores of postwar society. This ensured that lesbians would remain closeted and that the women agitating for access to contraception would "use the master's tools" in order to fight the system. For example, even though French lesbians flouted convention when they sought out other women, a traditional guilt and fear kept many women from telling their secret to others. Many French women mentioned that they had never told their parents the truth about their lives. Some thought their secret might actually kill their parents (figuratively or literally), while most lesbians knew that it would at least break their hearts. Patricia disclosed that because she was very feminine and men found her attractive, it was not hard to hide her life from her parents. However, she always regretted having to "trick" them.[71] She explained:

The subject was completely taboo ... I never spoke to my parents and I will never dare it. They are too old and I think that it is too late, I would cause them too much pain and a grief that would surely kill them since they both have heart problems.[72]

Others were frightened to tell their neighbors the truth about their lives for fear of rejection or ostracization. Georgette claimed that it was an unhappy society in which she had to pretend that she was in love with a married man from Lyon so that her neighbors would not become suspicious.[73]

This internalized traditionalism took other forms as well. "E." emphasized that having received a Catholic education she had had guilt "imprinted" on her from an early age. When she first struck up a romantic relationship with another woman, she felt guilty enough for two. "E." explained, "I knew that I had damned myself, which was my problem, but I had also damned another."[74] Because of their strong feelings of culpability, she and her lover felt it necessary to stop their sexual relationship. They lived together for months in uncertainty and doubt, until someone she trusted assured "E." that, "one can do anything with morality."[75] Relegated to a world of silence, many of these women refused to comply and instead navigated this space, creating personalized niches where they could live lives of their own choosing.

Hoping for public acceptance, other lesbians attempted to distance themselves from anything or anyone that would tarnish their image of respectability. Susan Daniel, who wrote for the homosexual review *Arcadie* insisted:

> If we want to make society accept a well-founded equality of sexual and social rights, it is indispensable that our moral attitude be unimpeachable. It falls upon us, homosexuals of both sexes, to ... embody ... a social and moral dignity that ... will succeed in attracting sympathy.[76]

"Unimpeachable" behavior often included homosexuals maintaining what the majority of gay and lesbian individuals considered "proper" gender stereotypes. Patricia, the nightclub owner, asserted, "It is necessary above all to conduct oneself well: women should not dress up like men and men should not dress like crazy women."[77] Patricia was also extremely concerned that the behavior of the more extroverted lesbians would reflect on her. She disparaged the "*garçonnes*" who came to her establishment, noting, "When they drink, they no longer know how to control themselves and ... become very aggressive, it is terrible."[78] Geneviève, as well, believed in traditionally gendered behavior, remarking that "manly" women "always gave her a good laugh because one is either a man or a woman."[79] However, Geneviève also delighted in dressing up in a suit and tie, and becoming "perfectly androgynous" for a night on the town. She insisted that one's choice of dress did not make one manly and that wearing pants or dress shirts was simply a matter of comfort.[80] Patricia, who passed her own judgment on the "*garçonnes*," was also mocked by other lesbians in the 1950s and 1960s, because she was a "pin-up," an ultra-feminine lesbian who was very blonde and wore make-up.[81] According to Patricia, being a pin-up was very different from the behavior of most lesbians, who refused to follow the social protocols for female beauty. Geneviève and Patricia's testimonies show us that even within the lesbian subculture there was much differentiation.

Women fighting for contraception in France were just as affected by traditional values. For example, when the respectable bourgeois women of *Maternité Heureuse* traveled to the city of Nancy soliciting support for the association, they were pelted with eggs for advocating the sexual liberation of women. Founding member Evelyne Sullerot explained that the association then "devoted [itself] to defending the family and became wary of those who were for absolute sexual freedom."[82] The women doctors, lawyers, jurists, and scientists who formed the association *Maternité Heureuse* were strengthened and unified by the fact that they were mothers. These women argued for women's legal access to contraception, not using the language of women's rights, but of motherhood.

Additionally, Dr Weill-Hallé had held an essentially conservative vision. She hoped that women would no longer be "scared of sex" and could experience a freer sexuality, but only so that married couples would be happier, their marriages more stable, and, as a result, the French nation stronger. It is clear that Weill-Hallé and other founding members of *Maternité Heureuse* had been socialized to believe in traditional gender roles and sexual mores in their families, schools, churches, and the greater society all the while promoting a more enlightened French society.

Some lesbians also believed that society would never accept the idea of "lesbianism," but that instead, each lesbian needed to change the minds of society, one individual at a time. For instance, Patricia suggested that each lesbian should educate her family, friends, and acquaintances about the realities of homosexuality and should thereby prove to her colleagues and loved ones that a lesbian was just like every other woman, with the same life and loves.[83] Patricia emphasized that the "lesbian movement," whose members yelled and paraded themselves through the streets, was "shameful," "lamentable," and "made one sick."[84] Instead of loud public displays to increase their "visibility," Patricia advocated a slow process of "integration" little by little. According to Patricia, one could make inroads in society by sharing with others in the workplace, in one's social entourage, or as she had done, by opening a "respectable" restaurant where homosexuals and heterosexuals could engage in a positive dialogue that would engender both acceptance and understanding.[85]

Daring to take a stand

Despite the strong bonds of traditionalism, in the 1950s and 1960s many European women "dared" to change society. The French women who formed the association *Maternité Heureuse*, those who volunteered at the planning centers, and those who volunteered to distribute informational brochures to educate women about birth control were willing to break the law in order to preserve the health of other French women. The women in France, harried by constant childbirth, put pen to paper and voiced their fears, hopes, and desires. They hoped to show other women that they were not alone and to convince the public and parliament of the necessity for immediate action. These women visited the illegal centers, spoke openly about their marriages, and faced their fears about their own sexuality.

In both East and West Germany in the postwar, women also made choices and took actions to safeguard their health and their lives. In East Germany, women took drastic steps to protect themselves from rape and to end pregnancies that were the result of rape. They also formed women's councils that battled (sometimes riotously) to maintain women's access to birth control and abortion, regardless of political trends or changes in the government.[86] In West Germany, youths (both male and female) openly resisted the government's efforts to dictate their morality and sexual lives by engaging widely in premarital sex and then marrying early. Responding to the restricted access to birth control in West Germany, many women also sought out illegal abortions to limit their family sizes.[87] Meanwhile, women in the Soviet Union fought against their successive governments' attempts to direct their sexual and reproductive lives. They employed abortion as a method to reclaim their bodies and therefore destinies from the clutches of the Soviet government.

British and French lesbians also flouted convention and lived lives that validated their own self-identity. British Bee Zed refused to marry. She insisted on "living life for herself," and when people asked her why she never found a husband she would "imperturbably" reply that she "just didn't have the time."[88] "E.", who was born in France in 1933, refused both heterosexuality and marriage, dreaming of one day living with a woman, although she believed at that time that this was impossible. Then, when her parents tried to force her to marry, "E." refused and left France to study abroad. For "E." this choice was a decisive step on the road to freedom in her life.[89] Both women refused to marry and crafted lives for themselves, far removed from the blueprint for women that their respective societies would have imposed on them.

In the postwar period, European women defined their own sexualities by making conscious choices. Many women refused to let Church doctrine or their respective governments dominate their sexual and reproductive decisions. Instead, women became agents, making decisions – sometimes very difficult or dangerous ones – that enabled them to take command of their sexual lives. Although many European women advocated a gradual transformation, they were not content to remain silent in societies that neglected their needs and desires. These women's actions were the first groundswell of rebellion that would metamorphose into the full-scale global revolutions of the late 1960s. Women in the postwar decades "dared" to push for change, whether it was doctors fighting to give women access to sexual education and contraception, lesbians refusing to be labeled and living lives that they chose for themselves, or women helping other women to control their pregnancies and thereby take control of their health and lives. Little by little, many women made inroads in societies mired in convention and helped create a more positive sexual space for women in postwar Europe.

Notes

1 Mouvement Français pour Le Planning Familial (MFPF), *Liberté, Sexualités, Féminisme: 50 Ans de Combat du Planning pour Les Droits des Femmes* (Paris: Éditions la Découverte,

2006), 20–21. Penelope Morris (ed.), *Women in Italy, 1945–1960: An Interdisciplinary Study* (New York: Palgrave Macmillan, 2006), 2–4 and fn 15.

2 "K.," Anonymous woman interviewed by Claudie Lesselier between 1986 and 1988, Claudie Lesselier, "Aspects de l'expérience lesbienne en France 1930–68," unpublished mémoire pour le DEA en sociologie, Université Paris III (November 1987), 62.

3 The *Place Pigalle* is a neighborhood in the Montmartre district of Paris that was (and is) famous for its dubious moral code.

4 Tyler Stovall, *France since the Second World War*, Seminar Studies in History, series eds, Clive Emsley and Gordon Martel (London: Longman, 2002), 32.

5 Stovall, 32.

6 Tony Judt, *Postwar: A History of Europe since 1945* (New York: The Penguin Press, 2005), 331.

7 *Ibid.*

8 *Ibid.*

9 Dr Pierre Simon, *Le Contrôle des naissances, Histoire, Philosophie, Morale*, 91 (Paris: Petite Bibliothèque Payot, 1966), 79–80.

10 Simon, *Le Contrôle des naissances*, 72–74 and 86–88. The details of the law can also be found in Janine Mossuz-Lavau, *Les lois de l'amour: Les politiques de la sexualité en France (1950–2002)* (Paris: Petit Bibliothèque Payot, 2002), 16–17.

11 Marie-Andrée Lagroua Weill-Hallé, *La Grand peur d'aimer, Journal d'une femme médecin* (Paris: René Julliard, 1960), 16–17.

12 Anne-Marie Dourlen-Rollier, *L'Avortement en France: colloque organize sous l'égide du movement français pour le planning familial* (Paris: Librairie Maloine, 1967), 180.

13 Anne-Marie Dourlen-Rollier, *La Vérité sur l'avortement* (Paris: Librairie Maloine, 1963), 115–16.

14 Weill-Hallé, *La Grand peur d'aimer, Journal d'une femme médecin*.

15 Marie-Andrée Lagroua Weill-Hallé, "Dix ans de lutte pour le planning familial", *Mouvement Français pour le Planning Familial, Dixième Anniversaire*. Bibliothèque Marguerite Durand (BMD). Dos 614.1 Mou.

16 *Ibid.*

17 Marie-Andrée Lagroua Weill-Hallé, *L'Enfant Accident* (Paris: Société des Éditions modernes, 1961). Cited in Catherine Valabrègue, *Contrôle des Naissances et Planning Familial*, L'Ordre du Jour (Paris: Éditions de la Table Ronde, 1966), 110.

18 This study focuses on the letters that discuss contraception; however, the letters addressed many different aspects of women's sexuality, sexual education, etc.

19 The Ogino-Knaus method was based on a mathematical calculation of the fertile periods in a woman's cycle. Jean Dalsace and Raoul Palmer, *La Contraception: Problèmes biologiques et psychologiques* (3rd edn) (Paris: Presses Universitaires de France, 1967), 90–92.

20 Madame L., Letter to the journal *Maternité Heureuse* by a woman from Seyrod, November 10, 1960, 2. BMD, Fonds Valabrègue 1 AS 30.

21 Anoymous letter to *Marie-Claire* (June, 1956). Cited in Marcelle Auclair, 'Le Contrôle des Naissances, Le point de vûe de l'Église,' *Marie-Claire* (June, 1956), 38.

22 Anonymous rural woman, cited in Marie Allauzen, *La Paysanne Française aujourd'hui*, Collection Grand Format Femme, (ed.) Colette Audry (Paris: Société nouvelle des Éditions Gonthier, 1967), 158. Allauzen printed the letters of many women from rural areas which were included in a survey conducted by Catholic bulletin *Clair Foyer* in 1967 called *3,000 foyers parlent*. Allauzen, 149–54.

23 Anonymous rural woman, cited in Allauzen, 155–56.

24 *Ibid.*

25 Anonymous female accountant, Compte Rendu d'une "Table Ronde" de 4 couples sur contraception et avortement (unedited), November 7, 1964, 4. BMD, Fonds Valabrègue, 1 AS 40. An edited version of this roundtable discussion was published in the *Nouvel-Observateur* (July 7, 1965).

26 In the postwar era, "fausse couche" (or miscarriage) was a term used by many for either a voluntary or an involuntary termination of pregnancy.
27 Letter to the journal *Maternité Heureuse* by a woman from Marseille, October 29, 1959, 1. BMD, Fonds Valabrègue 1 AS 30.
28 *Ibid.*
29 Letter to the journal *Maternité Heureuse* by an anonymous woman from Bourges, November 19, 1960, 1–2. BMD, Fonds Valabrègue 1 AS 30.
30 Mouvement Français pour le Planning Familial, *D'une révolte à une lutte: 25 Ans d'histoire du planning familial* (Paris: Éditions Tierce, 1982), 111.
31 Mossuz-Lavau, 26.
32 MFPF, *D'une révolte à une lutte*, 111.
33 *Ibid.*
34 Duchen, *Women's Rights and Lives in France, 1944–1968* (London: Routledge, 1994), 184–85.
35 Atina Grossmann, *Reforming Sex: The Germany Movement for Birth Control and Abortion Reform, 1920–1950* (New York: Oxford University Press, 1995), 8.
36 Bureau of European and Eurasian Affairs, "Background Note: Germany," *U.S. Department of State: Diplomacy in Action*, last modified November 10, 2010, accessed December 15, 2010, http://www.state.gov/r/pa/ei/bgn/3997.htm.
37 *Ibid.*
38 Grossmann, 193.
39 *Ibid.*, 192–94.
40 *Ibid.*, 196–99.
41 *Ibid.*, 196–97. The government also abolished paragraphs 219 and 220 of the criminal code, which forbid the dissemination of information on abortion. Grossmann, 149 and 196–97.
42 *Ibid.*, 196–98.
43 Dagmar Herzog, *Sex after Fascism: Memory and Sexual Morality in Twentieth-Century Germany* (Princeton, New Jersey: Princeton University Press, 2005), 122–23.
44 Herzog, 123.
45 See Ludwig von Friedeberg, *Die Umfrage in der Intimsphäre*, Beiträge zur Sexualforschung, vol. 4 (Stuttgart: Enke, 1953), 589. Cited in Herzog, 124.
46 See *Jahrbuch der öffentlichen Meinung 1958–1964*, ed. Elisabeth Noelle and Peter Neumann (Allensbach: Verlag für Demoskopie, 1965), 589. Cited in Herzog, 124.
47 Grossmann, 195.
48 Herzog, 127.
49 Barbara Alpern *Women in Russia, 1700–2000* (Cambridge: Cambridge University Press, 2004), Engel, 231–33.
50 Bonnie G. Smith, *Europe in the Contemporary World: 1900 to the Present* (Boston: Bedford St Martin's, 2007), 452.
51 I have used the term "lesbian" in this piece to facilitate comprehension. However, French women in the 1950s and 1960s (who might now refer to themselves as "lesbians"), refused to accept this label, referring to themselves either as "*comme ça*" ("women like that"), or as "women who loved women."
52 Mossuz-Lavau, 283–88.
53 Catherine Gonnard, "Les 40 Bougies de la RFSL," *Lesbia* 85 (Juillet–Août 1990): 25.
54 Geneviève, interviewed by Christiane Jouve for the article, "C'est comme ça," *Lesbia Magazine* 54 (October 1987): 14.
55 *Ibid.*, 13–14.
56 *Ibid.*, 13.
57 Patricia, interviewed by Christiane Jouve, "Vécu: Le pied à l'Etrier," *Lesbia Magazine* 20 (September 1984): 24.
58 Geneviève, "C'est comme ça," 13.
59 "Bee Zed," anonymous English woman interviewed by Catherine Gonnard, "C'était hier n'est-ce pas?" *Lesbia Magazine* 120 (October 1993): 25.

60 *Ibid.*, 25.
61 Françoise Gicquel (Police Commissioner of the Prefecture of Paris in 2005) provided me with the statistics for 28 individuals, although the report of July 5, 1950 states that 32 individuals would receive public hearings. The terms "perverted" and "perverts" are used throughout the police report.
62 Brigade Mondaine, "Rapport de 4 Juillet, 50 [1950]," Archives de la Préfecture de Paris, PJ Mondaine 36, "Les Annonces," 2–3.
63 *Ibid.*, 2.
64 The other ads sought "swingers" or individuals interested in sado-masochism.
65 Bee Zed, "C'était hier," 25.
66 *Ibid.*
67 *Ibid.*
68 Rachel, interviewed by Christiane Jouve, "Elle était tout pour moi," *Lesbia Magazine* 54 (October 1987): 24.
69 Rachel, "Elle était tout pour moi," 22.
70 Engel, 229.
71 Patricia, "Vécu," 24.
72 *Ibid.*, 23.
73 Georgette, interviewed by Christiane Jouve, "J'ai la haine des hommes," *Lesbia Magazine* 54 (October 1987): 20.
74 "E.," Anonymous woman interviewed by Claudie Lesselier in Lesselier, "Aspects de l'expérience lesbienne," 62.
75 *Ibid.*
76 Susan Daniel, *Arcadie*, 1954. Cited in Claudie Lesselier, "Formes de résistances et d'expression lesbiennes dans les années 1950 et 1960 en France", in *Homosexualités: expression/répression*, (ed.) Louis-Georges Tin (Paris: Éditions Stock, 2000), 114, author's translation. The gay periodical *Arcadie* (which ran 28 years from January 1954 to June 15, 1982) was in fact a fairly conservative review. This topic is covered more thoroughly in Cynthia Kreisel, "Between War and Revolution: French Women and the Sexual Practices of Daily Life, 1952–67" (PhD diss., Rutgers University, 2008).
77 Patricia, "Vécu," 24.
78 *Ibid.*
79 Geneviève, "C'est comme ça," 13.
80 *Ibid.*
81 Patricia, "Vécu," 23.
82 Mouvement Français pour Le Planning Familial, *Liberté, Sexualités, Féminisme*, 26.
83 Patricia, "Vécu," 24–25.
84 *Ibid.*, 25.
85 *Ibid.*, 24–25.
86 Grossmann, 193–98.
87 Herzog, 126–28.
88 Bee Zed, "C'était hier … ", 25.
89 "E.," in Lesselier, "Aspects de l'expérience lesbienne," 62.

8

POLITICAL PARTICIPATION, CIVIL SOCIETY, AND GENDER

Lessons from the Cold War?

Belinda Davis

In the 1960s and 1970s, West Germany witnessed the burgeoning of two kinds of politics.[1] The first was an intentionally provocative set of practices that deployed "theater" (visual as well as verbal communications), humor, and emotionally charged language to push beyond the more restrained, "reasoned" interventions supported by the post-fascist West German state. The second has been described as "kitchen table" politics, that is, "alternative" practices in non- or semi-public realms, often treated as representing a kind of retreat from politics. These practices were not necessarily specific to men or women, but they bore significant gendered aspects. In turn they affected gender relations, often disturbing existing hierarchies of power and perceptions of difference. Historians have provided useful models for understanding "kitchen table" politics in the context of civil society, particularly with reference to women in nineteenth-century Europe.[2] Social scientists have also addressed these "informal" politics, with special attention to the context of central and eastern Europe from the 1980s.[3] This chapter draws on such precedents to look at the ways in which these politics constituted attempts to expand the "pluralist and free community of communications"[4] that helps define civil society, which many had found wanting in West Germany. The two forms of communicative activity described here, often complementary, sometimes oppositional, flourished and ultimately gained legitimacy at some level, as a response to the limits of practical access to and influence on formal political channels. They exposed and challenged relations of power, sometimes with success. This does not suggest that official repression is a useful means to promote widespread political and societal engagement. It does confirm the value of using the concept of civil society to locate sites where politics often needed to play out, even in societies that legally guaranteed political expression through more formal channels. In turn, further exploration of such political sites in the Cold War West is consistent with the work of scholars who deploy the notion of civil society as a means to understanding self-expression and influence also in the Cold War East, thus before as well as after 1989.[5] I examine here what such political activity has "done" for participants as well as for the onlookers or "recipients" of this action.[6] I ask how such acts have influenced the understanding of politics, democracy, and political participation more broadly. I consider finally the kind of influence these politics have had on the "*Männerstaat*" (male state, men's state), a term that points up the long-lived association of the modern state and modern political authority with male privilege and social hierarchy. Answers to these questions may offer additional insight into debates around civil society, including concerning the full participation of women, as well as ethnic and religious minorities, and others, in current discussions of what is "Europe."

"Provo politics": Out in civil society

How might we use the concept of civil society to understand the role of provocative, or "provo," politics?[7] Analysts of civil society, primarily social scientists, identify four basic views of the concept: communitarian; democratic and participatory; liberal; and defined by communicative action.[8] They point to four basic modes of democratic engagement, as explicitly related to civil society, including representative liberal, participatory liberal, discursive, and constructionist.[9] These scholars have suggested that "participatory" engagement can include attention-getting and even provocative forms,[10] a range of styles that emphasizes not only the communicative effects of participants' acts but also the "empowerment" individuals themselves draw from participation. This in turn validates for them their continued contributions. These styles are not limited to the "reason" and "detached civility" idealized in dominant versions of modern politics. Emotion often plays an important role in both the appeal to and effect upon the participant. Indeed, the definition of "civility" itself can be challenged in this context. I argue for a notion of "deep civility" – that is, one that includes the potential to act with a surface incivility (minor destruction of property, ridicule of one's "opponent") that may appear to dismiss the value of communicative interaction but can in fact shore it up. It is vital to recognize that those deploying such forms in the 1970s, who often saw themselves as "revolutionary," overwhelmingly adopted strategies intended to *convince* others (rather than, say, shooting them – or, alternately, putting guns in their hands). They sought at least to get others to consider issues in new ways.[11] While acts of provocation may seem to fall outside many definitions of civil society, in the West Germany of the 1960s and 1970s, I argue that they helped deepen democratic participation and political communication, opening spaces for minority viewpoints and the perspectives of those otherwise less often heard – or listened to.

These "extraparliamentary" activists overall held free and open communications in high regard; many felt unable to make themselves heard, despite the range of formal channels, and/or misrepresented by others. One of the premier symbols of the "'68ers" throughout western Europe was the image of a person (gender indistinguishable, indeed individual features masked) with mouth pinned closed. In one example produced by the Parisian *atelier populaire* in 1968, the picture communicated the degree to which many young people, in this case also in France, felt closed off from "the public discussion."[12] The image was adopted by West German grassroots activists in the late 1960s and appeared with increasing frequency throughout the 1970s, above all in response to the 1972 *Radikalenerlass*, the Radical Decree. This draconian measure threatened the employment of all present and prospective public sector employees – professors, teachers, civil servants, clerks, and workers – who were perceived as in the broadest terms "hostile" to the existing state. By extension, the measure brought pressure on those employed in the private sector as well. Officials and segments of the media used this and like means to discredit the broad extra-parliamentary opposition, in order to marginalize and repress their voices.[13] Although photographic evidence shows that it was common for both men and women to tape up their mouths or wrap them in scarves during demonstrations (to be sure, also often to conceal their identities from officials), in West Germany, the face rendered speechless in posters and on leaflets most often appeared female. This very gendering emphasized the perceived impotence of men and women alike: feminizing the image powerfully communicated the sense of voicelessness experienced by both male and female activists.[14]

While provo actions have been characterized by some as distractions at best, and as prospective or actual violence at worst, they were often effective in introducing new ideas into public discourse. The physical violence associated with a tiny minority of such instances should not prevent us from considering the generally positive impact these practices had.[15] Certainly they startled and angered many, but that was the point: they were a way of attracting attention when more conventional means had failed – and in order to emphasize the limits of conventional means. In contrast to characterizing provo activists as irresponsible and irrelevant, if not dangerous to the fledgling "post-fascist" state, one could argue that, by insisting on being heard and working to produce spaces of communication, these activists espoused the principle of "responsibility" – the responsibility to participate – seen as both building and reflecting "mature" civil society.[16] If authorities often responded to such acts with violent repression, it is questionable to condemn the activists for bringing such a fate on themselves. Those engaging in provo acts often drew negative attention from the larger society. Nonetheless, they did succeed in making their own voices heard on issues they found important – from university reform to the Vietnam War and beyond – and in bringing such issues to broader discussion.

Provo politics also played an empowering role for the activists themselves, one with an important gender dimension. Some West Germans described these practices of fellow activists as a kind of "masculinist" intervention, as much a bullying insistence on one's own presence as a demonstration of serious political intent. Dagmar Seehuber, a member of the (in)famous "Kommune I," a small group of activists living and working together in 1967 and 1968 who led the way with provocative strategies, described such acts as a "men's thing" (*Männergeschichte*).[17] Yet she pushed herself to join in with these acts, as a way of combatting the silencing effects of prevailing gendered political–cultural practices. Robert A., who studied in the same period at the University of Heidelberg, recalls the feeling of being freed from a narrow, private world. Engaging in "small provocative acts" allowed him "to emerge out of [his] own background, to come out of the shelter of [his] own family, and to liberate [him]self," as well as to communicate a public message he found important.[18] Yet women spoke all the more of this sense of coming to feel as though they "existed," that they were a part of "the scene" – or at least some scene. These feelings in turn encouraged them to become further engaged, ultimately offering a range of rewards beyond remedying a "feminizing" silencing.

Further, this kind of intervention pushed many women in particular to rethink self-expression. Because such acts enabled a few to capture the attention of the many, as well as to ridicule those with power, provo action could be practiced effectively by a minority against the majority (numerically and in terms of power), by socially "lower" individuals against elites (including within organizations), by younger against older – and by women against men. It could challenge dogmatic, hierarchical, authoritarian, and totalitarian practices. Whether "masculinist" in terms of traditional practices, the appropriation of power, or otherwise, women as well as men used such means to gain visibility and convey their points within the larger society throughout this era. Such practices indeed helped mark the birth of the West German second-wave women's movement. They symbolized the assumption of a right to voice and a right to a response. In 1969, a group of mixed-gendered representatives of the West Berlin antiauthoritarian *Kinderladenbewegung* (a movement for cooperative childcare, independent of state authorities), one of the earliest West German feminist projects, staged a "dirty diaper attack" on the editor of the popular weekly magazine *Stern*. These representatives wanted to convey their dissatisfaction with the "shock" coverage the magazine had given them, which in their view trivialized their efforts, and cast them as ridiculous, when not "immoral." In this instance, registering their anger was one of the key goals, but the participants also showed that, like the magazine itself, they could communicate through tactics of surprise. The participants expressed considerable satisfaction with their efforts, which resulted in an uncommon acknowledgment of their concerns by *Stern*'s editor.[19]

Indeed the attention-grabbing tactics of media outlets including the liberal *Stern* and even the corrosively hostile "yellow press" contributed to informing activists' provocative practices. Activists saw their own use of the forms, however, as a means to spur critical thinking as well as find a voice for themselves. Certainly such press organs as *Stern* rendered successful many activists' efforts to make themselves heard (if most often however in mediated fashion). In 1971, West German feminist Alice Schwarzer and others, inspired by the French example, put together an article for *Stern* entitled "We've had an abortion," featuring the stories of nearly four hundred women, several of them prominent, who had undergone illegal abortions, in order to force fellow citizens to confront this reality.[20] Many women practiced provocative strategies of protest throughout this period, despite or even because of the strategies' perceived masculinist bravado and assertion of confidence. In a 1973 "Go-In," feminists in Frankfurt decorated anti-reproductive-choice Church leaders with baby powder and formula, to dramatize not just the theory but the everyday realities of responsibility for children. Others carried banners graphically suggesting that abortion would have been decriminalized if priests could become pregnant. While the history of abortion rights in (West) Germany has been rocky, the West German women's movement won considerable general support on this issue, resulting in an initial major parliamentary success in 1974.[21] In ironic emulation of the media practice of featuring bare-breasted women on the front page of newspapers, women used the disrobing of their own bodies in several public actions.[22] They not only thereby attracted attention to their words (often related to entirely different issues) by virtue of their bodies, but also commented cynically both on the culturally conditioned attention to women's bodies rather than to their words, and on the use of naked women to "sell news." Activists made a verifiable impact on this issue too, unleashing major public debate, and influencing national (public, at least) opinion against such media practices, even if losing a major court case – against *Stern* magazine.[23] This win in the court of public opinion proved the point for many. Many also felt pleased that the public had listened to them, at least somewhat more than before, rather than ignoring or attacking them – as women, as young people, and as activists.

Women also used provocative forms of politics directed toward the men within activist ranks. As was the case with feminists elsewhere, it was in part (if not exclusively) their frustration with fellow male protestors that led them to form what became the West German women's movement. At the 1968 national assembly of the West German Socialist German Students organization (SDS), female delegate Sigrid Rüger famously threw a tomato at the speechifying Hans-Jürgen Krahl, a leading theorist of the group. Krahl's speech followed an impassioned address by early feminist and filmmaker Helke Sander, in which she had identified the oppressiveness of patriarchy within the SDS; Krahl delivered his speech with no attention to Sander's words. Men in the audience, insofar as they responded at all to Sander, did so largely with sniggers and dismissive comments. Although Krahl followed customary practice in not referring to his predecessor's statement, Sigrid Rüger and others insisted that Sander's message be heard, acknowledged, taken seriously, and responded to directly. Certainly the tomato stopped the proceedings dead in its tracks, and the act took on iconic status associated with the idea of the need to listen to women's voices, and to unheard voices more broadly.[24]

As practitioners described their experience, provo acts also offered forms of satisfaction for the activists themselves. Participation in such acts could be joyous, gratifying, thrilling, socially enjoyable, and empowering. Certainly both men and women who engaged in provo acts recalled an emotional component, describing them as "fun," "inspiring," and "exciting." Kommune I member Susanne Kleemann found it "fabulous to throw eggs at Amerika Haus" in West Berlin – an act that captured considerable public notice, drawing attention to the war in Vietnam and West Germany's close relation to America.[25] It was as often a means of daring oneself to open up, to make oneself seen and heard. Robert A. found small-level provocation "crazily, crazily exciting," as he helped send the door of the university president's office down the river in Heidelberg, a symbol of protestors' demand for more open communications at the university. Emotion in political engagement has been dismissed as inappropriate to modern politics. Women's presumed "emotional" nature was long invoked as argument against their enfranchisement.[26] But emotion played a positive role in these politics, not least in keeping activists engaged over the long haul. In any case, the notion that humans divorce themselves from emotion when appropriately practicing politics is dubious at best. This emotional appeal does reveal a gendered dimension: provo acts and other forms of contemporary popular politics were about embracing fantasy and desire, casting off close constraints and expectations, including the highly gender-specific expectations of the early postwar decades. Provo acts reflected "disobedience" (*Ungehorsam*) in both the "familial" and "political" context (the two often closely related), and the challenge of existing limits. Author–activist Peter Schneider described such politics in retrospect as "organized self-liberation," constituted by "misbehavior," "insubordination, civil courage, and self-organization."[27] For cohorts of Germans who had grown up in the late Nazi period – and also in early West Germany – this was no small feat. In turn, and correspondingly, it appears it was not enough for the architects of the new West German state to respond to a dictatorial regime by erecting channels that reflected only the narrowest understanding of political participation. These kinds of acts, outside of formal political channels and anticipated political means, stretched political space and ultimately broadened the definitions of politics for the larger West German public.

"Politics of the kitchen table": *Back in* civil society?

This personal satisfaction illustrates yet another characteristic of these politics: the transcendence of a clear divide between "public" and "private," a linkage not only across issues (from abortion rights to everyday violence), but also between the parts of people's experience. Civil society emerged as a significant term for feminist historians in the 1980s in the context of activities "behind the scenes," outside of formal decision-making spheres. Catherine Hall and Leonore Davidoff used this concept to describe the ways in which women in nineteenth-century England participated in political discussions and collective associations on the local level beyond the family circle, to create for themselves a community identity and to participate in decision-making within their communities.[28] Their approach provides a vital tool for understanding participation and the practice of influence in the overlaps between "private" and "public" life in West Germany more than a century later. It helps us view political expression among those who had not yet reached majority status in that country,[29] as well as, and perhaps all the more important, among women and others who, though bearing formal political rights, did not feel able to exercise them satisfactorily. Indeed it leads us to question how sufficient franchise rights and membership in political parties can be in describing robust democratic participation. In the 1960s, sites such as schools and universities, neighborhood pubs, and churches were vital to these individuals' efforts to situate and express themselves, politically and otherwise. By the 1970s, activists had built their own such spaces, in such forms as women's and youth centers, the common rooms of non-familial shared residences (*Wohngemeinschaften* or *WGs*), and a flowering alternative press. Activity emerging from these spaces was, like provo politics, often politically successful, in a variety of ways.[30]

The "politics of the kitchen table" emerged out of perceived necessity, here again in part a response to the Radical Decree, as well as physical violence by police against protesters, and psychological measures of political repression exercised increasingly throughout the 1970s. They reflected a partial remove from particular sites of political expression, but not, as some have suggested, a retreat from politics.[31] "Extra-parliamentary" activists added new forms of activity to actions in the streets and other clearly public locations, creating lively alternative spaces of sociopolitical interaction and communication. These sites, often out of broad public view, became ubiquitous in the course of the decade, with the women's movement leading the proliferation. The impact of this development can be seen in the burgeoning of citizens' initiatives and the broader "new social movements," as well as in anticipation of the peace movement of the early 1980s, and of the Green Party.[32] These developments helped build vast alternative communication networks that also gave voice to women and to others who felt themselves unheard and even unable to speak. To be sure, authorities attempted to infiltrate these activist enclaves, as they had from the mid-1960s.[33] But as these sites both proliferated and became often increasingly "personalized," officials found them more difficult to penetrate. There is evidence too that officials' own often more narrow view of what constituted politics allowed many of these activities to pass below their radar.

As several activists have described, these alternative communication networks fostered a critical conjuncture of "public" and "private," even moving beyond any stark division between the two. Christiane W. emphasized how important it was for her political development that she met regularly with clusters of people of different ages and classes who found one another in a pub in the provincial Bavarian city of Hof. To be sure, there was nothing new about meeting and talking with others about politics in a pub. What was notable was Christiane's commitment to seeking out those who were "different," precisely those who were not likely to agree or see things from the same perspective, not part of the same groupings and presumed interests. Not only pubs but also private dwellings increasingly served as "semi-public" meeting sites, often bringing together surprisingly diverse groups. Christiane remembers that after moving to Regensburg, she and her friends used their tiny apartments to host innumerable meetings, for example, those of a women's group. The new, larger group house (WG) into which she then moved, with its "open-door policy," served this function even better; better still, the women's center she co-founded offered a site for many types of interaction and organizing. The center joined the imagined public and private within its walls, bringing hundreds in regular and shifting contact with one another.

Like the acts most closely associated with provo politics, the "politics of the kitchen table" became important for fulfilling specific needs. Women in this era, as well as many men, often found a greater comfort engaging with political discourse in more informal settings, both secluded and sociable. Katrin B. described how central it was for both her politicization and her ongoing political engagement to have discussions every evening at dinner with the members of her all-women WG, discussions regarding politics at every level and how they directly concerned her smaller community. These discussions around the dinner table were so central to its social and political functioning that when many members of the WG went on diets in the late 1970s and refused the collective meals, it ultimately destroyed the WG. Such venues expanded well beyond the literal kitchen table, offering a combination of "publicness" and intimacy, creating ease in speaking one's mind as well as in listening, and a sense that one had interlocutors, that one's thoughts reached others – ultimately, perhaps, many others. New lifestyle forms generally emphasized this transcendence of public and private, and allowed individuals to feel "whole" (*ganzheitlich*), as they saw it: living and eating with the same people with whom they planned and attended public events and engaged in political actions. Women's centers, which mushroomed in West Germany in the 1970s, were another major site, especially effective for linking women in smaller and more dispersed communities. Hosting a constantly transforming congregation of women, they provided permanent space for the exchange of thoughts at every level, and for forming communities in and through which individuals could move from ideas to forms of political action. This space was vitally important for women of all sexual orientations, and for those who came to pursue cultural, social, and/or political separatism.[34] Though she sought to make her voice heard widely, and to work in concert with broad groups, Susanne W. came to discover, "I can really only be a good activist in women's groups": for her, "as soon as there are men there, it is just crap."

Such activities were not limited to more controlled spaces like women's centers, nor were they restricted to women-only spaces. But their development in such communities bespeaks not only the impact of official repression but also the perceived limits of opportunities to speak and be heard even among one's peers in mixed-gendered settings. Teresa R. rued how in these contexts "the sons could be as bad as the fathers." Certainly individuals also could, and, did feel silenced and subjected to hierarchies of power in single-gender settings too. Wiebke H. found the "battles" among members of her feminist newspaper collective "depressing, yes, and also scary." Anna J. felt that, among the feminist groupings in Hamburg, it seemed she just didn't fit anywhere. But then she broke away from these circles and worked to create new political spaces. Women-only settings established one model for alternative public spaces and civil societies, one that was widely and effectively adopted by a range of citizens' initiatives and new social movements in the 1970s. These settings provided varied sites for a range of voices, while offering a level of comfort for participants. This might seem only a return to an older, institutionalized, single-identity politics. But in practice the landscape of innumerable, ever-changing, and overlapping groupings could offer sites of discussion at once open and connected, yet intimate and comfortable.

This landscape pushes us to look beyond any notion of a unitary, hegemonic "civil society" when employing such a tool. In many ways it appears the model of discussion that emerged in these intimate settings approaches conventional ideals of civil society, for all the reasons above, and because these sites did remain relatively impervious to official efforts at intervention. To some, such settings may suggest a lack of the transparency and openness that are deemed so important in democratic political engagement. But insofar as they allowed individuals to participate directly in communicative processes and thereby permitted so many different voices to be heard directly, they represented a summa of these values, in principle at least, and despite the acknowledged limitations in practice.[35] These contexts contributed to building trust as well as responsibility, elements also regarded as central to civil society.[36] To be sure, already in the 1970s, some feminists criticized what one termed "women sitting around drinking tea together." This might have been the most "comfortable" form of activism, she went on, but "we needed to get out there in the 'male society' (*Männergesellschaft*) to make our voices heard."[37] Yet, for hundreds of thousands of women (as well as men), "kitchen table politics" led also to other, and often more conventionally public, forms of activism as well. Despite the democratic impulses and other appealing attributes of the practices emerging from these settings, social scientists as well as some contemporaries have questioned activists' ultimate efficacy.[38] But these practices were no less functional in the event than other forms of popular politics and public self-expression of the period, from demonstrations to boycotts to strikes. The successes women and others achieved through this type of engagement – ranging from changes in abortion and family law, to the transformation of urban housing policy, to public awareness and new policy concerning nuclear energy – must be acknowledged.[39] The effects came too in other forms, by virtue of helping transform the expectations of and possibilities for interaction and challenging the necessity of existing power relations and the unchangeability of the existing social organization, from the level of personal and family relations on out.

These forms of alternative activities provided space for "one's own voice," a remedy for the voicelessness perceived as feminine. Former activists emphasize that they (usually!) felt encouraged to speak out and define and refine their own views against the sounding board of others in these contexts. They appreciated the broad spectrum of views these various settings offered. They saw these more intimate settings as being closely connected to larger networks of debate and discussion that moved across large populations. This in turn linked them to other forms of action and to results. Without exaggerating the breadth of this openness, it must be emphasized that in the 1970s, West German "extraparliamentary" activism was by no means dominated by the simpleminded orthodoxy by which some have described it.[40] Rather, alternative political spaces, situated as they were at the nexus of public and private, allowed marginalized voices of many types both to initiate discussions and enter a larger set of debates.

Transforming ideas of political practice

Ideas about civil society in the last centuries emerge from a modernist understanding that emphasizes individuation and independent thinking, education, and civic interchange. Because provo actions and kitchen table politics supported these qualities, civil society serves as a useful notion for examining the functioning and efficacy of these types of politics. The process of individuation, as these participants described it – finding one's own voice and having a chance to test it out against others – was central to their political participation. Robert A. described the "incredible feeling of self-possession and of strength" afforded by joining in both regular provo acts and evening meetings in local university pubs. These experiences forced him to define himself and speak his own positions clearly, thereby finding himself beyond the space of his family. This transformation did not always come easily. Anna J. described her shock after leaving school and heading to university to find that her comments were systematically ignored by members of the predominantly male political discussion group she joined, still dominated in the mid-1970s by longstanding characteristics of German university culture. But she credits her earlier experience both in small groups and with provo acts during high school with enabling her to successfully fight back. For example, she and a male fellow student conducted an experiment that successfully demonstrated to members of her political group how they ignored what women said. Gaby M. recalled her sense of inadequacy during her first year at the University of Cologne, as a young woman coming from a poor family in a farm village. "I felt completely out of place," she commented, "naïve, stupid, and ignorant ... [I] couldn't even talk to anyone." For more than a year, she ceased speaking altogether. But eventually she joined small group discussions, and found both her voice and good reason to speak. Soon, she claims, she and other group members found themselves "much better informed, [more] unorthodox and critical" than presumed extraparliamentary leaders in West Berlin, those some assumed spoke for her. A sense of being silenced led many who felt disenfranchised to find their own means of being part of the conversation. The sense was often associated with characteristics of gender, if not necessarily related to specifically gendered bodies.

Reading these experiences through the concept of civil society, we might consider that these practices arising in the 1960s and 1970s can be considered as part of the emergence of postmodern thinking, coming out of activists' own political experience. Postmodernism is characterized among other things by a rejection of grand theory and of totalizing ideologies. It challenges ideas such as a linear and progressive human history and development, universal truths and values, and other notions associated with Enlightenment thought. Postmodernism is often associated with more and less widely read political theorists, from Simon de Beauvoir and Frantz Fanon to Jacques Lyotard and Jean Baudrillard.[41] But through their political acts, the activists discussed here also contributed to developing the notions these thinkers described in their writings, and communicated them to a broad audience. Activists' de facto challenge to binaries such as "public vs. private" and "reason vs. emotion" also signaled this shift in thinking. Thus it should come as no surprise to discover that some of the most compelling recent models of civil society, such as the "participatory model," reflect precisely political understandings that emerged from the politics of the 1960s and 1970s.

Contemporary (and often later) critics of provo protesters of the period claimed that such activists represented a particularist view, hijacking a broader agenda and range of issues that "truly" represented West German interests, such as the growing stature of West Germany in the Cold War world order and an emphasis on societal order at home. But it was provo activists who through their acts demanded a respect for minority views, and for multivocality, in contrast with simple acceptance of "majority rule." These strategies demanded at the very least a toleration of different views – and even an emphasis on their value – though certainly these activists themselves could occasionally demonstrate the intolerance of which they accused others. By insisting on the need and possibility to attend to these different voices, provo and kitchen table political actors questioned an easy notion of a common good, the greatest good for the greatest number. In this sense too, the more recent philosophical view that communitarianism requires consideration of "minority" interests must be seen in part as coming out of the activism of these years, in West Germany and elsewhere.[42] At the same time, it is worth challenging the assumption that the views popular activists advanced were those of only a tiny minority. The numbers who shared such views grew to large numbers, in part a result of the efforts of activists themselves to communicate. By looking at the full panoply of sites we can describe as civil society, we discover that the activists represented a range of demographic characteristics in terms of age, class origin, and above all life experience – far broader than is often acknowledged.[43]

Conclusion

Early West German formal political leaders proclaimed an adoption of political ideals they saw as a stark contrast to the Nazi – and Weimar – past, and all the more to the new Cold War enemy. Many imagined reasoned discourse to encompass effectively a narrow stratum of educated participants, closely in concert with official sanction, in specified settings and forms, and manifesting a clear division between the public and private. Yet many activists argued in the course of the 1960s and 1970s that this model of sober, reasoned discourse, circumscribed to limited channels and controlled forms, engendered a kind of deep self-censorship that constituted an ongoing effect of the Nazi era rather than transcendence of its politics. This too was, not least, a gendered argument, as it emerged in these years. Christiane W. noted in retrospect, "'Big Politics' and private life could no longer be divided for the entire postwar generation, and certainly for women still less than for men." Contemporaries speak uniformly of the "excitement" and "satisfaction" this civil participation engendered, beyond building self-confidence and a sense of one's right to participate. Emotion and personal needs and desires were clearly significant in maintaining active participation and involvement. The hierarchy of gender has long inflected institutionalized political processes, even when such differentiation has been legally and constitutionally prohibited. The concept of civil society can allow us to see how women without formal legal rights have participated politically with some considerable efficacy, and also how women with these rights (among others) have still bumped up against limits to fully exercising their voices. The concept offers a means of viewing the practice of politics in highly complex form, transcending presumed boundaries of public and private and other "ideal" definitional features. This has direct implications for our understanding of gender and power.

Examining a broad terrain of civil society helps us to read political participation as being of a piece with participants' desires, helping us understand why so many gravitated to politics and their urge to frequent existing sites in fresh ways and create new places for themselves. The notion also helps us to read the significant and lasting transformations in German political culture that took place in this era, characterized in part by the legitimation of a wide range of forms of political participation. It is just these shifts that were of greatest interest in the post-Cold War era – even as those in former Soviet Bloc societies struggled, as had West Germans, with the complex political influences and pressures of both the recent past and the present. The transformations of 1960s–1970s West Germany do not overturn the idea that civil society may operate as a "safety valve," as leading scholars have asserted.[44] But they do offer evidence of some meaningful political change from the inside out, and also thereby challenge how we measure meaningful change, for example, in terms of notions such as "revolution."[45] As scholars have used civil society, it describes practices predicated on the ability of many to enter into discussions of broad significance, whether directly or indirectly. The forms of expression and communication that proliferated so expansively in the 1960s and 1970s overwhelmingly represented not, as some have asserted, a violation of ideals of civil society, but rather an expansion of it. In turn, consideration of such activity may add new utility to the notion of civil society – and fresh understanding of ongoing political change across Europe.

Notes

1 This piece is a slightly revised version of "Civil Society in a New Key? Feminist and Alternative Groups in 1970s West Germany," in Sonya Michel et al. (eds), *Civil Society and Gender Justice: Historical and Comparative Perspectives* (NY: Berghahn, 2008), 208–23. Thanks to Joanna Regulska, also to Frank Trentmann, Sven Reichardt, Jan Kubik, and Philip Nord, for discussion of civil society and related concepts over the years.

2 Among European examples, including those looking specifically at gender, see Leonore Davidoff and Catherine Hall, *Family Fortunes: Men and Women of the English Middle Class, 1780–1850* (London: Routledge 1987); Ute Frevert (ed.), *Bürgerinnen und Bürger: Geschlechterverhältnisse im 19. Jahrhundert* (Göttingen: Vandenhoeck & Ruprecht, 1988); Marion A. Kaplan, *The Making of the Jewish Middle Class: Women, Family, and Identity in Imperial Germany* (New York: OUP, 1991); Karen Hagemann, "Familie–Staat–Nation: Das aufklärerische Projekt der 'Bürgergesellschaft' in geschlechtergeschichtlicher Perspektive," in Hildermeier et al. (eds), *Europäische Zivilgesellschaft in Ost und West, Begriff, Geschichte, Chancen*, (Frankfurt: Campus Verlag), 57–84; Gunilla Budde, "Das Öffentliche des Privaten: Die Familie als zivilgesellschaftliche Kerninstitution," in Arnd Bauerkämper (ed.), *Die Praxis der Zivilgesellschaft: Akteure, Handeln und Strukturen im internationalen Vergleich* (Frankfurt/M.: Campus Verlag, 2003), 56–76. More generally among historians, compare James van Horn Melton, *The Rise of the Public in Enlightenment Europe* (Cambridge: CUP, 2001); Jürgen Kocka, "Zivilgesellschaft in historischer Perspektive," in *Forschungsjournal Neue Soziale Bewegungen* 16, no. 2 (2003): 29–37; Stefan-Ludwig Hoffmann et al. (eds), *Geselligkeit und Demokratie: Vereine und zivile Gesellschaft im transnationalen Vergleich, 1750–1914* (Göttingen: Vandehoeck & Ruprecht, 2003); Ralph Jessen et al. (eds), *Zivilgesellschaft als Geschichte: Studien zum 19. und 20. Jahrhundert* (Opladen: VS Verlag für Sozialw., 2004). As a still relatively rare historical application of the term in postwar Europe, see Paul Ginsborg, *Italy and Its Discontents 1980–2001: Family, Civil Society, State* (London: Penguin, 2003).

3 Again, specifically concerning gender, compare variously Joanna Regulska and Magdalena Grabowska, "Will It Make a Difference? EU Enlargement and Women's Public Discourse in Poland," in Silke Roth (ed.), *Gender Politics In The Expanding European Union: Mobilization, Inclusion, Exclusion* (New York: Berghahn, 2008), 139–54; Ann Graham and Joanna Regulska, "Expanding Political Space for Women in Poland: An Analysis of Three Communities," *Communist and Post Communist Studies* 30, 1 (1997), 65–82; Jasmina Lukić, et al. (eds), *Women and Citizenship in Central and East Europe* (Farnham: Ashgate, 2006); Barbara Einhorn and Charlie Sever, "Gender and Civil Society in Central Eastern Europe," *International Feminist Journal of Politics* 5, 2 (July 2003), 163–90; Susan Gal and Gail Kligman (eds), *Reproducing Gender: Politics, Publics and Everyday Life after Socialism* (Princeton: Princeton University Press, 2000); Jude Howell and Diane Mulligan (eds), *Gender and Civil Society* (New York: Routledge, 2004). See too John Keane, *Civil Society: Old Images, New Visions* (Cambridge: Polity Press, 1998); Thomas R. Rochon, *Culture Moves: Ideas, Activism, and Changing Values* (Princeton: Princeton University Press, 1998); Roland Roth and Dieter Rucht (eds), *Jugendkulturen, Politik und Protest: Vom Widerstand zum Kommerz?* (Opladen: Leske + Budrich Verlag, 2000); Grzegorz Ekiert and Jan Kubik, *Rebellious Civil Society: Popular Protest and Democratic Consolidation in Poland, 1989–1993* (Ann Arbor: University of Michigan Press, 2001); Matthias Freise, *Externe Demokratieförderung in postsozialistischen Transformationsstaaten* (Münster: Lit Verlag, 2004); Michael Edwards, *Civil Society* (Cambridge: Polity Press, 2004); Frank Adloff, *Zivilgesellschaft: Theorie und politische Praxis* (Frankfurt/M.: Campus Verlag, 2005); Sven Eliason (ed.), *Building Democracy and Civil Society East of the Elbe: Essays in Honour of Edmund Mokrzycki* (London: Routledge, 2006); also Ernest Gellner, *Conditions of Liberty: Civil Society and Its Rivals* (New York: Hamish Hamilton, 1994). The term has been used, to be sure, in some social scientific discussions of western Europe; see Myra Marx Ferree et al. (eds), *Shaping Abortion Discourse: Democracy and the Public Sphere in Germany and the United States* (Cambridge: Cambridge University Press, 2002); Hanspeter Kriesi and Ruud Koopmans (eds), *New Social Movements in Western Europe: A Comparative Analysis* (London: Routledge, 1995). Among recent efforts to bring together historical and social scientific perspectives, uses, and objects of understanding are: Nancy Burmeo and Philip Nord (eds), *Civil Society Before Democracy: Lessons from Nineteenth-Century Europe* (Lanham, MD, 2000); John Hall and Frank Trentmann (eds), *Civil Society: A Reader in History, Theory, and International Politics* (London: Palgrave Macmillan, 2005); Dieter Gosewinkel et al. (eds), *Zivilgesellschaft–national und transnational. WZB-Jahrbuch 2003* (Berlin: Edition Sigma, 2003); Norberto Bobbio, *Stato, governo, società* (Milan: Einaudi, 2006); Miklós Molnár, *La Démocratie se Lève à l'Est: Société Civile et Communisme en Europe de l'Est: Pologne et Hongrie* (Paris: Presses universitaires de France, 1990).
4 Sven Reichardt, "Civil Society: A Concept for Comparative Historical Research," in Annette Zimmer and Eckhard Priller (eds), *The Future of Civil Society: Making Central European Nonprofit-Organizations Work*, (ed.) (Wiesbaden: VS Verlag, 2004), 45.
5 Compare variously Ulrike Poppe et al. (eds), *Zwischen Selbstbehauptung und Anpassung. Formen des Widerstandes und der Opposition in der DDR* (Berlin: Links, 1995); Anke Silimon, *"Schwerter zu Pflugscharen" und die DDR. Die Friedensarbeit der evangelischen Kirche in der DDR im Rahmen der Friedensdekaden 1980–1982* (Göttingen: Vandenhoeck & Ruprecht, 1999); Andrea Genest, "Zwischen Anteilnahme und Ablehnung – die Rollen der Arbeiter in den Ereignissen 1968 in Polen," in Bernd Gehrke and Gerd Rainer Horn (eds), *1968 und die Arbeiter. Studien zum proletarischen Mai in Europa* (Hamburg: Vsa Verlag, 2007); Mark Pittaway, "Control and Consent in Eastern Europe's Workers' States, 1945–89: Some Reflections on Totalitarianism, Social Organization and Social Control," in Clive Emsley et al. (eds), *Social Control in Europe, Vol. 2* (Columbus: Ohio State University Press, 2004), 343–67; Mark Pittaway, "Retreat from Collective Protest: Household, Gender, Work and Popular Opposition in Stalinist Hungary," in Jan Kok (ed.), *Rebellious Families: Household Strategies and Collective Action in the Nineteenth and*

Twentieth Centuries (New York: Berghahn, 2002), 199–229; *International Studies in Social History Vol. 3* (New York and Oxford, 2002).
6 Compare Belinda Davis, "Provokation als Emanzipation. 1968 und die Emotionen," *Vorgänge* (December 2003), 41–49.
7 The term "provo" comes directly from practices in the 1960s in the Netherlands, though the roots of the idea are longer and broader. Compare Roel van Duyn, *Provo. De geschiedenis van de provotarische beweging 1965–1967* (Amsterdam: Meulenhoff, 1985).
8 Compare Reichardt, "Civil Society," 43–46 (Cambridge: Polity Press, 1998).
9 Compare Myra Marx Ferree et al., "Four Models of the Public Sphere in Modern Democracies," *Theory and Society* 31 (2002): 289–324.
10 See among others Paul Hirst, *Associative Democracy: New Forms of Economic and Social Government* (Cambridge, MA: University of Massachusetts Press, 1994); B. R. Barber, *Strong Democracy* (CA: University of California Press, 1992); John Gaventa, *Power and Powerlessness* (Oxford University Press, 1980); compare Ulrich Rödel et al. (eds), *Die demokratische Frage* (Frankfurt/M.: Suhrkamp, 1989). The forms discussed here do not fit exclusively into this category of democratic participation, but the characteristics marking the category are particularly critical here.
11 Naturally many revolutionary traditions rely on the notion of some number of people convincing others through argument or example. On the notion of violence in civil society, see Sheri Berman, "Civil Society and the Collapse of the Weimar Republic," *World Politics* 3 (1997): 401–29; Sven Reichardt, *Faschistische Kampfbünde: Gewalt und Gemeinschaft im italienschen Squadrismus und in der deutschen SA* (Cologne: Böhlau Verlag, 2002).
12 See Greil Marcus, *Lipstick Traces: A Secret History of the Twentieth Century* (Cambridge, MA: Harvard University Press, 1989), 35–36. Marcus's discussion of the Dadaist and Situationist roots of British Punk is equally relevant to the provo activism of the European New Left.
13 "Extraparliamentary," a term first used by the relatively small peace movement in early 1960s West Germany, was taken up by a far broader population of protestors in response to the "Grand Coalition" that ascended to formal Political leadership in West Germany in 1966, led by a former Nazi, Chancellor Kurt-Georg Kiesinger, and leaving no parliamentary opposition. For officials' habit of lumping together all on "the left," see Belinda Davis, "From Starbuck to Starbucks, or, Terror: What's in a Name?" *Radical History Review* 85 (December 2002): 37–57; Belinda Davis, "Jenseits von Terror und Rückzug: Politischen Raum und Verhandlungsstrategien in der BRD der 70er Jahre," in *Innere Sicherheit und Terrorismus in der Bundesrepublik der 1970er Jahre*, (ed.) Heinz-Gerhardt Haupt et al. (Franfurt/M.: Campus Verlag, 2006), 154–86.
14 On the impact of this image, see Belinda Davis, *The Internal Life of Politics: The New Left in West Germany, 1962–1983* (forthcoming publication), Chapter 3.
15 I would argue that even the violent activism of the Red Army Faction (RAF) represented, initially at least, a kind of "extreme" (if not necessarily useful or successful) communication, until the violence degenerated into signs devoid of meaningful signification, when not simple revenge. Compare Belinda Davis, "Violence and Memory of the Nazi past in 1960s–70s West German Protest," in Philip Gassert and Alan E. Steinweis (eds), *Coping with the Nazi Past: West German Debates on Nazism and Generational Conflict, 1955–1975* (New York, 2006), 210–37; see too Ingrid Gilcher-Holtey, "Transformation by Subversion? The New Left and the Question of Violence," in Belinda Davis et al. (eds), *Changing the World, Changing Oneself: Political Protest and Transnational Identities in 1960s/70s, West Germany and the U.S.*, with W. Mausbach, M. Klimke, and C. MacDougall (New York: Berghahn, 2010) 155–69.
16 Kocka, "Zivilgesellschaft."
17 See Dagmar (Seehuber) Przytulla, "'Niemand ahnte, daß wir ein ziemlich verklemmter Haufen waren,'" in Ute Kätzel, (ed.) *Die 68erinnen* (Berlin: Helmer Ulrike, 2008), 201–20.
18 Author's interview, "Robert A.," July 2004. (Many of these interviews are, at the request of the informants, referenced with pseudonyms.) My sources for this project

include contemporary documents, memoirs, and oral interviews. Though I cite relatively few interviews in this chapter, its arguments are based on themes that emerge in the interviews I carried out with fifty-five contemporary activists born between 1937 and 1957, as well as in research in archival and published sources.
19 Annette Schwarzenau, "Nicht diese theoretische Dinger, etwas Praktisches unternehmen," in Kätzel, Die 68erinnen, 41–59.
20 The French example appeared in August 1970 as "Le manifeste des 343 salopes," reprinted as "Je me suis fait avorter," in Le nouvel observateur 334 (April 5, 1971).
21 The West German law of 1974 allowed abortion on demand during the first trimester of pregnancy. The law was successfully challenged, however, and, in 1976, a range of restrictions were (re)introduced. The issue came to the fore again in 1990, when East German activists battled to save that country's more liberal abortion law, as the German Democratic Republic was dissolved and subsumed under the Federal Republic; they ultimately achieved a partial success in the prevailing 1995 law.
22 Compare the image reprinted in CheShahShit: Die Sechziger Jahre zwischen Cocktail und Molotow (Berlin: Espresso Press, 1984), 170, by Eckhard Siepmann et al.
23 Alice Schwarzer and other feminists brought Stern to court over this regular practice in 1978, charging that these images incited violence and hatred against women. Compare "Die Stern-Klage," Emma (July 1978), reprinted in Alice Schwarzer, Alice in Männerland (Cologne: Kiepenheuer & Witsch, 2002), 109–11.
24 Compare Halina Bendkowski et al. (eds), Wie weit flog die Tomate? Eine 68erinnen-Gala der Reflexion (Berlin: Heinrich-Böll-Stiftung, 1999).
25 Susanne Schunter-Kleemann, "Wir waren Akteurinnen und nicht etwa die Anhängsel," in Kätzel, Die 68erinnen, 108.
26 On the link between provocation, emotion, and emancipation, see Belinda Davis, "Provokation als Emanzipation: 1968 und die Emotionen," Vorgänge 164 (December 2003): 41–49. Compare among philosophical and historical studies concerning the association from the late eighteenth century of emotion with women and the relation to discrediting women's political participation, e.g. Geneviève Fraisse, Reason's Muse: Sexual Difference and the Birth of Democracy (University of Chicago Press, 1994); Anne-Charlott Trepp, Sanfte Männlichkeit und selbständige Weiblichkeit. Frauen und Männer im Hamburger Bürgertum zwischen 1770 und 1840 (Göttingen: Vandenhoeck & Ruprecht, 1996); Ute Frevert, "Mann und Weib, und Weib und Mann". Geschlechter-Differenzen in der Moderne (Munich: C. H. Beck, 1995); Manuel Borutta and Nina Verheyen, Die Präsenz der Gefühle. Männlichkeit und Emotion in der Moderne (Bielefeld: Transcript, 2010).
27 Cited in Peter Mosler, Was wir wollten, was wir wurden: Studentenrevolte, 10 Jahre danach (Reinbek bei Hamburg: Rowohlt Taschenbuch Verlag, 1977), 26; see also the flyer that translates as "Organize Disobedience to the Nazi Generation!" reprinted in Protest! Literatur um 1968 (Marbach, 2000), 43. Compare Belinda Davis, Internal Life, Chapter 3, on activists' efforts to open their mouths and overcome their fear of disobedience.
28 Davidoff and Hall, Family Fortunes (London: Routledge, 2002).
29 The age of majority in West Germany was 21 until 1970, when it was lowered to 18, as elsewhere, specifically in response to protest.
30 Compare e.g. Roland Roth, Demokratie von unten: Neue soziale Bewegungen auf dem Wege zur politischen Institution (Cologne: Bund-Verlag, 1994); Ruud Koopmans, Democracy from Below: New Social Movements and the Political System in West Germany (Boulder, CO: Westview Press Inc, 1995); and see especially Joanna Regulska's and Magdalena Grabowska's work on the "third space," e.g. "New Geographies of Women Subjectivities in Poland," in Samir Dayal and Merguerite Murphy (eds), Global Babel: Questions of Discourse and Communication in a Time of Globalization (Newcastle-upon-Tyne: Cambridge Scholars Publishing, 2007).
31 Some activists themselves claimed to have retreated from politics, but their own ongoing activity demonstrates clearly the ways in which they transformed the definition of politics. Compare too on redefining politics Joanna Regulska, "The Political and its

Meaning for Women: Transition Politics in Poland," in John Pickles (ed.), *Theorizing Transition: The Political Economy of Post-Communist Transformations* (New York: Routledge, 1998), 291–310.

32 "New social movements," characterized by the de-institutionalized networks of activism that burgeoned in the 1970s, usually describe the women's, ecology, anti-nuclear, and peace movements. Compare e.g. Roth, *Demokratie von unten* (Cologne: Bund-Verlag, 1994); Koopmans, *Democracy from Below* (Boulder, CO: Westview Press Inc, 1995); Dieter Rucht, (ed.), *Protest in der Bundesrepublik: Strukturen und Entwicklungen* (Frankfurt a.M.: Campus Verlag, 2001); Donatella Della Porta (ed.), *Democracy in Social Movements* (Basingstoke: Palgrave Macmillan, 2009).

33 There is good evidence of police "plants" from the mid-1960s, also regularly associated with instigation to violence from within. See variously Stefan Aust, *Der Baader Meinhof Komplex* (Munich: Hoffmann und Campe, 1989), 55 passim; Ulrich Chaussy: *Die drei Leben des Rudi Dutschke. Eine Biographie* (Darmstadt: Luchterhand, 1983), 253; Klaus Weinhauer, *Schutzpolizei in der Bundesrepublik* (Paderborn: Schoeningh Ferdinand GmbH, 2003); Davis, *Interal Life,* Chapter 5 (publication forthcoming).

34 Some of those women interviewed identified themselves as heterosexual separatists who had sex with men but chose to spend their time otherwise almost entirely in the company of other women. These centers would ultimately become one venue for confronting issues of gender identification.

35 There is a broad scholarly and journalistic literature emphasizing the limits of these practices. Compare e.g. Gerd Koenen, *Das rote Jahrzehnt. unsere kleine deutsche Kulturrevolution, 1967–1977* (Cologne: Kiepenheuer & Witsch, 2001); see too Davis, *Internal Life,* Chapters 3 and 4 (publication forthcoming).

36 Kocka, "Zivilgesellschaft."

37 "Autonome Frauendemo in Bremerhaven am 14.10," *Oldenburger Frauenzeitung* (November 9, 1983), 4–6.

38 See Koopmans, *Democracy from Below* (Boulder, CO: Westview Press Inc, 1995). In the West German context, compare Sibylla Flügge, "1968 und die Frauen – Ein Blick in die Beziehungskiste," in *Gender und Soziale Praxis,* (ed.) Margit Göttert and Karin Walser (Königstein/Taunus: Helmer Ulrike, 2002), 265–90. On East German women's disappointing confrontations with the West German state and society (including West German feminists), see also Ingrid Miethe, "From 'Mothers of the Revolution' to 'Fathers of Unification': Concepts of Politics among Women Activists following German Unification," *Social Politics* 6, no. 1 (Spring 1999): 1–22; Myra Marx Ferree, "'The Time of Chaos was the Best': Feminist Mobilization and Demobilization in East Germany," *Gender and Society* 6, no. 8 (1994): 597–623; Dorothy Rosenberg, "Women's Issues, Women's Politics, and Women's Studies in the Former German Democratic Republic," *Radical History Review* 54 (1992), 110–26; Lynn Kamenitsa, "East German Feminists in the New German Democracy: Opportunities, Obstacles, and Adaptation," *Women in Politics* 17, no. 3 (1997): 41–68; and Andrea Wuerth, "National Politics/Local Identities: Abortion Rights Activists in Post-Wall Berlin," *Feminist Studies* 25, no. 3 (Fall 1999): 601–31.

39 Compare variously Frankfurter Institut für Stadtgeschichte, Akte File S6b/72, Bd. 2, Dokumente und Materialien zum Bürgerkampf und die Hausbesetzerbewegung der 70er Jahre im Frankfurter Westend, compiled by Til Schulz; Dieter Rucht (ed.), *Von Wyhl nach Gorleben: Bürger gegen Atomprogramm und nukleare Entsorgung* (Munich: Beck, 1985); Rucht, (ed.), *Protest in der Bundesrepublik* (Paderborn: Schoeningh Ferdinand GmbH, 2003); Roger Karapin, *Protest Politics in Germany: Movements on the Left and Right since the 1960s* (Pennsylvania State University Press, 2007).

40 See Koenen, *Das rote Jahrzehnt* (Cologne: Kiepenheuer & Witsch, 2001).

41 Many have claimed that this era represented a major watershed of the postmodern turn, looking particularly to political theorists to make this case. Compare Hans Bertens, *The Idea of the Postmodern: A History* (New York: Routledge, 1995); also Marianne DeKoven,

Utopia Limited: The Sixties and the Emergence of the Postmodern (Durham: Duke University Press Books, NC, 2004); specifically on the West German case, Andreas Rödder, *Wertewandel und Postmoderne. Gesellschaft und Kultur in der Bundesrepublik Deutschland 1965–90*, "Kleine Reihe" vol. 12 (Stuttgart: Stiftung-Bundespräsident-Theodor-Heuss-Haus, 2004).

42 On communitarianism, see Cohen and Arato, *Civil Society*, 20–23 (Cambridge, MA: MIT Press, 1994). On the ability of small numbers to make their voices heard, see such fearful characterizations as "Herzlich wilkommen!" *BILD,* April 6, 1967.
43 Davis, *Internal Life,* Chapter 1 (forthcoming publication).
44 Antonio Gramsci questioned civil society's remove from the state and warned of its potential as a sphere for hegemonic cooptation, in which differing views could be easily neutralized. This anticipated Michel Foucault's assessment that civil society allowed self-expression while nonetheless controlling its power to produce change.
45 Compare Davis, *Internal Life,* Chapter 4 (forthcoming publication).

9

GENDER, RACE, AND UTOPIAS OF DEVELOPMENT[1]

Young-Sun Hong

> All human beings, irrespective of race, creed or sex, have the right to pursue both their material well-being and their spiritual development in conditions of freedom and dignity, of economic security and equal opportunity.[2]

In the late 1960s and early 1970s West Germany was embroiled in a number of international scandals involving the trafficking of young Asian women. The Indian public was enraged when it became known that 240 young Indian girls, many of them minors, had been forced to work for years as indentured workers in West Germany. Although these Indian women had been lured to Germany with the promise of a high-quality nursing education, they in fact spent most of their time cleaning toilets and mopping floors. Worst of all, many of them had to work in psychiatric institutions that were shunned by native German health care workers. The scandal became a national political issue in India, where the parliament asked the government to investigate the matter.[3]

The scandal was also publicized in Europe. In 1970 the British *Sunday Times* reported that European, and especially West German, religious orders were involved in the trafficking of Indian girls.[4] It turned out that, faced with an unprecedented shortage of novices, many religious orders were recruiting young women from Kerala because they needed someone to perform the necessary menial labor in their clinics and nursing homes. Although West Germany would have been lucky if this had been the only report on the matter, the Hong Kong *China Mail* also reported that Hong Kong girls were also being "sold" to West Germany.[5] As was the case with young women from other Asian nations, these Chinese women had been promised nursing training in West Germany, but were instead exploited as manual laborers in hospitals. Despite the gravity of these scandals, none of them led to a serious public discussion in West Germany about the plight of Asian women or the violation of their human rights.

Human rights emerged as an international policy discourse during World War II. The basic ideas were set out in Roosevelt's "four freedoms" and in the Atlantic Charter, which expressed the ideals that inspired the Anglo-American crusade against totalitarianism, and these principles flowed directly into the Universal Declaration of Human Rights. As Elizabeth Borgwardt has argued, the Atlantic Charter implied "that ideas about the dignity of the individual were an appropriate topic of international affairs" and, as such, it "marked a defining, inaugural moment for what we now know as the modern doctrine of human rights."[6] In Europe and the United States, the first payment on these promises came in the form of the postwar welfare state.

In the eyes of the European colonial powers, these principles applied only to Europe itself and to their former white settler colonies. In contrast, Asian and African peoples of color remained the object of "colonial development" policies pursued by the old metropolitan powers.[7] However, these assumptions were challenged at the 1955 Bandung conference, where the leaders of postcolonial states declared that the rights of their individual citizens depended on the rights of these nations to control their own destinies. This declaration transformed economic rights into an essential element of a broader conception of human rights, a shift that inaugurated the third generation of human rights discourse.[8]

The migration of Asian health care workers needs to be seen in the context of this redefinition of human rights in terms of the right to national development because it starkly posed the question of how to balance between the needs of the community and the rights of the individual to personal security and development. This chapter focuses on these migrant Asian health care workers who came to West Germany in the 1960s and 1970s – with a special emphasis on the South Korean women who made up the majority of these persons. Many of these Korean nurses ventured to the far side of the world in hopes of a better life for themselves and their families. However, the dreams of these young women were inseparably linked – in ways that only gradually became clear – to state-led modernization in Korea and the other countries of Asia. As Tani Barlow has argued, "What ... the post-World War II nation-state system, and later its globalization project, achieved was the materialization of women's labor in the contemporary zones of export production, sex labor, and piecework."[9]

Although the concept of development has fallen out of favor both in policy-making and academic circles in recent decades, at the height of decolonization and the Cold War it was the primary schema through which the nations of both the First and Third Worlds made sense of global patterns of socio-economic and political change.[10] However, development represented different things to different people. In the capitalist West, the ideas of development and modernization only made sense against the backdrop of the racialized representation of the Third World as a vast domain of archaism and underdevelopment that had to be carefully guided into the modern world. Development along the path marked out by modernization theory would save these countries from their own poverty and ignorance and inoculate them against the threat of Communism. In contrast, the countries of the Communist bloc saw the Third World as the object of international socialist solidarity in a common struggle against the vestiges of imperialism and the threat of neo-colonialism. But the telos of both of these narratives was an anticipated future whose realization ultimately depended on winning the hearts and minds of the peoples of Africa and Asia and reshaping them in their own image and likeness. However, these modernizing processes were not transparent, one-way processes. No matter how much the two blocs hoped to see themselves reflected in the mirror of the Third World, their Cold War blinders, reinforced by persistent racism, prevented them from seeing that these countries were themselves sovereign agents on the world stage and that they had local values and local interests that could not be fitted without remainder into either narrative of modernity.

For the nations of the Third World, development represented the path to their utopia of national independence, while for the United States and Europe development and modernization were viewed as alternatives to the socialist and Communist tendencies that were always latent – and sometimes manifest – in these nationalist projects. For many African and Asian developmental dictatorships, the collective dream of development was an important mobilizing force that evoked a deep resonance in their citizens. However, development also had its own subversive dynamism, whose contours were revealed with all desirable clarity in the case of those young, educated Asian nurses. They traveled to Germany in the expectation that their work would not only advance the government's economic development agenda, but that it would also enhance their own individual human rights by helping them escape from both material want and patriarchal rule. As I hope to show in this chapter, it is important to examine ways in which the diverse conflicts inherent in the idea of development were resolved, because this process of contention and negotiation was crucial in defining the concrete meaning of the otherwise abstract, universalistic notion of human rights. First, I argue that these development policies and the flow of migrant labor from Asia and Africa must be seen as related aspects of a larger process, one that gave rise to a transnational social space that cannot be adequately grasped so long as we attempt to conceptualize these developments in terms of categories drawn from the history of the nation-state. Second, although its conceptual and geographical borders are much more porous than was once believed to be the case, this does not mean that we must dismiss altogether the role of the state as a political actor. My chapter shows how the state serves as a "surface of articulation" between the global and the national – that is, how it influences the impact of global forces upon the interior life of the nation and, conversely, how it shapes the ways in which domestic forces are integrated into broader processes of globalization. While many scholars have defined the condition of globality in terms of flows, forces and networks operating at a variety of levels oblique to that of the nation-state, these metaphors tend to obscure the agency underlying these processes, the asymmetries embodied in them, and the all-important question of who profits from them. In contrast, I show how ideas on gender, race, and class helped structure global flows of migrant labor in the postwar decades and legitimize the unequal power relations that they embodied. Third, I argue that the construction of the postwar German welfare state cannot be fully understood unless we understand how the expanding need for low-wage health care workers in the West dovetailed with the developmental strategies of the Third World nations from which these women emigrated. Here, I hope to give the concept of globalization a more tangible, concrete form by showing how the specific features of these flows of reproductive labor were determined by states and societies competing with each other to control the local conditions under which these global labor flows would be produced and reproduced.

In recent years, it has become fashionable to use the concepts of "global woman" or "global care chain" to explain the commodification of the reproductive labor of Third World women. And, in fact, global domestic workers have become a potent symbol of contemporary globalization and its corrosive impact on the global South.[11] However, this process was already well under way in the 1960s, long before these "women on the move" became the symbol of the unevenness of contemporary globalization.[12] In countries like Korea and the Philippines during the 1960s and 1970s, the female labor force was mobilized in a variety of ways to support national, economic development: working abroad to earn vital foreign exchange and support their families, providing labor that functioned as form of a human collateral for Western development loans, working as "industrial soldiers" in the Export Processing Zone, and working as sex workers serving US soldiers and Japanese tourists. However, the terms of these employment arrangements were jointly determined by the governments on both ends of these chains. Since these governments were more interested in pursuing their own economic priorities than in the welfare of the individual women who were to be the agents of these policies, the result was to gender citizenship in ways that placed these women at a distinct disadvantage.

Yet this is only part of the story. Not only do we need to explore how the development policies of governments in both the Third and First Worlds led to the formation and reproduction of regimes of gender, race, and class at both the national and the global levels. We also need to examine how the experiences of these transnational migrant nurses often cut against the subaltern positionality into which they were forced by both their own states and racialized, gendered global labor markets. In this way, we will be able to uncover how the experience of living within these regimes sparked resistance to the inequalities on which these regimes were based, and how these women forged new forms of transnational identity and social action in the process. On the one hand, the expectations of these women would be bitterly disappointed concerning the work and way of life that they would encounter abroad, as well as their dreams of returning "home" with the education and property commensurate to their professional aspirations. On the other hand, though, these women also learned that, as much as their home was nowhere, they could make their home everywhere, but that this required a constant trouble to overturn the subalternity into which they had been positioned. In the end many of these women, whom West German contemporaries condescendingly called "girls from overseas" or "lotus girls," fashioned themselves into genuine cosmopolitans or citizens of the world.

Can the subaltern speak?

March 15, 2006 was a special day. It marked the 700th of the "Wednesday demonstrations" organized by the surviving Korean "comfort women," who had been forced to work in Japanese army brothels during World War II.[13] Since 1992, these elderly women have demonstrated – come rain or snow – every Wednesday in front of the Japanese embassy in Seoul to demand that the Japanese government admit that these women had been forced into sexual slavery for the Japanese military and to seek official compensation for the injustice they had suffered. On that 700th day, solidarity vigils were held around the world with Germany being one of the few European countries to participate in this action. On the same day, members of the Korean Women's Group (*Koreanische Frauengruppe*) in Germany performed a Korean cultural ritual in front of the Friedrich Wilhelm Memorial church in Berlin and then marched to the Japanese embassy on Hiroshima Street where they were joined by Japanese women activists.

The *Frauengruppe* was founded in 1977 by Korean nurses who were protesting against a proposed shift in West German government policy that would have ended the recruitment of nurses from non-European countries and thus forced these women to return to their country of origin when their work and residence permits expired. These women organized a campaign to gather signatures on a petition in support of their right to work and stay in West Germany, claiming that the proposed policy violated their human rights by treating guest workers as if they were "animals" or a "commodity" that could be exploited and discarded at will. Ultimately, the campaign was successful, and these women were allowed to settle permanently in Germany. The *Frauengruppe* had also supported other women's causes as well. For example, shortly after its founding, the group had raised money in Germany to support South Korean women textile workers who were fighting for the democratization of labor unions. The group also put on a piece of agitprop (entitled *Factory Light*) to win support for the Korean labor movement.

This politicization and radicalization of Korean migrant workers in West Germany and female wage workers in South Korea and the formation of such a transnational social movement took place in a specific international conjuncture. When West Germany first began to recruit Asian nurses on a mass scale in the mid-1960s, the Cold War was still at its height. By the second half of the 1970s, however, both blocs were pursuing a policy of détente, and this enabled West Germany to begin recruiting health care workers from one of the low-wage countries of eastern Europe and Yugoslavia. At the same time that the German need for Asian nurses was declining, rising oil prices and a global recession were putting pressure on those Asian states, especially South Korea and the Philippines, whose legitimacy depended on their ability to use foreign trade to fuel economic development at home. These pressures led to the unprecedented militarization of industrial relations in these two countries, which began to encourage the expansion of sex tourism to make up for declining remittances from abroad and a worsening balance of trade due to rising oil prices. It was the specific confluence of these domestic and global forces that gave rise to protest movements within each of the countries and fused them into a Korean transnational movement for human and labor rights. So how did it all begin?

"Last hope for (German) hospitals are Asians and the Third World"[14]

In an article entitled "The Federal Republic of Germany – An Underdeveloped Country," which appeared in the August 1961 issue of *Der Spiegel*, the author graphically depicted a catastrophic shortage of hospital beds and nursing personnel in West Germany. This exposé made a scandal over terminally ill cancer patients being placed in a makeshift hospital in old barracks surrounded by a rubbish heap and a morgue. The article also revealed that many overcrowded and understaffed hospitals in big cities had to turn away several hundred patients every day, and that, even if one was lucky enough to be admitted, patients were crammed together with more than a dozen other patients in small, grungy rooms.[15]

This personnel shortage was primarily due to two developments, both of which were products of the postwar modernization of German society. First, the aging of the German population, the growing importance of cardiovascular and other chronic illnesses (in comparison to acute, contagious diseases, which had dominated the health care landscape in earlier years), and the generous health care provisions of the German social insurance system meant that more nurses were required to care for the growing number of elderly persons who were being hospitalized for increasingly longer periods. This pressure on the health care system was being further intensified by advances in medical technology, which required more nurses with specific skills to monitor the new equipment.[16] But the gap between the demand for nurses and the available supply was being expanded by several social and demographic trends. The most basic problem was that German women were increasingly reluctant to move into a demanding but underpaid profession as long as the expanding economy was creating a steady stream of jobs with better pay and higher social status in industry, commerce, and trade. While religious orders had traditionally supplied a substantial proportion of the nurses employed in the nation's hospitals, by the early 1960s these orders were beginning to decline in numbers as they experienced growing difficulties in recruiting a new generation of nuns and deaconesses. In 1962, for example, West Germany faced a shortage of 25,000 such women, a grim situation that would only get worse in the next decade, according to one projection.[17]

German hospitals, however, were unable to meet their labor needs by drawing on other more industrialized European countries, which were suffering from similar shortages themselves. Nor could they draw from the less industrialized countries of southern Europe, where the underemployed female labor force lacked the necessary qualifications. The inability to find and recruit nurses from within Europe led German hospitals to look further afield to solve their labor shortage. However, this was anything but a straightforward process, and the history of Germany's "forgotten guest workers" – the tens of thousands of young Indian, Filipina, and South Korean women who came to West Germany to work as nurses from the 1960s through the

1970s – cannot be fully understood unless we take into account the connections between the expanding need for low-wage health care workers and the developmental strategies of the Third World countries that provided these workers. By focusing on this connection, I hope to show how the specific features of these labor flows, which have long been identified as one of the defining features of the current wave of globalization, were determined by states and societies competing with each other to determine the local conditions under which these global forces would be produced and reproduced and in this way to give the concept of globalization a more tangible, concrete form.

One of the key factors in determining which countries would be permitted to send nurses to Germany was what has traditionally been called "state strength." As early as 1962, the Foreign Office, the Labor Ministry, and the German Hospital Association had begun negotiating with the Filipino government to import a substantial number of nurses from that country. The Germans originally hoped to recruit Filipina nurses because they felt that the country's Catholic culture and the general knowledge of English would make it easier to integrate these women into German society. But the relative strength of the organization representing Filipina nurses, combined with traditional migration to the United States and the absence of a strong state capable of imposing its policies upon society, limited the ability of the Germans to recruit nurses on terms they found acceptable. The immigration of a large number of Germans to Central and South American countries during the nineteenth century made these Latin American countries potentially attractive places to recruit nurses. In fact, German businessmen (especially those in the medical field) frequently wrote either to German diplomatic officials in the region or to both state officials and hospital administrators in Germany itself, explaining that there were many nurses or nursing students who could be recruited to help alleviate Germany's nursing shortage. However, the German federal government was noticeably cool toward such offers. The Labor and Interior Ministries and the Foreign Office insisted that the German government retain a substantial degree of control over the entire recruiting process, and the German authorities did not feel that these countries had strong, centralized governments that would be able or willing to bring this process under their control and thus serve as reliable partners. However, the Germans found an eager and suitable partner in South Korea under the presidency of Park Chung-hee. Not only did the employment of Korean men to work in German mines, which had been going on since the early 1960s, provide a model for the state-organized sponsorship of transnational labor flows. Beginning in the mid-1960s, the Park regime, which hoped to make the steady flow of overseas remittances into a pillar of its developmental dictatorship, also asserted more direct state control over international labor migration.

However, reality did not always conform to such declarations of state principle. Despite these intentions, the Korean government only enjoyed intermittent success in controlling both the destinations of migrant women workers and their political activities, while the efforts of the German federal government to control such migration were frequently undermined by hospitals and officials of state and local government, who were more concerned with satisfying their immediate needs for nurses and nurse aides than with the niceties of national labor policy. Such factors explain why the recruitment of Indian nurses – primarily from Kerala – followed a distinctly different pattern. There, the traditionally strong direct (i.e. below the state level) connections between the Christian Churches in both countries permitted German hospitals to sidestep the efforts of the Indian state, which, despite its aspirations, remained relatively weak, to control the migration of nurses to Germany. Conversely, the policies pursued by the Philippines, where state–society relations were not dissimilar to those in India, began to resemble those of the Korean government after the 1972 coup by Ferdinand Marcos. Thus, it is this constellation of factors that explains: 1) the nature of the collaboration between the federal government in Germany and the developmental dictatorships in Korea and the Philippines to monopolize the migration of nursing labor; 2) the ongoing recruitment of Indian nurses by agencies operating below the level of the national state; and 3) the near absence of nurses from Latin American countries, despite the relative strength of their cultural connections with Germany. The remainder of this chapter, however, will focus on Korean nurses.

The German government had been bringing Korean men to Germany to work as miners since the early 1960s, and in 1964 the Korean government sought to extend this agreement to nurses. The German government, however, rejected the idea because it did not want to jeopardize ongoing negotiations with the Filipino government. That said, the slow progress of these negotiations and the initiative of the Koreans soon made Korea into the primary source of migrant labor in the health care sector. In April 1965 the Korean ambassador to Germany general Choi Dukshin authorized Lee Sukil, a Korean pediatrician employed at the Mainz University hospital, to act as an intermediary (though a few months later responsibility in this area was taken over by a government office).[18] Lee approached several hospitals in the Frankfurt area offering to recruit nurses on what the Germans regarded as very favorable conditions. The nurses would be contractually bound to the same employer for three years; air fare from Seoul to Frankfurt would be paid by the hospitals with the costs then being deducted from the nurses' monthly paychecks; and the hospitals would be permitted to select individual applicants from a list provided by Lee. The hospitals jumped at this offer, asking Lee to provide 210 nurses.[19] All of these hospitals were members of the Hofacker Association, and in the summer of 1965 the director of the association asked the Hessian Labor Office to issue work permits for these Korean nurses. In the hope of persuading officials to make an exception to German immigration law that prohibited the employment of non-Europeans in unskilled positions, the director painted a grim picture and made it clear that the government, not the hospitals, would have to bear the blame if clinics or nursing stations had to be closed due to personnel shortages.[20] Ultimately, the Hessian Labor Office granted visas to 128 Korean nurses.

On the other side of the world, the arrangement was supported by top officials, including president Park Chung-hee and the Minister of Health and Welfare, and the Korean government did everything in its power to expedite the process. Public opposition to the export of nurses by those who feared that this would endanger

Korea's own health care system were quashed by the Korean Central Intelligence Agency (KCIA), with agents beating a number of these persons and threatening them with jail sentences. This response by the Koreans gave German recruiters the impression that Korea represented an "inexhaustible" reservoir of nursing labor just waiting to be tapped by German hospitals and nursing homes.[21] The recruiting action was so successful that hospitals in other areas, including North Rhine-Westphalia and Lower Saxony, tried to get in on the action, and in response labor offices issued over 300 additional work permits for Korean nurses.[22]

The first group of 128 nurses left for Frankfurt on January 30, 1966; a second group left at the end of April; and two others followed in July of that year, along with two planes filled with men going to work as miners in Germany.[23] The German embassy in Seoul was inundated with paperwork for these nurses. The Labor Ministry, which was pleasantly surprised by both the qualifications of these Korean nurses and the relative speed at which they were recruited, instructed the Federal Employment Agency to grant permits as quickly as possible in order to avoid delays.[24] However, not everyone was happy with this program. In 1966 a Korean newspaper reported that one out of every five Korean nurses was being sent to Germany,[25] and German diplomats reported that the Korean government was subordinating the country's own need for nurses to the demands of the German market.[26]

The first groups of Korean nurses who were selected for work in Germany were especially well qualified. They had all graduated from either a four-year university or a three-year college of nursing and had already worked in one of the 21 general hospitals in Korea. And they were all young and pretty – a fact that the Korean media did not neglect to note. Their educational background alone was a marker of their privileged social position in postwar Korea, and this point was further reinforced by the fact that many of these women had arrived in chauffeur-driven cars to take the content test that they had to pass before being recommended for work in Germany. The women themselves were very excited about the opportunity to live and work abroad. For example, one of the women, K. Chang-Ja, was a classical music enthusiast who spent her free time singing in the Oratorio Choir at Yonsei University, the country's top private university. She planned to spend her spare time studying music in Germany, which was famous for its classical tradition.[27] Among the second contingent of nurses who left for Germany in April 1966 were two sisters, who were serving as nursing officers in the Korean military (the older of whom held the rank of captain). Not only did they expect to bring their professional experience to Germany, where they would have the opportunity to learn from the country's more advanced medical system. They were also planning to collaborate with their younger brother, who was then a medical student, to open their own hospital after their three-year stay in Germany.[28]

The recruitment of Korean nurses also needs to be seen as part of the West German history of efforts to make the nursing profession more attractive to young German women. The work week for nurses was steadily reduced from 54 hours in 1956, to 51 hours in 1958, to 48 hours in 1960, and finally to 40 hours in 1974. In order to forge a new, more professional image, measures were taken to relieve nurses both from unpopular housekeeping tasks – such as cleaning wards and corridors, doing dishes, transporting patients' meals, and doing laundry – and from such basic patient care tasks as bathing, feeding, bedding, and transporting patients. According to the 1958 survey, 30–40 percent of nurses' time was devoted to such activities.[29] In 1964, there were 100,000 nurses and 30,000 nurse aides in Germany. However, since the desired ratio of nurses to aides was 7:3, this indicated a shortage of about 15,000 aides. In 1966, it was estimated that there were as many as 30,000 vacancies in the nursing sector as a whole.[30] The obvious solution was to import workers from other European countries to fill this gap in housekeeping and basic-care labor, and by 1965 about 20,000 women from Mediterranean countries – Spain, Portugal, Italy, Greece, and Turkey – were employed in the health care sector, mostly as housekeepers. This represented a 400 percent increase since 1961 and a 200 percent increase since 1963. However, although German immigration policies against the employment of non-Europeans were based on the expectation that housekeepers and basic care workers could easily be recruited from the countries of the Mediterranean basin, German employers were uninterested in employing women from these countries. As the Labor Ministry pointed out with growing frustration, German hospitals actually deterred women from peripheral Europe from taking such jobs by imposing unreasonably high qualifications (they were expected to be single and have a basic knowledge of both the German language and nursing) on what was essentially unskilled work.[31]

One of the roots of this problem was the fact that German nurses had traditionally been responsible for a wide spectrum of tasks that ranged from skilled nursing duties to semi-skilled basic patient care to unskilled housekeeping. In contrast to Korea, where nurses were required to have a college degree, in Germany requirements for admission to nursing school and the social status of nurses were commensurately lower. The introduction of the new semi-professional position of "nurse aide" in 1965 was part of a broader effort to enhance the professional status of licensed nurses by "decompressing" this skill spectrum. But, in view of the persistent shortages of German women willing to take up work at the less skilled end of the spectrum of health care work, the status of German nurses could only be enhanced by displacing the problems of skill and status onto foreign nurses, who thereby found their skills devalued and their professional status diminished.

Despite their insistence on recruiting only highly qualified nurses from Korea, from the very beginning German politicians and health care administrators intended to employ these women primarily as housekeepers in their hospitals. Although German immigration law prohibited the employment of non-Europeans in unskilled positions, hospitals and nursing homes were desperate for such workers and tried to circumvent these restrictions. Both individual hospitals and the national hospital association began to pressure the government to permit the immigration of Asian women for such jobs. According to Rudolf Bernhardt, the executive secretary of the German Hospital Association, the future of the nursing profession itself would be endangered if foreign (i.e., non-European) workers weren't brought in and German nurses were forced to perform jobs that were beneath their professional expertise and status. In such a case, he argued, *German* (my emphasis) nurses would find themselves in

> [a] difficult situation in which they would have to take on cleaning duties in addition to their primary professional activity, with which they are already burdened to the extreme. It is, however, the patients who will have to bear the consequences ... If nurses are burdened to the limits of their physical and psychological capacity with tasks that lie beyond their professional responsibilities, it is likely that fewer and fewer young women will be willing to take up the nursing profession.[32]

This discrepancy had already become a topic of discussion in the German parliament (*Bundestag*). The state secretary in the Labor Ministry admitted that "Asian nurses whose degree of nursing education exceeded that of German nurses" were often exploited as housekeepers in German hospitals. But the Bundestag responded to this slippage not by insuring that these women were more properly employed in professional positions, but rather by working to liberalize immigration regulations to permit the employment of Asian women as housekeepers in the health care sector – and thus the de facto deskilling of licensed Korean nurses. For example, one Social-Democratic (SPD) parliamentarian reported that in North Rhine-Westphalia 661 hospitals and 641 old age homes were urgently trying to fill – but without success – more than 3,350 housekeeping positions. While she urged the government to recruit workers from outside Europe to fill these positions, three dozen hospitals and old age homes in that region sought to circumvent these restrictions by knowingly recruiting highly qualified Korean nurses to fill positions – in particular, in old age homes – that required far fewer qualifications and that would provide these women with far fewer opportunities to expand their professional knowledge.[33] These efforts of the hospitals to solve their labor needs by insisting on hiring only highly qualified Korean nurses, and then circumventing immigration law by employing them primarily in un- or semi-skilled work, was the source of most of the dissatisfaction of Korean nurses with their status and working conditions.

The agency of others

By the end of the 1960s, the recruitment of Asian women to work in German hospitals, which had appeared as a seemingly marginal and contingent phenomenon at the beginning of the decade, had morphed into something quite different. By 1971, there were 5,000 Korean, 3,000 Filipina, and 1,500 Indian women working in German health care institutions. In fact, German health experts agreed that their hospital operations would have collapsed without these women, especially the Koreans, who received 73–83 percent of all work permits issued to non-European health care workers between 1968 and 1970.[34] The Korean government did whatever it could to make its female labor attractive to the Germans, and by 1970, the Korean authorities had identified nurse aides as an "export" commodity for which there was high demand in Germany. In October 1969 the Korean government offered to send 500 licensed nurses, 1,000 nurse aides, and 5,000 nursing students to West Germany each year,[35] and in 1969–70, the Korean government agency for labor export signed a long-term agreement with the German government to supply "the requisite number" of nurses and nurse aides trained specifically to meet German needs.[36] This bilateral agreement marked the beginning of a second phase of nurse export, and the Korean government now set up special centers to rapidly train large numbers of nurse aides specifically to work in Germany.

However, there was one problem. Neither nurse aides nor nursing students would have any prospect of finding work in the health care sector when they returned after their three-year stay in Germany. These women were trained specifically for the demands and requirements of German hospitals, and their experiences in German hospitals were limited. As a result, those who opted to return to Korea were faced with the choice of either undergoing additional training or finding other kinds of work. Likewise, nursing students who were trained in Germany found it difficult to find employment in Korea because the German training system was considered inferior by international and Korean standards.[37] But such concerns about the welfare of individual women were quickly subordinated to the broader concern for national development, and it appears that the Korean government hoped that these women would continue to move from country to country and keep sending remittances home.[38] As the director general of the Korean Labor Office pointed out to the German Labor Ministry in December 1971, the women whom the government planned to send to Germany were "dispensable" at home.[39] But this was only one aspect of a much broader plan to exploit this surplus female labor to promote national development. The complement of this plan to send young women abroad was the opening of Korea itself to organized sex tourism for Japanese men and for "rest and recreation" for US soldiers serving in Vietnam.

Race, along with gender and class, also played an important role in the political economy of migrant female labor in West Germany. There were many factors behind the everyday racism that Korean nurses encountered in the German workplace. The long-standing bias against peoples of color was aggravated by the fact that Korean nurses did not have much exposure to the language before they arrived in Germany. However, instead of offering language courses, many hospitals used the language problem as an excuse for assigning trained nurses to work as cleaning ladies. Together with the belief that Third World people did not possess the requisite knowledge or technical skills, hospital officials felt justified in their expectation that even licensed nurses with many years of experiences in Korea should work as housekeepers for at least a year before taking on any nursing duties. According to one German nurse, "A Korean nurse, who comes to Germany without any knowledge of the language, is immediately put to work cleaning patients and dishes, because these jobs don't require much explanation."[40] According to a 1974 survey of about 700 Korean nurses and nurse aides in Germany (many of whom were skilled nurses, who had come to Germany during the 1960s), 32 percent of these women had to do *only* cleaning work, 25 percent bathing and washing patients, and 31 percent both cleaning and basic patient care. Not surprisingly, only 13.5 percent were satisfied with their work in their first year in Germany.[41] The first year was often the hardest because of the stark contrast between the expectations that these women had brought with them and the actual working conditions that they encountered. In the words of one nurse who arrived in Germany in 1971, "Initially I resisted this injustice and quietly protested. Sometimes it was very difficult to understand why I was required to do these lowly labors. But the more I resisted, the worse my situation."[42]

German prejudices against women of color were especially offensive to those nurses who had graduated from four-year nursing college and enjoyed much higher occupational status at home. Without doubt, those Korean nurses who began their first three-year contract in 1966 suffered most from the discrepancies between their professional qualifications and the menial nature of their on-site job assignments. In Korea, these nurses had been regarded as physician aides and performed advanced nursing responsibilities that had corresponded to their college or university education in nursing. In Germany, however, many of them were assigned to tasks that were intended for housekeepers and nurse aides. Working conditions were especially harsh for those Korean nurses working in nursing homes for the aged and the disabled, whose mobility was very limited. The following episode that Jung-Ja Peters experienced was not limited to one individual but widely shared among Korean nurses. She was assigned to a small Catholic nursing home for mostly bed-bound elderly in Berlin. On her first day at the new job, she got up early to get ready, and she wore a white gown, white socks, and shoes, her nurse's pin on her chest, and "what was most important – my hair was carefully combed underneath my nurse's cap. Everything was perfect and precisely done, and I looked just like a Korean nurse should have looked." However, when she arrived, she found a supervisor waiting for her with a bucket and mop. When she saw Jung-ja, without saying a word, she just gestured her to the direction of toilets and put both bucket and mop in her hands. "Without even saying 'good morning', she disappeared back to her breakfast table. At that moment, it was very difficult for me to maintain my composure. I took my cap, which was the symbol of our profession and our education, from my head and began to clean the toilets."[43]

Regardless of their qualifications, these women shared a common experience of mistreatment and discrimination, and many Korean nurses remember this as one of the most traumatic and degrading parts of their stay in Germany. In the words of one of these nurses who came to Germany in 1970:

> I am sometimes confused because I don't know whether I am a cleaning lady or a kitchen assistant. Every day, the work is the same. I remember my time in Korea, when I was responsible for medications and injections. When I applied to come to Germany, I thought about the highly developed treatment techniques that I hoped would allow me to expand my own knowledge. This has proven to be a delusion. The way things actually are now, they would be better advised to bring cleaning ladies and maids from Korea ... The result is

that I am even forgetting the techniques that I learned at the university and the hospital in South Korea.[44]

Another Korean also complained:

> I am really full of the cleaning work that I have been doing for months on end. Even maids in Korea don't do such work. The cleaning fluids that I use have made my hands so rough and swollen. Every day I hope to be assigned to some other kind of work, but they never free me from cleaning work.[45]

Again and again this common experience was most traumatic for most of Korean nurses:

> For the past two years I have worked almost only in the kitchen. My hope that in Germany I would be able to expand my professional experience has proven to be a false one. The inequality in the way they treat us is so great ... I want not only to work in the kitchen or bathe patients, but also to work at the bedside of the patients like my German colleagues ... I don't want to do the same thing all the time, but the Germans don't want to understand that.[46]

The growing number and increasing visibility of Asian health care workers in Germany did not necessarily mean that these persons had any more power to control their working conditions or combat the daily discrimination that they faced. First of all, even liberal Germans tended to dismiss what Asian nurses perceived as inequality as simply the expression of cultural differences. Although these women frequently complained about the discriminatory division of labor, German health administrators and officials portrayed the menial work which Asian nurses were required to perform as a valuable apprenticeship in work discipline and all of the other virtues of industrial modernity. These discursive politics of cultural and "developmental" difference thus served to veil both the exploitation of these women and the dependency of the German health care system upon Asian migrant workers.

Few of these women had what we might term a support network. Some attempted to commit suicide, and many more suffered from depression and other mental illnesses. While some women left Germany for the USA and Canada, others protested and sought to protect their own sense of dignity. There were many women who fought individually for their rights at work. One of these women later related how her work as a housekeeper in a German hospital made her look back on the good old days in Korea, where nurses enjoyed professional status and respectability. One day she appeared at the hospital wearing a nurse's cap, which she wasn't supposed to wear because she wasn't working as a nurse. For her this cap was a symbol of her self-esteem and dignity. But the station nurse went over to her and jerked it off her head without saying a word. When she put the cap back on, the head nurse reported her to a doctor, who then came over and jerked it off her head again. As the

Korean woman explained later, she was so humiliated and sad that these people didn't recognize her human dignity that she sat down and cried for a long time.

Here, it is important to note that the hegemonic nation-state system and its internal and exterior borders made the position of these transnational migrants more precarious and vulnerable because the collaboration between the Korean and German governments meant that there was no one to whom they could appeal to support their rights. Neither the diplomatic representatives of their home country nor German state officials were willing to intervene on their behalf because they felt that such actions would harm the public or national interests, whether this was understood in terms of the development of the German welfare state or the postcolonial economic development of the newly independent nation-states of Asia. On the part of the host country, where the Basic Law guaranteed social security to citizens, transnational health professionals were the object of a highly differentiated form of sovereignty in which they were to a much greater degree the objects of surveillance and obligation than the beneficiary of social rights. They also had few protections against being sent back home if they protested too loudly against their mistreatment or if the labor market changed. On the other hand, women occupied a notoriously subordinate position in Korean society, and Korean officials saw no reason to take vigorous action to protect their rights abroad, especially if such actions threatened or jeopardized the flow of foreign remittances that was crucial to the functioning of the regime's broader development strategy or to price Korean workers more generally out of the global market for cheap labor.[47]

"Where and what is my home (*zuhause*)?"

In the second half of the 1970s, labor market conditions in the health care sector were changing due to both the economic downturn and the changing geopolitical situation. It was against this background that the German government decided not to renew the contracts of the 16,000 non-EU nursing professionals working in the country (including approximately 7,000 Korean nurses and nurse aides). This shift represented a real threat to many of these women, who had worked for many years in Germany, because their work experience in Germany would not count for much if they returned to Korea. The Korean government did not provide any support and, in fact, pressured these women not to provoke German officials. It was at this point that it became clear to these women how much they had been exploited by both the German and the Korean governments. As one of the nurses – who became a leading member of the Korean Women's Group in Germany (*Frauengruppe*) – explained:

> At that point it became clear to me that we were only cheap labor, almost a commodity, but not humans. On top of this, German officials introduced new residence and work regulations. To get permission to work, one had to have a residence permit. However, when we went to the immigration office to get a residence permit, they told us that we had to have a work permit in order to qualify for residence. They played the same game at the labor office, and we

were bounced back and forth between the two offices. This game was set up so that we couldn't win, and we had to endlessly run the same gauntlet. They practically told us to our faces: Your contract has expired, now go home. That really opened my eyes. In their eyes, we were simply beasts of burden that could be set to work whenever one please and then sent away at will. The idea that people might have made friends, founded families, and led a personal life in the country where they worked played no role at all [in their considerations].[48]

Trapped between the two governments, neither of which was willing to support them, they decided to mobilize grassroots support from German citizens, and they eventually succeeded in achieving their immediate goal. This experience was quite a revelation for these women. As one of them later wrote, "Participating in this signature campaign was a turning point in my life. At that point, I was a young woman living alone, and cooperation with other Korean women was important. That opened my eyes for history and collective life." This campaign ultimately contributed in important ways to the development of both their character and their collective solidarity: "The signature campaign was not only a valuable experience for me; it also helped me grow. To go up to a stranger and explain my circumstances and then ask for a signature was by no means something easy."[49]

Participation in this collective venture also helped them learn how to deal with those Germans who looked down on them and disparaged their work. When one nurse first encountered such discrimination, she wrote:

> I was deeply wounded, even ashamed, so that I couldn't react at all … Later we laughed together about how afraid we had been at the beginning and how we changed in the course of the campaign, how we had become more self-conscious and assertive. Civil disobedience and resistance were concepts that were completely alien to us at the beginning. At first, it was everything but self-evident that we should stage protests and demonstrations. But we learned what was possible and that one can and must demand one's rights.[50]

The local associations of Korean nurses that had been formed in response to this threat became increasingly vocal in demanding that their grievances be redressed. The Göttingen group distributed a flier in which they complained that "the practice of making us into whipping boys for a situation that we did not cause by withholding information concerning our rights and claims and through neglect and indifference is inhumane and unjustified." They argued that, in view of how much they had contributed to West Germany, they were entirely justified in demanding that they be allowed to work in the country as long as they wished. "We believe that we are in the right," they insisted, "when we demand the right to determine ourselves when we return home so that we have the time and opportunity to prepare ourselves financially and socially for our return to Korea."[51]

The German government reversed its position, at least in part in response to these protests, and granted most of these women permanent work and residence rights. This experience led the various local associations of Korean women in Germany to form a national association in September 1978. Throughout most of the 1980s, most members of this association were nurses, many of whom were also working toward university degrees. Once they had achieved these first successes, the Korean Women's Group also encouraged its members to think in broader terms about the social, economic and political factors that conditioned their labor migration to Germany.

As mentioned earlier, this new perspective on their own situations also led these women to act in solidarity with female factory workers in Korea. Leading members of the Korean Women's Group tried to highlight the gendered nature of exploitation and subordination of women in society and the economy. The Korean Women's Group raised money on behalf of female textile workers on strike in Korea and found their sisterly act validated when Korean textile workers sent them a letter of thanks in January 1979. In this letter, these women, who were in their late teens and early twenties, explained that "we protested and opposed [the government's policy] because we could not tolerate the injustice," an experience with which the members of the group were able to identify.[52] However, it is important to note that even in West Germany it was not easy to show support for women workers in Korea. The Korean community in Germany was under the constant surveillance of the Korean CIA, and they had to censor themselves for fear of being branded as Communists. In fact, many Koreans in Germany referred to them as the "Red Groups" or "Red Communist Groups."[53] One man even threatened to divorce his wife if she did not leave the group.[54]

The twentieth century is now part of the past, and most of the founding members of the Korean Women's Group have witnessed epochal changes both in South Korea and Germany. Many of them are now in their fifties or older and work for refugees and migrants in Germany. How would they reflect on the past three or four decades of their lived transnational experiences? This mood and the underlying experiences are best described by a book entitled *Where and What is My Home?* that was published in 2006. These were the questions that a dozen members of the Korean Women's Group were asked to reflect upon, and their thoughts were gathered in this collection of essays. As the editors of the book, who are themselves daughters of group members, explain: "It is more a feeling of feeling comfortable and having arrived as a connection to a concrete place. In the end, the inner dividedness or lack of orientation that is often ascribed to migrants can't be found in any of the authors." In the end Kook-Nam Cho-Ruwwe captures the transnational experiences of these women and their multiple identities:

> I belong to both places, and at the same time I belong to no place. The search for a geographical home leads me to an inner division that permanently expels a part of me. But I want to include everything within myself. My home is everything that I was, am, and will be. It is in me. Therefore, my home is

everywhere where I was, am and will be. Every person possesses the wisdom to understand at some point the path through which she has become what she is. At such moments I sense how my previous paths from Korea, from Germany, flow out of the past and out of the future like rivers of time that flow together into the lake that is me. The separation between the spaces and the times where I have lived is dissolved beyond all delimitation. Nevertheless, I can distinguish the different colors and songs of these worlds without rending my soul. I often immerse myself in my deep sea and rediscover there my wonderful treasures. I want to flow even further in order to reach the sea.[55]

Notes

1 For an earlier version of this article, see Young-sun Hong, Verlag, 2007), 74–85.
2 May 10, 1944 "Declaration of Philadelphia" signed by representatives of the International Labor Organization.
3 West German embassy in New Delhi to the Foreign Office in Bonn, Archive of the Foreign Office (hereafter, AAA), B85/2196.
4 See also "Inderinnen für europäischer Klöster. Sklavenhandel unter christlichem Zeichen? – Heikle Situation für den Vatikan," *Badische Zeitung* (August 24, 1970).
5 According to a report from the General Consulate in Hong Kong (September 1, 1970). AAA, B85/2196.
6 Elizabeth Borgwardt, *A New Deal for the World. America's Vision for Human Rights* (Cambridge, MA: Harvard University Press, 2005), 4.
7 For more, see Daniel Maul, *Menschenrechte, Sozialpolitik und Dekolonisation. Die Internationale Arbeitsorganisation (IAO) 1940–1970* (Essen: Klartext Verlag, 2007), 201.
8 Pheng Cheah, *Inhuman Conditions. On Cosmopolitanism and Human Rights* (Cambridge, MA: Harvard University Press, 2006), 194f., citation 195.
9 Tani E. Barlow, "Asian Women in Reregionalization," *Positions* 15:2 (2007), 290.
10 Although we need to historicize the concept of the Third World and be sensitive to the heterogeneous histories, interests and ideologies that influenced the actions of these newly independent countries, I use the term to capture both the idealism of national liberation inspired by the non-aligned movement and the Eurocentric mapping of the post-1945 world that shaped the development policies and practices of donor countries in the global North.
11 See Cheah, *Inhuman Conditions*, Chapter 6.
12 Laura Hyun Yi Kang, "Si(gh)ting Asian/American Women as Transnational Labor," *positions* 5 (1997), 404, cited in Barlow, "Asian Women in Reregionalization," 290.
13 http://www.womenandwar.net. (Accessed March 4, 2009).
14 "Letzte Hilfe für Krankenhäuser sind Asien und die dritte Welt," *Welt am Sonntag* (July 27, 1969).
15 See also Anneliese Schulz, "Die Krankheit unserer Krankenhäuser. Mehr Geld – Heil Mittel gegen Schwesternmangel," *Berliner Zeitung* (date unknown, but presumably Ocotber 1969).
16 It is interesting to note here that the advancement in medical technology began to attract men into the nursing profession with the number of male nurses rising from 6.6 percent in 1950, to 8.9 percent in 1961, and to 12.9 percent in 1970. Susanne Kreutzer, *Vom "Liebesdienst" zum modernen Frauenberuf: Die Reform der Krankenpflege nach 1945* (Frankfurt/New York: Campus Verglag, 2005), 29.
17 "25000 Ordensfrauen fehlen in Deutschland," *Neue Presse* (September 29, 1962). In 1962 the University Hospital in Würzburg was forced to close three of its four

gynecology wards because the lack of younger members forced a nursing order to withdraw 36 of its members. "Eine Frauenklinik fast geschlossen," *Frankfurter Allgemeine Zeitung* (December 31, 1962).
18 Vermerk (March 17, 1966), Bundesarchiv Koblenz (hereafter, BAK) B149/22428. In the first half of 1966, Lee brought 434 nurses to the Mainz and Frankfurt area, and in the second half of that year another physician, Lee Jong-soo, recruited 638 Korean nurses to work in hospitals and nursing homes in Bonn and Düsseldorf.
19 Lee Sukil, *Building a Bridge between Han River and the Rhine* (Seoul: The Knowledge Industry Co., 1997; in Korean), 103–7.
20 Schultheis to Hessian Labor Office (August 2, 1965), BAK B149/22428. Schultheis's letter to the Korean embassy in Bonn (August 2, 1965) explicitly mentioned that Lee was acting "on behalf of" the Korean embassy, AAA B85/1319.
21 German embassy to the Foreign Ministry (August 6, 1966), AAA B85/1319, which also mentions corruption among both applicants and the Korean bureaucrats involved in nurse recruitment, and the Federal Employment Agency (hereafter, BAA) to the Federal Labor Ministry (BMA) (March 22, 1966), BAK B149/22407.
22 BAA to the Labor Ministry (April 29, 1966), BAK B149/22428. In 1966, there were 6,800 licensed nurses working in Korea, while it was estimated a few years later that some 24,000 were needed to fully staff the country's hospitals. Dr Corvoy, director of the Education Committee of the Korean Nurse Association, in *Korea Times* (March 12, 1971), AAA B85/1511.
23 German embassy to the Foreign Ministry (August 6, 1966), AAA B85/1319.
24 Vermerk (March 17, 1966), BAK B149/22428.
25 "Urgent Steps Asked to Halt Nurse-Drain," *The Korea Times* (September 14, 1966).
26 German embassy in Seoul to the Foreign Ministry (August 6, 1966), AAA B85/1319.
27 "With full excitement – to West Germany," *The Sunday News* (January 30, 1966).
28 *Chosun Daily* (April 28, 1966); and *Kyonghyang Newspaper* (April 28, 1965).
29 Susanne Kreutzer, *Vom "Liebesdienst" zum modernen Frauenberuf*, 260.
30 According to a report by the Federal Employment Agency (BAA), cited in Rudolf Bernhardt, "Die ausländische Arbeitskräfte in den deutschen Krankenhäusern," *Das Krankenhaus*, 11 (1966), 445–46.
31 The BAA to the Labor Ministry (October 20, 1966), BAK B149/22407.
32 Bernhardt, "Die ausländische Arbeitskräfte in den deutschen Krankenhäusern," 451.
33 Bundestag, 5. Wahlperiode, 69. Sitzung (October 28, 1966).
34 Irmgard Nölkensmeier, "Information über die Situation von asiatischen Arbeitnehmern und Arbeitnehmerinnen in deutschen Krankenhäusern" (January 1972), Archiv des Deutschen Caritasverbandes, 3291.024 Fasz. 6. See also the Federal Employment Agency to its service branches (July 2, 1970), and to Labor Minister (July 15, 1969), both BAK B149/22408.
35 According to Jörg Lauterbacher (German Hospital Association), cited in Labor Ministry's Vermerk (March 1970), BAK B149/22429.
36 Vermerk by Weidenbörner (April 1970), BAK B149/22432; Vermerk by Weidenbörner (August 25, 1970), BAK B149/22429. In October 1965 the Korean government created the Overseas Manpower Export Advancement Corporation (in November 1965 renamed as Korean Overseas Development Corporation, KODCO) to promote labor migration.
37 The German Development Ministry was fully aware of this problem. Ref. 314 to Ref. 102 (April 10, 1973) betr. Reise von Staatssekretär nach Korea. BAK B213/11962.
38 This point was made by the German embassy in Seoul in a memorandum to the Foreign Office (April 8, 1970), BAK B149/22429.
39 Memorandum by Wedenbörner (December 10,1971), BAK B149/22432.
40 Do-Jin Yoo, *Die Situation Koreanischer Krankenpflegekräfte in der Bundesrepublik Deutschland und Ihre Sozialpädagogischen Probleme* (Dissertation, Kiel, 1975), 209.
41 *Ibid.*, 211.
42 *Ibid.*, 212.

43 Heike Berner, Sun-ju Choi, and Koreanische Frauengruppe in Deutschland (eds.), *Zuhause. Erzählungen von deutschen Koranerinnen* (Berlin: Assoziation A, 2006), 85.
44 Do-Jin Yoo, *Die Situation Koreanischer Krankenpflegekräfte in der Bundesrepublik*, 208.
45 *Ibid.*, 225.
46 Yun-Chong Shim, *Aspekte der Sozio-Kulturellen Einordnung Koreanischer Krankenpflegekräfte in Deutschland* (Dissertation, Heidelberg, 1973), 47.
47 By the early 1970s the South-Korean government had become much more sophisticated in its surveillance of its citizens overseas.
48 *Zuhause*, 18–19.
49 *Ibid.*, 18.
50 *Ibid.*, 19–20.
51 Koreanische Frauengruppe (ed.): *Dokumentation* (no place, 1979), 13.
52 *Ibid.*, 99.
53 *Zuhause*, 23.
54 *Ibid.*, 25.
55 *Ibid.*, 40.

10

GENDER AND REFRAMING OF WORLD WAR I IN SERBIA DURING THE 1980S AND 1990S

Melissa Bokovoy

Introduction

This chapter examines the rewriting and reworking of Serbian national history that accompanied the break-up of Communist Yugoslavia, and the role historians, archivists, museum curators, intellectuals, public officials, and civic organizations played in reconstructing and resurrecting a distinct narrative of Serbia's national history as the liberator and unifier of the Balkan peoples. The historical methods and narratives employed to construct an "imagined community" are part of a web of "cultural representations and practices that produce and reproduce the meanings of the nation."[1] Embedded within the linguistic and visual representations of a particular national group is a strongly dichotomous construction of gender that gives men and women distinct roles in the family of the nation. Such gendered representations connect the perceptions, emotions, and memories of individuals with those of the collective to signify belonging.

Beginning in the nineteenth century, nationalists used essentialist ideas of the feminine and masculine when constructing national identity and the national citizen.[2] National movements and their predominantly male founders relied on the tropes of men as soldiers and fathers of nations and their states, and women as reproducers and mothers of the national (male) citizen.[3] Because the national project was initially defined by men and almost immediately became a masculine project, women's citizenship in the state and women's place in the nation have, in its nationalist context, been constructed in relation to men's. Thus, women, through their symbolic, moral, and biological reproduction, have often been portrayed as supporting the nation's creation, and rarely portrayed as its creators, founders, or geniuses.[4]

Similar assumptions operate into the present. While twentieth century European states allowed women into the political world, little thought or attention was paid to how these states continued to use constructions of gender to mark the cultural, social, political, and biological boundaries of belonging and citizenship. Even after 1945, the writing of histories in the postwar period perpetuated a gender-specific division of labor in terms of women's cultural and social responsibilities within the nation-state. Only now in the early twenty-first century, in an effort funded by the European Science Foundation, have scholars and educators in Europe come together to challenge "master narratives" of European states. Part of the purpose of this multi-country study is to examine the "construction, erosion, and reconstruction of national histories in relation to other narratives structuring diverse forms of historical writing, such as gender ... ."[5]

In the post-socialist states, historians and educators have been engaged in challenging and rewriting the master narratives bequeathed to them by both nationalist and Communist regimes. As these states rewrite and display their histories, they have been sensitive to domestic and external criticism concerning the exclusion of particular minority group's historical experience, obfuscation of their societies' culpability in the Holocaust or other genocides, and the portrayal of fascists, fascist sympathizers, or ultra-nationalists as misunderstood and misrepresented national heroes. They have paid less attention to the critiques that their newly constructed master narratives are highly gendered.[6] These master narratives, in both western and eastern Europe, still rely on nineteenth or early twentieth century nationalist histories and myths about the founding of their states, which used gender to construct national identity and belonging. Many of the new histories being written in the post-socialist states, and the public and civic remembrances celebrating their nation's past, their struggles for independence, their intellectual and military heroes, and enemy violence against their citizens, still rest on conceptions of gender polarity and binaries.

In the discussion that follows, I will examine a foundational story of Serbian national identity, Serbia's participation and experiences in the Balkan wars and World War I (i.e. "the Wars of National Liberation"[7]), as it was and is now being told, and how the telling of this story perpetuates gendered national identities. A most telling and simple example of how important it is to question the historical narrative of Serbia and World War I is illustrated by the display of an iconographic photograph of a Serbian soldier from World War I taken by Sampson Černov[8] on the cover of *History for the Eighth Grade of Elementary School*.[9] Displayed without comment or context, the soldier stares across time to students, and the photograph places the soldier at the forefront of Serbian history. Upon opening the book and reviewing the table of contents, the cover page takes on greater significance as chapter titles and subheadings represent Serbian history as "the sum of wars and suffering," and of individual and collective sacrifice and heroism on behalf of the nation and its liberation.[10] The male citizen–soldier is thus heralded as the most progressive and significant actor in Serbian history with a special place reserved for the experiences of soldiers in the Balkan wars and World War I.

During the wars of Yugoslav secession, Serbian discourses tapped into this reservoir of historical understanding as a way to explain contemporary Serbian trials and tribulations. Ivan Čolović, in his study of political symbolism in Serbia during the 1990s, noted how mass media, popular songs, advertisements and similar media appealed to the traditional values of the Serbian peasant soldier (manliness, bravery, masculinity and heroism), and to Serbia's suffering and heroism during World War I. He described how a popular Belgrade newspaper wrote of a match between Red Star, the Belgrade football team, and the Greek team, Panathinaikos, which was played in Sofia, Bulgaria in the early 1990s as a result of the sanctions against Serbia during the wars. The article opined:

> the army of the *Delijas* (Red Star fans) was as numerous as the army of Serbs led by brothers Mrnjavčević in the battle of Marica ... The miracle called FC Red Star ... can be compared only to the Serbian army in World War I. That army was also wretched and abandoned by allies and forced to leave the fatherland under the invasion of a more powerful enemy. But it survived and won on the front that was "abroad" ... "We cannot be saved, we must win." It seems that this sentence of Nikola Pašić from 1915 has become the way of life of FC Red Star.[11]

The notion of a "band of brothers," as inferred by the reference to the brothers Mrnjavčević who fought against the Ottoman Sultan, Sultan Bayezit I (r. 1389–1402), permeates this piece and highlights how brotherhood became an important concept in Serbian men's efforts to attain and defend national independence. In addition, alleged male values, such as virility, originality, vision and the search for truth were represented by great national men such as Nikola Pašić, longtime leader of the Serbian Radical Party and prime minister during the Balkan wars and World War I. These values and the camaraderie, gained by participation in war, implicitly exclude women from the nation and state building enterprise, political leadership, and the articulation of a vision for the nation. The examples demonstrate how the telling of Serbia's history is not simply the preserve of the professionals – historians, museum curators, or archivists – but also of Serbian novelists, poets, and journalists. Others such as amateur historians developing websites, civic associations established to commemorate World War I, and commercial interests selling World War I memorabilia also add to the narrative and mix memory, myth and history together. Remarkable is the consistent use of gendered language and images to tell and remember Serbia's history of its "wars of national liberation" among the narrators of Serbia's past.

Remembering and reframing World War I in post-socialist Yugoslavia

On June 28, 2001, men, women, and children of the Vojvodinian town of Karadjordjevo Selo in the Republic of Yugoslavia, now the Republic of Serbia, braved the hot and humid temperatures of early summer to gather in their town's commons. Here, in the center of their town and on the Serbian holiday of Vidovdan, the town's elite unveiled a modest statue of a World War I soldier and dedicated it to south Slavs from the Habsburg Monarchy who had fought on the side of the Serbian state during the "Wars of National Liberation, 1912–18." In attendance were a group of men who had resurrected an interwar veteran's association, the Association of Volunteers, which had been banned during the Communist period. This association not only helped raise the money for the statue but also financed a biannual journal that published articles and primary materials focused on the wartime experiences of the volunteers during World War I.[12]

Several years earlier, in the central cemetery of Zagreb, the capital of the new Croatian state, another ceremony commemorating World War I took place. This event, the rededication of the monument to fallen soldiers of World War I, was not only an act of remembrance but also one of erasure. This monument of a mother holding a dead soldier in her arms, a modern pietà, was first dedicated in 1939.[13] It had been conceived and sculpted by two prominent Croatian sculptors, Jozo Turkalj and Vanja Radauš. As the veil was lifted from the renovated monument, those in attendance saw the beautifully restored statue but its previous inscription, "To the Fallen of the First World War," had been changed to "To the Fallen Croatian Soldiers in the First World War, 1914–18."

In both of these events, local and national elites refashioned and reimagined past event. By celebrating these events ritually, they had made them present again, and mediated to the nation the meaning of World War I. The people of Karadjordjevo Selo, many of whom were descendants of the volunteers who had received land in this region for their service during World War I, laid claim to the idea that Serbia had fought for the liberation of all south Slav peoples. The name of the town, Karadjordjevo Selo, invoked memories of the two Karadjordjević monarchs Peter I, the Liberator, and Alexander I, the Unifier, who based their claims of political legitimacy in the interwar kingdom due to their wartime experiences and efforts to liberate south Slavs and create the first Yugoslavia. Members of the Association of Volunteers, not all of them descendants, had facilitated and created the means by which to commemorate and to remember World War I in the newly reconfigured Republic of Yugoslavia.[14] This ceremony, which had religious and civic leaders in attendance, reminded the audience and the citizens of Karadjordjevo about Serbian efforts and sacrifice to create a south Slavic state and brought the men who were in attendance into the brotherhood. Those organizing the event also wanted to highlight a widely held perception that these Serbian efforts had gone unrewarded and unrecognized by the Yugoslav Communists and other national groups in the Socialist Federal Republic of Yugoslavia (SFRY).

By reinscribing the pietà to only fallen Croatian soldiers, Franjo Tudjman, Croatia's first president, sought to establish a Croatian legacy of military sacrifice for national independence. During World War I, Croatian soldiers had fought on both sides of the conflict, as soldiers in the Austro-Hungarian Army and as volunteers in the Serbian Army. In addition, the original monument had recognized those who died making the first Yugoslavia a possibility, thus recognizing the sacrifices of other Yugoslav peoples. The new inscription honored only Croatian soldiers; absent were those whose national identity was not marked as Croatian. Most significant was how this monument contributed to the entire memorial site being created by the new Croatian national government in Mirogoj, Croatia's *de facto* national cemetery.

In the context of the history of the break-up of Communist Yugoslavia, the refashioned World War I monument that now represents only the Croatian fallen during World War I is symbolically and spatially connected to other monuments in Mirogoj. In addition to the pietà, there now stand two monuments that remember the Croatian fallen who suffered and died during Croatia's struggle for statehood: the monument to the Bleiburg victims and victims of the way of the cross (*Spomenik bleiburškim žrtvama i žrtvama Križnog puta*)[15] and the monument to those who fell during Croatia's recent Homeland War (*Domovinski rat*).[16] Grouped together, the three monuments remember the dead of Croatia's twentieth-century wars and create a memorial space which is designed to give Croatians "a sense of sameness over time and space."[17] The pietà, discussed above assigns to Croatian women the role of mothers and mourners of Croatian citizens. The young man lying in the mother's arm is the fallen male soldier, who, over the course of the twentieth century and three wars, sacrificed himself in order to forge a new nation. Through their efforts and sacrifices, Croatian male soldiers gave birth to the nation-state, bypassing women's procreative capabilities. In this newly refurbished public space, Croatian public officials in the 1990s narrated a story of male sacrifice for and procreation of the nation in World War I, and not during the more controversial war, World War II.[18]

The statue of the male volunteer and refashioning of the pietà are two obvious examples of the utilization of symbols and metaphors of femininity, masculinity, and family that were adapted from earlier periods of nation and state building in these states. How these statues are to be understood in their respective public spaces is that the male volunteer, represented as Serbian because of his dress, sacrificed himself for the Yugoslav ideal and ignored the selfish calls to create only a Serbian nation-state. By erecting or renovating these statues, the local and national elites of both Serbia and Croatia accepted a gender polarity – men fight battles and defend the nation, and women are the symbolic mothers and bearers of the nation. The mother in the pietà represents both a Croatian mother and "Mother Croatia," who is to mourn and remember Croatian soldiers, and is the ideal citizen. Erased from this monument are the non-Croatian soldiers who fought side by side with their Croatian compatriots to free themselves.

The public ceremony of renaming and repositioning the pietà by its national elites demonstrates but one instance, among many, when the history of World War I in the post-socialist states becomes a cultural and political instrument for constructing national identities in the twentieth first century. Serbia, however, had and has even more reason to focus its attention on its wars of the early twentieth century and Serbia's sacrifice in making the Yugoslav state. World War I was the war when Serbian declarations of heroism and defense of the western values of liberty and democracy and opposition to tyranny were unquestioned and even celebrated by the French and British during the interwar period. World War I and the creation of the Kingdom of Serbs, Croats, and Slovenes had been the pinnacle of Serbian national aspirations and resulted in the unification of all Serbs under one state, albeit a multinational one. By the late 1980s, Serbian national elites resurrected this history in order to remind their nation and other peoples of Yugoslavia that Serbia had a right to reassert itself in a post-Tito Yugoslavia.

Serbia in the 1980s

Discontent among Serbs about Serbia's position within the SFRY reemerged as a political issue with the passage of a new constitution in 1974. The constitution of 1974 created a more decentralized state, transferring power to the republics and dividing Serbia into three parts: the two autonomous provinces of Vojvodina and Kosovo, and Serbia proper.[19] With this act, some Serbian intellectuals perceived that Serbia's political power within the federation was diluted and its place in a post-Tito Yugoslavia insecure and uncertain. By the 1980s, the two northern republics of the SFRY, Croatia and Slovenia, were more economically dynamic and prosperous, and appeared poised to lead Yugoslavia toward greater liberalization of the economy and politics.[20] In addition, the two new autonomous provinces of Serbia, Vojvodina and Kosovo, did not always follow Belgrade's directives. Reflecting on Serbia's situation were some Serbian intellectuals who believed that Serbia and its male citizens were becoming disempowered and emasculated under Communist Yugoslavia.[21] Particularly disturbing to the more nationalist among them was the creation of an autonomous Kosovo and an emergent movement among Albanians to create an eighth and majority Albanian Yugoslav republic. In Serbian national history, this region had been portrayed as the "cradle of Serbian civilization" but one that had been ruled by the Ottoman Turks for five hundred years before it was (re)conquered and (re)occupied by the Serbian Army during the First Balkan war.[22]

In the first Yugoslavia (i.e., the Kingdom of Serbs, Croats, and Slovenes), public ceremonies, remembrances, and official histories fused the Balkan wars and World War I together as the "wars of national liberation," and Kosovo, as well as Macedonia, were areas that the Serbian state had "liberated" from the Ottoman Empire. Serbian soldiers had spilled their blood and died in order to free this region from Ottoman Muslim rule. The spilling of Serbian blood, first in 1389 and then again in 1912, consecrated this ground and despite a large Albanian majority living there, the idea of diminished Serbian influence in and Serbian control over this region in the 1980s generated the "Kosovo Question" (i.e., whether or not Kosovo should be granted republic status).

Beginning in the 1980s, Serbian intellectuals fixed upon the "Kosovo question" and how Kosovar Albanians had become the majority population. Despite efforts to (re)populate Kosovo with Serbian settlers over the course of the twentieth century, Kosovo always remained a majority Albanian province. However, by the 1980s, due to a variety of factors, the Serbian minority had shrunk to 10 to 12 per cent of the population. A 1986 memorandum by leading intellectuals of the Serbian National Academy of Arts and Sciences alleged systematic discrimination against Serbs and Serbia in the SFRY but that the most egregious acts were taking place in Kosovo where the Serbs of Kosovo were being subjected to "physical, political, legal, and cultural genocide."[23] In the memorandum's second section, titled "The Status of Serbia and the Serbian Nation," its authors reflected on the centuries-long struggle for independence by Serbs and how all of Serbia's sacrifices had been ignored and the final insult was when the 1974 constitution fragmented Serbia. They stated:

> A nation [Serbia] that has regained statehood after a long and bloody struggle, that has achieved civil democracy, and that lost two and half million kinsmen in two world wars underwent the experience of having a bureaucratically constructed party commission determine that after four decades in the new Yugoslavia it [the Serbian nation] alone was condemned to be without its own state. A more bitter historic defeat in peacetime cannot be imagined.[24]

The memorandum then asserted that Serbia's legal and political diminution in the institutional structures of twentieth-century Yugoslavia was not its only "defeat." Serbia was losing a demographic war in its historic heartland, Kosovo. The memorandum proclaimed, "The expulsion of the Serbian nation from Kosovo bears spectacular witness to its historic defeat." The Kosovo Albanians were not only intimidating and driving out Serbs from Kosovo but they were outpacing Serbs in their birthrates. By pointing out the declining birthrates among Serbs and that the Serbian nation in Kosovo faced "biological extinction," several highly charged sexual and gendered discourses emerged from the memorandum: Albanian women's fecundity, Albanian men's virility, Serbian women's sterility, and Serbian men's emasculation. Against the backdrop of the memorandum, rumors and unfounded accusations about Albanian men preying upon and raping Serbian women in Kosovo circulated and found outlets in Serbian media and popular culture. During the mid-1980s, newspapers wrote about and a play and a movie featured unfounded stories about the rapes of Serbian women by Albanian men.[25] Emerging from the discourse was a narrative that Serbian women had to be protected; added to this was the corollary that Serbian women also had to resume their natural roles as mothers and bearers of the national citizen. Socialism had deprived women of this natural role and had contributed to falling birthrates among Serbs. Another part of the discourse asserted that Serbian men, especially non-socialists, had to reclaim their rightful place in the state and protect the nation and Serbian women from a virile and prolific Albanian movement and its men.

The memorandum posited that socialism had emasculated the traditional manly, heroic and active Serbian male and that it was now necessary to embrace Serbia's non-socialist founding fathers, referred to in the memo as its "democratic bourgeoisie." According to the authors of the memo, it was the "democratic bourgeoisie" of the late nineteenth and early twentieth centuries who had begotten the liberation and unification of the Serbs in the first Yugoslavia. Denied to Serbs, and explicitly to Serbian men – was their proper place in the liberation story of Yugoslavia. This assertion had real poignancy for the President of the Serbian Academy at the time, Dobrica Ćosić. In the mid-1970s, he had published a novel about Serbia in World War I, *Vreme smrti (A Time of Death)* and his main protagonist, Vukašin Katić, was part of this "democratic bourgeoisie."[26] Ćosić was not alone. More than a few of Serbia's cultural and political elites set out to reclaim Serbia's preeminent position within Yugoslavia by highlighting Serbian sacrifices for and heroic role in the formation of the first Yugoslavia.

Serbian intellectuals, before, during, and after the wars of Yugoslav Succession (1991–95, 1999), narrated and commemorated Serbia's "wars of national liberation, 1912–18" through novels, films, photographic exhibits, websites, historical research, and the dedication and rededication of World War I memorials. These newly created or resurrected memory sites coded Serbian national identity as masculine, heroic, self sacrificing and exclusionary. In addition, this refashioning of World War I attempted to link Serbia to France, Britain, and other west European states to demonstrate how Serbs historically had fought on the side of democracy, liberty and freedom. Finally, when the wars broke out in the 1990s, most Serbian historians, museum curators, and archivists fixed on the suffering that the Serbian population endured in its earlier wars in order to highlight past Serbian victimization, violation and rape of Serbian women, and ethnic cleansing of Serbs. At the same time, many of Serbia's elites and its public ignored or denied the contemporary violence being committed by Serbs.

Reframing the Balkan wars and World War I in Serbia

The Balkan wars and World War I were ideal memory sites for Serbs to embrace because their positive, idealized past had been maintained and memorialized in Serbia's town squares during the twentieth century. Serbia's cultural landscape was and still is populated with World War I commemorative artifacts and activities and their offspring such as photographic exhibits, postcards, novels, textbooks, miniseries and reestablished or newly established veteran's associations. In her excellent examination of Serbia's intellectual opposition and the revival of nationalism, *Saviours of the Nation*, Jasna Dragović-Soso has observed how World War I underwent a complete historical makeover in the 1970s when Dobrica Ćosić published *Time of Death*, a three-volume historical novel about Serbia during World War I. In this novel, Ćosić portrayed how Serbs realized their dream for national unification during the Balkan wars and World War I. He touched on the themes of Serbia's greatness and hubris, its wartime martyrdom and naive belief in "brotherly South Slav nations, its constant struggle for liberation and unification" and its misplaced investment in the common Yugoslav state. As Dragović-Soso notes, "Ćosić, in his commentary on this work, wrote 'In every one of my literary heroes, I saw the people.' All of his characters were the embodiment of the nation as well as carriers of the national destiny as a whole."[27] Ćosić, who extensively researched this novel, defined Serbia's wartime drama not only as one of heroic enterprise but also as proof of the nation's tragic destiny to strive for liberty and greatness. But Dragović-Soso and others failed to note that all of these heroes and faces were male. Serbia's fate and destiny were solely in the hands of figures like Vukašin Katić who willingly gave up their lives but who learned their love of nation and need for sacrifice from their mothers.

It has been articulated and argued by Anne McClintock, Katherine Verdery, and others, that nationalism has typically sprung from masculinized memory.[28] However, to really interrogate such an idea means to look at how remembrances become collective and gendered even when women themselves are participating in creating masculinized collective memories or are used as symbols. In Ćosić's work women were conspicuously absent, as they were in the earlier commemorative activities. During the interwar period, not only were women's experiences excluded from the historical narrative of the war, but Serbian and south Slav women's memories appeared to be excluded from public ceremony and consolation as well. Remembering Serbia's war dead in the 1920s and 1930s honored the fallen soldier as the ideal national citizen, sacrificing his life so that the nation might live. In ceremony and ritual, a soldier's death was transformed from fatality into continuity through acts of struggle and war, and these practices of war were largely the preserve of men.[29]

The historical resurrection of World War I continued during the 1990s as Serbia sought to distance itself from the Wars of Yugoslav Succession (1991–95), the war in Kosovo, and Serbian culpability for the brutalities and atrocities committed. Turning to a moment in their history when the Serbian nation fought on the side of the western democracies, Serbian cultural, religious, and nascent civic organizations resurrected traditions, historical legacies, associations, publications, and war memorabilia that commemorated World War I. Activities included: the reestablishment of the Association of War Volunteers, 1912–18; the reissuing or creation of postcards, photographs, and memoirs from World War I; conducting oral histories with surviving veterans; curating museum exhibitions; holding academic conferences; selling and reselling cultural artifacts like photographs, uniforms, guns, flags, war albums, photographs, and postcards in antiquarian shops and in the markets; and producing movies and miniseries about Serbia and the World War I.[30]

The Serbs, as discussed below, sought a useable historical past in order to make sense of their experiences in the twentieth century, and World War I came to represent an experience whereby Serbs selflessly sacrificed and heroically died for a united south Slavic state. World War I and its memory were woven into a "system" of cultural representations and practices that produced and reproduced the meanings of the Serbian nation. As many have observed, these efforts are by no means simply explicit designations of the nation – the national flag, the national anthem, or national narratives. Explicit designations are ultimately connected to words and images that are understood within the community and that build on this understanding. Alon Confino writes that national memory can offer insights not only into "what people remember of the past, but also how they internalize an impersonal world by putting it in familiar and intelligible categories."[31]

World War I photographs: Then and now

During the 1990s, Serbian curators, researchers, and historians dedicated much effort to cataloging and publicizing the photography of World War I photojournalists, especially Rista Marjanović. Marjanović (1885–1969) was a Serbian photographer who took a leave of absence from his job as illustrations editor at the European edition of the *New York Herald* in order to document the First Balkan War and then

World War I in Serbia.[32] Not only were Marjanović's photographs featured in a 2002 exhibition of Serbian military photographs from the "wars of national liberation" but a compilation of his photographs from 1912–15 had been published earlier by the Archive of Serbia in 1987.[33] In the early twenty-first century, this compilation was made available on the World Wide Web by the *Rastko* project which presents "Serbian culture and history to the World Wide Web."[34]

During the Balkan wars and World War I, Marjanović framed his shots to capture the courage, heroism, and determination of the individual Serbian soldier, the selflessness and sacrifices of Serbian women, and the defeat of Serbia at the hands of barbarous enemies. Marjanović froze in time the grieving women, abandoned children, heroic men, and the tragic "exodus" of Serbs from their homeland in November–December 1915. After the "exodus," Marjanović gathered his photographs and at the behest of the Serbian High Command and royal government, both in exile on Corfu, made his way to Paris. There he assembled his photographs into an exhibition with the explicit purpose of showing Serbia's allies the "heroic struggle of the Serbian army, the pain and suffering of the Serbian people, and the crimes of the occupiers [Austrians and Bulgarians]." However, Marjanović's efforts were not confined to commemorating his people's struggles to the outside world. After the war, Rista Marjanović embarked upon an effort to publish his war photographs.

Asking for support from the Kingdom's Ministry of Education, Marjanović wished to compile his photographs into an inexpensive album. In his request for a subvention to the Ministry of Education, Marjanović detailed to the ministry the significance and importance of this commemorative album. Based on his expertise, the photographer argued that there was no more powerful medium for conveying a point of view than illustrations and photographs and that the publication of his photographs would commemorate "the horrible suffering and sacrifices of the Serbian people during the long war whose suffering during the war and the retreat through Albania is now being remembered only as a horrible dream. A free people must not forget the sacrifices made for this freedom."[35] After this appeal against forgetting, Marjanović asked the Ministry of Education that his photographs, as well as documents from the war, be copied and made available in the form of an inexpensive album "to the people, to schools, to the barracks, to cafes."[36] The commemorative significance of such an album was not lost on Marjanović as he ends his request thus: "This work represents a historical moment which the [Serbian] people will guard, love, and cherish."[37]

Marjanović proposed dividing the album into four chapters, each representing the four main periods of the Serbian people's struggle for liberation and unification, "The Balkan Wars, 1912–13," "The War Years, 1914–15," "The Exodus [through Albania]," and "Unification and Liberation." Marjanović never published this album. Instead, in 1926, Marjanović participated in a photographic exhibition at the Officer hostel in Belgrade. His photographs focused on 1912–15 with a special emphasis on the retreat of the "Serbian people and army through Albania."[38] The last photograph in the exhibition depicted the crossing of the Serbian Army into Albania in December 1915 and thus only the first sixteen months of the war and the two Balkan wars were on display.

Despite Marjanović's failure to publish his photographs, archivists at the Archive of Serbia in 1987 realized Marjanović's vision and published his photographs. Dr Dragoje Todorović in the introduction noted how the album captures the essence of the Serbian soldier by making available images from the Serbia's early twentieth century wars. He wrote:

> Aware of the historical moment in which he found himself, the Serbian soldier resolutely entered into an unequal fight by developing a broad banner of freedom and national independence. Armed with the sword of justice and truth, he found the strength to persevere in the difficult struggle, overcame all challenges, celebrated the victory won through force of arms, and trumpeted the ideals for which he fought. This time of great wars has left a deep imprint in the minds of the Serbian people. This crown of glory of legendary heroes and their history is bequeathed to his descendants.[39]

When placed in the same discursive space as Ćosić's *Time of Death*, the Serbian Memorandum, and historical research on World War I in Serbia, the publication and then later exhibition of Marjanović's photographs valorized the citizen–soldier as the leading actor in Serbian history.

Absent from Todorović's introduction is mention of those photographs that depict women, children, and civilians caught in the maelstrom of war − a lost child crying, mourners of the dead, families abandoning their homes, and soldiers collapsing and left for dead on the footpaths of the mountains of Albania. Nonetheless, the inclusion of these photographs reinforced an emerging narrative being written into Serbia's elementary and secondary school history texts during the 1990s and beyond, the idea of the nation as a "victim" or the "nation-victim." As pointed out by a leading expert on Serbian history textbooks, Dubravka Stojanović, children as young as nine years old read about Serbia's past as "a sum of wars and suffering" and that Serbs were "the historical victim of all neighboring … people."[40] The victims in these textbooks were highly gendered: Serbian women and children as victims were juxtaposed with those who had heroically sacrificed themselves for freedom, the Serbian males. Stojanović pointed to the valorization of two individuals from World War I, Gavrilo Princip, the assassin of the Archduke Franz Ferdinand, and Major Gavrilović, who according to myth, declared to his troops during the 1915 defense of Belgrade that their regiment had been erased from the list of the living and therefore should give their lives to defend Serbia. The public presentation of Marjanović's photographs which are now readily available on the internet paralleled these textbook narratives.

In addition to the publication and display of the Marjanović's photographs in the last two decades, additional visual records of the Balkan wars and World War I resurfaced: Dušan Šijački's illustrated periodical, *Balkanski rat* (1912 and 1913) and his World War I illustrated magazine, *Vidov-dan: Ilustrovana istorija srpskih rata, 1912–1918* (*Illustrated History of the Serbian Wars, 1912–1918*), and Andra Popović's massive photographic war album, *Ratni Album* (1926), which was reprinted in 1987. Šijački,[41] a Serbian journalist and publisher, utilized the cultural templates of medieval Serbia and

Serbia's century long struggle against its neighbors and the Ottoman Turks in his two short-lived illustrated journals. These two journals are replete with stories and photographs of male heroism, superhuman efforts and sacrifices, and with expressions of love for the Serbian nation. In *Vidov-dan*'s first issue, published in 1918 in Geneva, Šijački chose to represent Serbia's wars as wars for the liberation and unification of all south Slavs and accomplished by the sacrifices and heroism of the Serbian people. The title not only betrayed the journal's vision but the cover design tied the Balkan wars and World War I (1912–18) to the Battle of Kosovo in 1389. The journal's editorial statement declared that initially *Vidov-dan* would introduce to its readers "the history of our glory and our torment, our victory and our suffering" but that its goal would be "to protect from forgetting, to remember those wonderful heroes on whose graves rest our glory and from whose death will spring our life and our happiness."[42]

The task Šijački set out for the journal was to produce a visually accessible and readable history of the Serbian experience during the war for those who fought or whose loved ones had fought and died. In the first group of photographs,[43] Šijački displayed photographs of Serbia's wartime leaders, beginning with photographs of King Petar and his heir, Prince Aleksandar and then photographs of the Serbian parliament, the Yugoslav Committee, the prime minister Nikola Pašić, Prince Djordje, and Serbia's generals in 1918, Stepa Stepanović, Živojin Mišić, Petar Bojović, and Božidar Terzić. The editors introduced the picture of King Petar with two lines from the poem *Tomislav* by the Croatian writer Vladimir Nazor: "I guard the hearth of the fathers, a lion guarding native rivers and valley."[44] Above Prince Aleksandar's photograph they placed several lines from a Serbian national poem: "He is a child of generations of hajduks, a heroic heart of freedom." These lines were chosen in order to tie Petar and Aleksandar to well known figures from the south Slavic past. Followed as these photographs were by photographs of Serbia's political and military leaders left little to the reader's imagination about who had led the Serbs out of their exile and to victory and unification with the other south Slavs.

Lieutenant-Colonel Andra Popović, the wartime director of the Serbian Army's photographic division, worked for several years on a comprehensive war album, one that not only included the Balkan theater but all theaters of the Great War. Simply titled, *Ratni Album, 1914–1918,* Popović's album was a "monumental and voluminous" album of 448 pages and 1,500 pictures which was "a photographic collection of the personalities and events of the war in all countries." In this album, Popović gathered the photographs of wartime photographers, including Marjanović and Sampson Černov in order to create "a token of gratitude and glory for all the living and the dead participants in the Great War, to our own people, as well as to our Allies, the known and the unknown, to all those who, fighting for honor, justice, and Freedom, have with the help of God, contributed toward the realization of the Liberation and the Unity of our nation."[45] Popović's album celebrated a patriotism that tied Serbian history and military defeats, sacrifices, and victories to the foundation of the new Kingdom. He made reference in this album to the defeat of the Serbs by the

Turks at Kosovo Polje, Serbian victories during the Balkan war and first four months of World War I, the retreat through Albania, and then the late wartime victories along the Salonika Front.

While Popović claimed responsibility for the way he presented the photographs in the album, he was operating in a discursive space where these images had already been circulating and shaping the understanding of the Balkan wars and World War I for almost twelve years. By 1926, Popović's album elaborated truth claims that had been established during and immediately after the war at home and aboard. Popović greatly added to the discourse surrounding Serbia's heroic efforts to liberate and unify the south Slav nations, and his patriotic album was seen "as a lively panorama of the world war, as contributing to the patriotic upbringing and sense of purpose for the next generation, and internationally as the most significant record of the superhuman efforts and unbearable sacrifices of our [Serbian] people."[46]

Černov and Marjanović's photographs had served the purpose of narrating Serbia's war to its allies and those in exile. Popović's album sought to instill a "patriotic upbringing and sense of purpose for the next generation." This sentiment was echoed by others, like Marjanović, who believed it was a necessity to remember the suffering and sacrifices of the Serbs for the liberation of the south Slavs and creation of the south Slavic kingdom. What emerged from the wartime displays of photographs were distinct visual images: the fragile, yet determined liberator King, the successful military commander in the field and unifier of the south Slavs – the prince regent; Serbian military commanders as heirs to the hajduk tradition who were fighting infidels and conquerors; the loyal, tough, and patriotic Serbian peasant soldier; the south Slav volunteer fighting for the unification of all south Slavs; the selfless, fearless, compassionate, courageous, and victim–martyr Serbian woman depicted sometimes as mythical figures from Serbia's past or as the mourner.[47] Černov had grouped together many of these images into his postcard collection, *The Serbian Warrior*,[48] and sold it abroad to support the Serbian Relief committee. Popović, in his album, chose to redefine and re-remember those who were Serbia's warriors with the intent of constructing a narrative of sacrifice of the self to the collective ideal of the liberation and unification of south Slavs and the high moral purpose of protecting the new kingdom.

By the late twentieth century and immediately after the end of the wars in former Yugoslavia, the curators of the Military Museum in Belgrade utilized all of these visual resources to advance the argument that the Serbian people had been victimized and suffered, albeit at an earlier time. The photographs featured on the web and in the exhibition, "War painters, amateur photographers and photojournalists in the Serbian Army, 1914–18," were arranged and displayed in order to capture the struggle and sacrifice of the Serbian people against the backdrop of frightful and appalling conditions of war, conquest, occupation, and victory in Serbia's World War I. The photographs of women – especially those who had been killed or abused – served as metaphors of the homeland as a female body, one which had been trespassed upon, mutilated, raped, or murdered. These photographs drew public attention away from similar photographic images coming out of the Bosnian war of 1992–95 and the attempted 1999 ethnic cleansing of Kosovo. These conflicts were both the result of Serbian aggression and violence. Images from the Balkan wars and World War I reminded the Serbian public of their vicitimization and suffering with the goal of relativizing the violence being perpetuated by Serbs against the other nations of Yugoslavia in the late twentieth century.

The photographs circulating in these complex historical, mythical, and physical spaces contributed to the historical and fictional narratives constructed around Serbia's participation in the Balkan wars and World War I, not only during the interwar period, but also in the early twenty-first century. Of course, a photographer captures a specific moment in time, but the original context and intent of the image depend upon a viewer's experience, knowledge and sensibility. Thus, according to John Berger in *About Looking*, one ties an image to social and political context and often to a corresponding moment in the present.[49] In the twenty-first century, those who consumed these earlier images of the Serbian experience in World War I inscribed a meaning upon them but within a web of remembrances and the rewriting of history.

Conclusion: Remembrances and the rewriting of history

The introduction of new history textbooks for Serbian school children and high school students (gymnasium) which began in 2002 stirred an ongoing controversy about how Serbia's history was being presented.[50] One of the first textbooks published, *Istorija za III razred gimnazije prirodno matematičkog smera I za IV razred gimnazije opšteg i društveno-jezičkog smera* (for fourteen- and fifteen-year-olds), received well-warranted criticism. While critics found much to critique, the section on World War I is one of the longest and most significant parts of this text. It is thirteen pages, compared to two paragraphs on the late-twentieth-century wars in Slovenia, Bosnia, Croatia, and Kosovo. According to Keith Crawford, an expert on nationalism and textbooks, "these pages use powerful and emotive language to describe events, issues and historical themes such as liberation, democracy, freedom." In addition, the section included descriptions of Austro-Hungarian brutalities and acts of violence and utilized the reminiscences of a Serbian general from the early months of World War I in Serbia and quoted the following from him, "The Austro-Hungarian military is committing bestial acts and brutality in our villages. Everywhere I can find a group killed, most of them women and children, some had been hung and some shot, some children as young as ten."[51] This passage echoed the script of the public photographic exhibition on World War I mentioned above and the theme of a collection of documents published in 2000, titled *The Suffering of the Serbian People in Serbia, 1914–1918*. On the cover of this compilation was an oft-reproduced photograph of three dead women hanging from crosses in front of Austro-Hungarian soldiers.[52]

In the high school history textbook, the authors often referenced the heroism of Serbian soldiers and used the remembrances of soldiers. One passage quotes a Serbian general addressing the "defenders of Belgrade:"

> The soldiers who are called upon to fight for the town of Belgrade must shine like a light. You are all soldiers and heroes and all must fight until we are dead. When we die we die with glory, long live Belgrade.[53]

This passage might resonate among Belgrade school children. As they visit the main sports complex in Belgrade, located on the right bank of the Danube, they might pass by the 1988 monument to Major Gavrilović and the defenders of Belgrade and pause long enough to read the inscription, which reads:

> At three o'clock sharp, the enemy must be crushed by your mighty charge, torn to pieces by your grenades and bayonets. The honor of Belgrade must be spotless. Soldiers, heroes, The Supreme Command has erased our names from its roll. Our regiment is sacrificed for our King and Fatherland. You don't have to worry anymore about your lives that no longer exist. So forward, to glory! Long live the King! Long live Belgrade![54]

Another critic of the text, Olivera Milosavljević, a professor of history at the Philosophical Faculty of Belgrade, warned that nationalism was being rehabilitated in this textbook. She observed, "The word 'war' is mentioned more than 400 times in the history textbook printed in 2002. The word 'culture' is mentioned only 20 times, and the words 'general' and 'artillery' are mentioned more times than [is] culture."[55] She also stated "the textbook does not contain any photographs of pioneers in social democracy. But there are plenty of photos of Chetnik officers and more than 60 other generals, colonels, and majors."[56]

Critics of these textbooks pointed to the nationalist interpretation of Serbia's past, especially its reliance on World War I and military traditions in order to instruct the next generation on its duty to defend the nation. At the same time, these critics were silent about the gendering of this national history. Critics concluded that the textbook placed national sacrifice, the martial spirit, myth and legend at the heart of Serbian national identity but they ignored the implication of the choice of subject matter. By focusing on the war, especially World War I, the heroic sacrifice of male soldiers and the victimization of the Serbian nation, the authors of this high school textbook used women as symbolic capital.

The distinct narratives and collective remembrances now being mobilized are shaping new forms of national identity and citizenship in the successor states of Socialist Yugoslavia. School curricula, public holidays, and commemorative activities being developed in the region seek to provide a sense of belonging to their states and their nations, to define the nature of citizenship, and to integrate their communities into Europe. The instructional value of such activities is commented upon by Čolović, who writes, "nationalist ideology in Serbia, as elsewhere, has displaced historical and linear temporal conceptions and instead stopped time and transformed it into the eternal present or the eternal return of the same. In time conceived in such a way, the current wars which Serbs lead are merely the continuation of their previous history or, to be more precise, its mere repetition."[57] Not only have Serbian elites fixed upon their nation's past experiences in World War I in order to escape their nation's responsibility for the brutalities of the 1990s but they have embraced a gender ideology that promotes a martial and masculine spirit for its citizens, male and female. As Ann McClintock and others have pointed out, social representation, historical memory, and identity in national histories narrate a story where the nation has a deep patrilineal tradition, and men give birth to the nation, thus claiming the nation's procreative function. Women are left out of the national story.

Notes

1 Silke Wenk, "Gender Representations of the Nation's Past and Future," in Ida Blom, Karen Hagemann and Catherine Hall (eds), *Gendered Nations: Nationalisms and Gender Order in the Long Nineteenth Century* (Oxford and New York: Oxford International Publishers Ltd, 2000), 63.
2 *Ibid.*
3 Nira Yuval-Davis in *Gender and Nation* (London: Sage Publications, 1997).
4 Katherine Verdery, "From Parent-State to Family Patriarchs: Gender and Nation in Contemporary Eastern Europe," *East European Politics and Society* 8:2 (Spring 1994): 225–57.
5 European Science Foundation, "Representations of the Past: National Histories in Europe," http://www.esf.org/publication/171/NHIST.pdf. Accessed January 12, 2007. See also Stefan Berger and Chris Lorenz (eds), *The Contested Nation: Ethnicity, Religion, Class and Gender in National Histories* (Basingstoke: Palgrave Macmillan, 2009) and Jitka Maleková's chapter, "Where Are Women in National Histories?"
6 For examples, see controversies on Polish responsibility in the Holocaust caused by the publication of Jan Gross, *Neighbors: The Destruction of the Jewish Community in Jedwabne, Poland* (New York: Penguin, 2004).
7 The expression immediately used after 1918 in the kingdom to describe the two Balkan wars and World War I took on multiple meanings and usages. Depending on the context, liberation could mean liberation of the Serbs from the Ottoman Turks, the dominance of Austria-Hungary, the driving out of the Germans and Bulgarians from captured territories, the liberation of all of the south Slavs from their overlords, or a combination of all of the above. The political usage of the term must not be underestimated or overlooked when used.
8 During the Balkan wars and World War I, Sampson Černov, a Russian Jew with French citizenship, was sent to the Balkans by the Russian newspapers, *Novoe Vremya* and *Russkoe Slovo* of Petrograd, and also filed dispatches and photographs as a special correspondent for the French newspaper, *L'Illustration*. After the winter retreat of 1915, Černov compiled his photographs and created a touring photographic exhibition which first toured Great Britain and then the United States.
9 N. Gačeša, Lj. Mladenović-Maksimović and D. Živković, *Istorija za 8. razred osnovne škole*, 1st ed. (Beograd: Zavod za udžbenike i nastavna sredstva, 1998).
10 Dubravka Stojanović, "Slow Burning: History Textbooks in Serbia, 1993–2008," in Dimou (ed.), *Transition and Politics*, 145 and 146. Her critique implicitly points to the gendering of these narratives but stopped short of applying gender analysis to these narratives.
11 Ivan Čolović, *The Politics of Symbol in Serbia* (London: Hurst and Company, 2002), 267 and "Društvo mrtvih ratnika," *Republika,* 145/146 (1996), 4.
12 The Association of War Volunteers, 1912–18 (Udruženja ratnih dobrovoljaca, 1912–18) was established after World War I and had chapters throughout the Kingdom of Yugoslavia. After World War II, the association was banned by the Communists. In 1990, it was reconstituted and at that time the association began publishing the journal, *Dobrovoljački glasnik*.
13 This monument was dedicated in 1939 just as the Croatian banovina (province) was negotiating greater autonomy within the Kingdom of Yugoslavia and Nazi Germany was occupying Czechoslovakia and dismembering it. The monument, which had been

many years in the planning, was a gesture of reconciliation for the sacrifice of those who had died in World War I, regardless of nationality.
14 In 2001, the Republic of Yugoslavia consisted of the following regions and states: Vojvodina, Serbia, Kosovo, and Montenegro.
15 The monument, titled "Bleiburg victims and victims of the way of the cross" (Spomenik bleiburškim žrtvama i žrtvama Križnog puta), commemorated the deaths of over 45,000 Croatian Ustasha soldiers, opponents of the Communists, and civilians who fled the Independent State of Croatia into Austria and were executed or forced to turn back near Bleiburg, Austria. Tudjman's government also dedicated a memorial grave site to German soldiers who died on Croatian territory during World War II.
16 In the former Yugoslavia, even the act of describing the conflict during the 1990s remains contentious. The Croats call it the "Homeland War" and celebrate it as a war of independence.
17 Alon Confino, "Collective Memory and Cultural History: Problems of Method," *American Historical Review* 102 (December 1997): 1386–89.
18 The scale and nature of the wartime "Independent State of Croatia," remained highly contested in the post-Yugoslav period.
19 Nicholas Miller in *The Nonconformists: Culture, Politics, and Nationalism in a Serbian Intellectual Circle, 1944–1991* (Budapest: Central European University Press, 2007).
20 For a discussion see Dijana Pleština, *Regional Development in Communist Yugoslavia: Success, Failure, and Consequences* (Boulder, CO: Westview Press, 1992).
21 See Nevena Ivanović, "Appropriation and Manipulation of 'Women's Writing' in the Nationalist Discourse in Serbia in the Nineties," *REC: Časopis za književnost i kulturu, i društvena pitanja*, no. 59/5 (September 2000): 254.
22 In Serbian nationalist discourse, Serbia's defeat of Ottoman forces in the First Balkan War and annexation of a portion of the vilayets of Manastir of Kosova as result of the Treaties of London (1913) and Bucharest (1913) was portrayed as a "return" to these areas after almost 400 years of rule by the Ottoman state.
23 "Memorandum" (1986), Serbian Academy of Arts and Sciences (SANU) in Gale Stokes, *From Stalinism to Pluralism* (Oxford: Oxford University Press, 1996). Miller in *The Nonconformists* provides a succinct summary of the memorandum.
24 Ibid.
25 Wendy Bracewell, "Rape in Kosovo: Masculinity and Serbian Nationalism," *Nations and Nationalism* 6 (4), 563–90. Bracewell gives an excellent summary of these issues, as does Julie Mertus in her chapter about the alleged rape of a Serbian Kosovar by Albanians in the late 1980s. See Julie Mertus, *Kosovo: How Myths and Truths Started a War* (Berkeley, CA: University of California Press, 1999).
26 Miller in *The Nonconformists,* 215–27 points to how Ćosić believed the best way for understanding Serbia's past was through the novel.
27 Jasna Dragović-Soso, *"Saviours of the Nation"* (Montreal: McGill University Press, 2003), 90.
28 See Anne McClintock, "Family Feuds: Gender, Nationalism and the Family" in *Feminist Review: Nationalisms and National Identities* 44 (Summer 1993).
29 This idea has been developed in Jay Winter's *Sites of Memory, Sites of Memory* (Cambridge: Cambridge University Press, 1996).
30 Dobrica Ćosić penned the screenplay for *Kolubarska bitka* (1990) and in the late 1990s a mini-series about the English nurse Flora Sandes who became a commissioned officer in the Serbian army was produced.
31 Alon Confino, "Collective Memory and Cultural History: Problems of Method," *American Historical Review* 102 (December 1997): 1386–403.
32 The initial invitation to document the Balkan War came from Dragutin Dimitrijević-Apis, chief of Serbian Intelligence in 1912 and head of the secret society, Black Hand, which was implicated in the assassination of Franz Ferdinand.
33 Rista Marjanović, *Ratni Album, 1912–1915* (Beograd: Arhiv Srbije, 1987).

34 Rista Marjanović, *Ratni Album*. http://www.rastko.org.yu/fotografija/rmarjanovic/uvod_l.html. Accessed February 16, 2007.
35 Rista Marjanović to Press Bureau of the Ministry of Foreign Affairs, Predmet Piktorijalna Propaganda, 5 Novembra 1920. Arhiv Jugoslavije, Fond 66, Fascikle 631, Jedinica 1041.
36 Ibid.
37 Ibid.
38 "Izložba dokumenata o odstupanju srpskoga naroda i vojske kroz Albaniju 1915. godine," *Politika*, 4 January 1926, str. 5 and 20 January 1926, str. 4. Exhibition documenting the retreat of the Serbian people and army through Albania in 1915.
39 Marjanović, *Ratni Album*, p. ii.
40 Stojanović, "Slow Burning: History Textbooks in Serbia, 1993–2008," p. 145.
41 Dušan Mil. Šijački was the first president of the Belgrade section of the Yugoslav press association. Before the war, he had served as a correspondent in Slovenia, and was a member of the Serbian press association.
42 Review of *Vidov-dan: Ilustrovana istorija srpskih rata, 1912–1918*, *Vojni Vjesnik*, 1:8 (August 1921), 32.
43 *Vidov-dan: Ilustrovana istorija srpskih rata, 1912–1918* (Geneva: Srpski kurir, 1918), 1–15.
44 Original text: "Čuvar sam vjerni ognjišta otaca!, Lav stražar rodne rijeke i doline."
45 Andra Popović, *Ratni Album, 1914–1918* (Uredništvo Ratnog Albuma, Beograd, 1924), 4.
46 Ibid., 356.
47 The mythical figures are: Kosovo Maiden and the Mother of the Jugovići, the medieval persons of Queen Milica, the Lady Rosanda, and Princess Jerina.
48 In the collection there were fourteen colorized photographs which contained the following images: Portraits of King Petar of Serbia, the Prince Regent Aleksandar, Nikola Pašić, the Minister of War, and General of the Second Army, Stepa Stepanović; there were also cropped shots of a Serbian artillery colonel, a Serbian soldier on watch captioned "Eagle Eye," a little boy with an outstretched hand captioned "Please help my country," a soldier carrying a child in his arms, a young boy whose arm is in a sling captioned "Bomb thrower of Belgrade," and a dead soldier lying on the ground captioned "Last passenger." Some of these images are discussed later. Sampson Tchernoff, "Serbian Warriors," Getty Research Institute, Research Library, Special Collections. Malvina Hoffman papers, Box 31, Folder 3.
49 John Berger, *About Looking* (New York: Vintage, reprint 1992).
50 For a longer discussion of the controversy surrounding this textbook, see Keith Crawford, "Culture Wars: Serbian History Textbooks and the Construction of National Identity," *International Journal of Historical Teaching, Learning and Research*, 3:2 (July 2003) and Keith Crawford (with Marijana Mirković) "Teaching History in Serbia and English Secondary Schools: a cross-cultural analysis of textbooks," *International Journal of Historical Teaching, Learning and Research*, 3:2 (July 2003).
51 Crawford, 8.
52 Sladana Bojković and Miloje Pršić, *Stradanje srpskog naroda u Srbiji, 1914–1918* (Beograd: Istorijski muzej Srbije, 2000), 69.
53 Crawford, 9.
54 The monument is entitled "Spomenik majoru D. Gavrilović? u i braniocima Beograda 1915" (Monument to Major D. Gavrilović and the Defenders of Belgrade).
55 Cited in Goran Tarlac, "History Revised," *Balkan Reconstruction Report*, June 25, 2003.
56 Ibid.
57 Ivan Čolović, "Die Erneuerung des Vergangenen" in Nenad Stefanov and Michael Werz, eds. *Bosnien und Europa. Die Ethnisierung der Gesellschaft* (Frankfurt: Fischer, 1994), 91. Cited in Florian Bieber, "Nationalist Mobilization and Stories of Serb Suffering: The Kosovo Myth From 600th Anniversary to the Present," *Rethinking History* 6:1 (Spring 2002), 97.

11

POST-SOVIET MASCULINITIES, SHAME, AND THE ARCHIVES OF SOCIAL SUFFERING IN CONTEMPORARY LITHUANIA

Arturas Tereskinas

Introduction

Lithuania remains one of the most paradoxical gender regimes in Europe. Despite the implementation of a variety of gender equality directives and documents, including the Law on Equal Opportunities for Women and Men (1999) and the 2003–4 State Program of Equal Opportunities for Women and Men, the principle of gender equality is still more a slogan than reality in Lithuania. In public, patriarchal attitudes predominate.[1] According to the surveys, by the end of the twentieth century, Lithuania, along with other Baltic countries, Poland, and Hungary, represented ultimate patriarchal regimes marked by gender naturalization and a weak orientation to a dual-earner family.[2] In this type of regime, the attitude that the woman was a "kindler of the hearth" and the man a "family breadwinner" was very much alive and thriving. Furthermore, the low level of welfare services and inadequate benefits (underdeveloped childcare system, a strong male–breadwinner society and few opportunities for part-time work) not only hindered women's labor participation and their career achievements but also kept men from their involvement in family life. Men felt a disadvantage in the family because of the pressure of a good provider's role and their work outside home. Scholars note that, after the fall of the Communist system, political democracy and market economy in central and eastern Europe did not encourage gender equality, but rather "strengthened cultural and social hierarchies and gender-based inequalities."[3]

Such a state of gender affairs had negative consequences for both women and men constrained by the narrow gender roles and cultural expectations. Patriarchal gender norms and attitudes also affected the treatment of socially vulnerable groups, including sexual minorities. In Lithuania, as in other new European Union countries, the level of tolerance toward sexual minorities has been very low. According to the 2008 Eurobarometer Discrimination Survey, Romania, Lithuania, Latvia, Bulgaria and

Hungary are the countries with the highest proportion of respondents uncomfortable having a homosexual as a neighbor, while the old EU member states, such as the Netherlands, Sweden, Denmark, Belgium and France, have the highest proportion of respondents comfortable with a homosexual neighbor.[4] This is just one of many examples of intolerance, distrust and sometimes hatred toward sexual and other minorities in Lithuania and other post-Communist countries.

Such is the post-Soviet context of gender relations in which masculinities played a serious part. During the last two decades, Lithuanian men and women have faced a sudden, radical change. Socio-economic and cultural transformations have not been easy for either sex but men in particular have been affected. Government corruption, the rise in the crime rate, and economic impoverishment and pauperization not only diminished the democratic expectations of justice and well-being of Lithuanian citizens but also produced highly gendered and sexualized roles for men and women in a new post-Soviet gender regime. In this regime, men and masculinity have been inextricably tied up with issues of power. Masculine power has been expressed in multiple ways, from social or political power to financial worth, technical expertise, physical strength and sexual potency. For many men, however, post-Soviet masculinity entailed shame, despair, and powerlessness.

On the one side of this masculinity, there emerged nouveau riche men, some of whom accumulated financial and personal capital during the period of "wild capitalism" in the early 1990s. They became the new economic and political elite embodying the practices of "transnational business masculinity," to use Raewyn Connell's term. "Increasing egocentrism, very conditional loyalties (even to the corporation), and a declining sense of responsibility for others (except for purposes of image-making)" characterize these men.[5] They inhabit positions of power and wealth and reproduce the social relationships that generate their dominance in the Lithuanian society. They openly extol practices of hegemonic masculinity that legitimize patriarchy, guaranteeing the "dominant position of men and the subordination of women."[6] As a former member of the Lithuanian Parliament stated:

> Today men let women dominate them. I think it is a bad thing. I think that a real man must have as much masculinity as he wants to. ... That's why I am saying that a real man has to treat his woman honestly. First of all, he has to support her financially according to his abilities; he must give her money to take care of her appearance, for instance, to sign for aerobics classes. It is also possible to allow her to do some social work. There are a lot of various associations for animal care and so on and so forth ... However, a real man cannot let his woman dominate him ...[7]

This quote is symptomatic of the reinvention of a politically incorrect, ardently anti-feminist and patriarchal Lithuanian male: virile, brave, financially secure, proud, sexually potent and physically aggressive. The mass media and popular culture in general also produced oversimplified and one-sided discourses on men in which a flexible yet repressive norm of hegemonic masculinity embodied by a successful businessman or politician is pervasive.[8]

On another side of masculinity, a great number of men, affected by rapid social, economic and political developments, suffered severe marginalization due to their class, age, disability, sexuality and ethnicity. This chapter is about them, engaging the masculinities of two different groups: working-class and gay men. I argue that for these two groups identity is a place of suffering and misery. This is not to deny that other social groups experience constant political injuries and political humiliations in the post-Soviet world. The Lithuanian welfare state has failed to provide social security and an acceptable level of well-being to many groups of citizens. However, other groups, most notably women, are able to express themselves publicly through the rhetoric of equal rights and gender justice. The mass media most often publicizes the suffering of retirees, abandoned children, and mothers struggling with poverty. One of the most popular programs on Lithuanian national television (LTV), *The Market of Miseries* (*Bėdų turgus*), exposes the suffering of these groups and attempts to alleviate their pain by supplying them with charity. Yet men, with the exception of ones with disability and health-threatening conditions, are the minority on the program. "Inexpressive" male suffering is left unacknowledged and unaddressed.[9]

Examining the alignment of masculinity and suffering in life narratives of working-class and gay men may seem questionable to some. Gay men can be manual laborers, and working-class men can be gay. Although different reasons and bases determine the marginalization and social exclusion of these groups, some links between them can be traced. First of all, both experience relative invisibility and a single-handed rejection of their problems by the ruling elite and a cynical public sphere. Moreover, a public scandal involving the Lithuanian Gay League (the most active NGO defending the rights of Lithuanian homosexual people) and the Soviet sculpture of two workers which still adorns one of the Vilnius bridges demonstrated the complex relation between male working-class men and gays. The Lithuanian Gay League put the photograph of this public sculpture on their publication "Discrimination at Work: Practical Guide for Homosexual Employees" (2003). The author of this sculpture threatened to sue the organization for "defaming" and homosexualizing his work. The conflict was widely described by the mainstream Lithuanian press and it even inspired a short documentary film about gays entitled "Two Men on the Bridge." However, the Lithuanian Gay League did not breach any copyright laws, and ultimately the sculptor had to withdraw his complaint.[10] This example demonstrates that gay men have been more vocal in expressing their grievances. Yet their voices have been usually drowned in the plethora of extremely homophobic and offensive pronouncements by mainstream politicians and public figures.[11]

Statistical data on men and methodological notes

Problems related to men in post-Soviet Lithuania abound. Lithuanian men experienced much greater risk to their health than women. According to the data from the year of 2006, there were five times more chronic alcoholic men than alcoholic women in the country. The same data indicate that men committed suicide five times more often than women.[12] In 2006, the suicide rate for Lithuanian men between the ages of 45 and 59 was 92 suicides per 100,000 men.[13] The latest data showed that the Lithuanian men's life expectancy was twelve years shorter than women's (65 years for men and 77 for women respectively).[14]

Other problems related to the predominant traditional structures of masculinity. According to one of the most important representative surveys on men and masculinities entitled *The Crises of Male Roles in Lithuania* (2002),[15] the main features of a "normal" or "real" man emphasized by both men and women were (in order of importance): 1) his ability to earn money for his family (72 percent of respondents); 2) a man's capability to do male housework such as home-improvement and technical jobs (67 percent of respondents); 3) care and upbringing of his children (67 percent); and 4) his taking care of his woman (66 percent). Men themselves emphasized the following traits of a "normal" man: 1) his ability to earn money; 2) taking care of his woman; 3) care and upbringing of his children; and 4) his capability to do home-improvement jobs.

The survey demonstrated that the perceptions of masculinity and male practices in Lithuania did not diverge much from the model of traditional hegemonic masculinity based on heterosexuality, economic autonomy, breadwinning, professional success, keeping one's emotions in check, and not doing anything considered feminine. It should also be mentioned that 77 percent of Lithuanian men subscribed to this form of masculinity by stating that they were "real" or "normal" men. Only 10 percent of men thought that they did not conform to this image, and 14 percent did not know how to answer the question.

Both Lithuanian women and men considered the breadwinning role as the most important feature of a "real" man. However, this attitude no longer reflects the reality. According to the quoted survey, in about 50 percent of the Lithuanian families, women earned more and were the main providers. Furthermore, the 2006 data of the Department of Statistics indicate that both men and women's employment rates were increasing. Employment rates for women aged 15–64 increased from 59.4 percent in 2005 to 61 percent in 2006 and for men from 66 to 66.3 percent. Women's labor force activity rate was 64 percent, while men's was 70.5 percent. In 2006, 5.8 percent of Lithuanian women and 5.4 percent men were unemployed.[16] In 2007, the female and male unemployment rates were the same – 4.3 percent.[17]

Lithuanian men committed significantly more crimes than women. Unable to cope with social change, men often expressed their rage through violence against women, other men, and themselves. According to the data of the IT and Communications Department under the Ministry of the Interior of the Republic of Lithuania, in 2007, 2,500 women and 20,200 men were charged with crimes or misdemeanors. The average number of women suspected of criminal offences per 1,000 female population was 1, while the number for men was 13. In 2007, 1,400 women and 12,600 men were sentenced by the courts. As of January 1, 2008, 96 percent of convicted persons in imprisonment institutions were men. In 2007, per 100,000 male population, 14 men were murdered in rural and 12 in urban areas; per 100,000 female population, 6 and 4 women respectively. Some 37 women and

200 men suffered from serious bodily injuries.[18] These numbers indicate that men may not have been the main victims of the post-Socialist transition but their position has been as complicated as that of women.

Obviously, many of the problems enumerated here and faced by the Lithuanian men were not unique to post-Communist Lithuania. However, while we have excellent research conducted in western European and North American contexts,[19] there is a massive deficit in critical studies of men's practices in developing countries.[20] In Lithuania, the lack of a strong tradition of feminism and gender studies contributed to this deficit. Men have few cultural options, and the dominance of a single model of "real" masculinity at the expense of multiple masculinities makes them more vulnerable to acts of violence against themselves and their families.

The issues of men and masculinities in Lithuania have been largely overlooked, as they have been overlooked elsewhere. The same can be said about socially excluded and marginalized men. While there is almost no research on working-class men in Lithuania, several articles have been written on gay men and their masculinity.[21] Nonetheless, gay men remain one of the most stigmatized minorities, and working-class men are the least researched and visible social group in the country. This applies to a large part of post-Communist eastern Europe including Lithuania's closest neighbors Latvia, Estonia and Poland.[22]

Twenty semi-structured interviews with gay men and nine with working-class men are used in the chapter. Only working-class men involved in hard manual labor were used for the interviews. Four of them were loaders, three construction workers, one a welder, and one was involved in different temporary jobs. Only five informants had permanent jobs. None of the gay men could be described as hard manual laborers; some of them were service workers. This group of men included a hairstylist, a lawyer, a university teacher, a waiter, a bartender, a computer salesman, a post office manager, a journalist, a businessman, a croupier, a manager of cultural projects, a physician, a project manager at the Lithuanian AIDS center, and a state officer. The informants were mainly recruited through the so-called snowball method. The age of the interviewed gay men ranged from 17 to 55, and working-class men, from 22 to 68. The interviews with gay men focused on the broad issues of homophobia, masculinity, discrimination, coming out, and being public and private. The working-class men were asked about their work, social position, the difficulties they encountered in life as men and employees, and the male roles that they attempted to perform in everyday life.[23] Thus, the chapter presents some kind of ethnographic knowledge about masculinity, the importance of which has been emphasized by R. Connell.[24]

Social suffering and masculinities

The concept of social suffering has been popularized by the French sociologist Pierre Bourdieu and his co-authors in their book *The Weight of the World*.[25] It describes everyday miseries of the socially marginalized and exposes social factors contributing to their oppression and domination. "Small miseries" produced by the dominant system can contribute to the individuals' hopelessness, despair and diminished chances to participate in the public sphere. Social suffering cannot be reduced to suffering caused by class-based, globalized political and economic exploitation. Pierre Bourdieu uses the word "misery" to describe not only situations related to the lack of material resources but also to the situations in which persons or social group feel excluded and marginalized. The main victims are ordinary people surrounded by the invisible structures of domination and oppression. From the first glance, their lives seem "normal." However, these "normal" lives are marked by the stories of misery, lost opportunity, contextual constraints, degraded social environments and social relationships.[26] According to Arthur Kleinman,

> ... suffering is social, not only because social force breaks networks and bodies but also because social institutions respond with assistance to certain categories of sufferers (categories that institutions have constructed as authorized objects for giving help), while denying others or treating them with bureaucratic indifference.[27]

Poverty, alcoholism, violence in families and streets, and social tensions may be both causes and effects of social suffering. Social suffering is related not only to a larger framework of social distress – loss of the jobs, unemployment – but also to the vulnerabilities of gender, class, age, and sexual orientation.

Gendered and embodied experiences of social suffering are particularly powerful. This chapter explores the multiple forms in which gender, class and sexual orientation produce *la petite misère*, or ordinary suffering of specifically male subjects. Masculinity, a fragile and complex practice, is constantly produced, consumed, regulated and performed. Despite its instability, it is an incontrovertible fact. Masculinity as both a "place in gender relations" and a practice through which men "engage that place in gender, and the effects of these practices in bodily experience, personality and culture"[28] inflicts social wounds on the interviewed men.

Gay men and their masculine performances

While researchers speak of the disappearance of the homosexual in continental north European context,[29] in Lithuania the identity of the homosexual has remained in the stage of emergence. There are no openly homosexual public figures, and same-sex practices and desires are still considered socially illegitimate and unacceptable. Differently from western European and North American contexts, the gap between public and private homosexualities, or private heterosexualities and private homosexualities, is still rather wide.

It should be stated, at the outset, that while the public discourse of Soviet Lithuania glorified a heroic working man before 1990, the words "gay," "lesbian," "bisexual," and "transgender" were rarely heard in Lithuania. For a long time, homosexuality was a completely taboo subject, to be spoken about in only the most reluctant way. The situation changed after Lithuania declared its independence from the Soviet Union in 1990. With the advent of a new press and television, the problem of homosexuality came to be discussed publicly. Independent Lithuania inherited the Soviet prejudice on homosexuality, however. Despite the existence of constitutional guarantees of equality and privacy, the infamous article of the Penal Code (122 BK) against consensual sex between adult men was repealed only in 1993. Lithuania was the last among the three Baltic countries to abolish penalties for homosexual acts. However, it did not change significantly the public perception of homosexuality and gay men. The Lithuanian mass media, for instance, still present gay men as morally degenerate, deviant and perverted. They were and are often associated with pedophilia. The repeated labeling of male homosexuals as pedophiles and pederasts serves to underline a pathological character of homosexuality and to incite people's fears and anxieties. It is often assumed that homosexual males are effeminate and can be easily recognized by certain mannerisms, speech and behavior. The effeminate, handbag-waving "pansy" makes frequent appearances in Lithuanian sitcoms and the press.[30]

This public discourse has taken its toll on gay subjects. In their narratives, most interviewed gay males attempted to construct themselves as "normal" heterosexual subjects. But what are the ways to do so since gay masculinities, according to Tim Edwards, are a contradiction in terms? Male homosexuality has been widely represented in cultural discourses as the antithesis of masculinity, its vanishing point and its structural other.[31] Or, in the words of the interviewed gay males themselves, "Today a gay man ... is imagined not in a good way. I am trying to subvert this image as much as I can" (Marius, 28). Another man stated "If you're gay, you're an ultimate whore, ultimate anything ... Fruitcake ..." (Raigardas, 26).

What does it mean to subvert the image of a gay man? For the absolute majority, it is indeed self-subjection to the overwhelming imperatives of normalization and the construction of self-discriminating gay masculinity that distances itself from "abnormal" homosexual men, hides in apologetic secrecy and rests in peace and silence. By "abnormal" they have in mind "effeminate" gay men, or those "behaving in a feminine way." Most interviewed men tried to distance themselves from such individuals. Feeling like perpetual outsiders, they wanted to be "real men." One of the informants called feminine gays "girls" or "poofters" and said that they should be shot. "No person, no problem," he stated. The fear of being considered feminine or of being turned into women was most poignant. Therefore, feminine gay bodies came to be seen as "failing" or even abject bodies.

Being hostile to feminine gays, the overwhelming majority of the informants preferred "real men" as their partners. Anything that was beyond acceptable masculinity and gender order was not regarded with leniency. They openly articulated hegemonic embodied masculinity as their ideal: men had to be physically fit, masculine, straight acting and economically secure:

> To be a man? Mmm ... a man is bound to a family, money, wealth, sustenance and so forth ... I am not a specialist in these matters, but when you asked me

suddenly the image of what it meant to be a man appeared in my head: tough, strong, tall, well-groomed, volatile, one who is somehow above others ...

(Bronius, 28)

Consistently defining masculinity from a heteronormative perspective and drawing a sharp divide between feminized gays and themselves ("straight gays"), the informants enacted the heterosexist imaginary, so powerfully articulated by the Lithuanian mass media and public sphere. The several simple quotes can be interpreted both as an archive of traditional masculinity and a tribute to the naturalized gender dichotomies:

I act naturally. I mean ... I am not the one who walks around with painted nails and colored eyebrows or dressed in an extravagant way although sometimes I like to dress in a strange way just for fun ...

(Egidijus, 24)

You can see that I am not particularly well-combed; neither am I effeminate. On the contrary, I like sports and I attend to other masculine things like my car. I also have a motorcycle. ... I am not tender at all. Perhaps I am a bit sensitive but I don't have any [homosexual] mannerisms ... I am just a normal man.

(Viktoras, 33)

If you look at my appearance it doesn't tell anything about my orientation. ... I try not to emphasize and show [my sexual orientation].

(Andrius, 26)

I am masculine ... Look at my beard, I am not mannered and pedantically tidy ... I've got everything that a man has got to have biologically and in other respects.

(Giedrius, 30)

The quotes above demonstrate to what degree, in solving the riddle of their masculine identification undermined by the heteronormative stereotypes of them as "lacking" men, the interviewed gay men strove to conform to the norm of heterosexual masculinity. Some informants decided to become "masculine" and to learn bodily and linguistic practices of "real" masculinity. If you wanted to be a "real" man, you had to learn to act like one. A 22-year-old informant told about his female friend who had taught him to look masculine, to walk and talk in a "normal" way. According to him, if he had an effeminate male friend he would try to help him become masculine since almost every gay could become a "real masculine man." In his view, some gay men simply were reluctant or too lazy to change.

Moreover, to be an acceptable man and perform one's masculinity successfully one had to "play a role," "put a mask on," or learn the policies of "heterosexual passing":

You must constantly play the role in your family and at work ...

(Egidijus, 24)

Of course, I would like not to hide [my orientation] on the street, from other people ... but I already know that I have already adapted to this hiding, I have already developed some kind of mechanism: when you go to the street you must hide [your true self] and you must do the same in front of some people.

(Ramūnas, 21)

... and when I found out that [my sexual orientation] could not be public, I understood that I didn't have to think hard about it. ... I would put the mask on, and that's it.

(Giedrius, 30)

I accepted myself but I had to pretend sometimes ... for instance, to invent stories about my adventures with women, etc.

(Marius, 28)

Essentially, I don't want to reveal what I am ... I mean, it is easier for me than for other gays because I am not campy or mannered. I am just a guy ... And I live how I want to live. But I don't publicize [my orientation] because I don't need unnecessary problems ... It's so good to live quietly ...

(Paulius, 25)

The above narratives emphasize the essence of stigmatized Lithuanian manhood: Instead of democratic participation and public expressions of their problems these men succumb to survival and adapting to the cynical political sphere. They use their "most creative energy to cultivate intimate spheres while scraping a life together flexibly"[32] in response to homophobia, indirect discrimination and isolation. Since it was impossible to integrate homosexuality into conventional social worlds, shame, fear, and guilt dominated their lives. Some turned their intimate lives into an expression of painful obliteration, ecstasy, alcoholism, and promiscuity. To perform masculinity successfully in the face of homophobia they needed to eliminate any markers of gayness. To be successful meant to live carefully closeted lives ("to live quietly"), retain a decidedly masculine public presence in the public world and learn to enact tough and impenetrable masculinity.

The informants' narratives prompt us to ask: isn't the whole performance of masculinity, gay or straight, a spectacle, a masquerade, a play with fetishized signs of manhood? If gays wanted to be efficient and accepted, weren't they supposed to pass as public subjects with extensive resources of social, cultural, physical, and even emotional capital? The stories of the interviewed gay men show that as much as they tried to enjoy it, their performance of masculinity was devoid of pleasure, joy, resistance and feeling. Although the interviewed gay men did not manufacture themselves as victims, their masculinity was wrought with frustration, trauma, resentment, stress, and longing.

There was a slight difference among the interviewed older and younger gay men. Younger men were more defiant and uncomfortable in their silences. Older men were resigned to their privacy and felt the need to conceal same-sex sexual interests. Yet internalized homophobia and feelings of being an outsider were characteristic of both younger and older men. The pervasive imperative of successful performance of masculinity in the face of homophobia was overpowering in their stories. Almost all informants mentioned the risk of falling short of being a "real" man (manly, well-built, straight-acting, macho and in control of his life). It is not surprising. Coming into relative visibility after 1991 in Lithuania, homosexuality and gay men have been either erased and reduced or constituted as a "site of radical homophobic fantasy"[33] since gay sexuality presented a threat to established social order. Gay men disturbed mainstream conceptions of male sexuality, gender and sex and raise anxiety, ambiguity, and tension. An imperative to defy this homophobic fantasy was pervasive in the informants' stories.

The interviewed gay men were aware of their daily constraints; they attempted to contemplate consciously the forces and contexts within which they acted. In this way they differed from working-class men, whose speech was full of silences, gaps and discomfort. It can be argued that gay men's shame and powerlessness would also be acutely felt in the stories of working-class men. Manifesting itself in different ways and creating "different modes of abjection, marginalization, and self-abnegation,"[34] shame was pervasive in the lives of both groups of men.

Fallen working-class heroes and the narratives of shame

The situation of working-class men in post-Soviet Lithuania has been as precarious as that of gay men although in a different way. The independence of Lithuania brought sudden economic, social and cultural changes that to a great degree dethroned working-class people. The society of working-class heroes was replaced by a society of free entrepreneurs. The Soviet "super-hero" defying pain and striving for a better world and the leading role of the working class during the Soviet times disintegrated as a shadowy past along with the removal of most Soviet sculptures from town squares and parks.

It can be argued that, as in other Communist countries, Lithuanian "state socialism defined men so strongly as workers and soldiers – that is, as defenders of the country and of socialism – that there was no place left for any other aspects of traditional (or 'new') masculinity in the official discourse."[35] Soviets tried to constitute a compliant male subject who mimicked social norms, assumptions and values. As Libora Oates-Indruchova correctly emphasized writing on Czech Communist men, masculinity was "conceived of in terms of work, discipline, and work initiative."[36] In this society, which, at least on the level of the official state doctrine, was based on collective effort, the physical strength as the foundation of masculinity was valued, and everything that served the maintenance of this strong and heroic masculinity was highly esteemed. Adherence to this kind of masculinity brought patriarchal dividends for men while women remained subordinated and submissive to male authority. Women were not only employed but also did the biggest share of the housework.[37]

During the transition period from the declaration of independence in 1990 to the beginning of the twenty-first century, the existing hegemonic concept of masculinity based on the working-class ethos coming from the Soviet tradition has become increasingly marginalized in Lithuania. With the rise of a service economy that demanded more "naturally" feminine skills and emotions, the working-class male was somewhat emasculated rhetorically in the media and in policy statements.

The dethroning of a working-class hero was influenced not only by the disintegration of the Soviet state but also by the global social and economic processes. In the book *The Weight of the World*, Pierre Bourdieu explained the destructuralization and crisis of the traditional working class. Economic crises, industrial changes and social transformations have left workers in the past. It seems that they have become superfluous and unable to exist and act in the contemporary world. As a social group, they have become mostly passive and hopeless. Bourdieu's recounting of the factors that led to the crisis of trade unionism can also be applied to the post-Soviet context: "the disappearance of large factory areas, plants that brought together 4,000 to 5,000 workers and are now losing out to small companies with fewer than 50 employees that are always so difficult to unionize … the pervasive unemployment and the constant threat that it holds over those who have a job, driving them to submission and to silence."[38] The lack of strong trade unions as a legacy of the Soviet regime, low salaries, and overall passivity of working-class people also add up to their sense of hopelessness, financial insecurity and bleak future.

The interviewed working-class men were neither particularly cognizant of nor prepared to reflect on the circumstances of their lives. They did not feel confident to verbalize their lives – above all, their painful and traumatic episodes. They often fell silent. Theirs was silent suffering and inexpressive pain. They argued that their lives were unimportant and there was not much to be said about them: "I don't know much about this;" "This conversation won't be useful;" "I am an ordinary man; my life isn't special, I haven't achieved anything, I am just a simple worker" were often-repeated phrases. Another reason for their silences was their fear to appear unmanly since "no real man talked of suffering." Silence entrapped them in their suffering and denied their agency. In this regard, gay men were able to describe their experiences more openly and candidly.

Manual labor came to be devalued and did not guarantee a stable income in the Lithuanian society. Most interviewed men were hired illegally and did not have any social security. Thus, working-class men, particularly older ones, felt dominated and rejected by the society and relegated to the edges of social life. A 50-year-old man said that he did not have any dreams since he was too old for them: "Let younger guys dream …" Another interviewee said that employers considered working-class men "garbage" and did not respect them at all. Unlike the Soviet times when "superiors at work had respected people" (Julius, 60), contemporary bosses did not even say "hello" to them ("now they [bosses] don't even look at us; we are nothing to them, they can push us around as some old shoe … there's no respect for us at all … " Gediminas, 54). They knew that they had been marginalized and easily replaceable. Exploitative and even emasculating labor relations affected working-class men and made them vulnerable and even ashamed.

Older men argued that during the Soviet regime people were more connected at work but currently everyone stood for himself: "I don't feel a team member at work, now you work only for money, not for the love of work" (Gediminas, 54). Younger men did not care much for the unity of workers but they mentioned, as often as older interviewees, that their work did not guarantee them financial stability and was a source of tensions, stress, and constant worry.

Older working-class men talked, with a sheer heartache and grievance, about the drastic changes in the post-Soviet society. According to Saulius (50), "It was a big injustice done to people, that excessive destruction of factories and everything ... They destroyed them quickly, thousands lost their jobs ... ." Evaldas (49) said that "it was difficult ... to find myself, to adapt to the new system ... Well, it was even more difficult to find a job; factories went bankrupt, and our professions became redundant." The other informant stated that in the past he had held a good job and had been "respected and important." He continued, with sheer sadness in his voice: "But everything has changed, I am no longer needed; supposedly I don't know how to do some jobs ... I could learn everything but I am not allowed to try. To say briefly, I am redundant ... " (Rimas, 54). Most men felt that social injustices predominated in their native country. In an informant's words, "there [was] no justice now, only big injustice. Now you [were] exploited much more ... Previously much more depended on a person: if he didn't like the job he could leave and find another one. There were no problems ... " (Saulius, 50). Drastic change in their life conditions and the value orientations of the society made them feel redundant, isolated and asocial. Respected and valued in the past, they suddenly became secondary citizens.

One of the most important sources of their "small miseries" was their conception of manhood. Most interviewed men thought of a man as a breadwinner: "a man is stronger and he must be a breadwinner" (Vladas, 68); "a man and only he must be a breadwinner in the family ... I have been a breadwinner all my life" (Julius, 60); "I agree that perhaps a man has to be more responsible for the welfare of a family than a woman" (Tomas, 31). Several men felt that during certain periods of their lives they failed to achieve the foremost masculine ideal of a breadwinner; they could not take control of their lives because of their inability to rely on themselves as family supporters. To be supported by their wives was shameful. Some men even related the inability to fulfill the breadwinner's role to their divorce. During the times of unemployment they lost self-respect, felt emasculated and turned to substance abuse (two of the interviewed men struggled with it in the past, one was still struggling). It should also be mentioned that three interviewed men were divorced (31, 54 and 60 year-olds) and one (54 year-old) was in the process of divorce.

Thus, the interviewed men felt shame not only at work but also in their families. Shame as "a sense of failure or lack in the eyes of others," to use Rita Fielski's words, was provoked by the "infractions of social codes and a consequent fear of exposure, embarrassment, and humiliation."[39] The inability to live up to the expectations of society (i.e. the expectations of a self-reliant man) made them embarrassed and ashamed. As one informant said, "I would like to have a normal affluent life ... but at this moment it is difficult to achieve" (Saulius, 50). Even younger men longed for stability and security: "Well, I would like to have stability, clarity and the vision of my future ... sometimes you start to think, and sadness and anxiety overwhelm you ... Well, I would like stability ... but I don't feel secure ... " (Tomas, 31).

How have working-class men dealt with anxiety and shame, and constructed their masculine dignity? It appeared that they have done it through the repetition of gendered acts of hard drinking, banter, and violence. All these practices have been essential for temporarily reducing the stress and trauma of everyday life: "you know, there's a saying: those who don't drink are dangerous to society. I drink too; it is necessary to have a shot or two, I need it to restart my whole system ... " (Tomas, 31). By drinking huge amounts of alcohol these men demonstrated their strength, self-control and stamina. Through drinking they attempted to approximate hegemonic standards of masculinity. Heavy drinking for the working class men has been and remains to be a form of embodied masculinity construction. Violent sports served as another way to reproduce "powerful" masculinity. One of the informants boasted that when he was younger, he "trained, lifted weights, was very strong and often would get involved in fights" (Rimas, 56). Injuries caused by being dominated have been channeled into self-destructive suffering. According to several informants, they knew co-workers who lost control of their lives and drank themselves to death.

The excessive use of alcohol also served a different purpose for these working-class men. Drinking replaced other means of solidarity: it strengthened social relations within a peer group and helped men achieve recognition and authority among co-workers. Two informants mentioned that they had felt constant pressure to drink in their former jobs ("I remember how very hard it was to resist drinking; only drink, drink, drink ... " Vladas, 68). One of them left the job, and another pretended that he drank because a non-drinking man was ignored and stigmatized by others.

In her book *Masculinities*, Raewyn Connell talks of protest masculinity of marginalized men who pick up "themes of hegemonic masculinity in the society at large" and rework them in a context of poverty.[40] It can be argued that instead of questioning and fighting social inequalities and dominations, the interviewed men "reworked" them into practices of self-destruction, despair and silent suffering. But is it possible to call these male practices a protest?

While gay men mentioned corporeal aspects of "real" masculinity (tough, strong, fit), working-class men also talked of their bodies as the measure of their manliness. They equated masculinity with physical labor, strength, sports, power and good health. Muscles, endurance, and potency were crucial to them. The body was a model of pronounced virility, and male muscularity naturalized physical strength and domination. However, the interviewed older men have mutilated and worn down the bodies that symbolized their manhood. Four of them had some kind of disability; two were unable to work because of their current disabilities but hoped to return to work in the future. Their bodies acted as the screens on which the dramas of anxiety, insecurity and power have been projected. In R. Connell's words, "depression and disassociation are also experiences in the flesh."[41]

As S. J. Charlesworth emphasized, "Through the patterns of their embodiment, people radiate significances and instantiate differences of worth that manifest a form of positional-relation ... "[42] Self-devaluation and self-marginalization left marks on the interviewed men's worn-out bodies. In other words, social inequalities have been somatized and domination has been naturalized through their exhausted bodies. Although the interviewed men avoided expressing their miseries, fears and anxieties, the uncomfortable gait of their bodies and hesitant manner of their speech were quite telling. Only the bodies of two younger men exuded confidence, health and communicability. Prematurely aged faces, ill health, abused bodies, dirty hands, worn-out clothes, and lack of confidence characterized the rest of the men. Their appearance not only revealed their profession but also defined their place in both the labor market and social space.

Conclusion: wounded men and their masculinities

As was noted at the beginning, sociological surveys indicate that Lithuania, along with other new EU member states including other Baltic countries, Poland and Hungary, is still a highly paternalistic society.[43] In these societies, rigid gender norms influence the ways in which social programs assume and reinforce a family breadwinner role for men and a maternal and caring role for women. Family policy, population policy, labor force, regulation of sexual behavior and childcare provisions are a part of a broader set of power structures which act to perpetuate male power in these societies. However, very few scholars have analyzed different power dynamics in the post-Communist space. The research presented in this chapter contends that a great number of men affected by rapid social, economic and political developments, suffer severe marginalization due to their sexuality, class, and age. In many cases, the different bases of marginalization (for instance, class and age) intersect in men's lives.

The chapter focused on two very different social types: the fallen working-class hero of the Soviet times and the decriminalized homosexual man. Both expressed their views from the margins albeit differently. Both felt vulnerable but were hiding the wounds of their masculine identities. The chapter demonstrates that their marginalization is the effect of not only class-based, globalized political and economic exploitation. Their suffering and powerlessness are also related to situations in which men feel excluded, marginalized and surrounded by the invisible structures of domination and oppression. Not only was there a larger framework of social distress – loss of the jobs, unemployment – but also the vulnerabilities of gender, class, age, and sexual orientation caused social suffering.

Corporeal specificity of these men's suffering manifested itself in an attempt to imitate "acceptable" male norms, and, on the other hand, in succumbing to self-destructive behavioral practices. Both the interviewed gay and working-class men have become their own "gender police"[44] trying to conform to either tough heterosexual men or a macho work culture. While gay men did not feel inferior to heterosexual men, working-class men accepted their inferior status in the world of "successful" manhood. However, the pervasive sense of shame inflicted pain and suffering on both groups. It was shame for being lower class and shame for being different and "abnormal." It can be argued that the men's social suffering and exclusion were related to the capillaries of power: not only the sense of powerlessness but also the inability to resist it was inherently shameful for the interviewed men.

Deprived of power and authority in different life spheres, working-class and gay men have become social *Others*. Public invisibility of gay men and public marginalization of working-class men made their attempts at hegemonic normative masculinity look like some kind of a cul-de-sac. Powerful strategies of Othering present in the Lithuanian public sphere make the performances of alternative masculinity in public (and even private) tricky, unsaleable, and even excessive. Therefore, gay men desperately reiterated the compulsory norm of heterosexual masculinity in everyday life. Working-class men coped with it by adopting self-destructive practices. It seemed that the idea of hegemonic masculinity was the last refuge of the identity of these dominated groups.

These men's entanglement with powerlessness, shame and despair brings to the fore the issue of masculine normalization or male norms that have become more important in Lithuanian and other post-Soviet societies with the influx of western standards and male behavioral models. Violent forms of normativity and hegemonic masculinity attested to even by the cited public opinion survey not only create complicit men reaping the benefits of patriarchy but also produce "silent inequalities, unintended effects of isolation, and the lack of public access."[45] This is particularly evident when in such marginalized groups as working-class or gay men.

The pressures of normative subjectivities imbued the corporeal identities of gay and working-class men with depression, exclusion, anxiety and insecurity. It can be argued that the recreation of an independent Lithuanian state in 1990 went along with the political project of the normalization of the Lithuanian masculinity and even more intensive pathologization of different non-normative sexualities and socially marginalized male bodies.

Stigma, indirect discrimination, isolation, depression, anxiety – all contribute to ordinary suffering of these men. Their emotional wounding is largely invisible and "illegible" since the discourse of victimhood in Lithuania has been related mostly to women and other underrepresented groups such as disabled or ethnic minorities (for instance, Roma minority). However, as Pierre Bourdieu argues, there is "no worse deprivation, no worse privation, perhaps, than that of the losers in the symbolic struggle for recognition, for access to … humanity."[46]

Can the subjective experience of pain of these men travel from their physical bodies to the social body and become a part of collective life? It is difficult to think that in the post-Soviet cynical public sphere their social suffering has been or will be publicly voiced or politically articulated. The post-Soviet state institutions do not secure the implementation of social and economic human rights and are not sensitive enough to the needs of different social groups.[47] Furthermore, the legacy of the Communist regime does not encourage marginalized groups and individuals to engage in civic activities. The lack of trust, responsibility, and communal activity, and the limited solidarity and alienation of the Lithuanian citizens also lead to further inequality, marginality and even discrimination of these suffering men.

Notes

1 See Aušra Maslauskaitė, "Lytis, globa ir kultūriniai gerovės kapitalizmo barjerai Lietuvoje" [Gender, Care and Opportunities of Welfare Capitalism in Lithuania], *Sociologija* 3 (14) (2004): 39–51; Vlada Stankūnienė and Aušra Maslauskaitė, eds., *Lietuvos šeima: tarp tradicijos ir naujos realybės* [Lithuanian Family: Between Tradition and the New Reality] (Vilnius: STI, 2009).
2 Vlada Stankūnienė and Aušra Maslauskaitė, "Family Transformation in the Post-Communist Countries. Assessment of Changes," in Ch. Hoehn, D. Avramov and I. Kotovska (eds), *European Studies of Population: People, Population Change and Policies. Lessons from the Population Policy Acceptance Study*, 16(1): 119–49.
3 *Ibid.*, 132.
4 *Homophobia and Discrimination on Grounds of Sexual Orientation and Gender Identity in the EU Member States. Part II – the Social Situation* (Vienna: European Union Agency for Fundamental Rights, 2009), 9. Internet access: http://fra.europa.eu/ fraWebsite/attachments/FRA_ hdgso_report-part2_en.pdf.
5 R. Connell, *The Men and the Boys* (Cambridge, UK: Polity, 2000), 52.
6 R. Connell, *Masculinities* (2nd edn) (Berkeley: University of California P, 2005), 77.
7 *Tik vyrams* [For Men Only], no. 6 (2003): 31.
8 Arturas Tereskinas, "Kaip dėvėti savo kūną: vyriškumo normos šiuolaikinės Lietuvos masinės komunikacijos priemonėse" [How to Wear your Body: Masculinity Norms in the Contemporary Mass Media], in Arturas Tereskinas, *Bodily Signs: Sexuality, Identity and Space in the Lithuanian Culture* (Vilnius: Baltos lankos, 2001), 93–108.
9 It is also possible to speak of hybridized post-Soviet male subjects produced by the intersection of qualities associated with traditional masculinity – strength, heroism, and virility – and qualities previously associated with femininity – emotional vulnerability, empathy, parental affection, etc. But such subjects remain liminal and unarticulated in the public sphere.
10 For more on this, see http://www.advocate.com/news_detailektid09534.asp.
11 For more on this, see Arturas Tereskinas, *"Not Private Enough?" Homophobic and Injurious Speech in the Lithuanian Media* (Vilnius: LGL, 2007).
12 *Women and Men in Lithuania: Department of Statistics to the Government of the Republic of Lithuania* (Vilnius, 2007), 80–82.
13 *Ibid.*, 83.
14 *Ibid.*, 18.
15 *The Crises of Male Roles in Lithuania: A Representative Survey of Men's Values and Behavior*, 2002. Vilnius: SIC. Market research: http://politika.osf.lt
16 *Women and Men in Lithuania, 2006: Department of Statistics to the Government of the Republic of Lithuania* (Vilnius, 2007), 52.
17 *Women and Men in Lithuania, 2007: Department of Statistics to the Government of the Republic of Lithuania* (Vilnius, 2008), 46.
18 *Ibid.*, 81 and 84.
19 Michael Kimmel, *Manhood in America: A Cultural History* (2nd edn) (New York: Oxford UP, 2006); Michael Kimmel, Jeff Hearn and R. Connell (eds), *Handbook of Studies on Men and Masculinities* (Thousand Oaks, CA: Sage Publications, 2005).
20 F. Cleaver (ed.), *Masculinities Matter! Men, Gender and Development* (London: Zed Books, 2002).
21 See Arturas Tereskinas, *Esė apie skirtingus kūnus: kultūra, lytis, seksualumas* [Essays on Different Bodies: Culture, Gender, Sexuality] (Vilnius: Apostrofa, 2007).

22 On gay men in post-Communist Europe, see selected articles in Roman Kuhar and Judit Takacs (ed.), *Beyond the Pink Curtain. Everyday Life of LGBT People in Eastern Europe* (Ljubljana: Peace Institute, 2007). On working class, see Alison Stenning, "Where is Post-Socialist Working Class?" *Sociology*, vol. 39, no. 5 (2005): 983–99.
23 Four interviews with gay men were conducted by my MA student Lina Šumskaitė during the period of February–April 2005. I and the Lithuanian research team of the EQUAL project conducted the rest sixteen interviews with gay men in January–June 2006. The MA student Ieva Dryžaitė interviewed the working-class men in January–April 2008. I am grateful to my students for sharing their research with me.
24 R. Connell, *Masculinities* (2nd edn), 34.
25 Pierre Bourdieu et al., *The Weight of the World: Social Suffering in Contemporary Society*. Translated by Priscilla Parkhurst Ferguson, Susan Emanuel, Joe Johnson and Shoggy T. Waryn (Stanford: Stanford UP, 1999).
26 *Ibid.*, 1–5.
27 Arthur Kleinman, "Everything that Really Matters: Social Suffering, Subjectivity, and the Remaking of Human Experience in a Disordered World," *The Harvard Theological Review*, vol. 90, no. 3 (July 1997): 321.
28 R. Connell, *Masculinities* (2nd edn) p. 71.
29 Henning Bech, "Commentaries on Seidman, Meeks and Traschen: 'Beyond the Closet?' After the Closet," *Sexualities*, vol. 2, no. 3 (1999): 343–49.
30 See Arturas Tereskinas, *"Not Private Enough?" Homophobic and Injurious Speech in the Lithuanian Media*.
31 Tim Edwards, "Queering the Pitch? Gay Masculinities," in Michael S. Kimmel, Jeff Hearn, R. W. Connell, ed., *Handbook of Studies on Men and Masculinities*, 51–68.
32 Lauren Berlant, "The Subject of True Feeling: Pain, Privacy, and Politics," in Jodi Dean, *Cultural Studies and Political Theory* (Ithaca: Cornell UP), 43.
33 About the mechanisms of this process see Judith Butler, "Imitation and Gender Insubordination," in Diana Fuss, *Inside Out: Lesbian Theories, Gay Theories* (New York: Routledge, 1991), 20.
34 Judith Halberstam, "Shame and White Gay Masculinity," *Social Text*, vol. 84–85, no. 3–4 (2005): 223.
35 Libora Oates-Indruchova, "The Void of Acceptable Masculinity during the Czech State Socialism: The Case of Radek John's Memento," *Men and Masculinities*, vol. 8, no. 4 (2006): 429.
36 *Ibid.*
37 For more on this, see Dalia Marcinkevičienė, "Darbas ir šeima Lietuvos moterų biografiniuose interviu 1945–90 metais" [Work and Family in the Lithuanian Women's Biographical Interviews in 1945–90] in Dalia Marcinkevičienė, ed., *Moterys, darbas, šeima* [Women, Work, and Family] (Vilnius: Gender Studies Centre, 2008), 198–212.
38 Pierre Bourdieu et al., *The Weight of the World*, 317–18.
39 Rita Felski, "Nothing to Declare: Identity, Shame and the Lower Middle Class," *PMLA*, vol. 115 (2000): 39.
40 R. Connell, *Masculinities* (2nd edn), 114.
41 R. Connell, *Gender and Power* (New York: Routledge, 1987), 82.
42 S. J. Charlesworth, "Understanding Social Suffering: A Phenomenological Approach to the Experience of Inequality," *Journal of Community and Applied Social Psychology*, vol. 15 (2005): 301.
43 Vlada Stankūnienė and Aušra Maslauskaitė, "Family Transformation in the Post-Communist Countries. Assessment of Changes."
44 I borrowed this term from Michael Kimmel: "Our peers are a kind of gender police." Michael Kimmel, "Masculinity as Homophobia: Fear, Shame, and Silence in the Construction of Gender Identity," in Harry Brod and Michael Kaufman (ed.), *Theorizing Masculinities* (Thousand Oaks, CA: Sage, 1994), 132.

45 Michael Warner, *The Trouble with Normal: Sex, Politics and the Ethics of Queer Life* (Cambridge, MA: Harvard UP, 1999), 7.
46 Pierre Bourdieu, *Pascalian Meditations* (Cambridge: Polity Press, 2000), 242.
47 Rūta Žiliukaitė, *Socialinio kapitalo dinamika pokomunistinėje Lietuvos visuomenėje: socialinės ir kultūrinės efektyvios demokratijos prielaidos* [The Dynamics of Social Capital in the Post-Communist Lithuanian Society: Social and Cultural Preconditions for Effective Democracy]. Doctoral dissertation, Institute for Social Research, Vilnius University (Vilnius, 2005), 76–77.

12

POST-1989 WOMEN'S ACTIVISM IN POLAND[1]

Joanna Regulska and Magdalena Grabowska

Introduction

In the year 2004, fifteen new countries joined the European Union (EU), thus officially marking the end of the Cold War and underscoring the transformation from a bipolar to a unipolar world.[2] Although many post-state-socialist states are now considered part of the "developed" world, the old divisions – based on the east and west of Europe – persist, and make activists and scholars raise questions about the specificity of eastern European feminism. Approaches that focus on researching distinct genealogies and trajectories of eastern European women's movement, and recognizing various scattered forms of women's agency (before and after the transformation in 1989) move away from the 1990s paradigm that represented women as victims of "masculinist" politics of state socialism and transformation, and eastern European feminism as non-existent.[3] Instead, these new approaches tie the narratives of eastern European feminisms to broader theoretical debates about transnational feminist theory and practice.[4] They also speak to shifting definitions of eastern Europe, which in the past were often focused on geographical, political, and cultural proximity to western Europe. Eastern Europe is now more often conceptualized through the lenses of the post-structuralist critiques of the western European imperialist ideologies[5] and the studies of intra-European colonialism.[6]

Today's debates emphasize not only the ambivalent location of eastern European feminisms between east and west, south and north, but also the ambiguous role of state-socialism. The state-socialist project of "women's equality" should not only be considered as imposed on the eastern European locations by the foreign superpower of the Soviet Union. It also should be examined in the context of women's agency – as creators and critics of state socialism,[7] and as agents of transformation[8] and active subjects involved in reconstructing gender politics after the fall of the previous system.[9] The fresh, critical look on "peaceful revolutions" and eastern European transitions can lead to demystification of the transformation from a state-socialist to a capitalist economy by recognizing its often hidden aspects – "pathologization" of eastern European space and naturalization of capitalism as the only direction of the transformation and of their devastating effects on women's lives, particularly in the context of shrinking health and social services.[10]

From this new theoretical perspective, the process of the unification and homogenization of the globe after the fall of Soviet Bloc had contradictory effects on women's lives. On one hand, many – particularly working class – women paid a high price for the privatization of eastern European economies, as they experienced the decrease of job security, childcare services, and (in some countries) of the access to abortion. Yet on the other hand, globalization opened up new possibilities for women's organizing at the supranational level. The Fourth UN Conference on Women, in Beijing in 1995, presented numerous opportunities for eastern European women's organizations, both locally and transnationally to get involved in the transnational feminist debates and use transnationalism to forward women's rights locally. First of all, the UN process helped to establish women's organizations as important political actors at transnational and national levels. It led to the creation of coalitions of non-governmental organizations (NGOs) and consolidation of women's communities at the national level, and the establishment of various women's networks at the regional level (for instance, KARAT Coalition that was established in 1997, consisted of sixty organizations from twenty-four countries). Second, entering the transnational level initiated the introduction of the new language of equality into the vocabularies of eastern European organizations and governments. The concepts of "gender" as well as "gender mainstreaming" have entered and transformed the narrative of the women's activism in eastern Europe and elsewhere. Third, an introduction of the Beijing Platform for Action helped to reframe the focus of feminist politics by recognizing the "global" as a crucial level for feminist politics. Finally, the Beijing process facilitated an intense mobilization in the realm of women's organizations. From the service centers (reproductive rights, violence against women) that focused on diverse groups of women (older, lesbians, Roma, Jewish) through various forms of organizing (NGOs, informal groups and the gender studies units), women's movements transformed eastern Europe.[11] NGOs have been identified as a driving force behind women's mobilizations and women's groups as agents of change in the area of women's rights after Beijing.[12] This rapid development of women's non-governmental groups had also its downfalls. As the western donors sponsored the majority of NGOs, their rise instigated criticism about their lack of autonomy, professionalization, and detachment from various groups of women that they claimed to represent.[13]

Since the mid-1990s, the European Union has become another venue that facilitates organizing in eastern Europe. While initially the arrival of the EU represented a symbolic unification of the European feminisms and movements, after the brief period of what can be called "Euro-enthusiasm," women's activists faced significant questions regarding the EU's commitment and ability to create social change in eastern Europe.[14] Moreover, during the period of accession, women's movements from the candidate countries have been encouraged to utilize the framework provided by the European Union's "gender mainstreaming"; yet this process also challenged the solidarity within the region, while introducing the dichotomy between more "European" (the EU member states) and the non-EU feminisms.

For the last twenty years, eastern Europe was represented as a dynamic, yet somewhat homogenous space of women's mobilization. The current engagements call for a closer analysis of a variety of often contradictory developments that took place in the region. Many scholars and feminist activists in eastern Europe argue that the context of state-socialism, transformation, and the enlargement of the European Union requires building a more comprehensive narrative of Europen women's movements. Such a narrative would recognize building broader, European coalitions at the local and transnational level, and an understanding of the differences between east and west. At the same time, the debate of the transnational women's movement has to consider fragmentation and diversity of feminist mobilizations. While the scattered character of existing feminist activism is often interpreted as evidence of the complete demobilization of women,[15] one can now argue that post-socialist countries do not lack "women's consciousness," or experience "feminism by design"[16] or backlash "without feminism,"[17] but face new forms of women's mobilizations that are scattered and fragmented. These new modes of action, in time and space, recognize the coexistence of various sources and origins of power and oppression on multiple scales – local, national, and transnational – through which mobilizations take place.[18]

The year 1989 brought for Poland and other east European countries dramatic transformation. With it came the hope that women's positions would dramatically change and that in terms of their access to the public sphere, women would be acknowledged as equal partners in social, political, economic, and cultural realms. The momentous change of 2004, admitting Poland and others to the European Union, was seen as a renewed possibility to achieve gender equality and a way to address numerous violations of their political, social, economic, and reproductive rights. However, these recent events have not drastically altered women's position. Since 1989, progress has been made on some issues (political representation), while other spheres remained unchanged (the wage gap) or, even worse, clear losses have become noticeable (reproductive rights).

This chapter will examine how the post-1989 change in Poland's political and economic positioning within Europe – specifically, the admission of Poland to the European Union – impacted women's groups' strategies, agendas and actions, and how through these experiences women shaped their collective agency. We ask how this most recent turning point in Polish history influenced women's mobilization practices locally and transnationally. We are aware that analysis of the post-1989 women's mobilizations in Poland cannot be fully understood without para-feminist activism of conservative and Catholic women who have been involved in numerous social initiatives since the fall of Communism. For example, the post-1989 anti-choice movement in Poland consisted mostly of women, even though men held leadership positions in it. In this chapter, however, we will focus only on those active and visible women's mobilizations that aim at changing and improving women's position in various areas of public and private life, including the arena of politics, education, and culture as well as family.

Post-1989 women's activism: opportunities and challenges

Although in 1989 unprecedented opportunities opened up for citizens' mobilizations across central and eastern Europe, the origins of the contemporary women's movement in Poland have a long history dating back to the nineteenth and twentieth centuries.[19] Even nowadays, for many women's activists, the mid-1980s "Solidarity" movement is a template of the social movement itself. At that time, women – once again in the face of the absence of male leaders (taken into prison under the 1981 martial law) – took over the leadership positions in the Solidarity movement.[20] For a younger generation of women, who later became feminist activists, the Solidarity movement of that period remained one of the greatest sources of inspiration. One of them argued: "I realized that my experience of the mass movement concentrates around the national, patriotic and independent state narrative. I remember from mid-1980s Solidarity demonstrations, which were often initiated by people coming back from the Sunday mass … I think that Solidarity had a major impact on perception of the Polish feminism in the beginning."

During 1985–89, the period known as "Second Solidarity," the Communist state was still in power, but it already started to fall apart "from within." Society already knew that the end of Communism was approaching. There were no feminist organizations yet, nor "gender consciousness" as we know it from the western context. Feminist ideas, however, started to appear as a part of the "civil society" that was emerging quite fiercely, albeit illegally, across the country.[21]

The year 1989 brought a stunning emergence of new spaces of democracy.[22] In the case of women's movement, the year 1989, when the first women's organization the Polish Feminist Association was founded, marked the progression of the mobilization toward more institutionalized forms. A majority of the initially established organizations, however, emerged as a continuation of the previous grassroots mobilizations. These grassroots women's movements also continued throughout early 1989 and 1990, particularly in the context of the abortion debate. Women from across the country were protesting the proposed restrictive abortion law (particularly well attended were the March and May 1989 demonstrations in Warsaw, Kraków, Łódź, Poznań, Bydgoszcz and Wrocław) and spontaneously forming pro-choice initiatives. In the fall of the 1989, a number of informal pro-choice groups were founded, such as "The Movement on Behalf of Women's Rights" in Poznań or the "Women's Dignity Self Defense Movement" in Toruń.

Various NGOs, foundations, associations, and formal and informal groups, surfacing in large numbers between 1991 and 2001, shaped Polish democracy. As the political system was institutionalized through the rise of the civil society, the society was embedded mostly in the work of the non-governmental organizations. A similar process was in fact taking place in other countries of central and eastern Europe (CEE) that were undergoing transformation and where the emergence of the civil society meant a formation of numerous groups, networks, and alliances. However, there is no clear agreement among feminist scholars and activists about the degree to which the use of NGOs, as a mobilizing tool, benefited women's political engagement or allowed for making feminist agendas more visible.[23] Despite contradictory claims, women's organizations emerged rapidly, and by the year 2000 there were over 300 active women's groups in Poland. They have various goals and strategies as well as institutional structures. As we have mentioned above, the initial wave of mobilization was largely a reaction to the ways in which systemic transformation affected women. A number of the foundations and associations has been established as a follow-up of the pro-choice movement after the abortion law was changed (for instance the Pro-Femina Association, "Neutrum" Association and the Federation for Women and Family Planning). At the same time, a first group of service organizations focusing on violence against women and where a labor market has been established. Associations and foundations such as the Women's Right's Center, the Center for Promotion of Women in Warsaw, and the Association for Women's Activism in Rzeszów have been formed.

The influx of Western funds in the mid-1990s the most important of them being the Soros and the Ford Foundations, led to the creation of another set of women's organizations. Foundations and groups focusing on more general equality issues, such as promoting equal status of women and men in various domains of life: politics, leadership, education, art, and culture, began to dominate the women's NGOs scene. Through dissemination of information, conferences, seminars and publications, organizations such as eFKa in Kraków, OŚKa in Warsaw, and Konsola in Poznań aimed at developing the so-called political culture, in which equal opportunities for women and men will be promoted. Many of them, formally or informally, cooperated with various political parties at the national and supranational (i.e. European) level. Locally, branches of the reestablished League of Polish Women and Rural Women Circles have been focusing on improving women's position in rural areas through workshops and training in computer skills, and more recently, European grants proposal writing. At the supranational level, women's and feminist groups have been working on developing regional and transregional cooperation by focusing on areas such as reproductive rights (ASTRA), economic literacy (KARAT Coalition) or law (Network of East–West Women, NEWW). More recently, a number of informal groups and coalitions focus on making the feminist agenda more accessible to women representing various locations and age groups through feminist camps (Ulica Siostrzana) and street demonstrations (Women's Agreement). Finally, organizations focusing on the rights of particular groups of women such as lesbians (Lesbian Agreement) or mothers (Mama Foundation) have been gaining their visibility within the movement. The examples of formal and informal initiatives and mobilizations discussed above reflect the extensive diversity of women's needs. What they also indicate is the enormous resourcefulness and ingenious ability of women's and feminist groups to address diverse audiences and develop varied strategies and interventions in order to (re)shape women's agendas and public discourses.[24]

With whom then do Polish women work and what strategies do they use? How do these actions affect the formations of their political subjecthood? Using the examples of women's and feminist groups' mobilizations and interventions before and after Poland had become an EU member, the next section examines the processes through which these groups engage as political subjects.

Framing new political women's subjecthood: Poland's EU membership

Polish women's NGOs believe that social attitudes have to change in order to alter women's position in the society, but they differ in their perceptions of who should be the primary audience of these efforts. Ultimately, the strategies and audiences they have been choosing are wide-ranging. Should it be women themselves, state institutions, politicians, or all of them?

The heterogeneity of women's concerns, needs, and their varying life trajectories is directly reflected in a great diversity of women who are targeted by the groups' programs. Thus NGOs offer programs for women who have difficulty in adjusting to the free market (unemployed and those seeking jobs or looking for new carrier opportunities); for business women and managers; for young women (age 18–35, who work or study); for single mothers; for disabled or elderly women; or for women interested in running for political office. However, not all women's groups restrict themselves to work with women only. Some of these groups want to focus their actions on the whole society, as they would like to return to the notion of citizens' participation and the participatory energy that emerged around the regime changes in 1989.[25] These groups call for greater involvement at the grassroots level and for local mobilizations, arguing that as the country does not have sufficient financial resources (but also willingness and political will) to introduce social change, self-organizing is needed: "we need to refresh 'little society', so it feels again consolidated" (NPW12).[26,27]

The ambivalent relationship with feminism is critical for shaping the identities of women's groups, as well as their agendas and actions. Some groups make it explicit that while they offer programs for women, these are not feminist programs, and that they do not have any plans to depart from that position although they will continue to focus on a wide range of women's activities. Feminist groups almost exclusively focus on women: they want to create space for women, to work with women and only with women. In their view, such a space has to be independent from state structures; it has to be defended from the state and its actions; it has also to be protected from other movements. The primary efforts should focus on increasing awareness among women and engaging feminists in actions. For some, the only appropriate way of action is through feminist education: "We are doing feminist education, that means self-education and education. We would like to see more of feminism in Polish culture and in public life; more of thinking of just relationships between sexes and of course, women, first of all women" (NPW8). Some groups, like Ulica Siostrzana, perceive as one of their main political goals the necessity to negotiate and widen feminist discourses and make them more accessible for women, as one of their main political goals. Throughout the yearly feminist camp, members of Ulica hope to reach out to women from small towns and rural areas, and facilitate a debate about the meaning of feminism and women's rights. This informal group pays special attention to accommodating women with children – a separate camp for kids accompanies each summer action.[28] Other initiatives aim at developing closer relationships between feminists and labor unions. Collaboration between feminists and the medical staff employees' union during the 2007 nurses' strikes in Warsaw as well as feminist activists' involvement in the anti-discrimination mobilization of the TESCO unions in 2007 and 2008 are just some examples of such efforts.

Most recently, the focus of feminist activism has shifted toward addressing issues specific to certain groups of women, such as mothers, lesbians, women representing various ethnic backgrounds or girls. Initiatives such as Lesbian Empowerment (organized by Konsola in Poznań), Mama w Centrum and Mama Foundation (feminist support groups and policy development groups in Warsaw), Traveling Women (project focusing on women refugees living in Poland realized in Kraków), or Wen-Do for Girls (self-defense courses for young girls organized across the country) are just some instances of such a shift. The greater diversity is sometimes the cause of tensions within the women's movement as various ideologies (e.g. liberal, socialist) and approaches to women's rights are represented. As will be shown later, these distinctions in ideology of feminist and women's groups resulted in different approaches and strategies that are used by these groups.

State institutions represent another critical audience and target of NGOs' actions. These relationships are very fluid and have been changing depending on the political regime in power, with right-wing parties being more exclusionary and left-wing parties more open, but not necessarily more willing to address some of the primary women's concerns such as reproductive rights. In the early 1990s, despite many hopes for a quick opening of the public sphere for women, there was very little direct collaboration with state institutions. As economic and political transformation progressed and the results of these changes began to impact women's status and position, the contacts between NGOs and state structures became more frequent and deeper. They ranged from collaborations and cooperation to advocacy, lobbying, and open resistance. The direct threat and subsequent restrictions of women's rights to abortion was probably the single most important factor in consolidating and mobilizing the women's movement in the 1990s. The EU accession negotiations in the 1990s and Poland's consequent membership in 2004, have further shaped the intensity of these relationships as well as forms of collaborations and linkages. Equally critical for collective mobilization and relationships with the state was the reign of the right-wing party Law and Justice (2005–7) that has galvanized numerous actions and demonstrations.

Throughout the 1990s and 2000s, women's NGOs began to work more closely with local governments, with state offices, such as the Office of the Governmental Plenipotentiary for Equal Status or the Ministry of Labor and Social Policy, as well as with individual politicians. As numerous advisory councils emerged in the 1990s, women's NGOs were invited as members.[29] For some, especially feminist groups, the quandary of dual identity – remaining independent or engaging with the state and therefore sacrificing their autonomy – present a dilemma. While they do not see these relations as oppositional, they nevertheless do worry about being co-opted in their dealings. One of the representatives of a women's NGO engaged in lobbying on behalf of gender equality described this tension in the following way:

> Should we stay at the level of the grassroots movement, in opposition to state structures, or should we try to cooperate and possibly influence state structure, so that they would move more into the direction of equality of women and men or towards the issues that state should be involved in, although often it doesn't even know about them, yet these concerns are very important for women …
>
> (NPW21)

Some other groups, including feminist groups, often distrust and reject organizations as a tool for action: "I am a feminist, so I dislike organizations, because organizations were created by men" (NPW22). Women's and feminist groups believe that what makes NGOs attractive as agents of change is the fact that they can access a large group of people and they are not so bureaucratic; they have knowledge and a variety of channels through which they can work and collaborate channels that are not available to the government.

Politicians, both male and female, represent another distinct target group. Women's and feminist groups are aware that the level of knowledge varies tremendously between institutions and individuals, and thus the goals they set for themselves are strategically adjusted depending on circumstances. They use different forms of advocacy and lobbying; they send information, write letters, protest as well as invite politicians to their activities. In some cases, they were satisfied with what they perceived as a minimal accomplishment when members of government (which are predominantly men) reached, as one group put it, "the verbal level" – in other words, when these male politicians could talk about equality and show that this is important.

Far more attention of women's NGOs has been focused on working with women politicians, especially women in the government (to a lesser degree women elected to the parliament). The exception here was, for years, a close collaboration between NGOs and the Parliamentary Women's Group.[30] In many instances NGOs collaborated with the Parliamentary Group on various pieces of legislation, such as the Equal Status Act, or assisted in reviewing the pending legislation. The intensity of relationships with women politicians had been fluctuating, depending on the particular political moment and the emerging specific pressures. For example, during the negotiations with the EU, women's and feminist groups often attempted to work directly with members of the government or central institutions such as Minister Irena Boruta who was responsible in Poland during the EU negotiations for Chapter 13 on Social and Economic Policy (the only place where gender concerns were addressed). NGOs solicited her participation and established contact with her. Yet, groups felt that although these were very intensive contacts, they went only one way; Boruta never invited or solicited the assistance of NGOs. When Minister Jaruga-Nowacka (2002–4) held the office, and to some degree Minister Środa (2004–5), contacts with NGOs were very frequent and intense; however, when the right-wing Law and Justice party was in power, the Office of the Plenipotentiary was eliminated and many programs initiated previously were terminated. The arrival of the new Liberal–Conservative government has not brought much needed changes in the area of women's interaction with women politicians either. In March 2008, the newly appointed prime minister, who represents the Civil Platform party, refused the reinstallment of the Office of Plenipotentiary at its previous, ministerial rank.

How to make women's concerns visible: strategies for empowerment

The instances of women's activism across the world show how the use of particular strategies depends on a set of the objectives to be achieved, on resources available to particular group as well as on the skills and knowledge in their possession.[31] Chosen strategies depend on the social understanding and attitudes toward feminism or gender equality, and more generally toward the role of women in a particular society. Women's understanding of their own positionality and their sense of feminist identity affect particular strategic choices made by groups. Strategies differ depending on the audiences that they aim to address (e.g. state institutions, politicians, media, women or society) and vary across the geographical scale (e.g. local, national, transnational or global). Groups make choices and act independently or interact with each other as they exchange information, collaborate, form partnerships and networks, and/or compete for ideas and resources. Frequently, groups are simultaneously involved in several projects and engage several strategies that cross geographical scales, involve different locations, and require a use of diverse resources. As groups strategize and define their goals, conflicts of interest do emerge that sometimes preclude a formation of strategic partnerships, but other times result in a formation of new alliances.[32]

As women attempted to enter the masculinized and monopolized (by Polish men) public sphere, women's NGOs tried to create new entry points as well as to transform the existing political structures. The strategies that groups used reflected the specific moment in the history of the Polish women's movement that was shaped by its internal dynamic as well as by larger external conditions. These transformative strategies not only underscore the encountered struggles and resistances, but also reflect the ongoing process of strengthening women's agency that becomes increasingly political. In the 1990s, confronted with new concerns such as access to abortion, unemployment or limited political participation, women's and feminist NGOs became more strategic when developing their plans of action. By 2000, new concerns gained priority such as women's health, lesbian rights, sexual violence and the parenting laws in Poland. Within this context, the strategies that Polish women's NGOs utilized can be grouped along three dimensions: 1) empowering women;

2) strengthening domestic institutions and influencing national policies; and 3) engaging transnational resources. We discuss each of them briefly below.

Empowering women

Both women's and feminist NGOs saw consciousness-raising among women as a critical starting point for their work. They believed that women have to be aware of their status and have to understand how they can introduce change through their actions. Scholars and women's NGOs believe that such a process was started at the beginning of the 1990s from the abortion debate. As one representative of an NGO indicated, "the issue of women in Poland began from that legislation ... the discussion about women's role, their participation in political life, engaging with power, and creation of NGOs" (NPW1), and another added, "this was the base on which they began to develop women's NGOs" (NPW5). Raising women's consciousness is often a key element allowing women to realize that besides family roles, they could also have a professional and public role. In this context, "the consciousness raising process was about teaching women to reconcile these responsibilities and show such a model" (NPW5). For others, this was about gaining autonomy for self-realization.

Women's and feminist NGOs believe that Poland has strong gender-related law. Whether such a perception is correct might be too soon to judge, given that only a few legal cases have been tested in the courts so far. Women leaders have recognized that "Law is not enough, if we do not treat equally ourselves" (NPW12). They have often downplayed the fact that the legal framework exists and argue that attention needs to be focused on other mechanisms that shape the view of the society, such as education and/or media. The case of access to lawfully granted abortion for Alicja Tysiąc, successfully argued in the European Court of Human Rights in 2007, showed that using legal remedies both in Poland and on the European level might be, in fact, extremely important. This case prepared and argued by lawyers from women's NGOs has not only set a precedent, but it has also given visibility to the key concerns of women in Poland and to women's NGOs. In the opinion of women's NGOs, the main difficulty that exists is the gap between *de jure* and *de facto* reality: in theory, law is equal, but practices create inequality. Therefore, as argued by one respondent, what needs to be changed are these practices:

> We are aware that the legal framework in our region is relatively good; the main problem is with the implementation; equal status for us is primarily the implementation; searching for mechanisms how to implement law; we are concentrating on things that would equalize, that would strengthen [women's position].
>
> *(NPW9)*

During the two decades since the Polish political transformation began, many NGOs have fully engaged in generating new information, gaining new knowledge, producing materials and distributing them widely. Organizations such as eFKA, OŚKa, NEWW, Federation for Women and Family Planning, KARAT Coalition as well as more informal entities including Emancypunx or Women's Agreement, have pushed women's diverse agendas into the forefront. Through training, seminars, workshops, brochures, pamphlets, books, reports, exhibitions, manifestations, performances or websites, women's and feminist NGOs were able to reach other women and "give to our women and distribute knowledge, because this is very important" (NPW1). The Center for Women's Rights published all EU directives, as "the government didn't do anything in this regard, to publicize directives, to distribute information" (NPW15). Since 2000, yearly celebrations on March 8, "Manifa," and Equality or Tolerance Gay and Lesbian Marches exposed in public spaces the most pressing women's concerns.[33] Through performance, satire, and ridicule, thousands of women, children, and men, in many cities across Poland, express their collective frustration with the persistence of gender stereotypes, discrimination of women, gay and lesbians, and the lack of political will to address these concerns.[34]

The availability of the internet and the possibility of accessing websites and participating in discussion lists allow greater access for those who seek to be informed and who otherwise may not be able to do so. Perhaps the most successful example of an effective use of the information and communication technology was the website on EU negotiations launched by the NEWW. Other later instances include the feminist bookstore, portal and chatroom launched by Feminoteka in 2005. Success is the best way to publicize a particular cause and thus raise consciousness. The previously mentioned case of Alicja Tysiąc unquestionably raised the profile of the Polish women's struggle to secure reproductive rights. Leaders of women's and feminist NGOs repeatedly pointed to successes, and to their critical role in raising visibility and calling attention to domestic violence, sexual molestation, violence against children, and rape. Given the existing social stigma, talking about bodily integrity in a public space has been particularly difficult. Yet, feminist activists believe that fostering the process of community education is critical. They have pointed out that by focusing on sexual and domestic violence and bringing out the concern for women's safety into a public space, an increased sense of responsibility among people and neighbors can be achieved. Such campaigns set in motion a process of awakening and realization that domestic violence is frequently present although not acknowledged. Some examples of these actions include the "Safe Taxi" campaign realized by OŚKa in 2003, the workshops for police staff on dealing with domestic violence, and the campaign to expose sexual molestation in one of the political parties (Samoobrona) in 2007 and 2008 (feminist organizations assisted in the court trials).

Strengthening domestic institutions and influencing national policies

The strategies used by Polish women's and feminist NGOs have no doubt been affected by the state actions and state policies (or the lack of them). At the same time, these strategies have altered the level of knowledge and consciousness among creators and implementers of these policies – politicians, administrators, and bureaucrats, judges, police officers, doctors and nurses, academics and teachers, among others.

The persistent lack of political will to address women's concerns, and lack of knowledge about these concerns, are among the major obstacles that women's groups report.[35] Women also point to the little effort being made to include women's groups in discussions, including open hostility and a lack of domestic financial resources as main institutional obstacles. These challenges shaped in turn particular strategies that groups devised, such as protest letter writing, engaging with media, working with state institutions or focusing on institutional capacity-building.

Sending invitations to events, writing letters of inquiry, letters of protests and demands, has become a frequently used tool.[36] Letters have been written repeatedly, regardless of the political orientation of the elites in power. By continuously providing the elites with information, NGOs are engaging in their learning process and thus creating new knowledge-based instruments[37] that have become critical strategic tools. Women's NGOs spend a considerable amount of effort and resources on building different forms of contacts and relationships with state institutions. Faced with many challenges, the chief among them being the varying level of political will, groups have to adjust their activism accordingly. NGOs also believe that their inputs and effective working relationships have affected, in many instances, the agenda and the functioning of the various offices (e.g. the Plenipotentiary office).[38]

This process of building new partnerships and strategies that involved state offices, and the process of developing new directions of strategic thinking, reflect how women's and feminist NGOs came to understand the significance of their role in introducing social change. As groups became more aware of how various systems work, their understanding of the role that each of these systems plays and of the strategic entry points that could be utilized by NGOs has also increased. As one women's group summed up, "We were taking a very active role in shaping these changes, because we were speaking out" (NPW11). Many NGO leaders do believe, however, that in order to have an impact on the national policy-making process, women themselves have to realize not only that this is a continuous struggle, but also that it requires the consolidation of women's movement, as mass mobilization: "Without a strong women's movement, without lobbying, without self-organization nothing will change" (NPW2).

Engaging transnational resources

One of the striking features of Polish feminist and women's activism is that, notwithstanding its engagement on the transnational level, as in case of EU- and UN-related activities, it rarely defines and relates its experiences and activities to the transnational and/or international level in its everyday practices. Often it focuses on internal issues only, defines its objectives and goals in reference to the national scale, and rarely attempts to reach beyond the nation-state level. As a result, because it is not integrated and connected at the transnational level, Polish feminist and women's activism does not engage the international feminist discussions. It seldom defines its identity in reference to foreign feminism and/or transnational feminist debates at the European and international level (such as debate between East–West or South–North). Predominantly women's activism is concentrated on addressing the immediate problems of Polish women (such as abortion and violence against women, even though these are global concerns) or internal issues and debates concerning the feminist movement in Poland (such as the debate on the role of different generations in shaping feminism). Only a few of the largest NGOs are visible partners in the transnational women's movement and even that presence is confined primarily to the EU and the UN context. Groups such as the NEWW, the Federation of Women and Family Planning, and KARAT Coalition regularly participate, engage, and collaborate with the international partners. Over the years, they have become active members of coalitions and networks and actively engaged in advocacy and lobbying in Brussels, Geneva, and New York.

These transnational and international engagements grow over time as women's and feminist groups become more active and visible domestically, but also as global women's mobilization gains momentum. The 1995 Beijing conference on women was of historical significance for women in CEE as it was the first time that women from the Communist region could participate in large numbers in global women's mobilization. During the previous women's conferences in Nairobi and Cairo, Polish women as well as women from other CEE countries were absent. Preparation for the Beijing conference allowed Polish women to engage in advocacy work through the preparation of the "shadow report" on the status and position of women in Poland. This shadow to the governmental, official report mobilized women's groups to consolidate their efforts and present at the international forum the joint effort of their work that openly challenged state data, philosophy and claims of successes.

The process of maturation and of progressively deeper engagement in international and transnational networks, and advocacy and lobbying activities, can be illustrated by analyzing women's involvement in the EU accession process. Initially, groups saw in the EU a source of knowledge and benefits; they were eager to be introduced to new information, concepts and institutions. They were learning but not acting yet.[39] As the contacts between NGOs, state and international, and the EU institutions grew more frequent, and women's and feminist NGOs engaged in gathering information and in its dissemination, their role became more critical for increasing women's awareness and consciousness about the effects of the EU membership on women's lives. As a result of the groups' invitations to join meetings, participate in seminars, contribute opinions or present materials related to Polish women and women's concerns, nationally and internationally, new forms of networks of connections and engagements have developed. These relationships have become more interactive and multifaceted, and their impact has become stronger and more visible:

> NGOs were participating in these kind of discussions, they brought new knowledge, new information and the spectrum was getting wider, so in the last

[few] years there is this [new] link: the influence of Europe on organizations, organizations on us and we influence organizations ... this is such a connected system.

(NPW18)

While the EU has brought new layers of power, it has also opened new opportunities. The groups did not shy away from utilizing these links. For example, in 1998, a letter of appeal was written by women's and feminist NGOs to Mme Francoise Gaudenzi, chief EU negotiator for Poland's accession to the Union, expressing concerns with the lack of commitment, on the part of the Polish government, to gender equality policies and practices. Similarly, in 2002, when the Polish government entered into an agreement with the Catholic Church, women's and feminist groups participated in a protest letter address to the European Parliament and Anna Diamantopoulou, at that time the EU Commissioner for Employment and Social Affairs. By reaching across the borders and putting pressure on the EU institutions, women's and feminist groups wanted to draw EU members' attention to women's situations in Poland. While the European Parliament could not interfere directly into Polish affairs, nevertheless, it did pass a resolution stating that women in accession countries should have a right to choose.

The letter-writing was important and it became just one of the possible tools to be utilized. Increasingly women began to influence policy-making processes at the supranational level of the EU using the methods that were similar to those used by groups at national level. This required from them an understanding of how the system works, where the most effective entry points are for women to make their contributions, and what resources, knowledge, and skills they will need. One of the groups described this process as follows:

> We are focusing on the labor market within the context of European Union, it means we are researching, we want to research what the European strategy of employment looks like, how it is being translated into the national strategies of employment, and this is indeed a lot of work. Then we look how one can influence it. We know that European Union from 2001 ... introduced elements of social consultation with social partners and it believes that this will be an effective strategy. We can very precisely write in ourselves into these demands of the EU, because indeed, consultations with NGOs are required ... so it means that we have a chance to influence employment policy.
>
> (NPW9)

In another instance, NGOs learned about the ways through which they can make an intervention to the Convent on the Future Europe, and one of the three submitted contributions from Poland was from women's and feminist NGOs.

Learning to intervene in the political and policy-making process meant that these groups needed to know how and when to be critical. Although in the early stages of the accession process very few groups saw themselves as transnational critical agents, over time their actions and strategies have become more assertive. One of the leaders stressed: "We are not only looking at how to win various directives regarding employment, but also how to influence the EU, because this is also our task, not only wait what is flowing from Union, because some things are not relevant to women's situation" (NPW9). This shift from being a passive recipient of information to becoming an active agent of change indicates the process of maturing of NGOs and seeing themselves as playing a critical role in constructing transnational dialogues and building strategies that cross national borders. For groups working with the EU and its institutions, their interactions are a form of political and feminist activism; they want to secure the position of women as active participants in political life. While many NGOs feel that the hopes and expectations offered by the membership in the EU were never delivered, for some the integration with the EU presented a useful tool to become more active and to rethink the notion of citizenship in a new and multilevel way.[40] One of the leaders of women's NGOs was very conscious of this link: "Integration with the EU is an issue of citizenship, European citizenship. Being a citizen means being a conscious citizen, means participating, taking part" (NPW8). In their opinion, "it is about European citizenship of women – increase of women's participation in public and political life. Within the context of EU we want to be conscious, we want to be informed, we want to participate" (NPW8).

Conclusion

Since 1989, women's and feminist NGOs have emerged as active and knowledgeable agents that attempt to be informed about what is happening and have a vision about the kind of interventions and changes that need to be made to improve women's position in Poland. Through the process of inviting, questioning, evaluating, and promoting their points of view, NGOs have created new practices of political engagement that have not only positioned them as political subjects, but also revealed the formation process of their agency.

Over time, however, the initial desire for collective actions has been replaced by increased fragmentation. Feminist and women's NGOs' strategies have become increasingly more diversified and multidimensional; the organizations have also become strategic in selecting their partners, their tools of action and setting up networks of collaborators. Groups' missions have guided these choices and the tasks they wanted to achieve, but also were reflected in NGOs' organizational structures, financial resources, skills, and geographical locations. The groups' sense of being political in their work, or perceiving themselves as being feminist in their activities, has further shaped the choice of their strategies. While initial focus on reproductive rights has been replaced by a variety of mobilizations, a number of previously omitted questions have been raised, such as those of sexual minority rights, the relation between women's movements and neoliberalism, and the efficiency of previously dominating institutional forms of involvement such as through NGOs and political parties. Many activists are now asking if such fragmentation benefits or hurts feminists' long-term commitments to issues such as changing the existing abortion law. In the face of the lack of political will and mass women's support for the feminist goals in Poland, the new strategies of mobilizing have become scattered and do not always represent connected struggles. This seems to be one of the biggest challenges for the movement.

One way of achieving social support, questioned by many feminists themselves, is commitment to non-radical emancipation discourses. Despite the differences between feminist and women's NGOs in terms of the strategies they used and audiences they addressed, even the most "radical" groups represent very moderate (and we could argue restricted) notions of feminism. In most cases, women's and feminist NGOs have represented versions of liberal feminism and defined feminism in terms of rights and equality (as opposed to the focus on difference) and distanced themselves from the radical feminist activities. These definitions of feminism are very inclusive of men, but it is only to a limited degree that the groups see the need to recognize differences among various groups of women (e.g. lesbians, migrant women, rural women, elderly women). As the most vocal women's and feminist NGOs also have the most money at their disposal, they are the most visible and present in the public sphere, and therefore the most influential in shaping public discourse on women and gender.

Polish women's and feminist activism, before and after eastern enlargement of the EU, continues to experience an adversarial relationship with the state and the groups are aware of that. Some do actually want to establish a closer relationship with national institutions as well as political parties; others are suspicious of such relationships. Nevertheless, many groups work with state institutions recognizing that despite some voices about the demise of the state, the opposite is true: the state's role in controlling resources and selectively addressing gender and women's concerns is visible, and in many respects strengthened. Similarly, many of these groups have an ambivalent view as to their transnational involvement. By 2011, one thing seems to be much clearer for many groups, and that is their ability to achieve successes; they see these successes as resulting from their and their NGOs' hard work rather than an outcome of contributions by others.

Notes

1 The authors wish to acknowledge support from the National Science Foundation grant No. BCS-0137954. This research project involved three teams from the Czech Republic (Alena Krizkowa, Hanna Haskova, Dagmar Lorenz-Meyer and Lenka Simierska), Poland (Malgorzata Fuszara, Joanna Mizielinska), and the US (Magdalena Grabowska and Joanna Regulska), and was directed by Joanna Regulska. The results presented here are based on over 50 face-to-face interviews conducted during 2002–5 in Poland with women's NGOs, politicians and governmental representatives (both men and women).
2 Einhorn, Barbara. 2005. "Citizenship in an Enlarging Europe: Contested Strategies." *Czech Sociological Review* 41 (6): 1023–39.
3 Gal, Susan, and Gail Kligman, eds. 2000. *Reproducing Gender: Politics, Publics, and Everyday Life after Socialism.* Princeton: Princeton University Press.
4 Desai, Manisha. 2002. "Transnational Solidarity: Women's Agency, Structural Adjustment, and Globalization." In *Women's Activism and Globalization: Linking Local Struggles*

and *Transnational Politics*, ed. Nancy A. Naples and Manisha Desai, 14–31. London: Routledge.
5 Wolff, Larry. 1994. *Inventing Eastern Europe: The Map of Civilization on the Mind of the Enlightenment*. Stansford: Stanford University Press.
6 Cavanagh, C. 2004. "Postcolonial Poland", in: *Common Knowledge*, 10: 82–92.
7 Fidelis, Małgorzata. 2010. *Women, Communism, and Industrialization in Postwar Poland*. New York: Cambridge University Press.
8 Penn S. 2005. *Solidarity's Secret: The Women Who Defeated Communism in Poland*. Ann Arbor: University of Michigan Press.
9 Regulska, J. and M. Grabowska 2008. "Will it make a Difference?" *EU Enlargement and European Union*, S. Rothe (ed). Oxford, UK: Berghahn Books, 137–54.
10 Charkiewicz, Ewa. 2004 "From Communism to Neoliberalism. Pathologizing Eastern Europe(ans) as political technology," Paper presented at the Conference *From Cold War to European Union. Women and Gender in Contemporary Europe* at Rutgers University, New Brunswick, October 2, 2004.
11 Regulska, Joanna, and Magdalena Grabowska (forthcoming) "Social Justice, Hegemony and Women's Mobilizations." In *Justice, hegemony and Mobilization: Views from East/Central Europe and Eurasia*, ed. Jan Kubik and Amy L. Linch. New York: NYU press.
12 Lukić. J., Regulska, J. and D. Zaviršek (eds). 2006. *Women and Citizenship in Central and East Europe*. Aldershot: Ashgate. Einhorn Barbara and Charlotte Sever. 2003. "Gender and Civil Society in Central and Eastern Europe" in: *International Feminist Journal of Politics* 5 (2): 163–90.
13 Mizielińska, J. 2008. Przyjaciółki czy rywalki? Wpływ Unii Europejskiej na relacje pomiędzy kobiecymi NGO-sami ("Friends and rivals? The European Unions influence on the relations between women's NGOs"). In Fuszara, M., Grabowska, M., Mizielińska, J. and Regulska, J. (2008). *Kooperacja czy Konflikt?: Państwo, Unia Europejska i Kobiety*, (*Cooperation or Conflict? State, The European Union and Women*). Warsaw: Wydawnictwa Akademickie i Profesjonalne). (In Polish)
14 Regulska, Joanna, and Magdalena Grabowska. 2007. "New Geographies of Women Subjectivities in Poland." In *Global Babel: Questions of Communication in a Time of Globalization*, ed. Samira Dayal and Margueritte Murphy, 108–43. Newcastle: Cambridge Scholars Publishing.
15 Einhorn, B. 1993. *Cinderella Goes to Market*. London: Verso.
16 Ghodsee, K. 2004. "Feminism-by-Design: Emerging Capitalisms, Cultural Feminism, and Women's Nongovernmental Organizations in Postsocialist Eastern Europe," in: *Signs: Journal of Women in Culture and Society*, 29: 727–53.
17 Graff A. 2008. *Rykoszetem. Rzecz o kobietach seksualności i narodzie* (*Backlash: A thing About Women, Sexuality and Gender*). Warsaw: WAB.
18 Sandoval, Chela. 2000. *Methodology of the Oppressed: Theory Out of Bounds*. Minneapolis: University of Minnesota Press. Also see Desai, Manisha. 2005. "Transnationalism: the face of feminist politics post-Beijing" In: *International Social Studies Journal* 57 (187): 319–30.
19 For an extensive history of women's mobilizations in the nineteenth and twentieth-century representing various approaches (separatists or nationalistic) to women's issues and employing a variety of political strategies (from participating in military struggles, through the educational activism, publishing, journalism and politics) see (Borkowska 1996, Walczewska 1993, 1999, Mrozik 2007, Chyra-Rolicz 1992, Czajkowska 1992, Żarnowska and Szwarc 1996)) and virtual museum of women's history launched by Feminoteka Foundation (http://feminoteka.pl/muzeum).
20 As regional leaders of Solidarity (Barbara Labuda), editors in chief of the biggest underground newspaper (Helena Łuczywo) and day-to-day activists of the movement, women without a doubt have their share in the defeat of the Communist regime (Penn 2005).
21 Many activists recall this period as a time "when everybody was doing something, starting something; every decent person had a life beyond the dying and demolished socialist

state." See http://mss3.libraries.rutgers.edu/dlr/showfed.php?pid=rutgers-lib:26287. Women's consciousness rising groups emerged in Warsaw, Kraków and Poznań, and maintained strong ties with women émigrés in England, Netherlands, Germany, and the US. These women organized the first major feminist event, Women's Film Festival, in Warsaw in 1985.

22 One of the earliest expressions of citizens' power and ability to organize were the Citizens' Committees that sprung across Poland in thousands. The Citizen's Committees of Lech Wałęsa were initiated in order to engage a large number of citizens in support of the first free elections of 1989 (Regulski, Jerzy: Samorząd III Rzeczypospolitej: Koncepcje i Realizacja. (Warsaw, 2000). Numerous other local grassroots initiatives involved spontaneous responses addressing local concerns such as water pollution or traffic congestions, unemployment, need for services for single mothers, elderly, sick or children.

23 Alvarez (2000); Basu, Amrita. 2003. "Globalization of the Local/Localization of the Global: Mapping Transnational Women's Movements" in *Feminist Theoary Reader*, ed. by Carole McCann and Kim Seung-Kyung (New York: Routledge, 68–77). Kaplan, Temma. 1997. *Crazy for Democracy* (New York: Routledge). Sperling, V. 1999. *Organizing Women in Contemporary Russia: Engendering Transition* (Cambridge: Cambridge University Press). These writers among others, have been pointing out how women, in the regions of drastic political and economic transformations, by organizing and participating in NGOs, make visible their strengthened agency and how they challenge the old ways of being political. Others argued that using NGOs as a primary vehicle for such mobilization limits women's abilities to make their agendas visible and effective: Jaggar, Alison. 2005. "Arena of citizenship: Civil society, state, and the global order" in *International Feminist Journal of Politics* 7 (1): 3–25. Jacquette, Jane. 2003. "Feminism and the Challenges of the Post-Cold War World" in *International Feminist Journal of Politics* 5.3: 331–355.

24 For a more extensive discussion of diverse strategies and agendas world-wide see (Naples and Desai 2002, Ricciutelli, Miles and McFadden 2005, Kaplan 1997, Fuszara 2006).

25 These tensions between focusing primarily on the society as a whole or mainly on women were especially visible when respondents explored the meaning of gender equality and equal status and how their work is shaped by this terminology, which is to a large degree EU-induced. Two prevailing approaches seem to be utilized: those that believe that gender equality requires giving primary attention to women and increasing their rights in the first place (given their marginalized status within the society), and those who clearly included men in their understanding of the notion of equality.

26 NPW12 refers to coding of the interviews and stands for non-governmental women's organization in Poland number 12 (the number reflects the alphabetical order of interviewed groups).

27 Recently published data indeed indicate that the membership in NGOs has declined since 2005 and that this decline is especially visible among youth (Gumowska 2007). http://civicpedia.ngo.pl/files/civicpedia.pl/public/raporty/Poland_CSI_report_FINAL.pdf. For more data and discussion see Korolczuk, E. 2008. "Gendered Boundaries between the State, Family and Civil Society – the case of Poland after 1989." Unpublished paper.

28 Information about feminist camps is available at http://siostrzana.org.

29 For example, women activists joined the Advisory Council to the Office of the Committee for European Integration as well as the Advisory Council to the Office of the Governmental Plenipotentiary for Equal Status. Such participations were of great importance for NGOs not only because of enhancing their visibility, but also because these interactions allowed NGOs representatives to influence policy-making processes and to bring back new information and knowledge to their organizations.

30 A group of women, Parliamentary deputies, representing different political parties. The group was created in 1991 (http://pgk.kluby.sejm.pl/o_pgk.html).

31 Naples, N. A. and Desai, M. 2002. *Women's Activism and Globalization*. London: Routledge. Ricciutelli, L., Miles, A. and McFadden, M. H. 2005. *Feminist Politics*

Activism and Vision: Local and Global Challenges. Toronto: Inanna Publications and Education, Inc., and London and NY: Zed Books.
32 Mizielińska, J., 2008. Przyjaciółki czy rywalki? Wpływ Unii Europejskiej na relacje pomiędzy kobiecymi NGO-sami ("Friends and rivals? The European Unions influence on the relations between women's NGOs"). In Fuszara, M., Grabowska, M., Mizielińska, J. and Regulska, J. (2008). *Kooperacja czy Konflikt?: Państwo, Unia Europejska i Kobiety, (Cooperation or Conflict? State, The European Union and Women)*. Warsaw: Wydawnictwa Akademickie i Profesjonalne).
33 Regulska, J. and Grabowska, M., 2007. "New Geographies of women's subjectivities in Poland", M. Murphy and S. Dayal (eds) in *Global Babel: Interdisciplinarity, Transnationalism and the Discourses of Globalization.* Newcastle: Cambridge Scholars Publishing, 102–42.
34 See www.manifa.org.
35 The recent, unprecedented success in securing gender election quota shows that women and women's NGOs can intervene in a powerful way. From February 1, 2011 the 35 percent of women minimum must now be placed on electoral lists for parliamentary elections due in the autumn 2011.
36 For example, in 1997, when Buzek took over Jerzy as Prime Minister of a right-wing government, women's and feminist groups sent him an invitation to attend the Forum of NGOs that worked with the Office of the Plenipotentiary for Family and Women's Affairs. In the same letter, they stressed their position in support of the equal status act and called attention to the upcoming membership in the EU and therefore the need to adhere to the European standards and norms. They also openly protested the renaming of the Plenipotentiary Office by eliminating its focus on women. In another letter, women's and feminist groups attending II Annual OŚKa conference wrote another letter of inquiry to Prime Minister Buzek demanding progress report in regard to gender equality and pointing to the weak areas of Polish practices.
37 Liebert, U. 2002. "Europeanising Gender Mainstreaming: Constraints and Opportunities in the Multilevel Euro-Polity," *Feminist Legal Studies 10* (3): 241–56.
38 The NGOs' inputs and efforts enabled, for example, the creation of such mechanisms as the Forum of Women's NGOs, which secured their ongoing input into the design and implementation of many activities and programs undertaken by the Plenipotentiary office. Other forms of such collaborations included invitations to participate in advisory capacities, shaping legislation, writing experts' opinions, formulating new initiatives or helping to form new guidelines for grants.
39 Regulska, J. and Grabowska, M., 2008. "Will it make a Difference? EU Enlargement and Women's Public Discourse in Poland." *In Gender Politics in the Expanding European Union,* S. Rothe (ed). Oxford, UK: Berghahn Books, 137–54.
40 Lukić. J., Regulska, J. and D. Zaviršek (eds.) 2006. *Women and Citizenship in Central and East Europe.* Aldershot: Ashgate.

CONCLUSION

Joanna Regulska

Feminist scholars have written extensively about women's experiences in Europe after World War II. These contributions often focused on western Europe or Communist states, but rarely have the two bodies of writing been brought together. Moreover, little has been written about the implications of the Cold War period for women, yet the impact of women's carrying, nurturing, working, participating, and leading has been undeniable. The authors' contributions to this volume, written specially for it, attempts to fill these gaps. As the chapters have shown, the redefinition and reconstitution of the idea of Europe since 1945 had profound implications for understanding women's experiences across Europe, both in its eastern and western part. The Cold War period initiated spatial divisions and the ideological fragmentation of Europe into welfare states and Communist states. It also forged the emergence of drastically different social, economic and political agendas and policies, and as a result, produced patterns of regulation to which, in various degrees, women were subject. This changing institutional and political context, in the opinion of contributors to this volume, had major implications on how women's identities (individual and collective), as well as their practices and their everyday lives, were shaped at home, work, and in the public sphere throughout many decades. As authors in this book demonstrate, the Cold War era reverberated not only across ideological and economic domains, but also touched other spheres of everyday life such as motherhood, reproduction, sexuality, and formation of new gender roles and masculine identities. In Europe, ideologically divided for decades, women's position and status as well as struggles for rights and justice have much in common despite the great diversity between women, especially in terms of their historical circumstances, socio-economic conditions, cultural practices, and institutional structures.

As several authors demonstrate, the Cold War period exercised its most profound impact on women's lives by creating new economic conditions and opportunities. In the Soviet bloc countries, the tenets of socialism rested on the belief in equality between women and men. State socialist ideology claimed that women can participate equally with men in labor and politics, and that women have equal rights to education, employment, medical services, and other social benefits. The theory of women's liberation first and foremost assumed the liberation from oppressive capitalist exploitation and the elimination of the patriarchal family that was supposed to be replaced by the socialist family (which nevertheless continued to be oppressive to women). Yet, it also promised the equality of sexes. In practice, this meant for women massive participation in the production sphere combined with pressures and responsibilities to fulfill the reproductive and caring duties. The images of "women on tractors" – the heroine worker – and of a celebrated motherhood – in the form of the heroine mother – created a socialist gender regime that *de facto* was based on deeply rooted gender inequalities. For women, emancipation meant to produce, reproduce and provide care. It meant to carry a double or even a triple burden. The project of emancipation of women aimed as much to aid the expansion of the working class as to justify the imposition of a set of controls and duties over women to fulfill the needs of the paternalistic state. At the same time, the paternalistic socialist state generated numerous policies that advanced women's skills and provided them with access to education, wide-ranging services, and benefits. The en masse opening of educational opportunities to women across all levels of society created a phenomenally high level of educational attainment among women. In fact, in many countries of the region, women persistently achieved higher educational level than men.

In the welfare states of western Europe, much of the initial post-WWII context produced wide-ranging institutional and policy responses that aimed at reconstructing war-weakened Europe, rebuilding nation-states, fostering rapid economic growth and providing extensive social benefits. This dramatic expansion and growth altered women's more traditional roles as mothers and caregivers only to a limited degree, with public and political spaces remaining of limited access to them. Not all women in all locations benefited equally from these economic and social changes or were hindered by them. Nevertheless, over time, post-WWII welfare state policies resulted in the decline of regional disparities, in the convergence of social benefits and in the opening of employment opportunities for women, albeit many of these possibilities involved flexible, part-time jobs without benefits, with low wages and limited opportunities for professional advancement. Furthermore, the increased number of women in politics (from below and above), in particular in Scandinavian countries, and the emergence of the women-friendly welfare states resulting from that representation, to some degree did shift the focus towards empowerment and inclusion of women.

In the end, as this volume shows, it is not clear how much these diverse gender policies of the Cold War era, rooted in drastically different ideologies and implemented with varying degrees of success, differed in their ability to eradicate gender inequalities, as these disparities continued to exist both in "western" and "eastern" Europe. Despite women's entry into the labor force in the Soviet bloc countries, the persistence of occupational gender segregation, the wage gap and income inequalities indicate that the socialist project, contrary to its proclamations of equality, ultimately was not interested in equality. In fact, its policies aided the reproduction of inequalities, with women remaining to occupy the position of marginalized economic subjects. Although under Communism women's participation in the labor force increased, the fact that such a change was an effect of the imposition of the socialist regime from the outside made it unappreciated and unwanted. Yet the authors in this volume argue that it provided women with increased independence and self-esteem. The formal socialist top-down equality concealed discrimination despite women being key sources of cheap labor for industrialization and implementation of economic plans.

As some contributions to this volume argue, the diverse conditions, and thus varied individual and collective experiences, set different socio-economic, cultural and institutional contexts within which Cold War era policies were implemented. Although the socialist tenets did attempt to eliminate difference, inequality, as well as diverse traditions, and they strived to construct the Soviet block as a homogeneous entity, in the end they did not fully succeed. The privileging of some imaginaries, such as women on tractors, was paralleled by the silencing of others. This was the case of women's welfare work. The Communist leaders deliberately attempted to marginalize the existence of social work, seeing it as a petite-bourgeois women's occupation that should not exist under Communism, and therefore part of the class struggle. Interestingly, while across the Soviet bloc social work educational programs were being eliminated, Yugoslavia's schools of social work were expanded. Yugoslavia's different political trajectory, with its "third way," became realized through the establishment of "socialism with human face" in which social work became one of the vehicles for its implementation. In this context social work became a by-product of Cold War tensions.

Ultimately, both in the "West" and "East" the understanding of work as mainly taking place within the sphere of production meant that reproductive work that women were responsible for was seen as important, but certainly not of equal status. The need for the labor on the one hand, and the importance of preserving the nation on the other, required women to procreate. And these demands left a deep imprint on the reproductive agenda that emerged across Europe after World War II. To address these needs, in both the welfare state countries as well as in the socialist block, the state employed a wide range of tools and policies to increase women's fertility rates and to regulate women's sexuality. Simultaneously, however, Europe in the west and in the east has witnessed an emergence of competing sexual and reproductive regimes. Women mobilized, organized, talked and distributed propaganda in efforts to regain control over their lives by fighting for abortion rights or procuring illegal abortion, by attempting to control their fertility or by exercising their sexual choice.

The notion of motherhood became the subject of a multidimensional state's agenda that often reflected the specific social, economic and political realities of the moment. It also shows how such notions are deeply imbedded in national conventions, cultural traditions, beliefs and values. The dramatic expansion and growth altered women's more traditional roles as mothers and caregivers only to a limited degree, with public and political spaces remaining of limited access to them. The postwar shift from collective to a domestic form of citizenship emphasized the citizen's role in the making of nations through establishing families and home; indeed this was a dramatic need in a destroyed Europe. This process of constructing of fatherhood and motherhood was not limited however to the private sphere. The media and broadcasting industry was enlisted as a powerful tool to shape mother–child relationships and to introduce new norms, practices and interpretations of social relationships within a conservative family and where a child was seen as the future citizen of a democratic society. In many instances, the state played a major role by permitting and often facilitating interventions into women's bodies. While Romania under Ceauşescu represented the most extreme case of such abuse of the state power, the restrictive abortion law in different parts of Europe also points to the power of other institutions, such as the Church, in shaping women's rights discourses and practices in Europe regardless of ideological locations of "East" and "West."

Consumption and consumerism featured prominently in the process of engulfing and enlisting new spaces, both symbolic amd material. The power of consumerism was undeniable, as it shaped practices of modernity, sexual behavior and women's emancipation. These patterns of consumption and consumerism not only were gendered, but they were also racialized. But precisely because of consumerism's potential to instigate change, consumerism was perceived both as a positive and as a dangerous phenomenon that indeed could unleash desire for progress, social change and possibly political instability. In western European countries modernity tended to unfold alongside the rapid increase of material abundance, especially those for women's and household use, while women's idealized role of good housekeepers influenced public affairs. At the same time, the socialist regimes retained tight control over the citizen's access to consumer goods and used it strategically as a political tool to divert their attention in times of political uncertainties.

By the 1960s and 1970s in western Europe, there were new standards of living and patterns of economic growth and thus an increased demand for transnational labor. Cold War tensions fostered new imaginaries of First World superiority, and by doing so reinforced global hierarchies and made invisible the First World dependence on material and human resources from the global south and its continuing exploitation. These reinforced global hierarchies forged new migratory patterns that supplied western Europe with cheap labor of women and men from developing countries, thus marking the new era of transnational labor migration and pointing to the role that different parts of the world played in reemergence of postwar western Europe.

The ongoing reconfiguration of Europe was not limited only to ideological, cultural or economic changes. Many of these changes have to do with the continued processes of reterritorialization and deterritorialization that have been initiated by the creation of the European Commission and further pursued through the many enlargements and integration efforts that continued throughout decades. Hobsbawm,[1] in fact, argued that it was the Cold War that played a significant role in advancing the desire for European integration in response to the fear of superpowers and to the pressures for West Germany's integration into the anti-Soviet bloc. The growth and territorial expansion of the European Union as a supranational entity has altered gender relationships in member states (and also beyond EU in many potential candidates) discursively as well as implicitly. On the one hand, a large body of the EU directives that started with equal pay and subsequently expanded to encompass a variety of gender equality legislations, including the reconciliation of employment with family life as well as gender mainstreaming, was generated. On the other hand, the implementation, monitoring, and adaptation of this body of gender-related provisions have been unequal across member states. Their implementation as well as enforcement varied and were very much dependent on the already existing body of policies, political will, and the strength of women's advocacy and lobbying each of the member states. Not surprisingly then, even though there were unquestionable positive changes in many member states as well as at the EU level (such as a greater representation of women in the national parliaments as well as in the European Parliament), women in the EU member states have been often disappointed and have pointed out how women's economic status has paradoxically eroded despite the emergence of the EU's women-centered legislative framework.

The last two rounds of enlargements in 2004 and 2007 brought together on many levels the eastern and western parts of Europe in a historical integration. Yet the vast differences between the old and new member states with respect to gender not only remained but were in fact exposed and reinforced. Certainly the latest rounds of enlargements raised many hopes for women to achieve gender equality in central and eastern Europe. The transformation of 1989–91 in central and eastern Europe brought much attention to the impact that the arrival of the free market and neoliberalism had on the processes of democratization, institutional reforms, and the rule of law – as well as the emergence of civil society. Far less consideration has been devoted to how these processes translate into new forms of gender inequalities. This is not to say that processes of women's marginalization began only after 1989. In fact, as the authors point out, the period of the Cold War and of Communism in central and east Europe resulted in people's alienation from the oppressive Communist state and thus in the destabilization of the traditional male–female gender dynamic, in which men do politics while women stay home.

By degrading the public sphere, Communism brought politics into private homes, and this move resulted in the "domestication" of male leadership. The transition to democracy meant for many men the return to "normality," which often in the region equals patriarchy and women's exclusion from politics. Yet, as the contributions to this volume argue, this is only a part of the story of new masculine identities. The push for new forms of consumption in western Europe, discussed earlier, combined with the deindustrialization and commodification of the male subjects, began to destabilize the dominant discourses of masculinity in western Europe already in the 1970s. After 1989, in central and eastern Europe, while the hegemonic heterosexual masculinities dominated public discourse and popular media, new masculinities, previously marginalized as a result of class, age, sexuality, (dis)ability or ethnicity, rapidly began to emerge.

The post-1989 transformation has also opened the possibility for the telling and retelling of the national story of identity formation, participation and national experiences. The "master narratives" of European states constituted by nationalists and Communists became questioned and unraveled, and through that process the assigned gender roles of feminine and masculine were not only remembered, but also reconstructed and resurrected as a part of shaping a narrative (or narratives) of national history.

While the "privatization" of politics under Communism was a direct effect of the state's abusive control of individual and collective freedoms to associate, demonstrate, gather, speak or write freely, the emergence of "kitchen table" politics in Germany reflects the emergence of a subculture process that in many ways represents also a creation of new spaces of resilience where civil society was formed. In both cases, albeit at different times and different locations, private spaces of home served as fruitful training grounds where networks could be established, agendas formed and political subjecthood claimed.

This volume repeatedly asserts women's ability to claim their agency and to engage in creative and productive mobilizations, regardless of institutional, ideological, cultural, economic, and political constraints. From a historical perspective, marginalized groups such as women in different places and at different times were denied the possibility of acting on their behalf and even when it appeared that they did have power, these were, *de facto*, instances of limited agency that in reality amounted to theoretically given, but practically restricted, freedoms. Several authors call attention to the evidence of women's forceful and brave (to the point of sacrificing life) interventions that took place locally and nationally, as well as globally, as women engaged in peace-building campaigns locally and globally. While with different degrees of success these efforts shaped women's political identities and their political subjecthood, they served as role models to future generations. The pioneering work of the UN Commission on the Status of Women was indeed exemplary in its global scope and its attempt to unite and integrate women's diverse points of views at a time of major ideological tensions that divided the world and when many doors were closing with the onset of the Cold War. But, as we have seen, national- and local-level mobilizations were equally powerful be it during the Communist period in Czechoslovakia or in post-1989 Poland. Their diverse locations in formal party politics or within more informal structures of civil society indicate women's strategic ability to mobilize and struggle for their political and economic rights, gender equality and social justice.

The rapid growth of NGOs across Europe, run by women and for women, indicates the increased focus on women's agency and on their redefinition of the meaning of activism, echoing women's mobilizations around reproductive freedoms and sexual choices mentioned earlier. NGOs are seen as new entry points that have expanded the political space from which political actions can originate; they have created avenues through which access to policy decision-making can be gained across geographical scales. The emergence of supranational forms, such as the European Union, not only placed an emphasis on governance and action beyond the nation state, but it also opened up new possibilities for transnational mobilizations and actions that involve a multiplicity of actors and locations.

These diverse mobilizations reinforce what became clear to women activists across Europe (but also globally): the realization that the struggle for women's rights and women's participation in politics is a part of a global, universal fight for human rights and democratization, but it has to be addressed also as a particular concern within each specific context. The question then is not just how the meaning and consequences of women's agency are inflected by race, class, gender, sexuality, or ethnicity, but how the institutional and rhetorical constraints exhibited through socio-economic conditions, political ideologies, and particular historical experiences intercept this process.

The chapters in this volume repeatedly underscore that women did in the past, do now and will in the future matter for social, economic, political, and cultural identities of Europe. Women's productive and reproductive contributions, and their leadership at the level of home, work, community, nationally as well as internationally, are decisive not only for everyday life, but are also seminal for molding social relationships, constructing new gender regimes, producing institutional practices and policy-making, and empowering women's activism. Throughout the decades of the postwar era, Cold War period and more recently when the European integration led to the reinvention of a unified Europe, women engage, organize, and mobilize to transform power relations and to eliminate social inequalities; they use their capacities and skills to shape new European gender discourses. These engagements translated into transnational feminist collective actions and led to rethinking of what it means for women to be citizens in Europe. Thus the chapters in this volume demonstrate that past and current conditions raise important questions about how the history of a place, combined with the various structural barriers and ideological disputes, affects the formation of women's experiences and women's ability to act, and also how women are critical for our understanding of Europe.

Note

1 Hobsbawm, E. J. "An Afterword: European Union at the End of the Century," in J. Klausen and L. A. Tilly, eds, *European Integration in Social and Historical Perspective: 1850 to the Present* (Boulder, CO: Rowman and Littlefield, 1997) 267–75.

INDEX

Abortion 3, 4, 9, 10, 113, 122, 124, 125, 127, 128–129, 142, 143, 213, 215, 216, 218, 220, 221, 224, 227, 233; Abortion rights and laws 143, 144, 147, 13 n 21, 215, 216, 233
Addams, Jane 56
Advocacy 44, 218, 219, 224, 235
African Americans; discrimination against 38, 45
Albania 30 n2, 90 table, 181, 182, 185, 186, 188
Ali, Shareefah Hamid 44
All India Women's Conference 35, 47 n9
Anti-Fascist Women's Front (AFŽ) 57, 58, 59, 60, 61, 62, 64
Arcadie 133, 138 n76
Arko, Nika 59, 60
Arlt, Ilse (1876–1960) 54, 56
Atlantic Charter 157
Austria 20, 30 n1, 59, 89, 90, 185, 192 n15

Baby boom 13, 72, 123
Baader-Meinhof 10
Bandung Conference 157
Baranskaya, Natalya 8, 9, 87, 88, 90, 96
Bardot, Brigitte 3
Begtrup, Bodil 35, 38
Beijing Platform for Action 213, 214, 224
Belgium 41, 94, 95, 195
Benzie, Isa 72, 75, 78, 79, 80, 81
Birth Control (Contraception) 3, 10, 122, 123–129, 134; reproductive rights 213, 214, 216, 218, 222, 226

Birth rate 2, 3, 13, 72, 92, 123, 180, 182
de Beauvoir, Simone 7, 93, 148, 154 n41
Bourdieu, Pierre 198, 199, 204, 208
Bowlby, John 71, 72
Britain 3, 4, 7, 38, 44, 71–86, 109, 111, 123, 131–132, 135, 180, 183, 229 n21; United Kingdom 40–3, 94, 101 n 44; empire 40–43
British Broadcasting Company (BBC) 72, 74, 75, 76, 78, 79, 81–2
Brigade Mondaine 131
Bulgaria 30 n2, 90 table, 97, 100 n17, 178, 182, 185, 191 n7, 194

Capitalism 24, 27, 30, 109, 195, 213, 232
Catholic Church 4, 5, 10, 13, 124, 129, 133, 162, 168, 214, 225; Catholic politics 54, 60
Ceaușescu, Nicolae 234
Center of Italian Women (CIF) 115
Christian Democratic Party 115, 128
Churchill, Winston 16, 30 n 1
Citizens' initiatives 1, 145, 146, 215, 217, 229 n22
Civil society 46, 139–155, 155 n44, 215, 216, 236
Cold War 2, 3, 6, 7, 11, 16, 17–18, 20, 21, 22, 24, 25, 26, 29, 30, 35, 37–39, 44, 46, 49 n31, 59, 88, 92, 93, 105, 106, 107, 117, 122, 139, 148, 149, 150, 157, 158, 160, 212; methodology 52–3; stand-off 37–39; United Nations and 37–38, 48 n23

colonial rule 24, 35, 39–44, 157, 158, 212
Commission on the Status of Women (CSW), see United Nations
Communism 2, 4, 11, 12, 14, 16, 17, 22, 52, 53, 74, 88, 90, 106, 107, 116, 157, 158, 172, 176, 177, 179, 180, 181, 191 n12, 192 n15, 203, 208, 214, 215, 224, 228 n20 233, 235, 236; Communist Party 17, 18, 29, 20, 22, 26, 29, 52, 55, 56, 57, 58, 64, 65, 115; Communist Women 8, 19, 22, 23, 27, 29, 93; post-communism 14, 96, 195, 198, 207, 214
Collective agency 92, 171, 214, 233, 234, 236
concentration camp survivors 37; homosexuals 4; Ravensbrück camp, see Ravensbrück
Convention on the Political Rights of Women, see United Nations
Cosica, Dobric 182, 183
Cresson, Edith 11
Croatia 53, 54, 55, 59, 64, 179, 180, 181, 189, 191 n13, 192 n15
Czechoslovakia 17–33, 55, 89, 90 table, 95, 191 n13, 203; Council of Czechoslovak Women (CCW) 19, 20, 21, 22, 28; Czechoslovak Federation of Women 22, 23,24; political parties 18, 30 n1

decolonization 6, 39, 43–44, 157; United Nations and 39, 44, 45
Dembińska, Zofia 35
Democracy 4, 12, 18, 20, 21, 27, 30, 30 n6, 43, 62, 71, 73, 74, 78, 80, 82, 104, 107, 105, 118, 140, 180, 182, 183, 184, 189, 190, 194, 195, 202, 215
Denmark 13, 40, 47 n8, 94, 123, 195
Divorce 10, 60, 73, 76, 205
Domestic institutions; strengthening 221, 222, 223, 224, 234
Domestic citizenship 72, 75, 81, 234
Double burden see women's double burden

East Germany (SBZ) 2, 8, 11, 13, 30 n2, 89, 90 table, 92, 95, 116, 127–128, 129, 135, 153 n21; German Democratic Republic 127
Economic miracle 93, 94, 105, 110, 112, 117
Empowerment 141; strategies for 216, 218, 220, 222, 223, 225, 226; institutions 219, 221, 226; women 102, n63, 218, 220, 232

Estonia 97, 198
European Union 13, 95, 97, 98, 103 n71, 194, 195, 207, 212, 213, 214, 225, 235, 237; accession 213, 218, 224, 225; institutions 217, 219, 224, 225, 226, 227, 237
Everyday life 10, 59, 63, 72, 73, 80, 97, 107, 117, 122, 130, 142, 144, 167, 198, 223
Extraparliamentary activism 140, 141, 145, 147, 152 n13

Farkas, Edith 54
Feminism 7, 12; France 42; Italian 10; eastern European 212, 213, 214, 217, 218, 220, 224, 227; Irish 11; Lithuanian 198; West German 10
Feminist 30; activism 66, 142, 146, 213, 215, 218, 220, 223, 227; activists 93, 13 n23, 212, 213, 214, 215, 216, 218, 226; definitions 227; discourse 9, 53, 56, 93, 96, 98, 216, 218, 227, 227; education 215, 216, 217, 221, 222; groups 55, 146, 213, 214, 215, 216, 217, 219, 220, 224, 225, 226; identity 219, 220, 223; liberal 218, 220, 226, 227; mobilizations 213, 214, 215, 216, 217, 226, 236; movement 212, 213, 214, 215, 216, 220, 223, 224; perceptions of 58, 81; politics 212, 213, 216; programs 217, 220
Federation of Women and Family Planning 216, 222, 224
Fertility 73, 123, 128, 233, see also birth rate
Field visitors 53, 57
Four Freedoms 157
Fourth UN Conference on Women 213
France 1, 3, 11, 13, 42, 94, 104, 109, 113, 122–127, 129–135, 141, 180, 183, 195; "good morals" law 4; Law of July 23, 1920–124, 126, 127; overseas empire and 35, 36, 41, 43, 50 n53
French Medical Association 124
French Movement for Family Planning (MFPF) 126–127
Freud, Anna 71, 72, 75
Freud, Sigmund 71, 75, 80, 83, 93

Garçonnes 130, 133,
de Gaulle, Charles 123, 127
gender 25, 28, 29, 83, 106, 107, 116, 172, 176, 178, 179, 182, 184, 190, 199, 201, 203; and Cold War 18, 38, 88, 93; discourse 237; discrimination 39, 168,

169, 171, 198, 202, 218, 222; equality 13, 55, 94, 97, 98, 132, 194, 196, 214, 219, 220, 225, 232, 235; identity 58, 154 n34; mainstreaming 98, 213, 214, 227, 232, 235; politics 13, 38, 39, 53, 56, 59, 65, 98, 129, 141, 144, 149, 159, 177–179, 194, 212, 222, 232; regime 65, 93, 194, 195, 232, 237; related law 219, 221; relations 73, 96, 139, 195, 199; roles, norms and order 3, 14, 62–4, 65, 72, 73, 75, 79, 81, 82, 93, 115, 125, 127, 130, 133, 134, 177, 195, 200, 207, 231, 237, 237; wage gap 95
German Democratic Republic, see East Germany
Gobetti, Ada 117
Gorbachev, Mikhail 12
Gottwald, Klement 19, 20, 22
Greece 25, 45, 165, 178; Greek children 25, 36
Green Party 10, 145
Gulag 38

Himmler, Heinrich 128
Homosexuality 4, 13, 76, 129–131, 195, 196, 199–203, 207, see also Lesbianism
Horáková, Milada 19, 21–22, 24, 27–29
House Un-American Activities Committee (HUAC) 26
Human Rights, see rights
Hungary 12, 30 n1, 30 n2, 54, 55, 67 n3, 89, 90 table, 91, 92, 97, 102 n 55, 194, 195, 207.

Immigration 6, 122, 123, 162, 163, 165, 166, 170
Imperialism 24, 28, 39, 44, 158, 212
Independence; national 20, 158, 177,178, 179, 182, 186, 192 n16, 199, 203, 204; women's 64, 101 n5, 113
India 6, 45; All India Women's Conference 35, 47 n9; Indian women 156, 161, 163; status of women in 44, 50 n 48
Inter-American Commission of Women 35, 46, 47n9
Islam; attitudes toward 38, 44
Italy 1, 10, 13, 26, 89, 104, 105, 106, 107, 109, 110, 111, 112, 113, 115, 116, 122, 123, 165; Federation of Italian women 26

Jančar, Marija 60, 61

Kenyon, Dorothy 26, 47 n7–8, 49 n31, 50n66
Khrushchev, Nikita 88, 90, 109,129
Kinderladenbewegung– 142
Kingdom of Serbs, Croats and Slovenes 54, 55, 180, 181
"kitchen debate" 109
Kitchen-table politics 139, 144–47, 149, 236
Klein, Melanie 71, 75, 76, 77
knowledge based-instruments 223
Kool-Smit, Joke 87, 88, 93
Konsola 216, 218

La commessa 113, 114, 120 n37
Latvia 97, 194, 198
League of Nations 35, 46, 47n8
Lefaucheux, Marie-Hélène 36–37, 40–42, 43, 45, 47n11
Lesbianism 4, 9, 13, 122, 129–135, 199, 213, 216, 218, 220, 222, 227
Lithuania 97, 194–211
Lobbying 10, 35, 130, 218, 219, 224, 235
Loi Neuwirth 127
Lutz, Bertha 34, 46 n4
Luxembourg 94, 95

Macedonia 53, 55, 181
Majority rule 149
Mamonova, Tatiana 9
Manifa 222
"Männerstaat" 140
Marie-Claire 125
Marshall Plan 17, 24, 73, 90
Maternité Heureuse 124–126, 134
McCarthy, Joseph 26
Meinhof, Ulrike 10
Menon, Lakshmi N. 44
Mitrovič, Mitra 58

national policies; influencing 221, 222
National Productivity Committees 107
Nazi Regime 4, 16, 18, 36, 37, 56, 89, 128, 144, 149, 191 n13; medical experiments 36–37; opposition to 35, 57; postwar legacy 1,2, 18, 73, 74
Netherlands 2, 13, 93, 101 n44, 123, 152 n7, 195, 229 n21
Neo-liberalism 11, 94, 97, 226, 235
Neuwirth, Lucien 127
New Social Movements 145, 146, 154 n32
Non-governmental organizations (NGOs) 12–13; information 216, 221, 224; knowledge 221; Lithuanian Gay League 196; materials 216; women's 213, 215,

217, 221, 222, 226; feminist 219, 220, 222; organizational structure 213, 226; strategies 218, 219, 236
Non-violence 22
Norway 4, 13, 94

Obshchestvennitsy 58, 63

Pacifism see non-violence
Pakistan, status of women in 44
Paris 122, 126, 130, 131, 132, 140
Parliamentary Inquiry into the Conditions of Life and Work 114–15
Parliamentary Women's Group 219
Poland 10, 11, 12, 13, 30 n2, 31 n32, 55, 67 n5, 89, 90 table, 97, 98, 108, 109, 116, 120 n44, 194, 198, 207, 212–230, 236; accession 217, 218, 223, 225; government 213, 221, 223; politicians 219, 220; Polish Feminist Association 215
political participation 42, 45, 140, 144, 148, 150, 153 n26, 217, 220, 221, 226, 232, 233, 237
politicians 27, 61, 62, 92, 165, 196, 217, 218, 219, 220, 227
Popova, Elizieveta 38, 40, 44
Portugal 8, 13, 165
Post-fascist 139, 141
Postmodernism 148, 154 n41,
Private 17, 59, 60, 74, 132, 138 n61, 141, 144, 145, 146, 147, 148, 149, 198, 199, 208, 215
Produttivita 107
Prokopová, Julie 21, 22, 28
Provo politics 140–144, 145, 147, 148, 149, 152 n7, 152 n12,
Public 8, 9, 12, 13, 14, 21, 26, 27, 28, 29, 34, 38, 43, 55, 56, 57, 60, 65, 71, 72, 74, 82, 93, 98, 104, 107, 108, 111, 112, 114, 117, 118, 131, 132, 133, 134, 139, 141–9, 156, 163, 170, 177, 180, 181, 183, 184, 188, 189, 194, 196, 198, 199, 200, 201, 202, 208, 209 n9, 214–222, 226, 227, 234–6
Princess Ileana of Romania 54, 55

Quigley, Janet 72, 75–77, 82

Racism 6,12, 13, 26, 38, 45, 82, 158, 167,
Radical Decree [West Germany] 141, 145
Radlińska, Helena 54
Rape 2, 12, 82, 128, 182–3, 188, 222
Ravensbrück concentration camp, survivors of 36–37, 48 n21–22

reproductive rights 122, 159, 213, 214, 216, 218, 222, 226, see also birth control right wing parties and movements 12, 218, 220
rights 98, 105, 157, 158, 157, 160, 220, 227, 229 n26, 231, 236; equal 12, 65, 196, 232; human rights 11, 34, 47 n5, 156, 170, 208, 221, 237; property rights 18; sexual minority rights 226; women's 19, 40, 88, 98, 104, 144, 213,215, 218, 222, 232, 234, 237; worker's 94, 98, 161, 169
Rinascente 109, 113, 114
Robinson, Mary 11
Rodano, Marisa 104–05
Romania 14, 30 n2, 54, 55, 90 table, 91, 97, 194, 234
Roosevelt, Eleanor 25, 47 n8
Rüger, Sigrid 143
Rural women 13, 100 n27, 110, 120 n26, 125, 216, 227

Salomon, Alice (1872–1948), 54, 56
Sander, Helke 143
Schwarzer, Alice 142, 153 n23
Separatism 146
Serbia 55, 176–193
Siostrzana, Ulica 216
Slachta, Margit 54
Slovenia 53, 54, 55, 56, 57, 58, 59, 60, 62, 65, 69 n33, 97, 102 n63, 102 n68, 181, 189,
social work 5, 52–70, 195, 233; History of social work 52, 53; Professional social workers 53, 59; School of Social Work 60, 62; Slovene social work 53; Socialist social work 53; Yugoslav social work 62
Socialism 17, 18, 21, 22, 23, 24, 28, 29, 30, 35, 55, 61, 89, 91, 93, 95, 96, 97, 98, 108, 109, 143, 158, 182, 191, 212, 231, 233; influence on women 8, 60, 93, 102 n63, 182; post-socialist states 30, 177, 178–181, 198, 214; "Socialism with a human face" 59, 233; state socialism 63, 65, 89, 90, 91, 92, 100 n20, 100 n32, 102 n63, 105, 116, 203, 212–3, 214, 232, 233, 234
Solidarity 11, 215, 228 n20
Soviet Union 1, 8, 9, 12, 14, 16, 20, 25, 26, 37, 38, 44, 45, 52, 57, 58, 59, 88, 89, 91, 95, 105, 106, 107, 111, 113, 116, 122, 127–129, 132, 135, 200, 204, 212, 213; perceptions of 18, 24; post-Soviet 195–209, 209 n9; Soviet Bloc 2, 29, 293, 213, 231, 233, 234; Soviet women's organisation Zhenotdel 58, 59; women's status in 2, 8, 38–39, 45, 87, 90, 91, 111, 132, 135

242 Index

Spain 5, 13, 165
Stalin, Joseph 16, 29, 48 n25, 57, 58, 59, 63, 68 n24, 129
state 55, 58, 66, 140, 141, 142, 144, 157, 158, 159, 160, 162, 163 170, 177, 178, 179, 180, 181, 182, 183, 184, 190, 208, 217, 218, 219, 220, 223, 232, 234, 236; actions 109, 219, 227; independence 20, 36, 43, 44, 177, 182, 192 n15–16; institutions 39, 64, 65, 217, 218, 223, 227, 235; policies 105, 107, 108, 112, 127, 128, 157, 158, 215, 226, 232; socialism 63, 116, 129, 203, 204, 212, 213, 231; statelessness 36, 37
Štebi, Alojzija 56
Street, Jessie 34, 46 n4, 47 n8, 49 n31
Sullerot, Evelyne 134
Sutherland, Mary 38, 40–43, 48 n28
Sweden 3, 13, 59, 94, 95, 123, 129–130, 195

Thatcher, Margaret 11, 12
Third Republic 123
Thompson, Dorothy 26
Tito, Josip Broz 58, 61, 62, 64, 68 n24, 68 n26, 181
Transnational 158, 159, 160, 161, 162, 170, 172, 195, 236, 237; economy 13; labor 159, 161, 162, 170, 234; levels 213, 219, 235; networks 221, 224, 236 ; resources 223, 226
Truman Doctrine 17, 26

USSR, see Soviet Union
Unemployment 62, 94, 95, 97, 110, 197, 199, 204, 205, 207, 220, 229 n22
Union of Italian Women (UDI) 105, 115, 117
United Kingdom and empire see Britain
United Nations 34–46, 94, 95; Fourth UN Conference on Women 213; Cold War and 37–38, 48 n23; Commission on the Status of Women and 34–46, 237; Convention on the Political Rights of Women 44–45; decolonization and 39, 44, 45; Non-Self-Governing Territories 39–43, 45; Trust Territories 39–43, 45, 49 n35–36
United States 7, 16, 17, 18, 20, 25, 26, 37, 38, 59, 61, 89, 93, 105, 106, 108, 123, 157, 158, 162, 191 n8

Vichy 123
violence 2, 9, 24, 25, 64, 65, 77, 78, 141, 144, 145, 152 n 15, 153 n23, 177, 183, 189, 197, 198, 199, 206, 222, 224; domestic 6, 12, 222; sexual 216, 220 see also rape; sexual mutilation, claims of 40, 42; violence against women 2, 64, 153 n23, 197, 213, 216, 224
Vode, Angela 56
Vodopivec, Katja 56, 59, 60, 61, 62
Voice 82, 134, 141, 142, 143, 145, 196
Vyshinsky, Andrei 38, 48 n26

Weill-Hallé, Dr. Marie-Andrée Lagroua 124, 126, 134
Weimar Republic 127, 149; Constitution, Paragraph 218, 127–128
Welfare state 3, 5, 6, 11, 62–65, 72, 73, 75, 79, 83, 88, 94, 117, 157, 159, 160, 170, 196, 231, 232, 233
West Germany (FRG) 2, 4, 10, 101 n 44, 107, 116, 123, 127–129, 135, 139–155, 156–175, 234
Winnicott, Donald 71–2, 74, 75–81, 82
woman question 38, 55, 88
women's; access to public office 40; actions 215, 219, 224; activism 8, 12, 212, 216, 220, 227; agency 52, 100 n27, 212, 220, 223, 236, 237; agendas 216, 217, 223, 235; citizenship 72, 97, 98, 176; Conferences 9, 10, 24, 35, 47 n9, 128; double burden 87, 95, 96, 98, 104, 232; employment, work and wages 2, 12, 23, 53, 64, 73, 88, 89, 92, 94, 95, 96, 97, 100 n17, 100 n18, 113, 118, 125, 157, 197, 198; groups/organizations (international) 24, 25, 26, 27, 36, 46 n4; groups/organizations (national) 2, 9, 12, 17, 19, 20, 22, 23, 24, 26, 55, 57, 58, 59, 60, 61, 62, 64, 115, 135, 145, 146, 160, 216; health 10, 129; Identities 236; International Women's Day 20, 23; movement(s) 8, 9, 10, 17, 18–21, 22, 27, 29, 30 n9, 56, 58, 99 n2, 129, 142, 143, 145, 170, 172, 214, 215, 223; NGOs 216, 219, 221, 223, 225, 226; political engagement 153 n26, 198, 212, 237; publications and media 10, 55, 56, 76, 107, 111; mobilizations 212; strategies 215; subjectivity 7, 82, 184; work, see women's employment; voting rights 42–45, 55; women's rights, see rights
World War I 54, 127, 177–90, 191 n7–8, 191 n13
World War II 1, 7, 8, 16, 18, 28, 29, 34, 35, 36, 38, 54, 55, 57, 61, 66, 71, 73, 82, 88, 89, 92, 104, 118, 122, 123, 124,

127, 128, 157, 160, 191 n12, 192 n15, 231, 233; devastation 38, 71, 72

Yugoslavia 30, 36, 52, 53, 55, 58, 62, 63, 64, 66, 89, 104, 160, 176–84, 187–90, 233; Yugoslav social work 62; Yugoslav Women's Organisation 55; Women's Movement of Yugoslavia 56

Zedong, Mao 9
Zeminová, Fraňa 20, 27